Official Guide to Java

java

Created and Photographed by
Hans Johannes Hoefer

Written by Peter Hutton
Revised by Eric M. Oey and Melanie Hahn

Published by Apa Productions (Hong Kong) Ltd.
Fifth Edition 1983

If one assumes a "conspiracy of karma," it was perhaps inevitable that two utterly disparate personalities from opposite sides of the globe should have collaborated on a book that would take them deep into the heart of an ancient, equatorial civilization.

On the surface, it was a decidedly odd combination — a tall, ebullient, outward-going German and a slight, introspective, bookish Australian — but right from the start there was a complementary *yin* and *yang* association of ideas and attitudes.

Hans Hoefer and **Peter Hutton** first met in Singapore in 1970 at a time when Hoefer was enjoying acclaim for his first book, *Guide to Bali* (*Bali* in the current *Insight Guides* series), and Hutton was burning the midnight oil as creative director for the Singapore and Kuala Lumpur offices of an American-based advertising agency. Travel was their password.

Hutton

Hoefer had started traveling in earnest at the age of 15 with annual trips to Spain and North Africa. Before long he was driving second-hand Mercedes-Benz cars from Germany to Iran, selling them off at a handsome profit, and hitchhiking back to Europe (with time out in Jordan to indulge his passion for horses by riding with the nomadic Bedouin). These financial forays supported him through grueling years as an apprentice in the Bauhaus tradition, from which he emerged with a handful of diplomas in printing, book production and art direction. In 1967, camera in hand, he set out through Central Asia to India, photographing extensively before arriving in Bali for a year's painting — and, as karma dictated, the seminal *Guide to Bali.*

Hutton's peregrinations had seen him as a stockman and papaya-pollinator in Queensland, a shearers' cook in New Zealand, a truckdriver and dishwasher in London, a seller of the *New York Herald Tribune* in Paris, and a film extra in Rome. Between times he wandered in and out of the world of journalism before settling into a long-term stint in advertising which took him to Kuala Lumpur in 1967 and Singapore in 1969, and which also give him the chance to travel extensively in Iran, Uzbekistan, Afghanistan, Nepal and Northern India.

The odd couple met. Ideas flowed back and forth. Hoefer completed the first editions of new guides to *Singapore* (1971) and *Malaysia* (1972). Hutton was getting itchy feet. What next?

"Java," said Hoefer. "I've never been there," said Hutton. "Well, let's go," they both said. So they did. Eighteen months and 17,500 kilometers later (in an island only 1,100 kilometers long), Apa Productions' *Insight Guide: Java* rolled off the presses and the champagne corks popped.

Hoefer

It was not, of course, a wholly two-handed venture: "no man is an island." The voyage became an enduring love affair with a unique and extraordinarily resilient culture. In traveling as extensively and intensively as they did, the authors noted in the book's first edition, "We feel that we must have met half of Java's people. They are remembered with gratitude and affection. We hope some day to meet the other half."

This edition of *Insight Guide: Java* has been updated by **Eric M. Oey** and **Melanie Hahn.** Oey was born in the United States and is an American citizen, but traces his roots to Java itself. He is the progeny of an Indonesian-Chinese father and an American mother. Oey spent early 1983 in Java, updating and revising this volume while studying on a Fulbright fellowship in Surakarta. He is working on graduate degrees in Indonesian literature and history and in Chinese studies at the University of California at Berkeley. Oey speaks fluent Javanese, Indonesian and Mandarin.

Hahn, who put together the expanded and updated Guide in Brief, is an academic specialist at Berkeley, involved in programs for students of English as a second language. An American of Korean heritage, she has a masters degree from Harvard's Graduate School of Education. She presently teaches English in Korea but has traveled extensively in Java.

Oey

The current edition of *Insight Guide: Java* was pulled together by Apa Productions' editor **Paul Zach.** Zach produced Apa's *Insight Guides* to *Jamaica* and *Florida* and was involved in the production and revision of other volumes in the series. He worked in Jakarta for nearly three years as a free-lance journalist for the *Washington Post,* Reuters News Agency, ABC News and McGraw-Hill World News.

Many others, both Javanese and then-resident "expats," offered their knowledge, suggestions, interest and encouragement; and, above all, they shared their love and enthusiasm for Java. Particular thanks are due to **Anderson G. Bartlett III,** without whom the project could never have got off the ground; to **Raden Tumenggung Hardjonagoro** for his kindness and generosity with which he put his time and encylopaedic knowledge at the *Insight Guides* team's disposal; and to **Charles Levine,** whose editorial expertise and wisdom helped eliminate grammatical errors and put subtle restraints on a romantic prose style.

Wendy Hutton, who shared the agonies inherent in the birth of a book, deserves special mention for her dual role as mentor to the book's author and as *mater familiensis* to two small children; her contributions to many sections of the book — language, food, women's roles, sociological insights — are acknowledged with gratitude.

Java is also indebted to Aji Damais, Tjiptono Darmadji, S.T. Lie, Liem Thian Khoen, Muktia Mashud, Dameria Nainggolan, Gloria & Soepomo Podjosoedarmo, B.P.H. Poeroebojo, Poerwoko, Soelijastowo, R. Soetedjo, Franz Surjanto, Bernard Suryabrata, and Connie Tan; Kate & Doug Clendon, Sergio Dello Strologo, Rosemary & Geoffrey Forrester, Joan Ogden Freseman, Caroline & Peter Jurgens, Lim Kim Guan, Anton Lucas, Janelle & Les Murphy, Barbara & Robert Pringle, Warwick Purser, Charlie Thomas, Don van Dall, Annemarte & Peter Paul van Lelyveld, Joan Webster, and Judy Bird Williams.

Hahn

Additional photographs are by Max Lawrence (pages 72–73, 192, 200), Peter Hutton (pages 195, 197, 235, 237) and Kal Muller (page 92). For permission to reproduce photographs, thanks to Charles Hardeman (page 129), Raden Tumenggung Hardjonagoro (pages 178–179), Cornell University Press (page 219 from *Art in Indonesia* by Claire Holt, copyright 1967 by Cornell University; the Jakarta City Museum (page 219); and Affandi for his painting *My Mother* (pages 66–67).

— Apa Productions

TABLE OF CONTENTS

A CHANCE TO BE PERSONAL

If the soul of Java could be captured in oils, the result would be subtle and great: a balance of light and shade, nuances of warmth and softness amid brush-strokes with an edge of honed steel; there would be highlights of diamond brilliance, green flowing into burning gold, and ruby fire touching fathomless azure.

But to begin with there is a clean canvas and a preliminary sketch of a restless, contradictory subject.

The sketch is of an island lying 6° to 9° below the equator, more than 12,000 kilometres from London, 17,000 kilometres from New York, and 7,300 kilometres from Tokyo. An island which is the fifth largest in the Indonesian archipelago after Kalimantan, Sumatra, Irian Jaya and Sulawesi. Overlaid on a map of Europe the archipelago stretches from the west coast of Eire to the Ukraine and Sevastopol in the east, from Berlin in the north to Belgrade and Bucharest in the south, covering an area of more than 10 million square kilometres . . . and even though much of the archipelago is warm sea and ocean, the total land mass is the size of Mexico, and Java the size of Greece.

That is the bird's-eye view. As you draw closer, as the outline of Java assumes a palpable third dimension, the quirks and delights of a beautiful island make themselves apparent and reveal its panorama, through time and space, of history, culture and people.

Java is people. Including the island of Madura there are more than 100 million of them in an area of 133,000 square kilometres (the size of England), representing an average density of roughly 800 per square kilometre, or more than twice that of Holland or Japan. There are more than eight million in Jakarta, and over 1.5 million in Bandung and an estimated four million in Surabaya, but fewer than 25 other cities in Java have more than 100,000 inhabitants. About 85 percent of the population live in rurual and semi-rural areas, with 60 per cent of the work force engaged in agriculture.

A dancing master from Yogyakarta in Central Java personifies a highly refined traditional Javanese art.

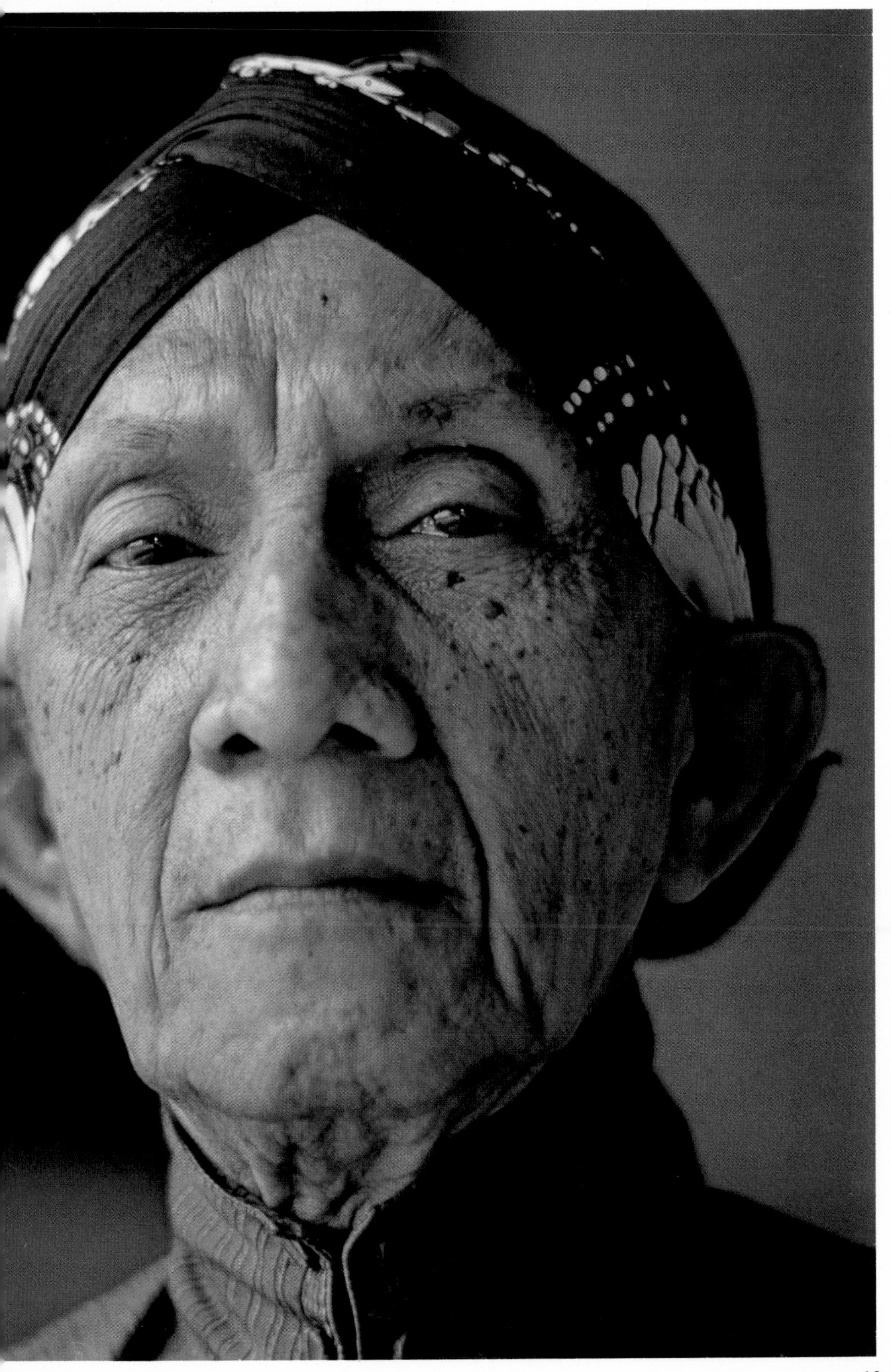

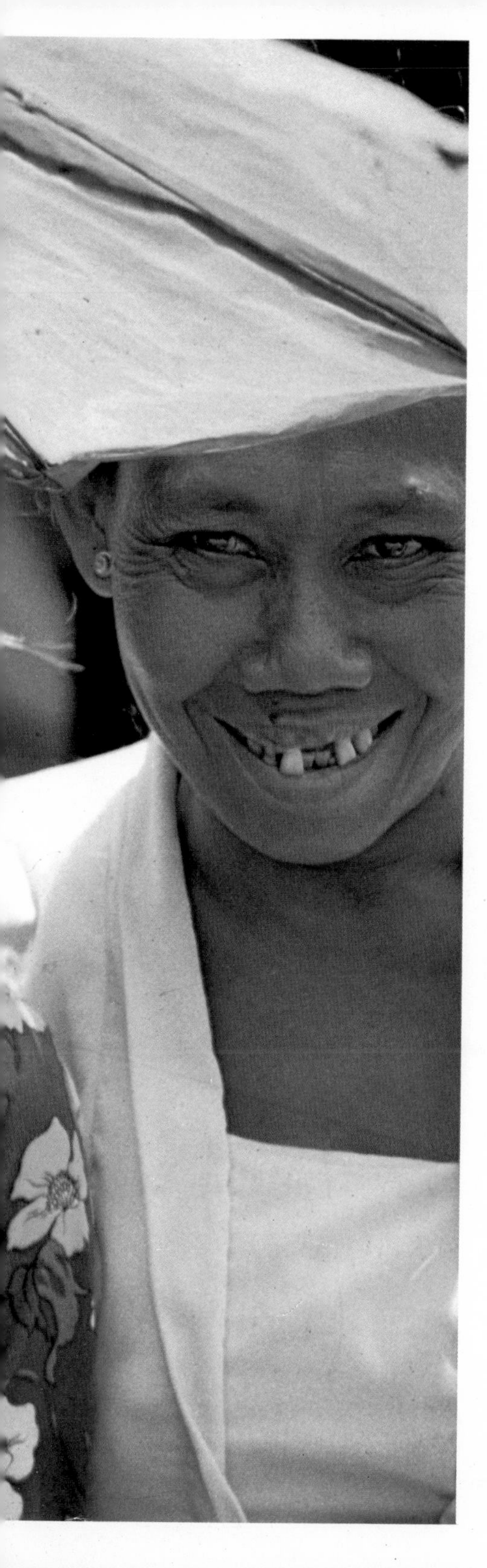

Not everyone is 'Javanese'. In the uplands of West Java the majority of the population is Sundanese; the Javanese proper come from Central Java and a part of East Java; and the Madurese come from the island of Madura, though many now live in East Java. Each group has a different heritage in customs, culture and language; although *Bahasa Indonesia*, the Indonesian language, is the lingua franca throughout the island, in many small towns and villages day to day communication is still carried out in Sundanese, Javanese and Madurese.

Coming to terms with Java means coming to terms with people . . . and in Java, perhaps more than in any place else in the world, the travel experience offers the chance to be personal.

This opportunity is scarcely new: 'The Javans . . . were sociable, full of vivacity and beyond description happy. They were likewise hospitable to strangers.' That was the impression of Captain Francis Drake, master of the *Golden Hind*, when he landed in Java in 1580.

The words still apply, though of course there are exceptions. In the anonymity of airport waiting rooms and international hotel lobbies, personal contact is fleeting and brusque; and the disaffections of 20th-century life afflict a few of the young and the well-to-do.

These are minor blemishes . . . and often, when voices are raised and tempers fray, it is a frenetic Westerner at fault: not in tune with the rhythmic flow of time, but obsessed with the seconds, minutes and hours of schedules.

Java is like a hot bath. You can jump in and scald yourself, and shriek. Or you can ease in, adjusting to the warmth, until there is nothing to do but luxuriate and let the world go by.

The people of Java do things with a 'we' consciousness. There is a strong sense of community, of sharing, of warm involvement with the lives of others. That anguished cry from the psychiatrist's couch, 'Doctor, I don't know how to relate to people!', has probably never been heard in Java. The idea of being a

In Java laughter and good spirits are always just around the corner. 'Life may not be entirely a bed of roses, but there are flowers. And they bloom.' It's easy to make friends.

loner or a recluse while living amongst others, a Simon Stylites detached from the world and the people around him, is not yet anathema: it is simply not understood. The notion of 'an Englishman's home is his castle', or the Western obsession with privacy, are foreign to Java.

The average Westerner, enmeshed in a private world, also shrinks from physical contact. The Javanese do not. A seat meant for two will always take three, buttock to thigh. It doesn't matter. Proximity means friendliness and warmth; people are people. Men hold hands and embrace. Boys stroll arm in arm.

Outside of the larger towns, personal contact becomes even more vital and apparent in its expression.

The arrival of a foreigner is an entertainment, an event which adds spice and flavour to an ordinary day. It is something else to talk about. You'll be greeted with shrill cries of '*Belanda! Belanda!*' (which originally meant 'Hollander', and now applies to any paleface); half a hundred children envelop your car; dozens of eyes fix on you as you tuck into a plate of *nasi goreng* at a food stall. Giggles, cheekiness and laughter. Sometimes, tired and fretful after the rigours of a journey, you may feel like screaming. Having withstood the noisy overtures, you will find it easy to slip into the life of the community and find warmth, generosity and friendship in the most unexpected circumstances. Java *is* people.

Java is also a wonderful place for the tourist, the traveller and the explorer. Exploration, in fact, is another aspect of the island's charm, another segment of the chance it offers to be self-indulgently personal, for there are discoveries to be made which will titillate the palate of even the most jaded, world-weary voyager.

An island of great and varied beauty, a treasure of historic and outstanding temples, a casket of cultural gems, Java is full of surprises, not the least of which is the realisation that the outside world knows little about what it has to offer. There are dozens of ancient temples and

Across the desolation of the Sea of Sand, around Bromo in East Java, a rider makes his solitary journey at dawn, at home in the vast solitude.

monuments, most of them older than Europe's great cathedrals, all of them completed long before the first colonists set foot on North American soil. There are heavy jungles and savannah, boisterous coastlines and manicured *padi*-fields, majestic stands of bamboo and groves of coconut palms, mangrove swamps and high plateaux on which the temperatures can plummet to freezing-point, and a long line of mountain peaks, crater lakes and smouldering volcanoes.

Culturally, Java is a giant *pot-pourri*. There is a repertoire of dance, drama and comedy which draws its inspiration from Hindu epics thousands of years old, from the exploits of Islamic warriors, and from tales of ancient Javanese heroes; there are trance rituals whose origins are as misty as mankind's own beginnings; there are puppets in leather and wood who entrance local audiences through all-night performances; and there is a music of gongs and chimes which is as glistening and fluid as quicksilver, yet as textured as the face of the land.

It is not a forced culture. Older than Java's memory, it is as relevant now, in the continuum of living, as it was yesterday or a thousand years ago. This sense of immediacy and timelessness also animates the work of Java's artisans and craftsmen: the woodcarvers, the waxers and dyers of *batik* cloth, the potters and silversmiths, and even the journeyman painters who decorate the island's three-wheeled pedicabs. The survival of these traditions (not merely intact, but aglow with vitality) through the turbulent years of this century says much about the strength of Java's spirit.

Java's ability to absorb outside influences, and to reshape them for use within the context of its own needs and tastes, is as old as the island's recorded history. New arts and interests of Western origin are increasingly evident, and many have already assumed a Javanese veneer and have taken their place alongside the older forms with little or no conflict.

An island of such depth and complexity as Java naturally has a darker side to its personality.

'Java is perhaps best looked at as a mosaic of small portraits': farmers of Tengger who till and toil in the eastern foothills near Bromo.

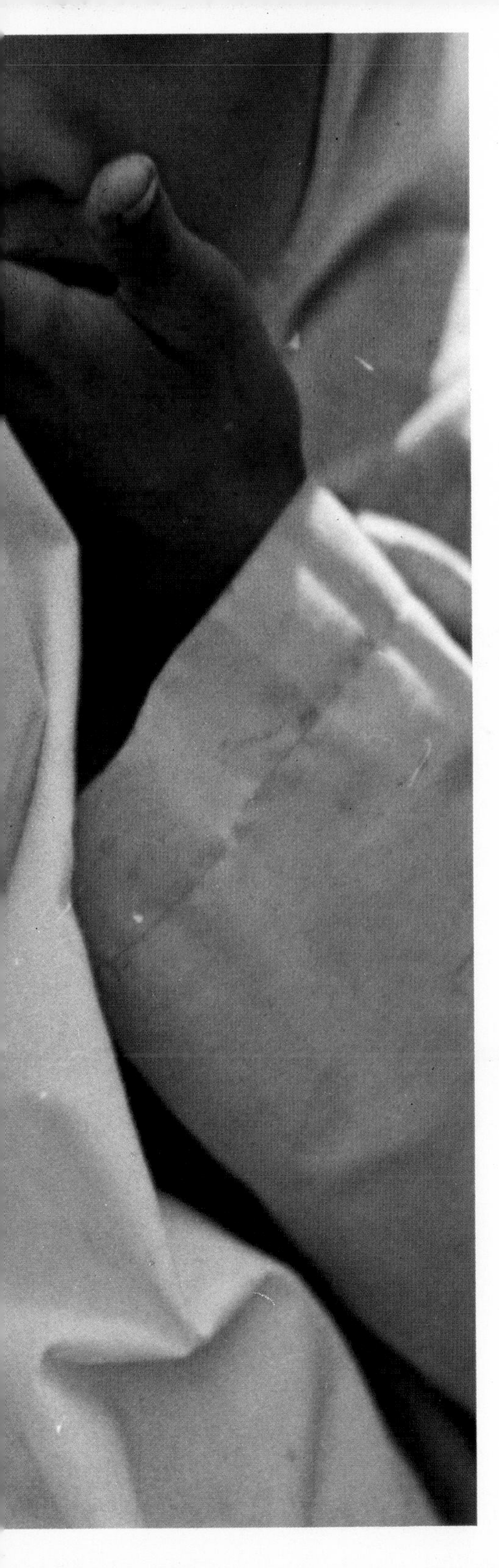

No country in the world, after hundreds of years of domination by a foreign power, has ever been able to achieve social and economic perfection in a quarter of a century. (Remember that it is more than 150 years since the states of South America wrenched themselves free from the yokes of Spain and Portugal . . . and yet!) And, it would be dishonest to suggest that over-populated Java is without problems. The distance between the privileged and the poor is obvious; there is a need for more educational and medical facilities; there are signs of youthful alienation (that world-wide malaise), coupled with an overt rejection of older communal and cultural values.

Yet one of the joys of Java is the sensation that Java will pull through. Despite certain social and economic problems, there is an underlying current of hopefulness, not of self-destructive resignation. Life may not be entirely a bed of roses, but there are flowers. And they bloom. Desperate people cannot laugh with the spontaneity of the Javanese; nor can they find real pleasure in simple things; and least of all can they be as generous in action and in spirit as the people of Java.

The great canvas of Java is perhaps best looked at as a mosaic of small portraits, an assembly of beautifully executed miniatures, each one delineating and capturing the essence of a mood, a place, a time. Individually, the portraits are fascinating. Seen together, they illuminate the complex interrelationships within the island, imbuing them with an aura of strangely compelling magic.

Java offers a unique chance to be personal. Take the chance. You will find yourself engulfed in a world of extraordinary variety and vitality, of compassion, subtlety and drama; you will find it impossible not to become involved; and the least of your rewards will be an appreciation and an understanding of a remarkable island. You may also become the happy victim of a great and enduring passion.

In Java, as anywhere, there are children who take to strangers immediately; others, like this little Muslim schoolgirl at Banten, are more reticent .

Dawn in Java. The hour when shadows cast by moonlight dissolve and disappear, that brief hiatus when all the earth's colours express themselves in mingling tones of grey, uncertain of their daylight form.

The scarlet hibiscus, soon to flame at the sun's touch, is dark against darker leaves. The virginal frangipani blossom, blinding white at noon, is now as soft and shapeless to the eye as an empty grey-velvet glove: only its sulky, sensual perfume has not been dulled by the darkness. The coconut palms, mop-headed, slightly drunken telegraph poles, lurch blackly against silvery space. The nodding fronds of bamboo are etched ostrich plumes, silhouettes from a mystic dreamworld.

In the pillared forecourt of an old house, temporarily roofed with woven palm-leaf, a flat piece of beautifully cut and coloured parchment mounted on a stem of buffalo-horn, a gunungan, *the symbolic magic mountain and tree of life of the shadow plays, stands alone at the centre of the informal stage. The puppet-master intones the last ritual phrases of his night-long tale, the last tremulous note of a bronze gong fades into silence. The amplifier snaps off with a click. The crowd inside the forecourt stirs. Sleeping children are lifted gently in their parents' arms. Sarongs are tightened. Bare feet glide silently across the floor mats and slip into sandals at the entrance. Bicycles move off into the half light as the puppet-master carefully packs his puppets into a large wooden chest. The musicians unknot themselves from the cross-legged position they have maintained for nine hours. There is a flare and a crackle as someone lights up a clove-flavoured* kretek *cigarette. The white screen is folded. Another* wayang kulit *performance has finished, and the shadows of the night shall sleep until night falls again.*

* * *

A sixteen-year-old pedi-cab driver huddles in the passenger seat of his becak *and counts his night's takings by the light of a street lamp . . . 210, 215, 240, 250, 255* rupiah. *A handful of small change and a few grubby notes. He stretches his muscular legs. 255* rupiah. *A better night than most. But there are 100* rupiah *to go to the* becak *owner. And a kilo of rice to be bought. Another hundred. He shrugs. It is time to sleep.*

* * *

On a windswept ridge a trio of barefoot horsemen pauses, each huddled in his sarong, worn like a poncho against the biting cold. They have seen this spectacle before, countless times, as did their fathers before them, and yet they pause as participants in a timeless ritual. On the other side of the crater rim on which they stand a segment of burning orange rises inexorably from behind a jagged black wall. Bridle bits catch the golden fire and fling it back in glints of tawny silver. Behind them, tall pines whisper, and the wind carries the fragrance of acacia blossom on its breath.

There is a primeval quality about dawn in Java, as though it were not today but a thousand thousand years ago, the very awakening of the earth itself. It is a moment of pristine peace, a transcendental moment that seems to affect the sun itself, for in Java the sun does not merely rise. It leaps. It gallops into the sky, hot on the trail of that haunting first light: red, then orange, then golden fingers touching the peaks and spires of nature and of man.

At the Hindu temple of Prambanan the sun lays a roseate garland over the knobs and gargoyles, the pinnacles and contours, touching first the apex and quickly enveloping the monument with the bloom of a new day.

At the top of Mahameru, Java's highest mountain, it catches a billow of smoke from the crater's core and transforms it into pink candyfloss.

In Jakarta, at a single stroke, it adds more gold to the gold-jacketed 'Freedom Flame' and more silver to the silver crescent surmounting the brilliant white dome of the Istiqlal Mosque.

And as the sun moves higher, embracing the island in its mantle of warmth, its turns padi-*fields and windows of high-rise buildings into dazzling mirrors. It silvers the splash and struggle of fish enmeshed in salt-drenched morning nets, evaporates the mist on high plateaux, and chases its own image in the shimmer of jets rising skywards on errands of commerce.*

* * *

Mankind may have experienced its first dawn in Java, that island so richly endowed with history. The remains of Java Man, the celebrated *pithe-*

Light of a new day breaks upon the 10th-century Prambanan shrine to Siva in Central Java.

canthropus erectus (no longer an ape, yet not quite a man), were discovered in 1891 at Trinil in Central Java. Probably 1.5 million years old, and one of the earliest known hominid fossils. Java Man died out when today's Java was still an integral part of the Asian mainland. The skull of *homo soloensis* (Solo Man, a more highly developed creature, a maker of flint tools, and a cousin of early *homo sapiens*), was unearthed in the 1930s not far from Trinil, and is 60,–100,000 years old.

Neither Java Man nor Solo Man was a *direct* ancestor of Indonesia's 20th-century inhabitants (Charles Darwin's 'missing link' has not yet been found), but both lived along what is now known as the Solo River, *Bengawan Solo*, immortalised in a popular Indonesian folk-song, and for thousands of years a vital waterway.

When Java Man lived, the melting waters of the last great Ice Age were already rising and beginning to alter the face of the earth. By the time of Solo Man the mainland and islands of Southeast Asia had assumed the outlines that we know today. About 20,000 years later small bands of men wandered through the Chinese province of Yunnan down into Indo-China, Thailand, the Malay Peninsula and eventually into the western islands of the Indonesian archipelago . . . and probably farther afield into the Pacific Islands.

The remains of Wajak Man, about 10,000 years old and the earliest known true *homo sapiens*, were found along the Brantas River in East Java. He was, perhaps, the Cristofero Colombo for later generations of immigrants who trickled into Indonesia, and of course Java, over several thousand years. It was once thought that there were two distinct waves of migration, the Proto-Malays being earlier, the Deutero-Malays being later, but the divisions are cloudy. The only certainty is that the neolithic and bronze age men who arrived between seven to three thousand years ago from Asia were the real ancestors of the people of today's Java, perhaps leavened with boat-loads of explorers and voyagers from Oceania who travelled from the Pacific Islands as far west as Madagascar, and who almost certainly settled in small numbers in parts of Indonesia.

At Singosari a 600-year-old temple guardian, bedecked with skulls, holds no terrors for the local children.

The first Henry Ford roundly declared that 'History is bunk!'. Nevertheless, knowing something of what has happened in Java in the last two thousand years serves two purposes: it clarifies one's comprehension, and it enhances one's travel experience. There is plenty of visible history in Java. Most of it is easily and pleasurably accessible, and is a fine excuse (if an excuse is needed) for walking and exploring.

Everywhere there are elements of the past. At an obvious level there are splendid monuments in stone, temples like Borobudur, Prambanan and Penataran. But Java's awareness of its past is not limited to the adulation of piles of stone: it also celebrates the names and deeds of its outstanding sons, ancient and modern. Roads and streets throughout the island record nationalist leaders and thinkers like Haji Agus Salim and Husni Thamrin; military heroes like General Sudirman who, wasted by tuberculosis, often led his guerrilla forces from a litter, and whose likeness adorned the older series of Indonesian banknotes; popular heroes like Prince Diponegoro, leader of the bloody but futile rebellion of 1826–30; Hayam Wuruk, the greatest king of the Mojopahit dynasty; Gajah Mada, the amazing *patih* (prime minister) who was largely responsible for Mojopahit's most glorious period of power and influence; Falatehan (or Fatahillah), the Islamic warrior-missionary who in 1527 flung the Portuguese back from Sunda Kelapa, today's Jakarta.

Even older memories are kept alive at the highest levels of the nation. Indonesia's motto, *Bhinneka Tunggal Ika*, 'They are many; they are one' (more commonly translated as 'Unity in Diversity') is a Sanskrit phrase; so too are the words *Panca Sila*, the 'Five Principles' on which the Republic is based; the 'supporter' of the Indonesian coat-of-arms is the *garuda*, the mythical sun-bird which has played an important role in Javanese legend and which earlier still occurs in Hindu mythology as the 'vehicle' of the god Visnu.

In two thousand years Java has been influenced by, and had thrust upon it, a variety of religious, social, political and commercial forces. All of

them have in some way left their mark: one has only to peel back the layers of modern Java to find an astonishing array of customs and beliefs that have maintained themselves through the centuries, no matter how many times or in how many different ways they have been overlaid with a new influence. Java is famous for this 'syncretism', about which so much has been written ... the ability to absorb and adapt external influences without necessarily discarding older beliefs, practices and values. What is obvious is a mere fraction of what *is*.

* * *

Any history of Java is also, to a large degree, a history of Indonesia. Although much smaller than its neighbours Sumatra and Kalimantan (Indonesian Borneo), Java was (and still is) agriculturally richer, and easily maintained a larger population; it controlled the trade route east to the fabled 'Spice Islands' of Ternate, Tidore, Banda and Ambon, all of which traded with Java for rice; it exerted a powerful influence on the important north and nor'nor'east sea-lanes to Indo-China and the Chinese mainland, a source of silk and porcelain; and it had a say in the trade that moved northwest through the Straits of Malacca to Burma and farther on to India. Whether a muddle of competing kingdoms, a reluctant colonial vassal, or a trio of provinces in an independent republic, Java has never, in two thousand years, relinquished its joint roles of political linch-pin and entrepôt centre for the Indonesian archipelago.

It seems that Java was known by Indian chroniclers as early as 600 B.C. The earliest plausible reference to Java in the Christian era occurs in Chinese annals of the Han dynasty, recording the visit in 132 A.D. of an embassy from 'Yavadvipa'. A little later, about 160 A.D., the Alexandrian geographer Ptolemy mentions the East Indian islands, and while it is doubtful that Roman traders ever reached the archipelago, Roman beads have been found in Borneo, presumably carried by Indian merchants.

India was to have a profound influence on Java.

The cool tiles of a mosque are conducive to study for this Muslim on Java's north coast, where the tradition of Islam is strongest.

The great modern Indian poet Rabindranath Tagore, visiting Java, said 'I see India everywhere, but I do not recognise it.'

'I do not recognise it.' That phrase is a key to understanding Java. Whatever the island accepted from outside, it changed ... yet the changes were subtle. 'I see it, but I do not recognise it.' These could be the words of almost any outsider: a Christian priest or parson, a Muslim from Saudi Arabia, an expert on the classical dances of India, a scholar immersed in the complexities of the Hindu caste system. There are, to the orthodox mind, apparent inconsistencies and even heresies, but it is the very fact of being unorthodox that has imbued Java with its rich diversity.

It is easy to find examples. At the celebration of *Idul Fitri*, the feast-day marking the end of the Muslim fasting month, immense conical mounds of rice are carried to the *Masjid Besar*, the Great Mosque, in Yogyakarta ... mounds known as *gunungan* or mountains, a direct reference to the sacred mountain, the *mahameru*, which is the abode of the Hindu gods. Beneath the otherwise severe, unornamented throne of the *susuhunan* of Surakarta, a titular Muslim prince, is a tiger skin symbolising his role as the embodiment of Siva. In a *ketoprak* play retelling the Christmas story, *Kelahiran Jesus Kristus*, Mary and Joseph wear traditional Javanese dress, the Three Kings wear court clothing ... and Joseph approaches his father-in-law with the stifling obsequiousness (lowered head and eyes, a soft whining voice) that still dominates Javanese social contacts between inferiors and superiors.

* * *

Under the northern Gupta dynasty (300–600 A.D.) India enjoyed one of its 'golden ages'. Buddhism, that gentle, contemplative offshoot of Hinduism, penetrated China, and many Chinese Buddhist pilgrims chose to take the sea voyage through Southeast Asia to India rather than face the perils of the mountainous overland route. This sea voyage sometimes led to Java, and always to Sumatra.

One such pilgrim, Fa-hsien, observed in 414 A.D. that Hinduism was practised in both islands. The oldest inscription in Java, found near modern Bogor, dates from the same time, and records in Sanskrit the name of King Purnavarman of

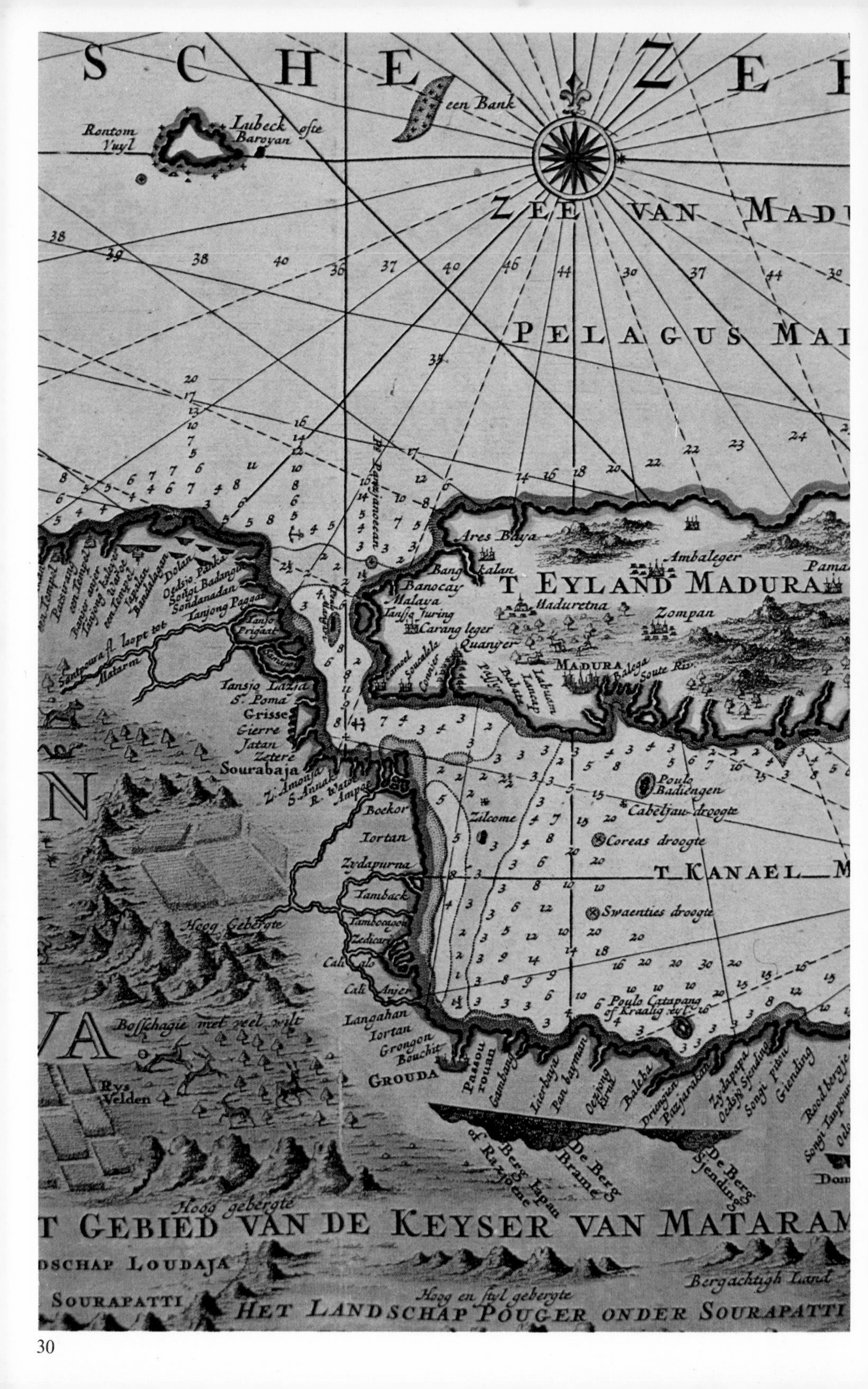
S C H E
Z E
een Bank
Rontom Vuyl
Lubeck ofte Baroyan
ZEE VAN MADU
PELAGUS MA
Ares Baya
Ambaleger
Bang kalan
Banocay
Malava
Tansjo Juring
Carang leger
Quanger
T EYLAND MADURA
Maduretna
Zompan
MADURA
Balega
Soute Riv.
Dolan
Oedsjo Panka
Tanjong Paggat
Sentpoura fl. loopt tot
Mataram
Tansjo Lazia
S. Poma
Grisse
Gierre
Jatan
Zetere
Sourabaja
N
Poulo Badiengen
Cabeljau droogte
Zilcome
Coreas droogte
T KANAEL M
Swaenties droogte
Bockor
Iortan
Zydapurna
Tamback
Hoog Gebergte
Cali Calo
Cali Anjer
Langahan
Iortan
Grongon
Bouchit
GROUDA
Poulo Catapang of Kraalig eyl.
VA
Bosschagie met veel wilt
Rys Velden
De Berg Brame
De Berg Sjending
Hoog gebergte
T GEBIED VAN DE KEYSER VAN MATARAM
DSCHAP LOUDAJA
SOURAPATTI
Bergachtigh Land
Hoog en steyl gebergte
HET LANDSCHAP POUGER ONDER SOURAPATTI

Taruma . . . but virtually nothing is known about his kingdom.

Another pilgrim, I-tsing, travelled from 671 to 695 and spent ten years at a Buddhist monastery school in Sumatra: 'If a Chinese priest wishes to go to the west [India] in order to hear and read he had better stay here one or two years and practise the proper rules and (then) proceed to Central India.'

I-tsing's monastery may have been a part of the great thalassic empire, Srivijaya, then rising rapidly at the site of present day Palembang. At the same time the Sailendras, 'Lords of the Mountain', were carving out a rich kingdom in the heartland of Central Java. Apart from the fact that they were were Buddhists, and were related to the house of Srivijaya, little is known of them: but they were powerful enough to erect Borobudur's prayer in stone, one of the most splendid of all Java's ancient monuments. For reasons unknown the Sailendras soon afterwards moved their centre of power to Srivijaya, and the leadership in Central Java passed to the first short-lived dynasty of Mataram. The change of rulers also occasioned a change in religion, for Mataram followed the Hindu faith, and erected the magnificent Loro Jonggrang temples at Prambanan (see page 24) in honour of Siva. By the year 1000 A.D. Mataram was in eclipse, and new kingdoms were rising more than two hundred kilometres away in East Java.

The dozens of temples erected on the plains, plateaux and hills of Central Java between the years 732 and 928 are proof enough of the cultural and artistic vitality of these early kingdoms, flourishing at a time when much of Europe was languishing in the gloom that preceded the Early Middle Ages, its northern frontiers harassed by Vikings and Spain firmly in the hands of victorious Muslim armies. It is inconceivable that Sailendra and Mataram burst into life like a mushroom: it is assumed that the great kingdoms had accumulated their wealth and prestige over several centuries and that they had begun as indigenous Javanese states which later employed artisans, teachers and scholars from India. There is nothing to suggest that Java was ever colonised or conquered by Indian forces; rather, the cultural exchange was free and open (even if a little one-sided), and it is known that Javanese and Sumatran monks attended the school of Mahayana Buddhism at Nalanda in Bengal during the 9th century.

The four centuries between 900 and 1300 are obscure, though a few names emerge to find their place in a mixture of myth and history. The best known of the early East Javanese kings is Airlangga, who ruled somewhere to the south of Surabaya from 1019 to 1049. Before claiming the throne and uniting East Java, Airlangga spent years as a hermit, accumulating wisdom and magical powers through fasting and meditation. Significantly, it was during his reign that the ancient Hindu story of Arjuna's ascesis and temptation, the famous *Arjuna Wiwaha* (see page 92), was first translated into Old Javanese.

Airlangga was followed by the Kediri dynasty (1049–1222), during which another Hindu epic, the *Bharatayuddha* or 'War of the Bharatas', was translated. The translations were important, for these popular tales (combining entertainment and instruction) are an integral part of Java's modern cultural tradition. For the rest, Kediri's fame is essentially negative, since in later dynastic chronicles it invariably appears as the force opposing the establishment of a new and 'rightful' regime.

The next dynasty, Singosari, which lasted a mere seventy years, was engulfed in a welter of gore, with all the elements of a Shakespearean tragedy: successive rulers vainly tried to thwart a curse that seven kings and princes should die by a sword fashioned for the dynasty's usurping founder, Ken Angrok . . . who tested his new weapon by murdering the smith who forged it. Singosari also saw the building of some of East Java's more striking temples, and the introduction of a unique sculptural style that owed little or nothing to original Indian models, with figures in a flat, two-dimensional style derived from the *wayang kulit* (shadow puppet) theatre.

Distinctions between Buddhism and Hinduism, always slender in Java, had evolved into a form of Tantric Syncretism, heavily imbued with overtones of magical and arcane practices that had originated in Tibet and spread down towards and into the archipelago under the influence of India and of the Mongol ruler Kublai Khan. The last

Singosari ruler, Kertonegoro, refused to pay obeisance to the Great Khan. This shocking effrontery was set to rights by a military expedition of 20,000 men who invaded Java, achieved minor victories, and were then surprisingly thrashed by Kertonegoro's son. However, since Kertonegoro was dead (he died before the arrival of the Khan's forces), the Chinese troops felt that honour had been satisfied, and the new king was enthroned. The year was 1293 and Majapahit, Java's greatest dynasty, was on its way.

* * *

In the previous year, 1292, Marco Polo had passed by though not landed in Java. He was not the first European in the area, but his informative memoirs survived, and his notes on Java (although second-hand) are interesting:

'... *(Java) is the biggest island in the world, having a circumference of more than 3,000 miles. The people are idolators ruled by a powerful monarch and paying no tribute to anyone on earth. It is a very rich island, producing pepper, nutmegs, spikenard, galingale, cubebs and cloves ... It is visited by great numbers of ships and merchants who buy a great range of merchandise, reaping handsome profits and rich returns. The quantity of treasure in the island is beyond all computation.*'

His estimates of Java's riches were indeed correct, though the size of the island was greatly exaggerated, and nutmeg and cloves never grew there. Nevertheless, knowledge of such wealth was shortly to inflame the cupidity of Europe, and within three centuries Java was brutally wrenched into the orbit of Western influence. Another of Marco's observations (this time first-hand) was equally important to the future of Java:

'*You must know that the people of Ferlec* [modern Peureulak, on the far northeast coast of Sumatra] *used all to be idolators, but owing to contact with Saracen merchants, who continually resort here in their ships, they have all been converted to the law of Mahomet.*'

Islam had planted its first, and irreversible, step

A thousand years ago, this panel at Candi Mendut anticipated a common scene in today's rural Java: fruit trees, children, mother.

in Indonesia. Marco Polo's 'Saracens' were almost certainly Gujeratis (themselves only recently converted) making the long voyage from Cambay, north of modern Bombay. The progress of Islam from northern Sumatra to Java was slow, but considerable, for it set in motion a power struggle between the lords of the coastal ports and the kings of the agrarian, inland states for whom rivers like the Solo and the Brantas were the only means of contact with the outside world.

Majapahit's wealth lay principally in the rice it grew on rich alluvial plains and on terraced *padi*-fields. In its heyday, when it controlled or at least received tribute from most of today's Indonesia, there was no problem finding coastal merchants who were happy to trade imported cloths and luxury goods for Java's rice. But Mojopahit was never a maritime power in its own right, for its rulers, like 'proper' Victorian families, disdained to soil their hands with trade, and relied on more enterprising, business-oriented souls to 'do the dirty work'. This lapse, though understandable in the context of a rigidly structured society, was to prove fatal.

The now famous dynasty got off to a promising start under Wijaya, who had bested the fearsome troops of Kublai Khan and established his *kraton* (palace) some sixty kilometres southwest of Surabaya where the little town of Trowulan now stands. For almost forty years it ambled along, sometimes bumpily, without seeming to anticipate its greatness. Other minor kings and princes nibbled at its borders. Java was anything but unified. Then, towards the end of the 1320s, the miracle occurred. A lowly officer in the palace guard put down an anti-royalist revolt and was rewarded with the title of *patih* or prime minister. Shortly afterwards he quelled another uprising, and thereupon vowed to devote himself to the reunification of Java. He was almost laughed out of court, but his time came, and eventually it was Gajah Mada who had the last laugh.

During the regency of Queen Tribhuvana, and through the first fourteen years of the long reign

Two serious young Muslim boys are enthroned as kings for a day on the occasion of their ritual circumcision, one of the most important moments in their lives.

of Hayam Wuruk (who ruled from 1350 to 1389), Gajah Mada skillfully expanded and consolidated Majapahit's territories, reorganised its administrative structure and brought peace to a troubled land. How much was achieved by conquest, and how much was simply the acknowledgement by weaker rulers of Mojopahit's strength, will probably never be known, but the extent of the kingdom is said to have stretched from Sumatra and part of Malaya through Borneo and east to the Moluccas.

Gajah Mada died in 1364, Hayam Wuruk in 1389. Neither prime minister nor king left a worthy successor, and Mojopahit's brilliant but brief flame was reduced to a mere flicker within a generation. By the time Cristofero Colombo had discovered the West Indies in 1492 while looking for a route to the East Indies, and Vasco da Gama had rounded the Cape of Good Hope and reached India in 1498, Mojopahit was snuffed out forever. With it died the last of the great Hindu-Javanese kingdoms, for Islam was now firmly established along the north coast of Java.

* * *

The people of Java, before the arrival of the Buddhist and Hindu faiths over a thousand years earlier, had been animists and ancestor worshippers. Even now it is hard to imagine a land more likely to enhance a belief in the reality of supernatural forces and spirits, for along the island's rugged, mountainous backbone there lie more than a hundred volcanic cones and craters: 35 of them are active and seven are under constant supervision by volcanologists (running west to east, they are Tangkuban Prahu, Papandayan, Merapi, Kelud, Mahameru or Semeru, Lamongan and Ijen; Kelud, with its hot crater lake, was on the 'very dangerous' list in 1973, and Merapi sends frequent flows of mud and lava down its western flank).

Volcanoes ravage. They also replenish. It was on the island's richly productive soil, much of it the residue of old eruptions, that the early Javanese established their crops. Today, about 63 per cent of Java's land area is cultivated (exclude the mountain peaks and urban con-

Throughout Java, children naturally accept the responsibility of caring for their siblings.

centrations, and the percentage is getting close to saturation point), and of that area more than a third is irrigated. The most familiar form of irrigation, the flooded *padi*-field known as *sawah*, is hardly a newcomer: some of the terraces, especially those in West Java, are probably two thousand years old, and appear to have been built by people who combined a doctorate in civil and hydraulic engineering with a lifetime of mountaineering experience. On the plains *padi*-fields dominate the landscape in many areas, with silvery sheets of water or the brilliant greens of young growth or the gold of a ripened crop surrounding small islands of bamboo, coconut palms and banana trees that mark the site of a village.

Rice, of course, had its spirit or soul. To do it the least possible injury the heavy heads of grain were delicately cut with a small wood-mounted blade tucked into the palm of the hand, and no more than three or four stalks were severed at a single stroke . . . a method of reaping still widely used. Since Hindu times the rice spirit has been identified with the goddess Dewi Sri, and offerings are still made to her before a crop is harvested.

Pre-Hindu Java, with its animistic and ancestor-worshipping beliefs, seems to have had two classes of society: those who owned or controlled the land, and those who worked it. At the top, the king. At the bottom, the peasant. The advent of Hindu Brahmanism introduced a different but nonetheless compatible concept of the god-king, the divine ruler, a concept that helped to consolidate the position of the Javanese rulers. The older two-level class division was also modified by the influence of the Brahmanistic caste system, with its pecking order of *brahmans* (priests and teachers), *satriyas* (warriors, kings and courtiers), *vaisias* (traders), *sudras* (peasants and artisans), and *pariahs* (outcasts or beggars).

The rural village or *desa*, wedded to its surrounding rice-fields and plantations, was the hub of the economy and the source of the kingdom's wealth. The harmony and welfare of such communities was, and still is to a large degree, dictated by the observance of *adat* or customary law. The most striking element in *adat*, at least to Western minds, is the way in which problems and disputes are resolved through discussion (*musyawarah*) and a consensus of opinion (*mufakat*): the issue is debated and analysed, opinions shift, subtle compromises are made, until there is unanimous agreement on a fair and just decision. The so-called 'democratic' mechanism which perversely allows 51 per cent to overrule a dissenting 49 per cent is a foreign concept in the tight village communities of Java, for majority rule is considered divisive and unequitable because it leaves an often sizeable minority unsatisfied.

A familiar sight in Java for thousands of years: carefully transplanting the tender rice shoots by hand to the flooded padi-fields.

The villager and the agricultural worker, far removed from the direct influence of the courts, retained many of their animistic beliefs, and even the missionary spirit of Islam has never succeeded in eradicating all vestiges of the old practices. Some 90 per cent of Java's people are classified as Muslims, but with few exceptions (principally along the north coast from Banten through to Surabaya) the Javanese version of Islam would scarcely satisfy an orthodox *mullah* (teacher) from the Middle East.

Clifford Geertz, in his *The Religion of Java*, distinguished three observable types of religious practice and the social role or status of the people who practised them. The divisions tend to overlap, for an individual may observe several types of practice simultaneously, but the distinctions are useful. The first group, the *abangan*, are mostly peasants in whom the animistic strain is dominant. The second, the *priyayi*, are broadly the upper middle class and are in some ways the successors of the old Hindu *satriya* caste (as are the heroes of the dance dramas and puppet plays); their religious observances are flexible and eclectic, and the *priyayi* tend to be found in bureaucratic or white-collar positions. The third, the *santri*, are defined as the more-or-less orthodox Muslims who, not surprisingly in the perspective of history, are generally traders and merchants.

The *selamatan* or ceremonial meal is the most common of the *abangan* ceremonies. It may celebrate such important events as a wedding or a birth; it may acknowledge a death or a ritual circumcision; and it may be occasioned by a hundred smaller and different events such as

moving into a new house, a bad or ominous dream, a decision to make a long trip, or the return of a prodigal son. Although one person or one family is usually the originator of the *selamatan* it is invariably a communal affair. It may be extremely simple and modest; it may be restricted entirely to men; it may be lavish.

Every *selamatan* includes 'rice mountains' (*gunungan* or *meru*) which, even if the size of a cup-cake, are an important part of the ritual meal. In addition to the meal there is often a performance of puppet plays or of mask dances (*wayang topeng*). The name of the ceremony comes from the word *selamat*, which variously means safe or happy, welfare, prosperity, congratulations or good luck, and the *selamatan* ritual meal, with its religious overtones, is designed to bring about and enhance *keadaan selamat*, the 'state of selamat'. However celebrated, or wherever seen, the *selamatan* is still a lively and involving aspect of Javanese life.

* * *

Majapahit, and the other Hindu kingdoms that preceded it, have left their mark on modern Java: their heroes are also today's heroes, the tales and stories-within-stories they introduced are still highpoints in the Javanese cultural tradition, their beliefs are the bedrock of many current attitudes and social observances. But the decline and fall of Mojopahit was hastened by the advent of one of the two great forces that helped mould Java as it exists today: Islam.

Shortly after Majapahit's fall from grace the strongest power in the area was Malacca, initially a modest trading centre on Malaya's west coast. Under the leadership of Iskandar Shah, a Sumatran from Palembang who became a Muslim around the year 1420, Malacca set forth on a path of glory that was to last, under Muslim, Portuguese, Dutch and English rulers, for more than 300 years. Strategically placed on the eastern shore of the Straits of Malacca, the new city (for it quickly became a city) controlled the trade route linking, in the east, China, Indo-China and the Moluccas, with the great Indian and Arabic ports to the west.

A carpet of young rice, bordered by coconut plams and surrounded by misty hills.

A century later an ill-fated Portuguese 'ambassador', Tomé Pires, destined to die in a Chinese prison at Canton, reported that many 'foreign merchants' had settled in Java's north coast ports. They were no doubt Gujerati Muslims from Cambay, with a leavening of Omanis and Persians, whose predecessors had slowly ranged eastwards from Aceh to Surabaya, bringing with them trade goods, the *Qur'an*, the *Hadith* and an inseparable proselytising fervour (though without the fanaticism of a *jihad* or holy war . . . it was the Portuguese, confronted with Muslims, the 'heathen Moores', who were to mingle blood and steel with trading ambitions).

By 1500 every major port, from Aceh through Palembang, Malacca, the Javanese north coast (Banten, Cirebon, Demak, Tuban, Gresik) and across to the Spice Islands, was in Muslim hands. The cloves, nutmeg and mace from the Moluccas and Amboina, the pepper from Sumatra and West Java, were moved on Muslim ships through Muslim traders to Muslim middlemen who sent the treasures through more Muslim ships to Muslim merchants in the Gujerati ports of India. 'Because of the expansive, missionary nature of Islam,' said Jacob van Leur (a brilliant Dutch historian killed at the age of 34 in the Battle of the Java Sea), 'every Muslim is . . . a propagandist of the faith. That is why the trader from the Muslim world was the most common "missionary" figure in foreign regions. That is why . . . the faith was certain to follow the routes of trade.'

Islam's penetration of Java was essentially peaceful. Dominating the seaways, the Muslim sailors and traders effectively stifled (or absorbed) the commercial advantages of inland Mojopahit. Power at sea, during the 15th century, was the key to success.

* * *

The Portuguese knew this too. Spices were available in Europe, but were exorbitantly expensive by the time they had been carried overland from the Far East to Constantinople and through the clearing houses of Venice. The answer, with its promise of great profit, was to find a sea-route to Southeast Asia and then to control it.

In 1498 Vasco da Gama established a base at Calicut on the west coast of India. In 1508 a

hard-hitting Portuguese fleet demolished a combined Egyptian and Indian force off Diu, at the mouth of the Gulf of Cambay, and thus made the Indian Ocean safe for Portuguese merchant shipping. In 1510 the irrepressible Afonso d'Albuquerque established what was to be a long-lasting enclave at Goa, and the following year took the powerful trading city of Malacca by storm. By 1512 the Portuguese had reached the Spice Islands, and in 1522 they founded a trading post in the town of Sunda Kelapa, then controlled by the Hindu state of Pajajaran in West Java; their *padrão* or commemorative stone can still be seen in the Central Museum, *Musium Pusat*, in Jakarta (as Sunda Kelapa is now called). The Portuguese were thrown out of Sunda Kelapa in 1527, but they virtually monopolised the spice trade for a century until the Dutch captured Malacca in 1641.

* * *

The 15th century saw Islam's penetration and expansion, the 16th century its consolidation in Java. Wealthy trading ports like Demak and Surabaya flourished, and feuded with the Portuguese; Jepara rose for a brief moment of glory, and under a war-like queen despatched two fleets against Malacca. At the end of the century, two important events took place.

The first was the rise of the last great Javanese kingdom, another Mataram founded by Senopati, expanded by the conquests of Sultan Agung. The second was the arrival of the Dutch, who were eventually to control the archipelago.

The Dutch, religious and trade rivals of the Catholic Portuguese, were initially interested only in trade and not in territorial aggrandisement. Their first exploratory fleet of four ships anchored off Banten in 1596 and bought a cargo of pepper. Other fleets followed. Appalling shipboard conditions, a high mortality rate, and the dangers of shipwreck and foundering were regarded as a trivial price to pay for profits that could (with luck) run to as high as a thousand per cent. In 1602 the United East India Company was formed under the aegis of the States General; better known as the VOC (*Vereenigde Oostindische Compagnie*), it controlled Dutch trading fortunes in the East Indies until its demise in 1799.

The VOC was, first and foremost, a trading company; it was not entitled to be a colonial administrator. This was its strength and its weakness, for its oligarchic powers, and the high-handed manner in which those powers were exerted, made the Indonesian islands colonies in fact if not in name. The 18th-century's Age of Enlightenment, with its noble philosophies of liberalism and humanitarianism, held little appeal for hard-bitten traders whose main aims were gold and an early retirement (providing of course that they survived the rotten fevers in swampy, malarial Batavia). There were honourable exceptions, but they were voices crying in the wilderness when rapacity was apparently next to godliness.

The first inroads of the VOC had little effect on the people of Java. The Dutch were chiefly interested in establishing a handful of strong trading posts, in destroying the power of the long-established but thinly distributed Portuguese, and in thwarting the ambitions of the English. Occasionally, great men emerged. One of the first was Jan Pieterszoon Coen who founded Batavia (Jakarta) in 1619 and successfully defended it against Sultan Agung in 1629.

Had the value of the spice market remained high, the VOC might never have become an obtuse and often unfeeling despot. Ironically, the improvement of farming methods and especially of animal husbandry in 18th-century Europe meant that animals could be kept alive during the bleak winter months, and therefore the need declined for spices to disguise the foul taste of autumn-slaughtered meat preserved in brine. Pepper, cloves and nutmeg were no longer worth their weight in gold. The new luxury commodities were sugar and coffee. Thus began the inimical system of 'forced deliveries', in which cash crops were (from the traders' point of view) much preferable to subsistence agriculture . . . but

Under the lopped cone of Gunung Slamet in Central Java, villagers harvest the ripe heads of grain by hand—taking care not to offend Dewi Sri, the rice spirit. Abundant and cheap human power helped the Dutch exploit fertile Java, beginning in the 17th century, and make it their spice, sugar and coffee garden.

peasant farmers, invariably in debt under a corrupt and semi-feudalistic chain of command, could not live on cash crops. Many did not live.

The Javanese rulers themselves had always been autocratic, and the Dutch pragmatically (if unjustly) utilised a system in which the limitations of individual authority were clearly defined. The Javanese 'regents', acting on behalf of the VOC, were even in some cases worse than the voracious Europeans when it came to 'emoluments' and blatant financial chicanery.

Two foreigners attempted to rectify some of the glaring inequities, though with only partial success. The first was Herman Willem Daendels, appointed Governor-General by the Bonapartist regime in The Hague, and who was in Java from 1808 to 1811; the second was Thomas Stamford Raffles (better known as the founder of Singapore) who, through the strange international repercussions of the Napoleonic Wars, was Lieutenant-Governor of Java for the English East India Company from 1811 to 1816, and who must always be remembered for his monumental and enthralling *History of Java.*

The 18th century also saw the growth of an economically powerful class of Chinese merchants and middlemen, and the decline of Mataram, the last autonomous Javanese kingdom. The Chinese, not renowned for their ability to assimilate in foreign lands, were frequently the targets of local resentment over the next two hundred years; though their financial powers were eventually limited, they generally remained a strong and prosperous minority.

In Central Java, at the court of Mataram, fifty years of dynastic in-fighting had ruptured Sultan Agung's empire, and in 1755 the Dutch finally split the old kingdom into the royal houses of Surakarta, Mangkunegaran and Yogyakarta, all with greatly reduced powers. The Javanese were daring and accomplished warriors (as the Dutch discovered to their cost after 1945), and had they managed to set aside their differences and come to terms with each other and with their Sundanese and Madurese neighbours there is

Women and children throng the rural markets, such as this one at Kejajar in Central Java, making it a lively social event each day.

no doubt that they could have pushed the Hollanders back into the sea. Though numerically immensely stronger, they did not, and Java was lost.

* * *

In 1815 the population of Java was a little more than four million. By 1920 it had reached 35 million and was climbing steadily. Pressure was mounting for social, educational and economic reforms. Some of the advocates of change were Dutch, though the majority of the Dutch in the East Indies and in Holland were colonial conservatives, deeply committed to maintaining the unequal *status quo*. Progress was slow. Indonesians were admitted to the *Volksraad* (People's Council) in 1918: '(It) gave political experience to a small handful of Indonesian leaders . . . from different parts of the country, enabled them to work together and to realise their common grievances and aspirations. It provided a forum for criticism of the government and for contact between government and governed, but had no real share in governing, as both its criticisms and suggestions could be overridden' (Ailsa Zain'uddin). Education was also a problem, for anything more than the most basic primary education was denied to most Indonesians. Nevertheless, the unexpected Japanese victory against Russia in 1905 and the fall of China's Manchu dynasty in 1911 had given many Asians new hopes of a brighter future: Europeans were not invincible; corrupt and reactionary regimes could be overthrown. Indonesians reacted.

Parties rose and fell all over the archipelago; they co-operated and they quarrelled; they differed on the role of religion and on the benefits of passive resistance. But an awareness of nationalism spread, fanned by courageous and capable leaders like Sutan Syahrir, Umar Said Cokroaminoto, Haji Agus Salim, Mohammed Hatta, Tan Malaka and Sukarno, among others. Many of them suffered imprisonment and exile. By 1940 the pressures, from the Dutch point of view, were becoming intolerable, with their homeland occupied by German troops and the seeds of unrest blossoming in Indonesia. In 1942, the Batavian government surrendered Indonesia to the Japanese. After nearly three and half centuries the Dutch presence was coming to an end.

The Indonesian leaders took advantage of the brief Japanese reign, buoyed up by an ancient prophecy, attributed to King Joyoboyo of Kediri, that Indonesia would emerge victorious after a long period of suffering and humiliation. When the Dutch returned, three and a half years later, it was to find that the Declaration of Independence had been read (17 August 1945, three days after the end of the Pacific war) and that the Indonesians were determined to throw off the colonial yoke. The struggle was painful and bitter, and heavy Dutch attacks were launched against the 'rebel' Republican forces in 1947 and again in 1948 and 1949. After several abortive agreements had been broken world opinion swung against the Dutch, the United Nations intervened, and on 27 December 1949 Queen Juliana of the Netherlands officially transferred all sovereign rights over the territories of the Dutch East Indies to the Republic of Indonesia.

* * *

Arguments will always rage about how far and how fast colonial countries would have developed if they had not been colonised. The debate is invariably unresolvable and acrimonious, for the idea of development is generally couched in terms of 'Western capitalistic progress', a questionable virtue. Java, more than a thousand years ago, had generated a civilisation of exquisite sophistication when much of Europe was gambolling in the mud. In certain areas Java does owe a debt to the Dutch presence, for if nothing else it inherited a sadly battered but workable administrative infrastructure.

Major cities and towns are still dotted with heavy, columned, colonial mansions which are now mostly occupied by civil servants, the military, the police, and huge bundles of manila files. The Dutch administrative divisions, themselves based partly on the old feudal order, have been maintained, largely intact: the three provinces (*propinsi*) of West, Central and East Java,

The ubiquitous becak, *found all over the island and especially in small towns, provides a pleasant, breezy and unhurried way to travel. But, this hold-over from simpler times means a hard life for the drivers, who are exposed to the elements and to the crush of modern transport.*

I WANT YOU FOR

and the two Special Areas of Jakarta and Yogyakarta; the regencies (*kabupaten*), districts (*kewedanan*), subdistricts (*kecamatan*), and villages (*desa*).

Nevertheless, in rural Java, from west to east, the cyclic pattern of village life continues much as it has for centuries. Here it is difficult to imagine the presence of foreigners or the *Belanda*, the Hollander, for at this level vestiges of colonial rule are as good as non-existent. The following words turn back the clock two hundred years, to 1768, but in many ways the description still applies:

'Rice is the principal grain that grows here. They have also plantations of sugar, tobacco, and coffee: their kitchen gardens are well replenished with cabbages, purslain, lettice, parsley, fennel, melons, pompions, potatoes, cucumbers, and radishes. Here are also all manner of Indian fruits, such as plantains, bananas, cocoas, ananas [pineapples], *mangoes, mangosteens, durians, oranges of several sorts; limes, lemons, the betel and arek nut; gums of several kinds, particularly benjamin* [benzoin]*: in March they plant rice, and their harvest is in July. In October they have the greatest plenty of fruit, but they have some all the year. They have good timber, cotton* [kapok], *and other trees proper to the climate, besides oak, cedar, and several kinds of red wood. The cocoa-tree* [coconut] *is very common, which is of universal use, affording them meat, drink, oil and vinegar; and of the fibres of the bark they make them cordage; the branches cover their houses, and they write on the leaves with a steel stile, and with the tree, and the great bamboo cane, they build their houses, boats and other vessels. Here are buffaloes and some oxen, and a small breed of horses. The few sheep we find here have hair, rather than wool, and their flesh is dry. Their hogs, wild and tame, are the best meat we find there, or in any other countries between the tropics; and their venison is good; here are also tygers and other wild beasts, crocodiles, porcupines, serpents, scorpions, locusts, and a multitude of*

Becak*s, bicycles and motorcars vie for space in the ancient capital of Surakarta. With a notion of balance and harmony, the city moves at its own pace into a new era.*

YAMAHA
APECO

insects. Monkies of various kinds are found here, also flying squirrels.'

* * *

The palm-thatched houses are now tiled, the *lontar* scroll has given way to pen-and-paper, there are only a handful of tigers left, there are immense rubber plantations, there are two and sometimes three rice crops a year . . . yet that 200-year-old picture of rural Java is still essentially accurate. The incursions of foreign powers, and the drastic system of 'forced deliveries', created great hardship for many peasants, but the nature of Javanese life, the cycle of events within a small village community, remained largely untouched by the outside world. *Adat* continues to be observed; balance and harmony are still virtues, for the Javanese abhor excess, and an obsession with deadlines and schedules is not an indigenous trait.

Trains and planes depart and arrive on schedule. Most other things can wait. It is not quite the *mañana* syndrome, for things do get done . . . but they happen in their own sweet time. A favourite phrase is *jam karet*, which translates literally as 'rubber time'. Rarely must a social event or a meeting start at the appointed hour; time can be stretched to suit the occasion.

The notion of balance and harmony is also important in personal contacts. Great respect and deference are shown to superiors and elders, and there are distinct speech levels that are used according to the status of the person being spoken to. These fine social divisions may hark back to the Hindu caste system as yet another example of Java's heritage. To lose face, to be made ashamed (*malu*) is something to be avoided, and many Javanese will suggest that something can be done when they know perfectly well it cannot . . . but in this way they do not give offence, and the listener knows as well as the speaker that the answer has in fact been a polite, graceful 'no'. *Halus* or refined behaviour is also infinitely preferred to *kasar* or coarse deeds and actions.

Sometimes this carefully controlled bottling up of emotion (at least on the surface) tells only half the story. Occasionally something goes snap and repressions flood out: the state of *amuk*, running amok, when pressures can no longer be borne, or when there is no communally agreed response to or precedent for a totally new and emotionally jarring experience. It seldom happens . . . but it should be remembered that the Javanese often fought with great savagery during the battles for independence.

The children of Java: 'Cheeky, mischievous, wide-eyed, laughing, they are visible everywhere.' They are also trendy.

* * *

'Javanese' is useful but inaccurate shorthand when speaking about the people of Java as a whole, for the Sundanese in the west and the Madurese in the east must both be reckoned with. Their languages are different (though related) and in parts of the island there are obvious physical differences. In the coastal parts of East Java there are faces that seem to have come straight from the *souks* of Arabia. Generations ago, they probably did. Inland, around Surakarta and Yogyakarta where the Mataram dynasty slowly withered, there are gentle, aristocratic old men with long, thin, epicene faces; and many of the daughters of the ancient noble houses can be recognised not only by their almost ethereal prettiness but also by heavy-lidded eyes that seem almost about to pop. Different again are the broad, snub-nosed faces of the peasants.

Over two hundred years ago the women of Java were described as being 'much fairer than the men, (with) good features . . . a soft air, sprightly eyes, a most agreeable laugh, and bewitching mien, especially in dancing . . .'. One could hardly disagree, especially when watching the exquisitely composed features of a court dancer, eyes downcast, her slender body moving as fluidly as the notes of a *gamelan*, through poses as rigid as Hindu temple carvings, fingers shivering as gently as falling rose petals. And there's the other side of the coin, the rough peasant woman, her remaining teeth stained red through chewing great black wads of tobacco, a swatch of green paste stuck to her forehead to ward off ills, her bare feet planted firmly on the ground. There is the corseted middle class woman with her bosom thrust high, her movements hampered by a tightly wrapped sarong and teetering high-heeled sandals, her hair rolled

in a huge black bun padded out with green wool, the whole effect a caricature of the other Javanese woman . . . the natural beauty like the brown-eyed, golden-skinned *padi*-field worker or the T-shirted young student with glossy black hair flowing freely over her shoulders.

Benedict Anderson, in his *Mythology and the Tolerance of the Javanese*, pointed out two obvious stereotypes of Javanese women, Sumbadra and Srikandi. Both are wives of the *Mahabharata* hero Arjuna, but that is all they have in common. Sumbadra is the aristocratic ideal, meek and ladylike, devoted to her husband, and unquestioningly loyal; Srikandi is lively and independent, strong-willed and warm-hearted, sufficiently courageous (or foolhardy) to take on a passing knight in battle, quick-witted enough to indulge in philosophical debate.

The visitor, thinking that Java is ostensibly Muslim, may be surprised to find Srikandi. But she is everywhere, has never worn a veil, and has always enjoyed an active and important role in the family and in the society around her. The Srikandis may be the women who run the great markets, bringing in their produce for sale, haggling with other fishwives, gossiping with ribaldry as they sell their tortoise-shell hairpins, prawn paste, meat and mangoes; or they may be the *padi* workers who (after the men have done the ploughing) transplant the young rice shoots and who later harvest every head of rice by hand; and they can be found in offices, shops, schools, hospitals, universities, lawcourts, the armed forces . . . in fact, everywhere that men work.

Talk is one of the joys of life for the women and the men of Java. The theatricality of an evening gathering of 'the boys' is a delight, for it is a form of entertainment, and everyone is a storyteller who has his say without interruption. Each performance is a masterpiece of the orator's art. The scene is set with a droning preamble. Soon come the dramatic gestures and pregnant pauses, the voice rising to an appropriately high pitch of indignation before dropping to a conspiratorial *basso profundo*; then a staccato *entre-acte* before the next set piece, the seemingly interminable monologue occasionally punctuated by passive grunts from the rapt audience . . . which waits, with indefatigable patience, for its turn will come.

The people of Java have an extraordinary capacity to find pleasure in simple things: watching the flight of a bird, smoking a cigarette, or playing endless games of dominoes (with cards, not chips) in the coffee stall of a small market. Often, of course, there is not the money for anything more diverting that what one can see in the trees and fields . . . no television, no magazines, nothing that can be done without. Children display incredible ingenuity in making toys out of improbable materials, and a rudimentary truck with wooden wheels, pushed along at the end of a length of fine bamboo, will provide entertainment for weeks. Village life can be difficult and even monotonous. Yet because the villagers can accept and enjoy the presence of a butterfly or an insect, or even the fleeting relevance of ephemeral things, there is always something about which to small-talk or in which to be involved.

The children of Java are a delight. Cheeky, mischievous, wide-eyed, laughing, they are visible everywhere. They are also extraordinarily self-possessed little bodies. Never ignored, always loved, and yet firmly controlled by an invisible discipline (they are never chastised in public, for they rarely misbehave), they are part of the family and community group from birth; not just a cipher, but an active and quickly contributing member. It is not unusual for a little girl of five to care during the day for younger brothers and sisters while her parents work in the fields, an assumption of responsibility that often seems astounding to foreigners. There is no child beating, no cruelty. Their lives are often poor, but in these respects rich.

Children, loved as they are, represent one of Java's major problems. The island is grossly overpopulated, and has long ceased to be agriculturally self-sufficient. Family planning units get close to their targets each year, but the targets are modest to the point of being ineffectual. There are too few teachers, and too few schools, and at the beginning of each school year several million school-age children have no place to go;

East of Surabaya, fishermen set out at dusk in their high-prowed boat full from stem to stern.

they cannot be taught at home, for many of their parents are themselves illiterate. The gap between the haves and the have-nots is enormous.

* * *

Java's problems of overcrowding are more intense than any other island in the archipelago; Jakarta's population has increased ten-fold since 1930. Widespread birth control and transmigration are only partial answers to the problem. Nonetheless, Java is also the island of opportunity. It is in Java that industry is booming, and Java is the heart of a top-heavy bureaucracy. At least jobs are increasingly available.

The accomplishments since 1949 involve, inextricably, Java and the rest of Indonesia. The late President Sukarno did much for the morale, if not for the physical wellbeing, of his people. Through Sukarno, Indonesia was, at various times, a reasoned spokesman for the non-aligned nations, a courtesan of Russia, a xenophobic anti-foreigner, a builder of grandiose and generally ugly monuments, a short-sighted sabre-rattler angered by the apparent designs of NEKOLIM (neo-colonial imperialists). The attempted communist *coup* of 1965, bloody in its aftermath, set the stage for a wind of change. President Sukarno's powers were drastically reduced. On 12 March 1967 General Suharto was sworn in as Acting President, and on 29 April 1969 he was acclaimed President of the Republic of Indonesia.

Since 1969, under Suharto's series of REPELITAs, "Five Year Plans", the infrastructure of Java has improved radically. Foreign investment capital has poured into the country, and the outskirts of Jakarta are bright with dozens of new factories (pharmaceuticals, textiles, milk foods, batteries) that have sprung up in recent years. The government, a mixed civilian and military authority, is firmly in the saddle. Although slow and often erratic, progress is being made. The problems are great, but hopes are correspondingly sanguine. Java, having survived so long, is not likely to throw in the towel now.

At right, a fisherman checks his catch hauled from the relentless southern surf in one of Java's oldest industries. Following pages: a West Java village sparkles in the sun.

THE PERFORMANCE

Novelty, and the idea of change for the sake of change, are the antithesis of cultural life in Java. Rather, Javanese culture finds its roots and its strength in a continuing statement of the validity and relevance of ancient forms.

The variety of Java's cultural offerings does not begin and end with the 'fine arts', for there is no arbitrary division between the sublime and the vulgar, the culture of the courts and that of the market place. The expressions, and the degree of refinement, may be different, but they are also linked by their relevance to daily living and entertainment. The people of Java enjoy spectacle; they love colour and form; they revel in both simple and complex beauty. Plastic roses and crystal chandeliers are part of the same continuum. The brilliant colours of cordial drinks (the soft white meat of young coconut afloat in a sea of crimson syrup), multi-layered rice cakes in pink and green, and hectically ornamented bullock carts and *becaks* are as much a part of the cultural fabric as the magnificent gold-and-glitter costumes of dance heroes and heroines . . . complementing the view of the art historian A.K. Coomaraswamy: 'The basic error in what we have called the illusion of culture is the assumption that art is something to be done by a special kind of man, and particularly that kind of man whom we call a genius. In direct opposition to this is the normal and humane view that art is simply the right way of making things.'

The West, always self-conscious, was amazed at its own audacity in producing a mini-cult of 'Pop Art'. A can of Campbell's soup, said Mr. Warhol, is a work of art. The people of Java have known that for centuries: they accept functional beauty, and don't expect to have it pointed out to them because they know it is there. It is there in superbly woven rice baskets, in the cleanly simple lines of village pottery, in the gaudily painted hats of south-central Java; it can be found in the sun-ray patterns on horse-carts near Jepara and in the harnesses of Garut; and it is visible everywhere in endless varieties of *batik* designs, colours and patterns.

Preceding pages: a quiet, country road leads to the spires of the Candi Plaosan temple complex near Yogyakarta. Left, a wayang topeng, *mask dance, the entertainment at an elite wedding in Solo.*

Repeated expressions and manifestations of well-known traditional themes were, and in many cases still are, the core of Javanese culture. Ancient beliefs were continually reaffirmed through repetition which, far from dulling the senses, actually amplified the experience and confirmed the rightness of a dance movement, of a sculptural form, of a puppet's visual characteristics.

Two strong cultural influences in Java's history have been the great Hindu epics *Ramayana* and *Mahabharata*, which established ethical and aesthetic codes that are still followed in many respects. There are obvious parallels between the impact of these immortal sagas on the life of Java and the impact of Old Testament heroes and villains on the life of medieval Europe. The difference, now, is that while in the West such characters as Lot, Job, Joshua, Goliath and David have become little more than ill-remembered names, the inhabitants of the Hindu epics still strut upon the stage in Java. They have done so for more than a thousand years, and they are unlikely to fall from favour in the next thousand. The West celebrates change. Java celebrates tradition.

Tradition, reinforced by religious, moral and social pressures, naturally imposed limitations which inhibited originality. As in many parts of Asia, in Java the maxim 'hasten slowly' was scrupulously observed: *Achieve perfection within limits you understand, do not attempt to surpass your masters for the sake of surpassing*. This was the philosophy of Middle Eastern, Indian, Chinese and Japanese artistic masters for centuries, just as it was during the great flowering of Western religious art from the 5th to the 15th centuries.

But in Java, as in medieval Europe, the following of established precepts, the imitation, the repetition, did not mean that artistic expression became static or moribund. In time, however gradually, changes did occur, and Java's culture assumed a distinctive personality; influenced by Indian artistic tenets, it nevertheless put its own mark on a rich and complex heritage: 'I see India everywhere, but I do not recognise it.' The *panakawans* (clowns, servants and heroes) were a peculiarly Javanese addition to the Hindu epics; *wayang kulit*, the theatre of shadows, influenced sculptors and masons in a way not seen anywhere else in Asia. The traditional arts which survived for so long survived because they continue to answer spiritual and emotional needs. The concept of a secular culture is largely foreign to Java.

The pressures of modern life, of commercial competition, are naturally being felt, but their influence on *traditional* cultural forms has so far been small. The movies, television, rock groups and 'modern art' have taken space on the Javanese cultural stage, but have merely expanded the options rather than destroyed the old heritage.

Many young Indonesians do flock to the cinema. Lust and gore are high on the list of movie preferences, which is hardly surprising: there is a tradition of overt violence in all of the ancient epics. The same youngsters, almost without exception, will be enthralled by a performance of *wayang kulit*. Although there are groovers who are more likely to pluck the strings of an electric guitar than to wield a hammer in a *gamelan* orchestra, even those with the long hair and Afros who eulogise Elton John will generally be more familiar with the intricacies of the *Ramayana* than their Western counterparts will be with the Old Testament, Chaucer or Shakespeare.

In rural Java conservatism is still strong, and there are reminders of the life style in towns and hamlets in old Europe: annual harvest festivals, Maypole and Morris dances, celebrations of Midsummer's Night, the feeling of being part of a tightknit, harmonious community. At this level Europe absorbed the new spirit of Christianity, yet kept alive (symbolically at least) the old pagan rituals of the Christmas tree, the mistletoe, the holly leaves and berries. In the same way, and beginning about the same time, animistic, ancestor-worshipping Java accepted Buddhist and Hindu beliefs, and then Islam . . . and elements of every faith and belief can still be found in Java's traditional cultural expressions.

It is not only at the village level that a sense of timelessness pertains. The courts of Yogyakarta and Surakarta maintain *gamelan* orchestras that were old when Bach was a young organist seeking royal favour. The refined art of classical Javanese

Palace guards at the kraton *in Yogyakarta.*

dance is taught within the walls of the old palaces. The profession of *dalang* or puppet-master is still honourable and necessary.

If half the population of Java were suddenly swept off the land and into factories, the role and nature of this cultural continuity would undoubtedly change. But it is unlikely that it would change radically, for Java's folk heroes animate much of daily life, far beyond the confines of a stage or a single night-long performance. The Javanese still describe another person's strengths or foibles through epic characters: he's a Bima, she's a Sumbadra, he's a Rama, she's a Srikandi. Countless shops and *warungs* throughout the island are named after the same heroes and heroines. *Becaks* are gaily adorned with scenes of volcanoes, the Apollo moon-landings, pretty landscapes . . . and events and characters from the *Ramayana* and the *Mahabharata*; there are hundreds of household products, from cigarette papers to noodles, named after characters from . . . the *Ramayana* and the *Mahabharata*; and panels of woodcarving, *batik* paintings and comic strips portray episodes from these epics because the epics still impinge upon daily life.

The apparent timelessness of many of Java's arts and crafts has not meant stagnation or a refusal to change, for tradition and repetition have in fact reinforced the vitality and relevance of expression. Many outside influences have been absorbed and utilised in the last fifteen hundred years. Hindu and Buddhist iconographic principles were accepted and subtly modified in their application to temple architecture, bas-reliefs, free-standing sculpture and bronze-casting. Elements of Chinese design added a distinctive touch to the crafts of woodcarving and *batik*-making. Furniture makers borrowed freely from imported styles, producing 'Dutch' chairs and tables and magnificent 'Chinese' wedding beds (often decorated with scenes from Hindu mythology), 'Chinese' chests and herbal cabinets. The popular lute music of 16th-century Portugal was taken up in the eastern islands of the archipelago and still influences the gentle, bitter-sweet *kroncong* melodies of modern romantic pop songs.

Some arts, like stone sculpture and metalworking (especially the armourer's art), died

A village performance of slapstick wayang topeng.

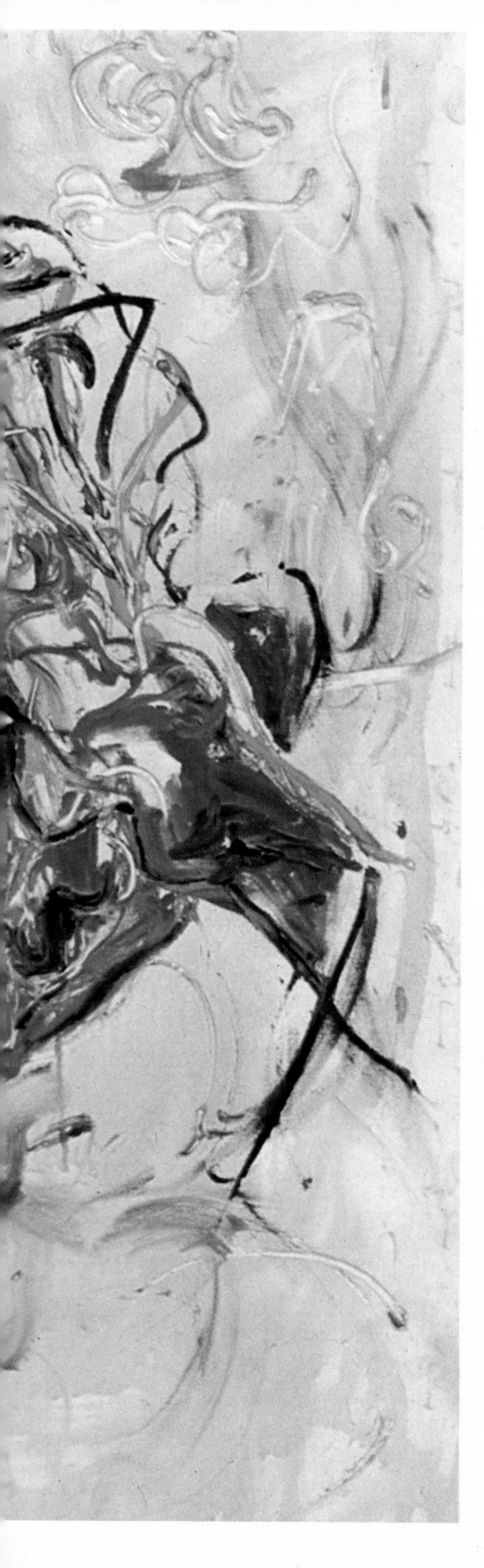

out for religious or historical reasons. Others, like the two-dimensional *wayang klitik* wooden puppets of East Java and the ancient art of *wayang beber* pictorial scrolls, are virtually dead.

* * *

PAINTING on canvas is a Johnny-come-lately on the Javanese scene. Although there are written records of portrait painting more than four hundred years ago, nothing has survived. By the beginning of the 19th century the art had so declined that Raffles was able to write that the Javanese 'have a tradition, that the art of painting was once successfully cultivated among them, and a period is even assigned to the loss of it; but the tradition does not seem entitled to much credit.' A certain amount of illustrative work, in a crude 'comic-strip' style, continued to be done on calendars and astrological charts, but it could hardly be called painting. Much finer was the highly stylised artistry of the old *wayang beber* narrative scrolls which are still being reproduced (though not originated) by artists in Surakarta.

The first modern painter of note was Raden Saleh (1816–1880). He spent twenty years in the *salons* and courts of Europe, and later painted some memorable portraits of the royal families of Central Java, but after his death there was a gap of fifty years before a number of schools of modern art surfaced. In later years Yogya and Bandung became the two crucibles of Indonesian painting, and many accomplished artists appeared. Their work was invariably modelled on Western norms, and whilst Hendra Gunawan, Suromo, Rusli, Yudhokusumo, Lee Man Fong, Affandi and others developed highly personal and often compelling styles (subtle, boisterous, 'primitive') there was nothing apart from the subject matter to make their works specifically Indonesian.

Ironically, painting in Java has remained virtually untouched by the island's older cultural traditions. It is adamantly 20th-century in inspiration and expression. Yet, knowing Java's extraordinary capacity for absorbing and adapting outside influences, painting may yet wrench itself out of the doldrums and assume a strongly

Somewhat surprisingly in an ostensibly Muslim society, women in Java are often independent, vigorous and proud. 'My Mother', by Affandi.

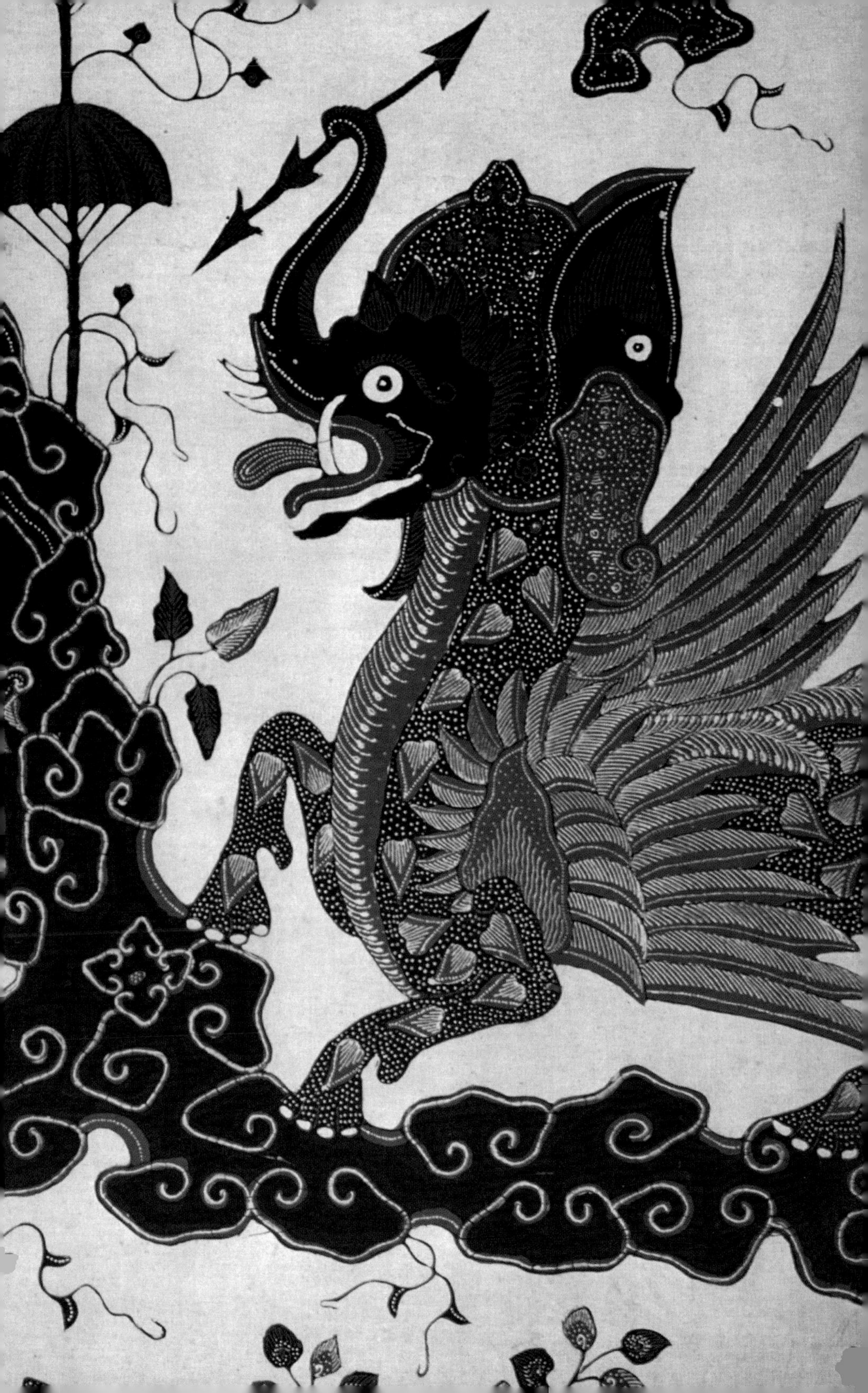

Indonesian (if not Javanese) personality.

Only in the realm of *lukisan batik* (*batik* painting) has a new form blended with an ancient technique. It is a curious encounter. In some cases it is merely a vehicle for illustrating incidents from the Hindu epics; in others it is an imaginative medium for portraying age-old symbolic figures and heroes; it is also effectively used as a means of self-expression, though here the wax-and-dye process in the hands of people who are not experts in the *batik* technique has sometimes resulted in repetitive, easily executed visual themes that would be rejected as canvases.

BATIK has long been one of Java's foremost arts, and can be seen in multitudinous colours and patterns all over the island: severely classical brown-and-cream designs in the courts of Central Java, faded floral *batiks* in the rice-fields, gay *batiks* worn as shirts, more subdued patterns worn as school uniforms; there are millions of *batik* sarongs in new and old designs, there are precious *batiks* of soft old silk, and there's a thriving industry churning out *batik*-patterned shoes, bags, hats, table-cloths, napkins, place-mats and anything else that can use a printed cloth in a functional or decorative manner. For the visitor, *batik* is probably the most vivid visual memory of all.

The word *batik* means a length of cloth printed with a wax-and-dye process, though recently it has included machine-printed fabrics with designs based on the traditional *batik* patterns.

Genuine *batik* is normally printed on fine cotton or linen, and more rarely on silk. Molten beeswax, impervious to dyes, is applied to those areas of the cloth on which a colour is *not* required. The basic pattern is first finely outlined in wax, and the areas not to be coloured in the first dyeing are then filled in with wax. Both sides of the cloth are treated in this way. The cloth is then steeped in the dye, and once the desired colour has been achieved the wax is removed by boiling or scraping. Once again wax is applied to those areas on which the second colour is not required, and the process is repeated as many as four or five or even more times according to the number of colours needed for the finished design.

Both men and women are involved in making *batik*, and can be seen at work in tiny home workshops or in large co-operative groups that are virtually factories. Apart from the machine-printing of *batik* designs (which is not strictly *batik* at all) carried out on a large scale, the size of a *batik* workshop has no bearing on whether the design is hand-drawn or stamped. Women normally do the designing and the waxing, men normally look after the dyeing, but there is no hard and fast rule, and men often do the waxing of stamped designs.

It is comparatively easy to make crude *batik*, but the finest hand-worked materials can take up to nine months to make, and require the eye of a hawk, the patience of Job, and the combined skills of a chemist and a magician. In the hands of a skilled artisan, *batik* is much more than a craft. In delicacy and subtlety it can touch sublime heights. It can be bold, subdued, as richly coloured as a full spectrum, or monochromatic. There are motifs three thousand years old whose origins can be traced back to Assyrian times; there are others that date from the neolithic period of Southeast Asia.

The origins of *batik* are obscure, though it probably developed in Java. Iwan Tirtaamidjaja, a modern authority and designer, suggests that '*batik* may have begun as a kind of painting' and that later, when Islamic influence led to stylisation and abstraction, 'this stylisation in painting made it more easily adapted for clothing and dress material, and . . . slowly a marriage of painting and textile design took place (and) may well have produced the art of *batik* as we know it today.'

There have been three major influences on the development of *batik* printing since the 17th century. The first was the introduction of the *canting*, a short piece of bamboo with a brass or copper reservoir at one end; the reservoir holds the molten wax, which runs onto the cloth through one, two or even three spouts of varying thickness. The *canting* is the 'pen' for hand-drawn or *tulisan* work. The second influence was the *cap*, a copper stamp introduced about a hundred years ago.

Preceding pages: a classic batik executed by the Ibu Masina workshop of Cirebon. Right, a highly-stylized Cirebon batik with rocks and clouds motif.

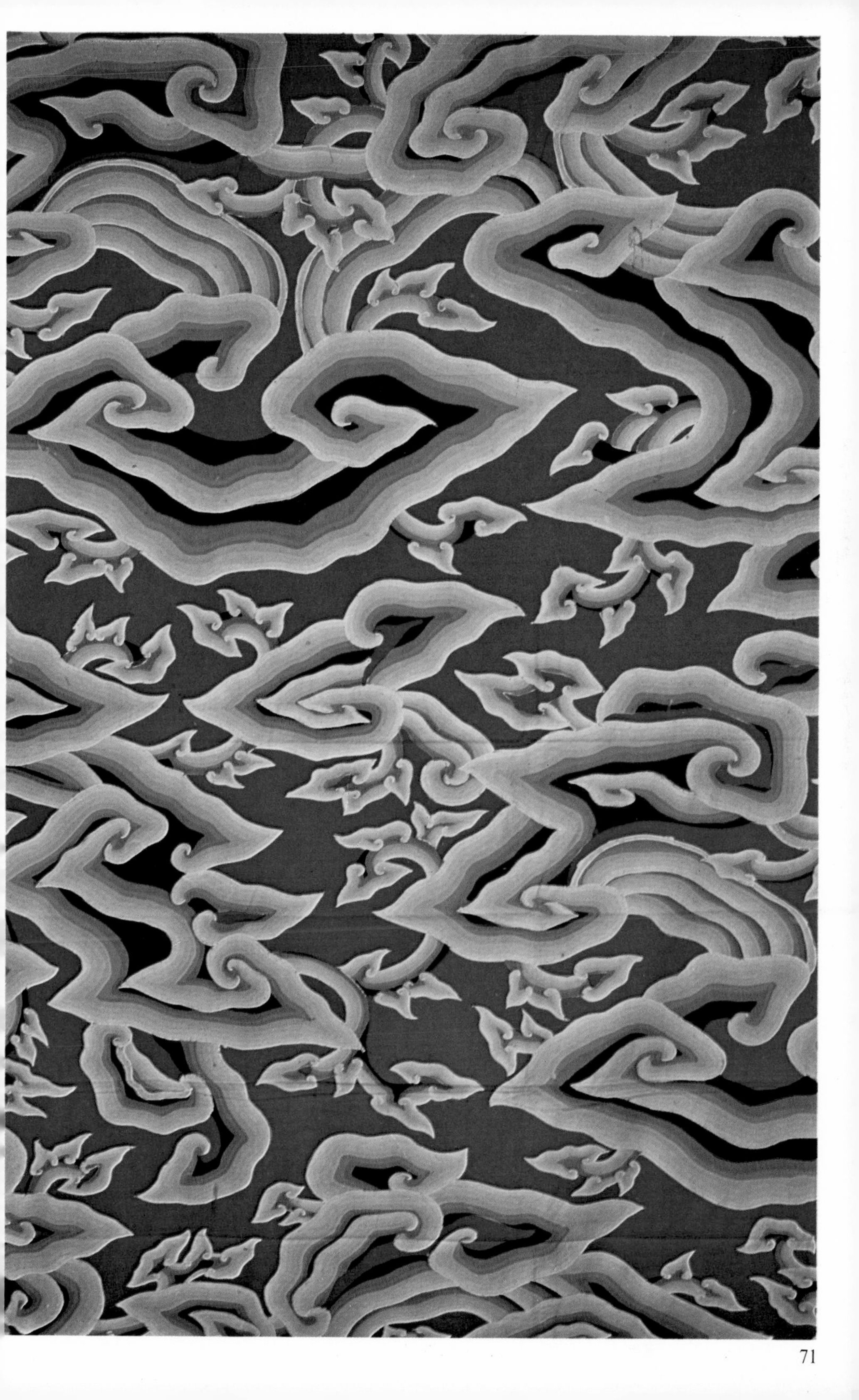

It greatly speeded up *batik* production and helped popularise *batik*, but being semi-mechanical it lacks the individual touch and imagination of the *canting* . . . nevertheless, it almost put the *batik tulis* artisans out of business, but happily the hand-drawn product is now in increasing demand. The third influence was the introduction of chemical dyes. New colours and colour combinations developed, especially in the north coast *batik* centres, and even some of the traditional patterns of Central Java (long restricted to indigo, brown and cream or white) are now being produced in brighter colours.

In the last decade the old wax-and-dye process has been applied to an increasingly varied range of modern designs. Some are combinations of motifs from Central Java and the north coast, others have been inspired by modern abstract designs and by Western motifs, whilst others still have 'modernised' ancient stylised motifs with considerable success.

Machine-printed cloths can generally be detected easily because the colour strength on one side will be much stronger than the colour on the other side; only true wax-and-dye *batik* has equal colour density on both sides.

* * *

TEMPLES are the most striking archaeological remains in Java. For more than 750 years, from about 732 A.D. to the middle of the 15th century, kings, emperors and conquerors ransacked their treasuries to build a magnificent series of temples which still dot the island from the Dieng Plateau in Central Java to the Brantas River in East Java. Many of those erected in Central Java between 750 and 900 A.D. were inspired by the ideals of Buddhism: Borobudur (one of the world's greatest Buddhist masterpieces), Mendut, Kalasan, Sewu, Plaosan. Others were built at the same time in honour of the Hindu pantheon: the temples on the Dieng Plateau and the Gedung Songo group above Ambarawa, and the magnificent soaring pinnacle of the Siva temple (*Loro Jonggrang*) at Prambanan.

After the centre of Java's kingly power shifted to the eastern end of the island during the

Preceding pages: the stupas of Borobodur. Left, the 9th Century Candi Sewu, Central Java.

10th and 11th centuries, a second spate of temple building activity occurred to the south and south-west of Surabaya. The majority were dedicated to Siva, though some represented a blending of Hindu and Buddhist principles (never far removed in any case) in which Buddha was seen as the elder brother of Siva, Buddha being the spiritual superior while Siva held the temporal reins. Major sites where impressive remains can be seen include Kidal, Jago, Singosari and the huge sprawling complex of Penataran. Unique amongst Java's temples are the sites at Sukuh and Ceta, on the western shoulder of Gunung Lawu on the border of Central and East Java, where in the middle of the 15th century a so-called 'Bima cult' based on a puzzling mixture of Hindu and animistic beliefs practised fertility rites. These strange, forbidding temples were the last to be built in Java, for Islam had forced a strong beach-head along the north coast, and the power of the Mojopahit kingdom was crumbling fast.

A temple is generally known as a *candi*. Strictly, *candi* means a sepulchral monument housing some of the ashes of a dead monarch, but it has come to refer to any religious edifice.

Borobudur, discussed in more detail in Part Two, is exceptional amongst Java's temples for its size (it is the world's largest *stupa*), shape and overt religious statement. Most other temples adhere to a plan which, although fairly rigid at its core, is nevertheless flexible in detail: a square platform (also an ambulatory) surmounted by a straight-walled temple body which is in turn crowned by a high pyramidal roof; the body of the temple contained an inner chamber or *cella* in which stood a statue of the deity to whom the temple was dedicated. In more ambitious projects there were sometimes smaller *cellae* entered from the remaining three sides of the temple structure, and perhaps an intervening 'base' between the platform and the body of the main temple. Buildings which appear to have combined the function of both temple and monastery were rare, but there are fine two-storeyed, three-celled examples at Candi Sari and Candi Plaosan in Central Java.

In the early years of Java's temple-building period sculptural ornament was sparing and essentially simple. The shrines on the Dieng Plateau carry little carving apart from figures of deities and fierce guardian *kala* heads above the lintels of doorways. A little later reliefs were used on the walls and balustrades of immense undertakings like Borobudur and Prambanan, but even then many temples were simply decorated. It was not until the East Javanese period that ornamentation came into its own with an exuberant and obviously Javanese flavour.

Borobudur's relief panels, fascinating for their domestic, pictorial and narrative detail, are formal and sometimes static; at Prambanan there is a stronger sense of freedom and movement. Three to four hundred years later at Candi Jago and the Penataran complex the relaxed naturalism of Prambanan's panels had almost disappeared, replaced by a strikingly different sculptural style in which figures and animals were carved in a two-dimensional *wayang kulit* manner, surrounded by lush intertwinings of foliage, clouds and rocks where demonic *raksasa* faces and threatening wraiths can be discerned or imagined; every square centimetre of a panel is filled with voluptuous, sinuous forms.

It is believed that some of the later East Javanese temples were roofed with wood and thatch above the body of the temple, in much the same way as the multi-tiered Balinese *meru* roofs are constructed today.

Temple building had ceased by the end of the 15th century, and the *masjid* (mosque) became the new place of worship. In Java the rapid rise of Islam was not accompanied, as it had been in India and Iran, by a flowering of art and architecture: there are no tiled glories like the great mosques of Isfahan and Shiraz, and only at Sendangduwur (near Bojonegoro) and Mantingan did Islam leave a legacy of fine ornament in brick, stone and plaster. The greatest Muslim monument in Java is the new Istiqlal mosque, still being built in Jakarta.

The architectural art of temple building, and the skills of the sculptors who fashioned the accompanying bas-reliefs and free-standing statues,

Preceding pages: Dancers and muscicians of Central Java's 8th Century perform in the stony silence of a sculpted relief that ornaments the side of the Borobodur.

disappeared hundreds of years ago. More recently another art has moved to the point of oblivion: there are no longer any *mpu* (master) armourers who can forge a classical Javanese kris or dagger. Although the art has died, the mystique remains, and even today amongst old Javanese of wealth and means, and amongst what is left of the court aristocracy, a man's most prized possession is his *keris*, followed by his gongs and *wayang kulit* figures.

THE KRIS, perhaps more than any other weapon in the world, has been endowed with an aura of myth and mysticism. There are krises which, legend has it, removed from their scabbards, refuse to return until they have drawn blood; others are credited with the power of flight; others can reject or even turn on an unworthy owner. One of the strongest and most popular beliefs is that the blade of the kris contains the soul of its first or most valiant owner.

The kris has probably existed in something like its present form for a thousand years. The earliest dated kris was made in Java in 1342, but earlier examples exist. Francis Drake, visiting Java in 1580, noted that the people were warlike, 'well armed with swords, targets [shields] and daggers, forged by themselves and exquisitely wrought'. Some of the finest krises were made during the Mojopahit and Mataram dynasties, and as late as the early years of this century talented smiths were still employed by the *susuhunan* of Surakarta.

The kris is essentially a thrusting weapon, held not like a dagger but with a 'pistol grip'. The double-edged blade may be 30 to 45 centimetres long, and is either straight-edged or wavy; including both edges the number of waves varies from 7 to 25 (always an odd number). Although hilts and scabbards have often been elaborately decorated in ivory, gold, silver, rare woods, precious stones, and chiselled and repoussé work, the sacred blade has always been the most important part of the weapon.

The finest blades were forged from at least two kinds of iron, one of which was generally meteoric iron with a high nickel content (in fact a form of steel). Bars of the different metals were hot-forged together, cut, rolled, hammered . . . and re-worked again and again until the resulting blade contained layer upon layer of varying grades of iron and steel. Immersed in an arsenic solution, the impure iron turned black, the nickelous iron turned silver-white, revealing an astonishing range of patterns. These patterns are known as *pamor*, and are highly prized as a sign of craftsmanship. An ability to anticipate the final pattern was an inherent part of the *mpu*'s artistry, and it is easy to understand why an *mpu* armourer was often credited with magical powers.

Many blades were valued on the originality of their *pamor* work. Others were further embellished with raised gold inlay of superb workmanship. Floral motifs were popular, especially on straight blades, whilst on wavy blades a sacred serpent (*naga*) would weave from the haft almost to the point. Kris hilts in Java were often fashioned in the form of a guardian demon, variously a *raksasa* or a stylised half-man, half-bird figure (possibly an anthropomorphic *garuda*). Later, perhaps as a result of Muslim influence, the hilt figure lost its representational form, and most Javanese hilts now show only the faintest hint of a demon on the inside curve of the carved wooden hilt.

In the course of centuries, and even of decades, outstanding blades received new hilts and new scabbards, though the blade itself remained inviolate. Today, the finest krises, whether *pusakas* (sacred heirlooms) or not, are reverently enveloped in 'gloves' of velvet. They are treasured for their beauty and for their history. Krises are still worn with ceremonial court dress and on formal occasions in Central Java, when they can be seen tucked into the back of the colourful waistbands of courtiers, aristocrats and gentry. The krises among the royal *pusakas* are the most valued and revered possessions in the old courts, and regular offerings of *melati* flowers and fragant incense are still made to them. Only female attendants in the palaces are permitted to clean the royal krises, though once a year in Yogyakarta the sultan himself is expected to perform that duty in a special ritual.

Following pages: a pair of rare kris daggers *from a private collection in solo. The one on the left is reputed to have belonged to the 11th Century king Airlangga, and its decoration tells the story of Arjuna's ascesis.*

THE PERFORMING ARTS, of all Java's cultural achievements, are at once the most deeply rooted in the past and the most dramatically evident in the present. There are instruments in the *gamelan* orchestra of Java that have links with the Bronze Age cultures of Central Asia. There are shadow puppets whose origins can be traced back to animistic beliefs that shadows are the manifestations of ancestral spirits. There are masks that once helped village communities protect themselves against demons, and which are still used as aids in exorcism rites. There are dances that were once seen only within the sacred precincts of royal courts (one at least, the *bedoyo ketawang* still performed in Solo, is never likely to emerge as a public entertainment). There are trance-inducing dances harking back to ancient beliefs and tribal myths. There are tales and stories based on Hindu, Islamic and indigenous Javanese legends.

Java's performing arts are found everywhere, in much the same way that morality and mystery plays were almost the bread of daily life in medieval Europe, that Punch and Judy puppet shows were regularly performed at fairs and on village greens until recent times. Java still has its strolling minstrels and its mobile theatrical groups; it has famous troupes who work in one place, others who wander through a district or subdistrict like touring repertory companies, always ready for a *selamatan* or for a series of one-night stands.

It is a rich, vibrant tapestry of colour, dance, sound, movement and charm, a finely interwoven mixture of religion, story-telling and entertainment. There has been a constant cross-fertilisation: court dances have become part of the farmer's heritage, the shadow plays of village rituals have developed into one of the island's most consummately sophisticated art forms.

Inevitably, somewhere in Java, the visitor will come across a *wayang* performance of some kind. *Wayang* literally means 'shadow', but since all theatrical forms are, in a sense, abstractions, *wayang* has become a handy expression embracing

Red faces and staring eyes identify the ogres, giants and demons of the wayang kulit *world.*

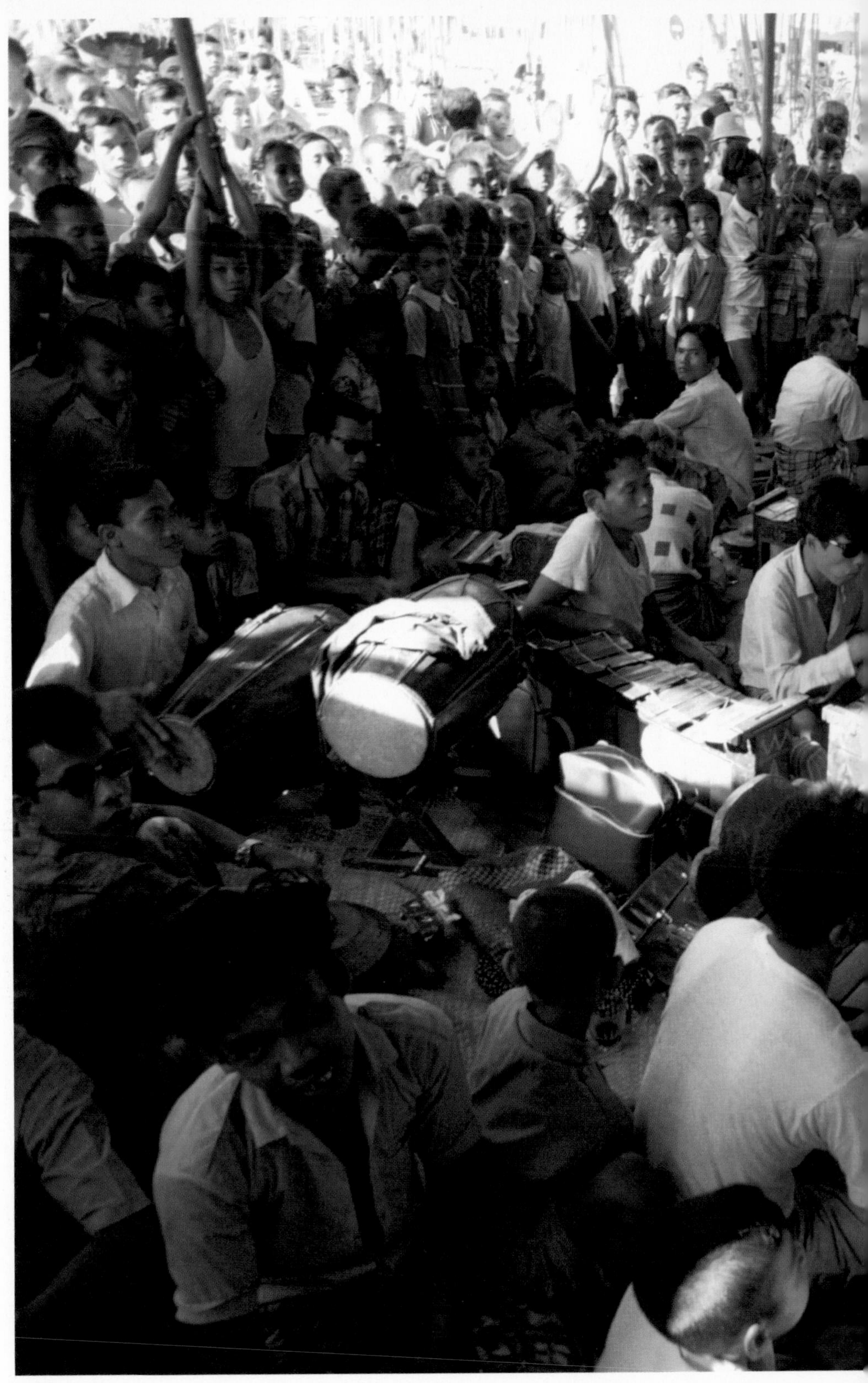

most types of theatre in Java.

Wayang kulit (less commonly known as *wayang purwa*) is the theatre of the flat leather shadow puppets; *wayang golek* is the theatre of three-dimensional wooden puppets; *wayang wong* (Javanese) or *wayang orang* (Indonesian) is the human theatre; and *wayang topeng* is human theatre in which the actors wear masks. Separate again is classical dance, once the exclusive prerogative of the Javanese courts, but now an important element in *wayang wong* performances. In all forms of *wayang* the dialogue (whether spoken by the *dalang* or the actors) is in Javanese or Sundanese, and the chants are often in *kawi*, the Old Javanese language. *Bahasa Indonesia* is sometimes used in humorous exchanges between the clowns, or in direct repartee with the audience, but except in the modern *ludruk* plays it is never used as the main language.

A *wayang kulit* performance requires a white cloth screen, a puppeteer or *dalang*, a *gamelan* ensemble (the size varies), the trunk of a banana tree, a light source to cast the shadows (once an oil lantern in the shape of a *garuda* or sun-bird, now generally an incandescent bulb), and of course the puppets. All are assembled on one side of the screen, the *dalang* sitting cross-legged on the floor from where he manipulates the puppets, directs the *gamelan*, intones or sings special songs, narrates story outlines, and provides the voices for every character. The puppets are arrayed to the left and right of the centre of the screen, stuck into the soft pulp of the banana trunk: the 'goodies' are on the *dalang's* right hand, the 'baddies' on his left. The audience, as it chooses, can sit on the *dalang's* side of the screen (the best place to appreciate the colours of the puppets and their master's extraordinary skills) or on the 'shadow' side of the screen, a marvellously exciting world of hard-edged blacks and subtle, wavering, ghostly greys.

In addition to his other skills the *dalang* is a master of improvisation. He works from a basic

Preceding pages: The audience watches a daylight performance of wayang kulit *from backstage. Right, a dance of welcome at a Solo wedding.*

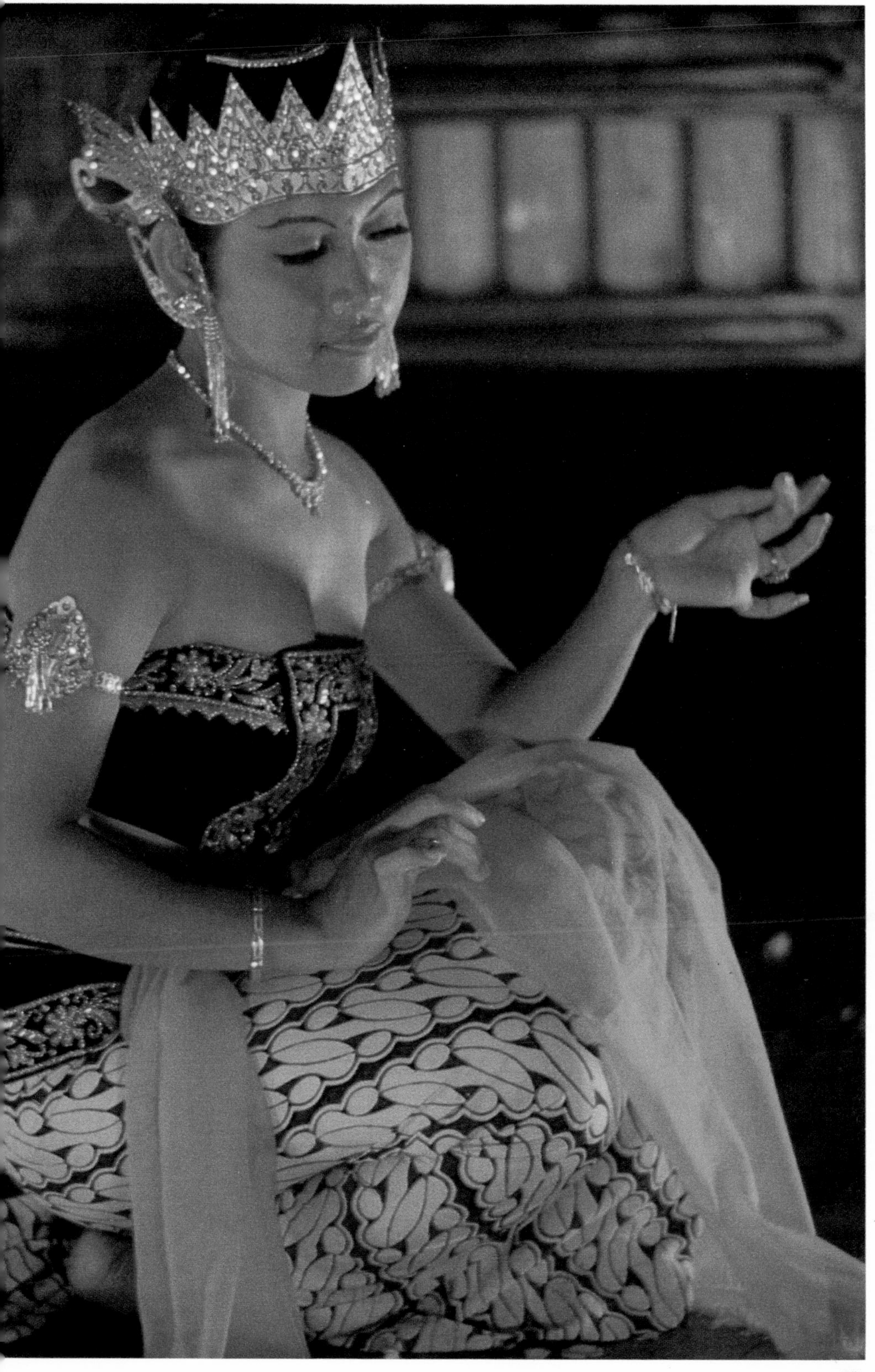

story outline or *lakon*, but there is no formal 'script' in any *wayang* performance. The outline naturally dictates much of the content of the dialogue, but it is the *dalang* who injects originality, humour, satire and even social commentary into the presentation.

A performance begins at 8.30 or 9 o'clock at night (though daytime shows are not uncommon). The first three hours up to midnight introduce characters, establish the story line and provide occasional skirmishes and conflicts. At midnight the second part begins, invariably introduced by the *panakawans* (clowns), and this is always the most vigorous and enthralling segment of the play. Some three hours later, after a multitude of battles and sundry adventures, the resolution of the action and plot takes place, and the performance ends just as the sun is about to rise.

Wayang golek performances follow a similar pattern, though naturally without the need for a screen, and the audience normally sits facing the *dalang*. Daylight performances of *wayang golek* are quite common.

Shadow puppets are most popular in Central Java, where they enact episodes from the *Ramayana* and *Mahabharata* cycles; wooden-puppet plays are much less common, and normally tell stories from the Amir Hamzah tales. In West Java, *wayang golek* is far more popular than *wayang kulit*, and follows the *Ramayana* and *Mahabharata* repertoire.

Wayang wong (or *wayang orang*), with live actors, is extremely popular throughout Java. As in the puppet theatre, the plays are mostly based on the Hindu epics, though there is a considerable store of tales from East Javanese history and legend. *Wayang wong* also uses a *dalang* who chants songs and conducts the *gamelan* orchestra, but his role is less important than it is in the puppet plays. The human players move with rigid adherence to stylised steps and actions, many of which are astonishingly similar to those of the puppet characters. Dance has a very important role in *wayang wong*, and although some of the verbal encounters which help set the scene are boring to look at (but full of philosophical subtleties to anyone who understands Javanese) the dancing more than compensates for the dull patches. Every town of any size has a resident *wayang wong* troupe. *Sriwidari* performs each night in Solo, and is the oldest and most famous troupe in Java, acknowledged throughout the island as the best.

Good presentations of *wayang wong* are brilliantly colourful spectacles, with sumptuous costumes and a golden glitter of bracelets, armbands and head-dresses. For the visitor the *Ramayana* performances on the open-air stages at Prambanan 16 km east of Yogya and at Pandaan's Candra Wilwatikta 45 km below Surabaya are exciting introductions to a complex but superbly alive world of theatre. In both instances the dialogue has been dropped, so that the dancing and the music become all-absorbing.

Wayang topeng is now seldom seen as a full length performance, though a revival is taking place in Cirebon in West Java, and *wayang topeng Cirebon* can sometimes be seen in Jakarta.

A variation of *wayang topeng* is *tari topeng* (literally 'mask dance'), in which two or three masked dancers perform short excerpts from the Panji stories (see page 92). These are invariably danced with great skill, and the beautiful, stylised masks seem to acquire a living, mobile quality. The Panji cycle is also of probable historical interest, representing a unique Javanese synthesis of indigenous with Hindu elements.

Until the early years of this century Javanese classical dance was not seen outside of the courts, where it had developed over the centuries into a serenely stylised and immaculately precise form. Originally of ritual and religious significance (Siva was more easily propitiated by dance than by any other form of worship) it became one of the most highly regarded and polished of all Java's arts. Happily for today's visitor many of the movements of court dancing can now be seen in the *wayang wong* dance dramas, and the formal art of classical dance is now taught outside of the old palaces ... though dancing masters at Yogyakarta's *kraton* can be seen instructing their pupils as they must have done for centuries.

Pure dance, as opposed to the dance dramas, still exists in two famous forms, the *serimpi* and

The microphone is the only anachronism in an otherwise ageless performance of wayang golek *wooden puppets near Cirebon.*

the *bedoyo*. Both are danced solely by girls, and both are exquisitely subtle in their grace and elegance. The *serimpi* is a stylised combat between two pairs of girls, and is apparently based on the old Amir Hamzah stories. The *bedoyo* (or *bedaya*) is a beautiful series of undulating and gently flowing movements performed by nine girls. The *serimpi* and the *bedoyo* are still danced within the Solo court, and can also be seen in Yogyakarta at special functions held by relatives of the sultan or by members of the old aristocracy, though dance performances are no longer staged within the *kraton*. Any opportunity to see either of these beautiful dances should not be missed.

Ketoprak and *ludruk* are two other theatrical forms that might be encountered. The *ketoprak* repertoire is based largely on indigenous East Javanese tales (part myth, part history), and the acting style is essentially realistic; dance and singing may be used at the opening of a performance, but not within the fabric of the play. *Ludruk* was created this century, and is the closest thing in Java to modern Western theatre, with plots generally based on conflicts arising out of the generation gap or thwarted love trysts. Female roles in *ludruk* are played by men and young boys.

The most famous folk-dances in Java are the *reog Ponorogo* (in which the lead dancer wears a horrendously heavy tiger mask) and the *kuda kepang* 'horse trance dance' which is sometimes seen in conjunction with the *reog Ponorogo* but more often seen alone. It is known by several different names, but the action is essentially the same: dancers, astride 'hobby horses' of plaited bamboo, whirl themselves into a state of complete trance, during which they dismount from their steeds and proceed to eat unhulled rice, glass or anything else that is offered to them.

* * *

The two main stories informing Javanese theatre and dance are the *Ramayana* and the *Mahabharata*, brief synopses of which are given on page 88. Both are moral tales, full of instructions and examples on how to lead the good life; both praise the rectitude, wisdom and perseverance of the noble *satriya* or warrior class; both stress faithfulness, integrity and filial and fraternal devotion; and both acknowledge that the trek along the path of virtue demands humility, self sacrifice, deprivation and compassion. They are cautionary tales, like *Everyman*, but are less a battle between good and evil (in which evil must always lose) than a recognition of the perpetual ebb and flow of the spirits of darkness and light. They are far older, and far more popular, than Chaucer's *Canterbury Tales*, but like the *Tales* they are filled with action, wit and imagination. Their partly religious, partly philosophic content has remained absorbing and relevant because it has been presented in such a consummately entertaining manner.

In the *Ramayana* the chief characters are Rama, his wife Sita, his brother Laksmana, the monkey general Hanuman, the demon king Rawana, and Rawana's brother Wibisana. In the *Mahabharata* the 'good guys' are the five Pandawa brothers, of whom Arjuna and Bima are the best loved, and the semi-divine Krisna; the 'bad guys' are the hundred Korawas (ninety-nine brothers and one sister).

Arjuna and Rama have certain characteristics in common: both are semi-divine (Arjuna is descended from the god Indra, Rama is an incarnation of Visnu), and both are consummate archers; Rama, however, does not have Arjuna's awesome predilection for the fairer sex, but devotes himself to Sita.

The most popular figures of all are the four *panakawans*, the clownish servants of the Pandawas: Semar the father, 'short-legged, fat, hermaphroditic . . . flat-nosed, with a hypertrophic jaw, a wise, tired eye, an enormous rear part, a bulging paunch, and heavy, almost feminine breasts' (Claire Holt), and his three sons Gareng, Petruk and Bagong. They are much more than clowns. Whilst they are often uproariously funny (even to those who can't understand a word of Javanese), their role is akin to that of the medieval court jester: a source of wit and humour, and also of valued counsel. Semar, especially, appears to carry the accumulated wisdom of the ages. Although Arjuna is semi-divine, he is not impervious to the displeasure of the gods. Yet gross, grotesque Semar, with

A topeng *dancer clowns for a village audience near the ancient sultanate of Cirebon.*

his rheumy eyes, not only confronts the gods but often bests them: he alone could have the effrontery to throw the great god Brahma into a well.

* * *

In a complete set of *wayang kulit* figures there may be as many as four hundred individual puppets. In the course of a village performance of *wayang golek* upwards of a hundred characters might be seen. Even *wayang wong* calls for a large number of human actors, and the Prambanan *Ramayana* troupe puts a hundred people on stage.

Although many participants in the larger 'crowd scenes' will be nameless monkey warriors or crude, destructive giants and demons, there are still dozens of leading characters whose identity is established visually according to age-old precepts. The clue may be the way in which a dancer moves, the shape of his head-dress, the colour of his face or his mask (*wayang topeng*). Wooden and leather puppets can be unmistakably identified in the same way. These visual characteristics, however, tell much more than 'who', for they also illuminate the personality of the character.

Rama and Arjuna are obviously of noble birth for they move in a refined (*halus*) manner. Even in battle they are graceful and delicate, using their minds as much as their muscles, whilst their demon foes rant and rage with the fury of a wounded bull elephant. As dancers, they are always slimly built. As puppets, they have long, straight downward-pointing noses and narrow downcast eyes, both symbols of nobility, and their faces are generally gold in colour. Arjuna and the twin brothers Nakula and Sadewa always wear their hair in an upward-curling roll like a scorpion's tail: their elder brother, Yudistira, wears a flatter, more compact style, denoting his more gentle, introspective nature.

Bima is stupendously strong. He is also impetuous, generous, loyal, and a ferocious warrior. In *wayang kulit* he towers above his four brothers, and has wide-awake eyes and an upturned nose similar to his Korawa opponents, though his 'scorpion-tail' hair style automatically marks him as royal. In *wayang wong* he moves with abrupt, angular steps resembling vigorous isometrics. His most singular feature is a pair of huge, talon-like thumbnails, fearsome weapons in time of war.

At left, veteran Javanese dancers put young students through the paces of refined dances of the Yogyakarta kraton *during a weekly Sunday morning training session.*

Krisna, a god incarnate, is an ally of the Pandawas. As a shadow puppet he has a black face, is small, and has the long straight nose and narrow eyes of the gentleman warrior. His brother Baladewa, who sides with the Korawas, has a rose or red face, is much taller than his brother, but nonetheless has a refined nose and almond-shaped eyes: he is not a complete ogre.

Rawana, Rama's implacable foe, thrusts and struts upon the stage, every step filled with menace. His head turns sharply with each movement, his legs move like pistons in the *gagah* or *kasar* style which is an attribute of all demon nobles. His eyes are fixed rigidly ahead of him, symptomatic of intractability; his face (whether a grease-painted human one, a mask, or a puppet's head) is an impassioned, furious red in keeping with his aggressive, hostile nature.

The *raksasas* and *butas* (giants, ogres, demons) who inhabit both the epics normally have red faces, huge round eyes and bulbous noses.

Voices, too, are helpful in identifying a type, if not a specific character. The *halus* characters speak in a soft, often inaudible monotone (delivered by the actors in *wayang wong*, or by the *dalang* in puppet plays). The *kasar* characters variously shout, rage, scream and bellow. Wheedling ministers (*patih*) and ill-meaning teachers (*guru*) often whine and sniffle.

* * *

In their homeland, the vast subcontinent of India, the *Ramayana* and the *Mahabharata* have been known for three thousand years. With the spread of Indian religions and culture through Southeast Asia, the two epics became part of the mythology of Burma, Thailand, Laos, Cambodia, the Malay Peninsula, and especially of Java and Bali. Both epics are long and complex, even in the barest outline. Thus, the following synopses offer a thread, but not the rich texture.

THE RAMAYANA*: Rama, Laksmana and their*

half-brother Barata are the sons of the king of Ayodya. An accomplished bowman, Rama wins the hand of beautiful Sita in an archery contest, but through the intervention of Barata's mother Rama is prevented from succeeding his father as king. Rama, Sita and Laksmana go into exile, refusing Barata's entreaties to return. In the forest they meet a sister of Rawana, king of the demons (raksasas)*; she falls in love with Rama, is spurned, and then turns to Laksmana who promptly cuts off her nose and ears.*

Rawana, determined to avenge this indignity, sends off a servant in the form of a golden deer. Rama stalks the animal and kills it. Its dying cries sound like Rama calling for help, and Laksmana, taunted by Sita, goes in search of his brother though he has been forbidden to leave his sister-in-law. In his absence Rawana appears as a holy beggar and confronts Sita, who refuses his appeals to desert Rama. Rawana assumes his natural terrifying form, abducts Sita, and flies off with her. The gallant bird Jatayu attempts to rescue her but is mortally wounded. Before dying he tells Rama and Laksmana what has happened.

Searching for Sita, the brothers meet Hanuman, a general in the kingdom of the apes, who takes them to meet Sugriwa, his king. Sugriwa, who has been usurped by his brother, seeks Rama's aid in regaining his throne. Rama kills the errant brother, and the grateful monkey king places his army at Rama's disposal. Rama and Laksmana set off with Hanuman and the white ape army, and learn that Rawana has carried Sita across the sea to the island of Langka, Rawana's homeland. Hanuman undertakes a daring reconnaissance of Langka and finds Sita in a garden of Rawana's palace. He gives her a token from Rama, and Sita in turn gives Hanuman one of her rings, but Hanuman is discovered by Rawana's guards, is captured after a desperate fight, and is sentenced to be burnt at the stake. With the pyre blazing, he wrenches free, his tail a mass of flames, and sets fire to the palace before fleeing from Langka.

Hanuman carries Sita's ring to Rama, and the ape armies gather on the shore opposite Langka

Lustful Rawana threatens Sita in the Pandaan Ramayana festival.

and build a giant causeway across the sea. On the island a tumultuous battle ensues. One of Rama's magic arrows eventually fells Rawana, and the victors return home with Sita to a boisterous welcome. In the kingdom of Ayodya Rama receives the throne from his half-brother Barata.

THE MAHABHARATA*: The ninety-nine Korawas, led by the ambitious Suyudana, believe that the kingdom of Ngastina should belong to them and not to their cousins, the Pandawas. Egged on by the evil chancellor Sakuni they resolve to destroy the Pandawas: Yudistira, Bima, Arjuna and the twins Nakula and Sadewa. Although brought up together under the regent of Ngastina, and instructed by the same teacher Durna, the cousins have never been close, and the superiority of the Pandawas in any kind of contest has only heightened the resentment and jealousy of the Korawas.*

Plot follows plot. Arjuna is poisoned, but revived by the gods; Yudistira is imprisoned, but released by Bima, the greatest warrior amongst the famous five; and finally a drastic attempt is made to burn the Pandawas alive. Tiring of torments, the Pandawas and their wives take to the forest for some years and form an alliance with Krisna. Yudistira has married the beautiful Drupadi, oft-wed Arjuna marries Sumbadra (Krisna's sister) by whom he has a son Abimanyu, and Bima has married the giantess Arimbi and produced a son Gatutkaca . . . who, like his father, is a fearsome warrior but who has also inherited from his mother the ability to fly.

A truce is reached with the Korawas, but the peace is short-lived. Yudistira, an inveterate gambler, is inveigled into a rigged dice game and loses everything (palace, wife, himself and his brothers) to Suyudana. The Pandawas are forced into a thirteen-year exile. On returning they find that Suyudana will not return them their little kingdom as promised. They hold a council of war with Krisna. The Bharatayuddha, *'The War of the Bharatas', begins.*

In eighteen gory days the cream of the Bharata nobility is destroyed. The Pandawas' losses are heavy, and of the Korawas there is only one survivor.

Rama, the royal hero, of the Ramayana epic.

In microcosm, the *Bharatayuddha* is the archetype of the fratricidal conflict: the House of Lancaster against the House of York, Union against Confederacy. Yet the whole cycle is filled with soft interludes, with humorous tales of mistaken identity, with reflections on the court life of the Pandawas.

Arjuna Wiwaha, 'The Wedding of Arjuna', is one of the most popular stories in the cycle, relating the temptations imposed on Arjuna during his ascetic devotionals on Mount Indrakila, where he has gone to seek strength and guidance for the forthcoming battle against a demon king who threatens the abodes of the gods (the gods, in many of these tales, are far from infallible, and frequently seek human aid in thwarting the demons and netherworld creatures who assail them). In ordinary life a redoubtable warrior with a fatal charm with women, Arjuna is tempted by seven divine nymphs, whom he resists; the god Indra tests him further by promising *nirvana*, but Arjuna persists in his ascesis; he is attacked by one of the demon's giants, defeats it, and then joins forces with the gods in a series of escapades which bring victory . . . and as a reward spends a month with each of the nymphs.

Three other legends (part myth, part history) are popular to varying degrees in different parts of Java.

PANJI is a royal prince who loses his beautiful bride Candra Kirono (Kirana), a princess of Kediri, on the eve of their wedding. Panji's subsequent adventures in searching for his true love have been embroidered and embellished in scores of variations on the simple theme. There are disguises, the inevitable lusting demon kings, innumerable cases of mistaken identity, wild battles, false leads . . . in fact, everything that 'True Love Stories' could ever hope for. Candra Kirono, though deeply in love with Panji (described by Claire Holt as being 'in many ways the East Javanese Arjuna, the ideal noble prince, unconquerable in battle and irresistible in love'), often manages to complicate matters by assuming the role of a warrior, but love always wins out.

The *Panji* cycle probably developed in East Java about five hundred years ago. Today it is most often seen as a mask play (*wayang topeng*) or in shorter mask dance versions (*tari topeng*) and is a popular and apposite entertainment at wedding parties: guests may be treated to a half hour episode featuring Candra Kirono in a white mask, Klono (an ardent but ill-fated kingly suitor) in a red mask, Panji in a beautiful golden mask . . . and a clown who will have the guests in tears of laughter as he mimics the delicate movements of Candra Kirono and the bold severity of Klono (waving a feather duster instead of a kris) until the *gamelan* refuses to play for him and he feigns sleep in the middle of the floor.

DAMAR WULAN, another semi-historical tale from East Java, is a favourite in the *ketoprak* repertoire. Nephew of the prime minister of the Mojopahit queen, Ratu Kencana, Damar Wulan is employed at the court as a lowly grasscutter but he falls in love with and secretly marries his beautiful cousin Dewi Anjasmara. The handsome couple are discovered and imprisoned but Damar Wulan wins his freedom and honour when he succeeds, after many adventures, in vanquishing Menak Jingga, the 'Red Knight' who is advancing with an army on the palace of Ratu Kencana. (Menak Jingga, though classically cast in the bad-guy mould, is interesting and colourful enough to warrant stories of his own.)

AMIR HAMZAH is a fanciful interpretation of Persian history and the rise of Islam in the 7th century. It was probably composed about 800 A.D. during the reign of Haroun al Raschid and reached Java (along with Islam) in the 15th century. *Amir Hamzah*, also known as *Menak*, relates the trials and tribulations of Prince Menak Jayanegoro Amir Hamsa Putro Puser Bumi Mekah, and mainly consists of battle after battle after battle, interrupted by frequent love affairs. The noble prince is credited with laying the groundwork for Mohammed's warrior missionaries, and his boisterous adventures are by far the most popular stories in the *wayang golek* theatre of Central Java.

Hanuman, the mercurial monkey general, is a favorite with Ramayana audiences. Following pages: the moon rises over Mount Bromo in East Java and an ancient auto that still runs.

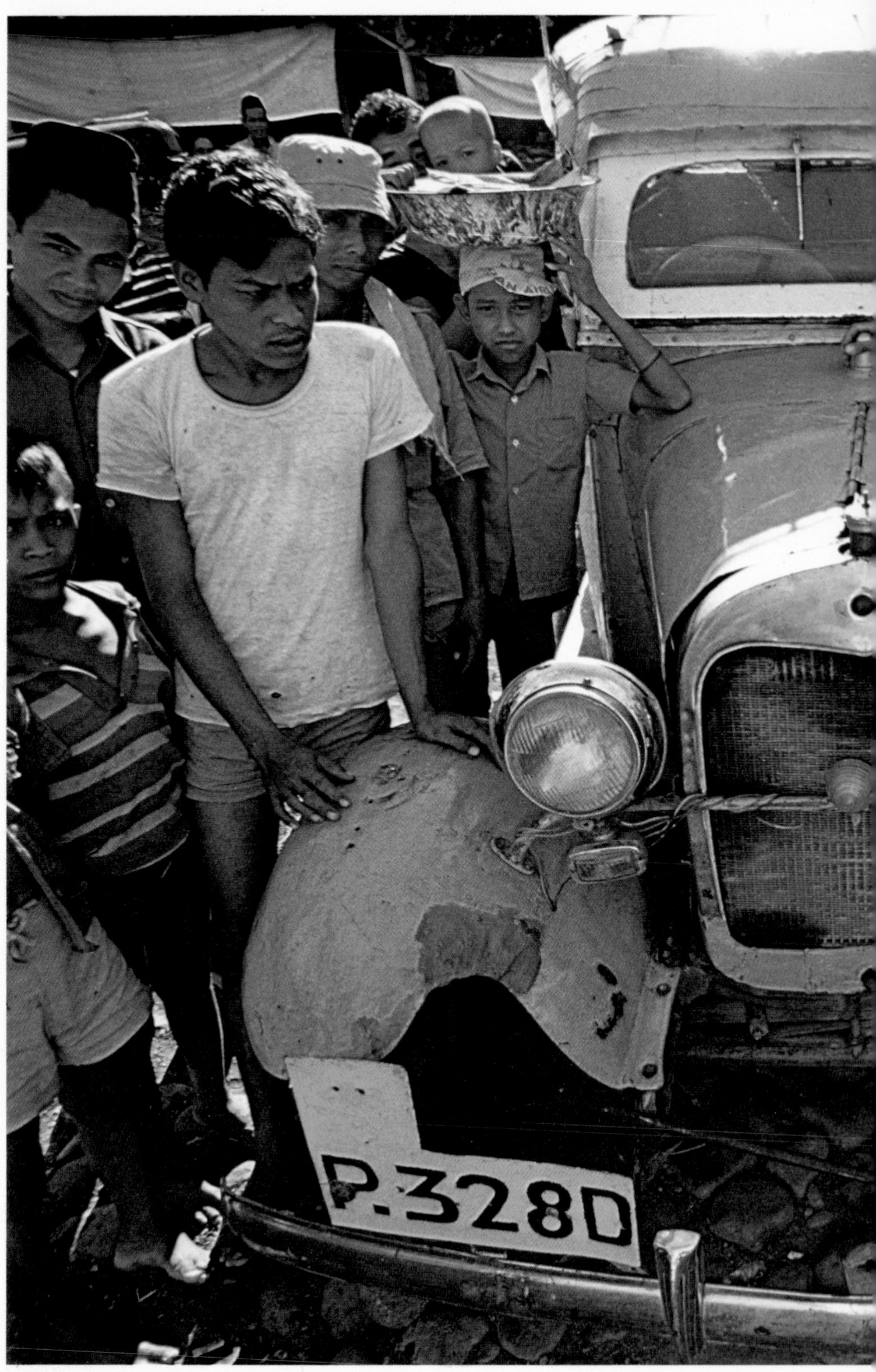
P.328D

B 5135

TRAVELLING IN JAVA

It is possible to see a little of Java in the sublime detachment of airconditioned splendour. But it is impossible to explore Java, to enjoy the magnetism of its landscapes and people, its culture and historic remains, without a certain amount of discomfort. And even though the tried-and-true itinerary from Jakarta through Yogya to Surabaya has much to recommend it, a real understanding and appreciation of the island's riches can only be gained if you diverge from what has, until now, been the regular tourist track.

Java is a land for the travelin' man (or woman). Although in tourist terms it is comparatively unexplored and certainly unexploited, it is remarkably accessible. With a jeep or similar four-wheel-drive machine you can get almost anywhere; a rugged car can show you most of the island; and local buses and trucks penetrate seemingly impenetrable areas. There is even one volcanic crater (Tangkuban Prahu) which can be reached by car; most other peaks involve pony-trekking or hiking.

Travel by road is the best way to see Java. Train services can show you much of it, but many routes (such as the airconditioned *Bima* from Jakarta to Surabaya, or the service from Jakarta to Yogya) are night runs. Only Jakarta, Semarang, Yogya and Surabaya can be reached by scheduled domestic airlines; light aircraft and helicopters offer regular flights to Pulau Seribu (the 'Thousand Islands') north of Jakarta and to Pelabuhan Ratu on the south coast; helicopter charters can take you to a few other places, including the wildlife reserve at Ujung Kulon; and in some cases fishing boats, launches or speedboats will be the only transport available.

Time. Java needs time. A day in Jakarta, two days in Yogya and another day in Surabaya are just not enough. Give yourself two weeks (if you can), and Java begins to come alive, begins to assume a form and pattern which become increasingly complex and increasingly compelling.

Time, unfortunately, is a luxury that few can afford. In allocating precious hours or days, be guided by your interests: for *batik*, the best centers are Yogya, Solo, Tasikmalaya and the north coast between Cirebon and Semarang; for temples, Yogyakarta and Malang are musts, and Dieng, Gedung Songo and Sukuh are also recommended for their scenic beauty; for cultural activity, including dance and puppets, Yogya and Solo are the high points, and Cirebon (though less organised) has much to offer; for museums, allow time in Jakarta (*Musium Pusat* and the new Jakarta City Museum), Yogya, Solo, Trowulan and Mojokerto; and for spectacular scenery, include Bromo and the southern part of East Java.

At left, an old steam engine still in use in Central Java.

Off the trunk routes (and even in major towns if you're travelling on the cheap) be prepared for minor inconveniences. Most small towns have a *losmen* or *penginapan* (cheap hotels): some *losmen* are very pleasant, some are downright appalling, and most are adequate. In villages, the *lurah* or *kepala desa* (the local headman) can generally find accommodation for visitors.

Mosquitoes and cockroaches are unavoidable in many areas. Slow-burning aromatic coils will keep the mosquitoes at bay, but you'll have to learn to live with the roaches.

Although the people of Java are scrupulously clean in matters of personal hygiene, the means to the end are not always sanitary. Away from expensive hotels in large towns and cities hot water is rare and there are no Western-style bathrooms. The answer is the cold-water *mandi* or bath: the bathing area contains a large tub filled with clean but non-drinkable water. Never, under any circumstances, plunge into the tub. Instead, learn the gentle art of the 'elephant shower': stand outside the tub, and douse and de-soap with the dipper supplied. On cold mornings in mountain areas the effect of the first dipperful can be shattering, but during the heat of the day a cold *mandi* is deliciously refreshing.

The pedestal toilet is rare. The ubiquitous hole-in-the-floor is easily managed, but be sure to use the water dipper to flush the bowl. Wear rubber thongs or sandals in bathrooms and toilets.

Take plenty of tissues and/or toilet paper. A 'sleeping sarong' is necessary, since top sheets are seldom supplied and bottom sheets are sometimes damp.

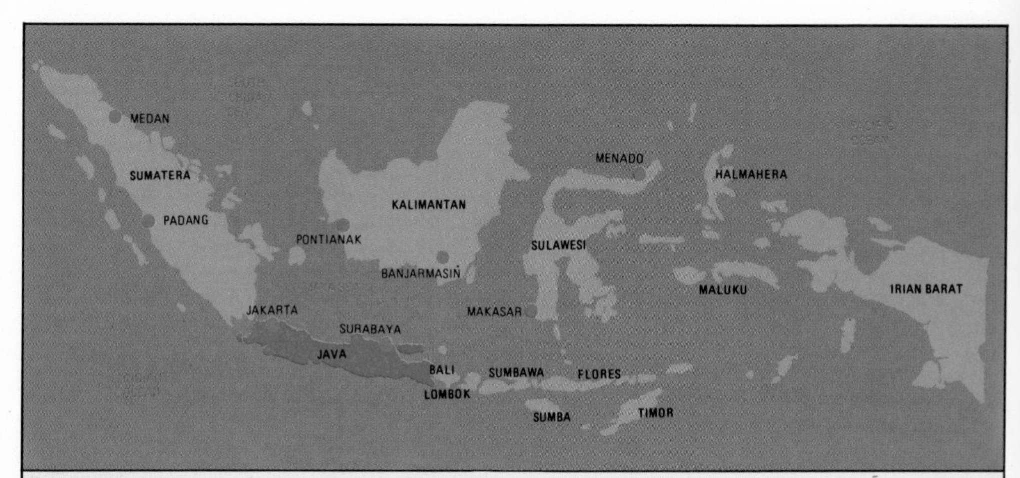

Indonesia (above) lies between 6° north and 11° south of the equator; to the north are the Philippines and the Malay Peninsula, to the south is Australia. The archipelago's 13,667 islands, of which less than 1,000 are inhabited, stretch more than 5,400 km from the Indian Ocean eastwards to the edge of the Pacific Ocean.

Java (below), including Madura, represents only 7% of Indonesia's land area, and is the same size as England or Greece. It is 1,100 km long, but is home to 65% of Indonesia's population of more than 120 million.

Exploring Java is an experience that is at once rich, beautiful, generous and tantalising. Often demanding, sometimes infuriating. It is a time to adventure. And if it gives you one tenth of what it gave to us, you won't be satisfied until you come back for more.

Right, the antique market on Jakarta's Jalan Surabaya. Following pages: A prahu *on the black sand beach at the inappropriately named Pantai Putih in East Java; the misty mountains of West Java; maps of the island; night lights illuminate Jakarta's Medan Merdeka; and the Indonesian flag waves in a Javanese breeze.*

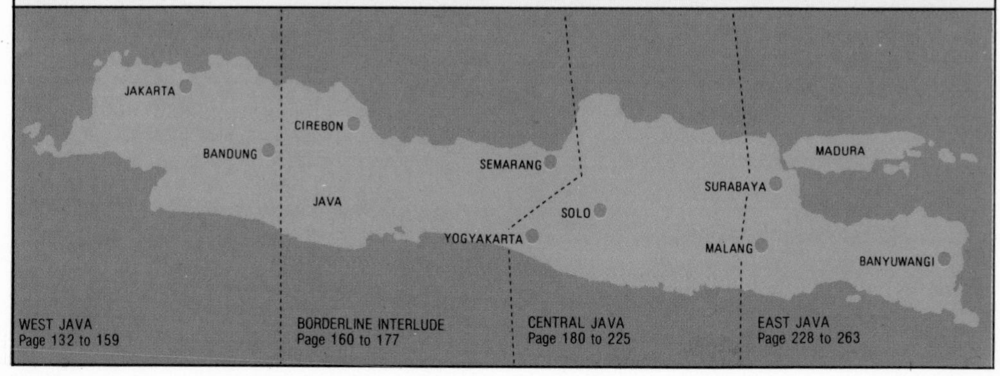

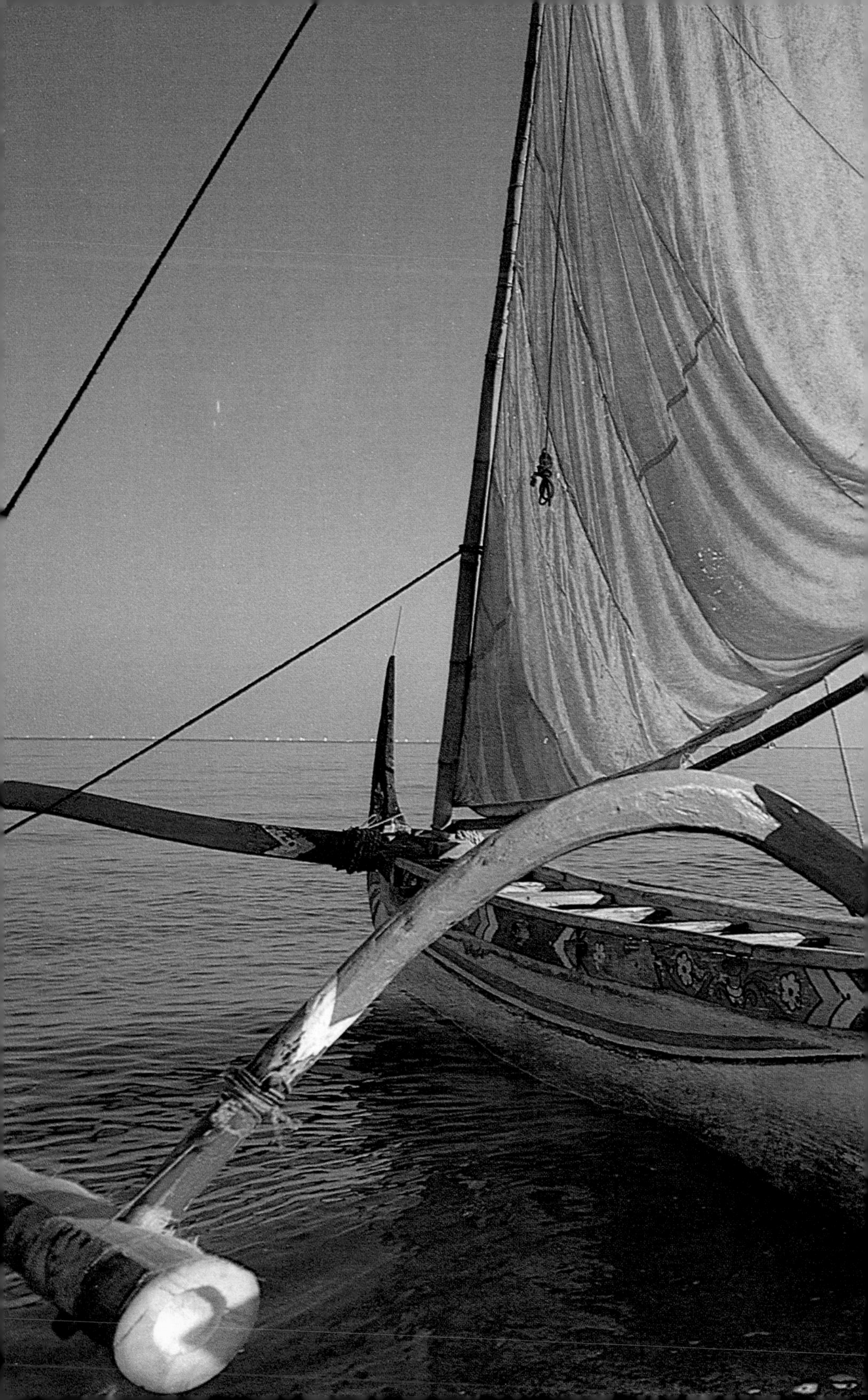

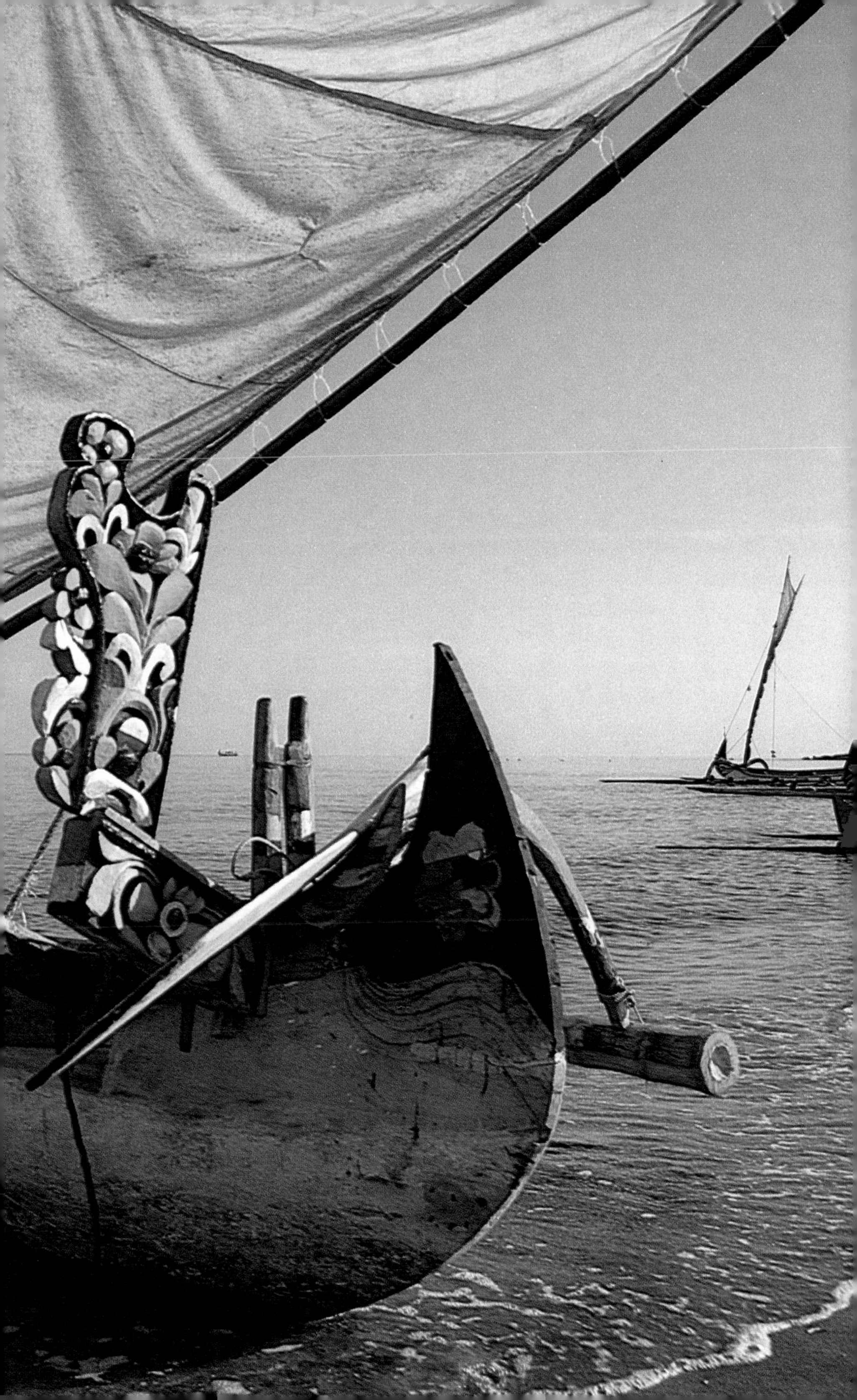

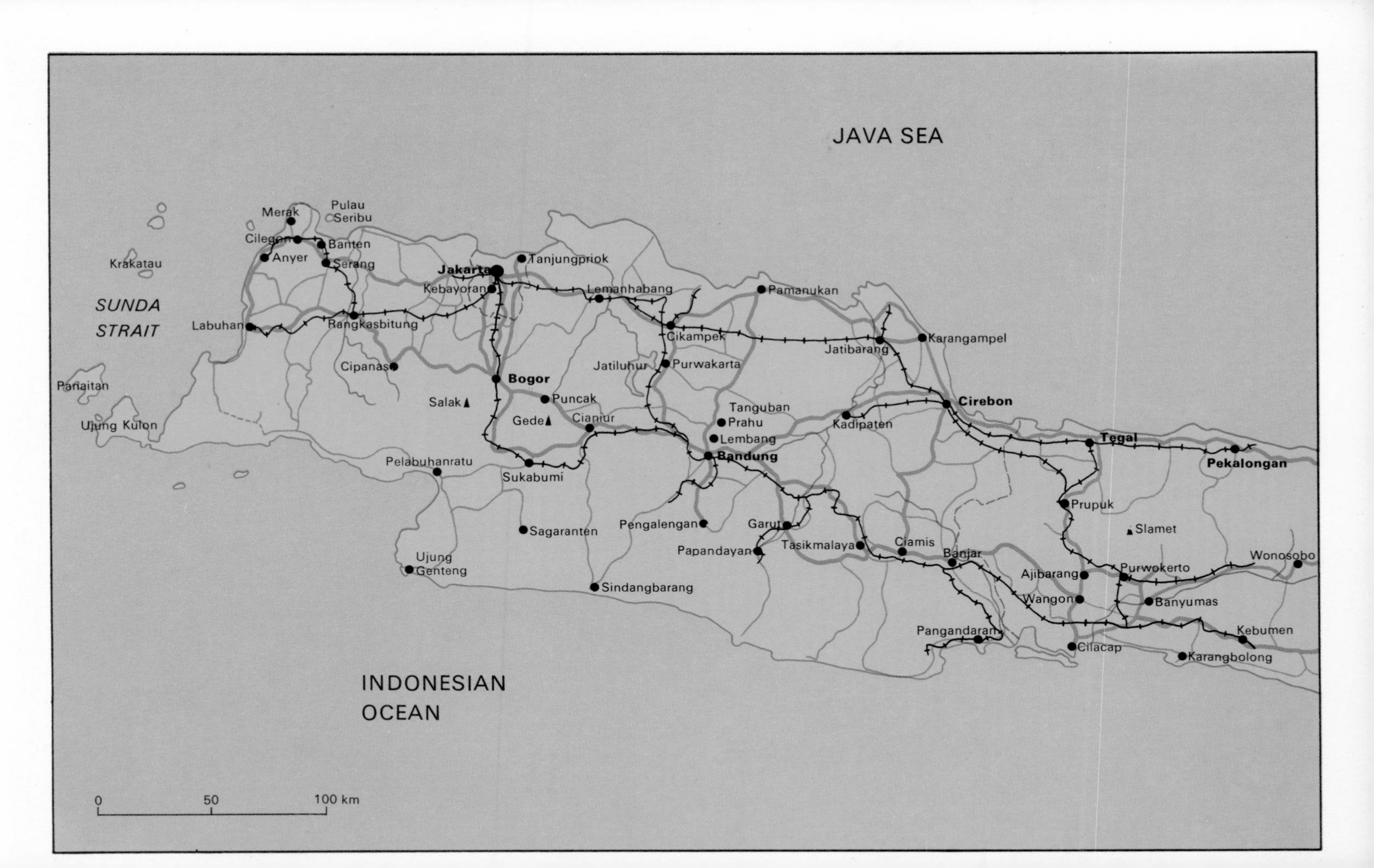
JAVA SEA
Merak
Pulau Seribu
Cilegon
Banten
Anyer
Serang
Krakatau
Jakarta
Tanjungpriok
Kebayoran
Lemanhabang
Pamanukan
SUNDA STRAIT
Labuhan
Rangkasbitung
Cikampek
Jatibarang
Karangampel
Cipanas
Jatiluhur
Purwakarta
Bogor
Panaitan
Salak
Puncak
Cirebon
Tanguban Prahu
Kadipaten
Ujung Kulon
Gede
Cianiur
Lembang
Tegal
Pekalongan
Bandung
Pelabuhanratu
Sukabumi
Prupuk
Slamet
Pengalengan
Garut
Sagaranten
Ciamis
Tasikmalaya
Papandayan
Banjar
Wonosobo
Ujung Genteng
Purwokerto
Ajibarang
Sindangbarang
Wangon
Banyumas
Pangandaran
Kebumen
Cilacap
Karangbolong
INDONESIAN OCEAN
0
50
100 km

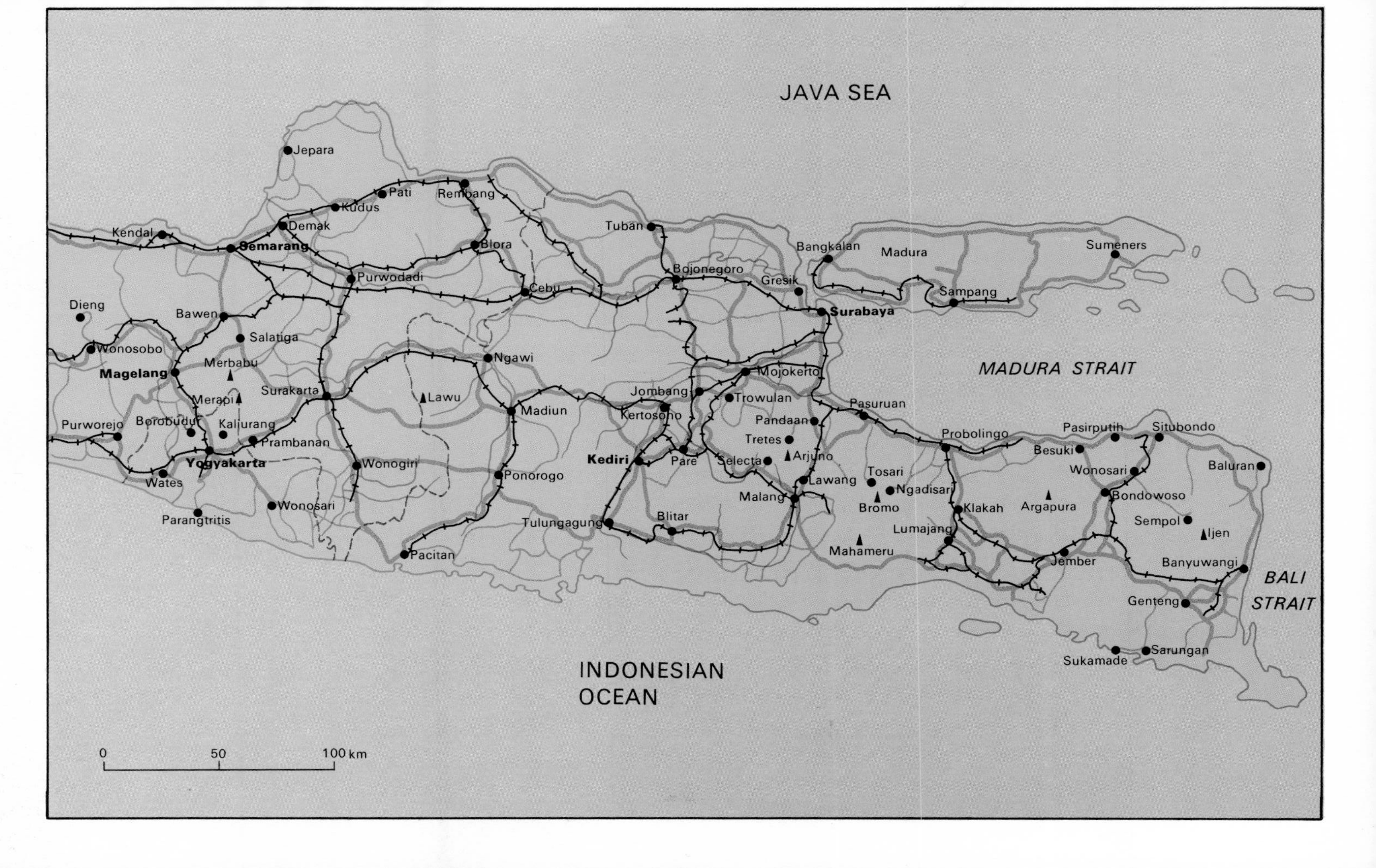

JAVA SEA
Jepara
Pati
Rembang
Kudus
Demak
Kendal
Semarang
Blora
Tuban
Purwodadi
Cebu
Bojonegoro
Gresik
Bangkalan
Madura
Sumeners
Sampang
Surabaya
Dieng
Bawen
Salatiga
Wonosobo
Merbabu
Magelang
Surakarta
Ngawi
Lawu
Merapi
Madiun
Purworejo
Borobudur
Kaliurang
Prambanan
Yogyakarta
Wates
Wonogiri
Ponorogo
Wonosari
Parangtritis
Pacitan
Tulungagung
Blitar
Kediri
Pare
Jombang
Kertosono
Mojokerto
Trowulan
Pandaan
Tretes
Arjuno
Selecta
Lawang
Malang
Pasuruan
Tosari
Ngadisari
Bromo
Mahameru
Probolingo
Klakah
Lumajang
Argapura
Besuki
Pasirputih
Situbondo
Wonosari
Bondowoso
Baluran
Sempol
Ijen
Jember
Banyuwangi
Genteng
Sukamade
Sarungan
MADURA STRAIT
BALI STRAIT
INDONESIAN OCEAN
0
50
100 km

KARTIKA
PLAZA

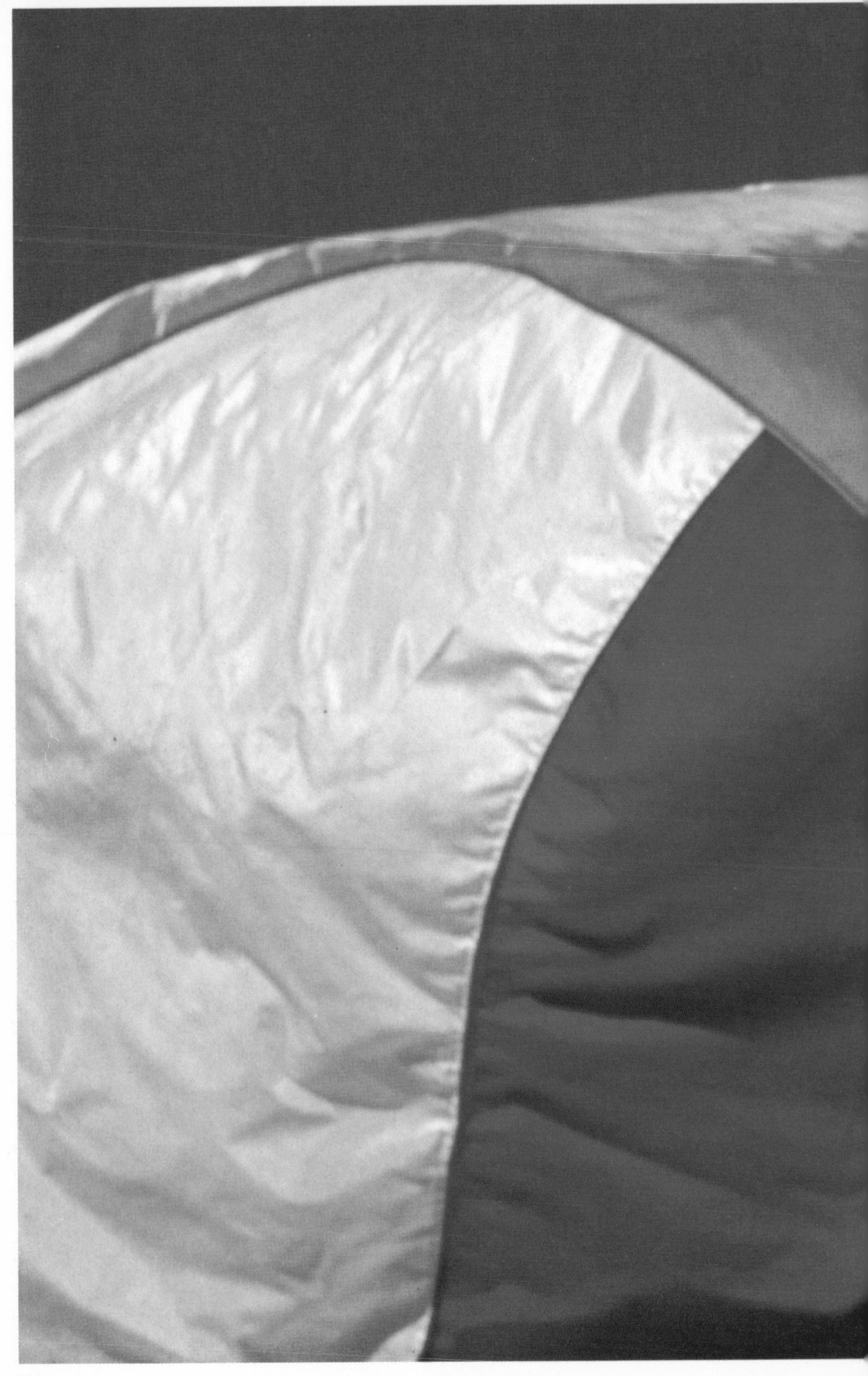

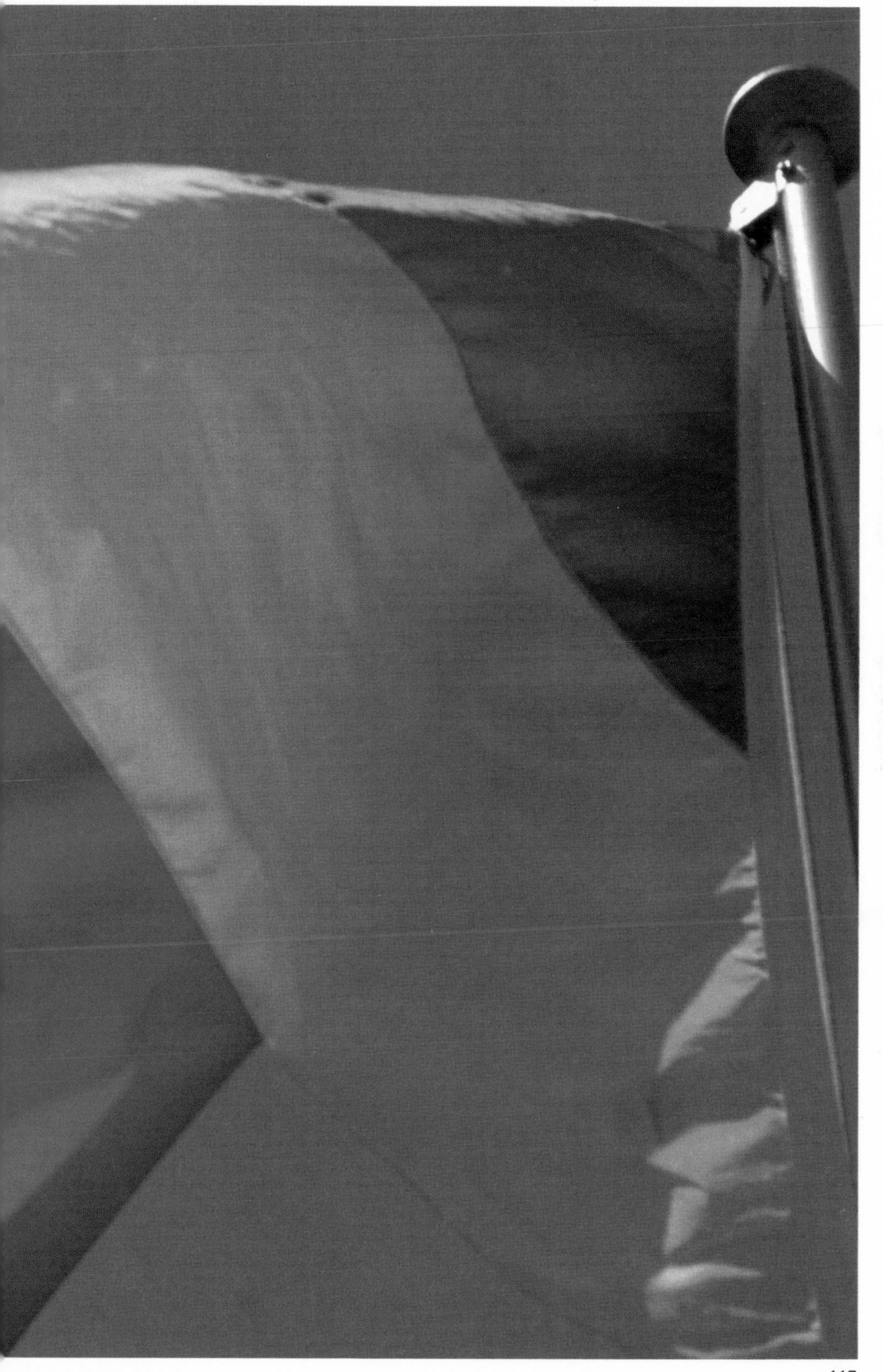

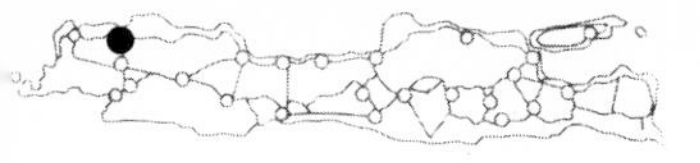

JAKARTA CITY OF VICTORY

Alexander the Great solved the problem of unravelling the impossible Gordian knot by slicing it through with his sword. Similar drastic measures are needed in attempting to compress all that could be said about *Daerah Khusus Ibukota Jakarta*, the 'Special Area of the Capital City Jakarta'. Thus, what follows consists more of highlights than details.

Jakarta is no Rio de Janeiro or Sydney or San Francisco. Situated on a broad alluvial plain, which every year thrusts farther northwards into the sea (part nature, part reclamation), it has no attractions in geographic terms. Not until the foothills of the Parahyangan (Preanger) District, 50 km to the south, does the landscape begin to offer any natural beauty.

It has also grown too fast. Its population has jumped more than 25 per cent in the past ten years and there are now thought to be more than 9 million people living in Jakarta. To accommodate this growth the city has sprawled outwards rather than upwards (most high-rise buildings are hotels or offices, not apartment blocks). Jakarta has also suffered from unsympathetic stories carried abroad by many foreigners: businessmen who found the place tough-going a few years ago, or tourists who refused to give it a chance because they were told it wasn't much of a place.

They are wrong. A great deal has happened since the frustrating 1960s, and successive city administrations, led by military men Ali Sadikin and Tjokropranolo, have applied a mixture of rigorous planning and common sense to beat some of the city's most pressing problems: roads and communications have been vastly improved; new hotels have sprung up like desert flowers; office blocks now throw long shadows on broad expressways. Although there is still much to do, particularly for the city's poorer residents, it is no longer possible to dismiss the place out of hand or (as the joke went in the 1960s) to say when speaking of someone working two blocks away in the city that he is "an hour away by car, an hour and a half by phone".

It is likely that the mouth of the Ciliwung River (modern Kali Besar) has been settled for thousands of years. By 1500 it was Pajajaran's port town, known as Sunda Kelapa, and it was here in 1522 that the first Europeans made contact with a Javanese kingdom. The Portuguese, aware of the turmoil in Central Java, thought (erroneously) that the struggles were religious rather than political, and sought a trading alliance with the Hindu kingdom of Pajajaran. This was granted. Returning five years later the Portuguese found that Pajajaran's control of Sunda Kelapa had been destroyed by Islamic troops led by Falatehan (Fatahillah) on 22 June 1527. The name of Sunda Kelapa was changed to Jayakarta, or 'Great Victory', and the date is still celebrated annually as the birthday of Jakarta.

As a vassal town of the powerful Banten sultanate, Jayakarta survived virtually unmolested for almost a hundred years.

In the first decade of the 17th century, Dutch and English traders established posts in the town. The presence of the interlopers was initially peaceful. Then, in 1618, Sultan Agung of Mataram destroyed the Dutch post at Jepara. The Dutch fortified their trading centre in Jayakarta. In a rapid series of events the Sundanese posted a gun battery against the Dutch, who in turn destroyed the battery and the English trading post; Banten captured the town but not the Dutch fortification.

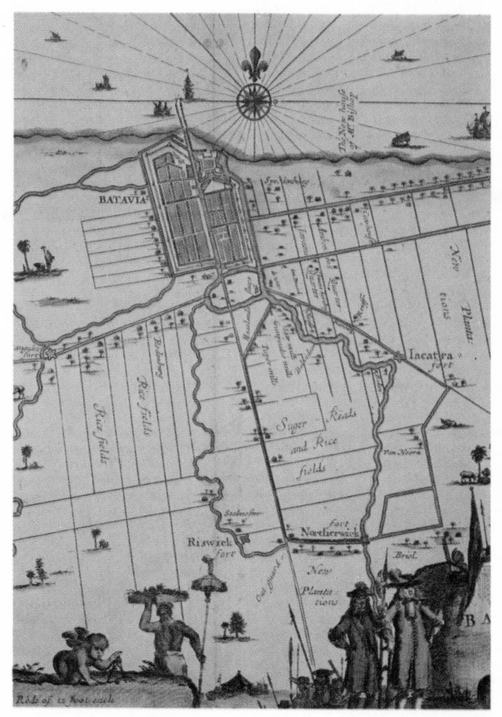

In Jalan Veteran, behind Istana Merdeka, *the official residence of the President, cleaners polish the Republic's gilded coat of arms. The* Istana *faces* Medan Merdeka, *a site known in 1703 as the 'New Plantations', below Fort Northerwick (lower right). The walled town of Batavia, then less than a century old, was only 1,600 metres long from the southern gate,* Pintu Besar, *to the northernmost bastion. The walls, gates and* Kasteel *have vanished, but today's streets still follow the layout of the old town.*

Sunda Kelapa became the Dutch capital of Batavia—and then the Jakarta of today.

which the beleaguered garrison named Batavia; on 28 May 1619 the Dutch governor-general, Jan Pieterszoon Coen, arrived from the Moluccas (Maluku) with a fleet and soldiers which, two days later, sallied forth to capture and destroy the old town.

Jayakarta remained in Dutch hands for the next 330 years.

A massive shoreline fortress was built on the northeast bank of the Ciliwung River. The fortress survived a critical attack by Sultan Agung in 1629, and a new walled town slowly developed within the protective range of its guns. The rigorously geometric layout of that town, laced with canals (see the map of 1703, previous page), is still preserved in the streets of 'Old Batavia'.

About 1730 'the pestilence' arrived in the form of decimating malarial plagues. The appalling death toll over the next century, encouraged by the lack of proper sanitation, greatly hastened Batavia's spread to the south. Many citizens moved into more salubrious dwellings along the southern reaches of the Ciliwung and in the new suburb of Weltevreden or 'well contented', and in 1741 the governor-general moved out of the old castle to a healthier clime.

The old town nevertheless maintained some of its former grandeur. Captain James Cook, who landed there in October 1770 and stayed almost three months, left a detailed and generally favourable account of the town, its suburbs, the countryside and the people. At one place in his journal he wrote:

> The environs of Batavia have a very pleafing appearance, and would in almoft any other country, be an enviable fituation. Gardens and houfes occupy the country for feveral miles, but the former are fo covered with trees, that the advantage of the land having been cleared of the wood that originally covered it, is almoft wholly loft; while thefe gardens and the fields adjacent to them are furrounded by ditches which yield a difagreeable fmell; and the bogs and moraffes in the adjacent fields are ftill more offenfive. For the fpace of more than thirty miles beyond the town, the land is totally flat, except in two places, on one of which the governor's country-feat is built, and on the other they hold a large market; but neither of thefe places is higher than ten yards from the level of the plain. At near forty miles from the town the land rifes into hills, and the air is purified in a great degree; to this diftance the invalids are fent by their phyficians when every other profpect of their recovery has failed, and the experiment fucceeds in almoft every inftance, for the fick are reftored to health; but they no fooner return to the town, than their former diforders revifit them. On thefe hills the moft opulent of the inhabitants have country feats, to which they pay an annual vifit. Thofe who refide conftantly on the hills, enjoy an almoft perpetual flow of health; and moft of the vegetables of Europe grow as freely there as in their native ground.

During the nineteenth and early twentieth centuries Batavia's life was centred around Weltevreden and Kiningsplein — "King's Square" — the area which is now Medan Merdeka, dominated by the 137-metre National Monument capped with a flame of pure gold - 37 kilograms of it. In the nineteen twenties and thirties new residential streets were laid out in the Menteng area to the east of present-day Jalan Thamrin. Later during the Japanese occupation, the name 'Batavia' was changed to 'Jakarta' an abbreviated form of the older name for the city "Jayakarta". After Indonesia's independence was secured the republican government moved back to Jakarta from Yogyakarta and in 1966 the city was proclaimed as the "Daerah Khusus Ibukota", literally the "Special Region of the Mother City". In spite of grumbles about the heat (from everyone — foreigners or Indonesians) and the occasional regret that the Dutch never decided to shift the capital permanently to Bandung, Jakarta is here to stay as Indonesia's capital.

Since Independence the city has grown out in

In the pestilential 17th and 18th centuries a man who lived to 59 had attained a good age. This magnificent bronze tombstone in the grounds of Jakarta's 'Portuguese Church' commemorates Henricus Zwaardecroon (1667–1726), twentieth governor-general of Nederlands India.

all directions. The orderly development of the Dutch-planned satellite town of Kebayoran Baru (now a fully integrated part of the Jakarta municipality) has been matched by a vast growth in squatter settlements and by "*pemukiman liar*" — lit. "wild inhabitation" — especially in the east and south. The city creeps out year by year and the experts are predicting a solid urban strip from Jakarta to Bogor by the end of this century.

Many visitors experience Jakarta without seeing **TAMAN FATAHILLAH,** the heart of "Old Batavia". It is reached by heading straight north from Jalan Thamrin to Jalan Gajah Mada and Jalan Pintu Besar Utara. On the southern side of this square, renovated during 1973-4 with the help of a **UNESCO** grant, is the old **STADHUIS,** the town hall built in 1710. The building now houses the city's Historical Museum and it contains a rich collection of antique furniture, European porcelain and stoneware, portraits, maps, old tombstones, weapons, coins and other paraphernalia dating right back to periods of pre-history. Special sections of the museum are also devoted to the successive kingdoms that once controlled the Jakarta area. Admission to the museum, as is the case with every government-subsidised museum in Jakarta, is still amazingly cheap.

On the east side of the cobbled square is the **BALAI SENI RUPA JAKARTA,** which serves as the city's art gallery, as a repository of a fine ceramic collection and as a storehouse of information about the arts. The *Balai*'s gallery is perhaps the best example of contemporary Indonesian painting. This museum is housed in a restored neo-classical building dating from the Dutch period.

Directly across from the *Balai* and northwest from the old Town Hall is one of Indonesia's most fascinating special purpose museums, the **WAYANG MUSEUM**. Here the great complexity of the *wayang* tradition in Indonesia is captivatingly displayed and the proximity of the Museum to the Taman Fatahillah square means that every month there is at least one all-night *wayang* performance in the courtyard, as well as a *wayang* workshop each Sunday inside the Museum itself.

Overlooking the north side of the Square, and above a ground floor curio shop is the Restaurant Fatahillah. An evening meal above the Square, which watching a *wayang* performance or spiritted Sundanese street theatre underway below, is one way to recapture the spirit of old Batavia.

North of Taman Fatahillah and slightly to the west is a famous small Dutch drawbridge over the centuries-old *Kali Besar* — the "great canal". The bridge, looking for all the world like a Van Gogh study, has also been restored with UNESCO's help and it sits on the spot where Coen built the old *Kasteel,* Batavia's venerable fort. Although its walls were almost seven metres high the fort had a comparatively short life: a Dutch historian's records say that during the 18th century the walls looked formidable enough, but "the garrison was forbidden to fire too many salutes from its batteries lest the walls crumble under the shock!" Unhappily for posterity, the fortress was demolished in the early nineteenth century.

Northwest of the bridge within easy walking distance is **PASAR IKAN** and the adjoining area known as **SUNDA KELAPA.** This is a fascinating area: fish from each day's catch is sold beginning at the first light of dawn (a good — and cool — time to visit) and vessels from the world's last great commercial sailing fleet can be visited and explored.

The Pasar Ikan area is full of myriad lanes, bursting with stalls selling all manner of nautical gear: ropes, chains, pulleyblocks, winches, sailcloth, hooks, lanterns, and tackle of all descriptions.

The restoration of historic parts of Jakarta included refurbishing a line of splendid old Dutch warehouses, one of which now houses the city's *maritime museum.* (called the *"Museum Bahari"*) Sadly, the museum is not well maintained but it's an invaluable guide to understanding the Buginese *pinisi* and Sumateran *lambok* sailing ships that are massed just outside the museum's windows. Nearby the museum is the restored Dutch watchtower and adjoining buildings, now used by the city administration. The view from the top — you can sometimes get permission to climb — is superb.

The most enthralling part of the Sunda Kelapa area is undoubtedly the sailing ships; a polite request for entry onto the wharf at the entrance way is rarely refused, and the crews of these ships are anything but camera-shy. Sunda Kelapa is one of the major ports for this sailing fleet that ranges all over the Archipelago. Some of the bigger *pinisi* are over two hundred tonnes deadweight, built entirely of teak by craftsmen who use no nails and work to no plan except what they carry in their heads. If you're game, persuade the crews to let you scramble up the monkey ladders affixed to the mainmasts of these vessels. The view is sensational but hold on tight!

Many travellers moved by an adventurous spirit try to arrange passage on the schooners to other destinations in Indonesia. The best time to attempt this is during the west monsoon (March to September, more or less) and the easiest destinations are on the cross-wind tack to Borneo or (tacking to Surabaya first) across the Java sea to Ujung Pandang in Sulawesi. If you are minded to try, you should talk over the idea with one of the

Restoring the heart of old Batavia, atop the Jakarta Historical Museum.

rows of *expedisi* (shipping agents) offices that face the moored ships; permission is also necessary from the *Shahbandar* (harbour master) and sometimes too from the local police before you can sail into the sunset.

Jakarta's sea-faring past is also kept alive in **KALI BATU**, about ten kilometres east along the coast road. This port area has none of the restored and rather orderly atmosphere of Sunda Kelapa; on the contrary it is raw harbour life. A rigid distinction is traditionally preserved between the mooring places for Buginese sailing ships and those for the Madurese *lete-lete:* at Kali Batu Madura sailors tie up singlemasted, wide-beamed ships that bring in salt from Gresik, near Surabaya. For the nautically-minded these intricately carved and painted ships are something not to be missed.

Also to the east of Sunda Kelapa, but much closer is an interesting reminder of past European influence in Java: the old **PORTUGUESE CHURCH**. The church, located on Jalan Pangeran Jayakarta No. 1, was completed in 1696 and was once used by the many Portuguese descendents who then lived in Batavia. The pulpit is elaborately ornamented, and the inside of this plain-looking edifice is an unexpectedly beautiful example of baroque art, a testament to the variety of peoples attracted to the Indies.

MUSEUM NASİONAL (formerly Museum Pusat) is found to the south of the old Kota area, on the west side of the huge **MEDAN MERDEKA**. Housed in an old Dutch neoclassical building, once known as "*Gedung Gajah*", the Museum is the nation's repository of historical and cultural artifacts. The central courtyard is filled to overflowing with stone friezes, reliefs and free-standing statues from the Hindu and Buddhist periods. Examples of traditional architecture, musical instruments and household items from each of Indonesia's twenty-seven provinces are presented in the right ground floor gallery. A fine library completes the ground floor attractions while upstairs is a treasure chest of bronze dieties and Hindu artifacts.

There is also an outstanding collection of Chinese porcelain in the Museum. The expert in T'ang horses and Sung platters will be disappointed but the devotee of Chinese porcelain made for export will find himself confronted with one of the finest collections in Asia. Every piece has been located somewhere in the archipelago, and anyone thinking of buying Chinese porcelain in Jakarta or elsewhere in Java will be doing himself a good turn if the examples in the Museum are studied closely.

The best part of the National Museum undoubtedly is its treasure room, which is opened on Sundays, revealing gold ornaments from various Javanese kingdoms and other precious artifacts. The Museum deserves a full day. Hours are: 8.30

Pasar Ikan, the fish market, and a cluster of Bugis schooners.

a.m. to 2.00 p.m. on Tuesdays, Wednesdays and Thursdays; 8.30 a.m. – 11.00 a.m. on Sundays; and 8.30 a.m. – 1.00 p.m. on Fridays.

The area adjoining Medan Merdeka is crowded with places to visit The **RRI** (Radio Republic Indonesia) **BUILDING** is host to concerts of Western music on alternate Thursday nights. For information and invitations enquire at the ground floor reception desk. On the north side of the Square is the brilliant white **PRESIDENTIAL PALACE,** formerly a merchant's mansion. It is only the official residence of the current Indonesian President however; President Suharto actually resides in a relatively modest home on a small back street in Menteng.

Other Medan Merdeka attractions include the new **ISTIQLAL MOSQUE,** said to be the largest in Southeast Asia, with its celestial but massive white dome and rather rakish minaret. The vast new headquarters of the Pertamina Oil Company is on the northeast side and from every angle "**MONAS**", the National Monument, towers above the Square: it can be visited each day from 9.00 a.m. – 5.00 p.m. The Monas has a lift up to the top of its tower and a series of relief murals depicting the struggles of the independence war may be viewed in the ground area.

The other structure of interest on Medan Merdeka is the **IMMANUEL CHURCH**, a building evoking Jefferson's Montecello in Virginia with its circular expanse and strict neoclassical porch. It is on the eastern side of this vast square. Both it and Istiqlal can be visited, but with the latter it is best not to go during Friday's prayers and to ask directions at the gate. (Remember to always remove your shoes when entering any mosque.)

The best thing about Medan Merdeka may not be the imposing buildings on its sides but the day and night time activities which are going on. During the weekend the **TAMAN RIA JAKARTA** is usually going full bore: it's an amusement park catering to all tastes. There are night-time concerts and sometimes *ludruk* (Javanese light entertainment) performances in Medan Merdeka. Best way to find out what's on is to ask at Taman Ria.

Another entertainment area — in the broadest sense of the word is at **ANCOL** (pronounced "Anchol"), in northeast Jakarta by the coast. A fabulous complex of drive-in-cinemas, golf courses, hai-lai arenas, bowling halls, marineland, type aquarium called the Gelanggang Samudra, and an eight-storey hotel named the Horison which caters to planeloads of Chinese gamblers from Singapore. Every cabdriver knows about Ancol and a visit especially at night-time — is a must for every visitor who really wants to know Jakarta.

A major step in the preservation of Old Batavia was the restoration of the early 18th-century Stadhuis *at Taman Fatahillah. The old town hall now houses Jakarta's excellent City Museum. Streets run north to Pasar Ikan where clusters of Bugis schooners (right) prove that the days of sail are not yet over.*

Entertainment of a more special kind is provided by two clusters of massage parlours, bars, hotels and restaurants. One group is found on Jalan Gajah Mada near the Glodok Chinese quarter (the latter also worth a visit, especially for fine street-stall Chinese food) and the other is on Jalan Blora, close to the Hotel Indonesia. Around both these areas is a sumptuous choice of the various world cuisines: there are Japanese, Korean, Thai, Indonesia, Chinese and European restaurants on these streets, to name but a few.

Although a detailed shopping guide to Jakarta would need dozens of pages, there are some areas which you cannot afford to miss. Although all the international class hotels (and there are many now in Jakarta) have curio shops, some of them quite good, a better bet for the cost-conscious and/or adventurous is an excursion to places like **JALAN AGUS SALIM** (sometimes called Jalan Sabang) where there are many "antique" shops filled with some unexpectedly good bargains — if you look hard. Less impressive are the shops that line **JALAN KEBON SIRIH TIMUR DALAM** (running perpendicular to Kebon Sirih and Wahid Hasyim) although the occasional "find" is

Musium Pusat houses a treasure of Hindu-Javanese antiquities.

still there. A staggering array of some really first-class antiques, ranging from colourful Madurese guardian ducks carved from teak to elaborate Chinese influenced canopied beds, is found on Jalan Majapahit, especially in "N.V. Garuda." Fabrics are found in many shops, a good start can still be made in the **PASAR BARU** area (within sight of Istiqlal on the west side of Jalan Dr Sutomo) and batik stores are scattered around town. One of the best: GKBI, a batik makers cooperative which has stores on the west side of Jl. Sundirman just north of the Hilton Hotel and on Jalan Agus Salim. There is also Batik Danar Hadi, an excellent shop on Jalan Raden Saleh Raya, just east of the Menteng area. There is also a variety of batik boutiques in the smarter suburbs such as Kebayoran Baru, Kemang and Menteng, and it is easy to find out where they are, find them in the yellow pages of the telephone book. There are not many single stop shops in Jakarta but an exception is the Sarinah department store on Jalan Thamrin, close to the Hotel Sari Pacific. For the traveller with only a little time in Jakarta, Sarinah offers the totality of Indonesian handicrafts at set-out reasonable prices.

Any traveller to Asia worth his salt is attracted to the life and pace of open air markets, whatever their wares. The Jakarta city administration has zealously tried to impose some order on the more chaotic markets, mainly by building some rather dreary multi-storied concrete leviathans to house the small traders. Fortunately the bustle of Jakarta's main markets has survived these transplant operations, and the large general markets (such as **PASAR CIKINI** and **PASAR MINGGU**) are as alive as ever. Small special purpose markets also hold many surprises. **JALAN SURABAYA** is probably the largest special purpose market for antiques and bric-a-brac in Jakarta: it's located off Jalan Diponegoro in Menteng. Although it has been flashed up with permanent aluminium awnings and is somewhat rather overrated now, it's still possible to find a bewildering assortment of domestic vanities: heaps of old Delftware porcelain from Holland, great collections of "Chinese porcelain" (most of which are copies from a Bandung factory), old coins, hot-out-of-the-mold bronzeware, eastern Indonesian textile and other goodies. Try to come early to Jalan Surabaya, well before the tourist buses that now make regularly scheduled stops at this once-chaotic, now-tame market.

Another special purpose market is **PASAR BURUNG**, one of the real attractions of Jakarta. Located just off Jalan Pramuka in an area called Kayu Manis, orinthologists will experience heaven or (if they happen to be conservationists too) suffer agonies. Here are captive birds from all over Indonesia: macaws, parrots, the Javanese *perkutut* and other tropical curiosities, almost all captured illegally. **TAMAN ANGGREK** (Orchid Park), off Jalan S. Parman in the northwest part of town is another special purpose stop (Indonesia is justly famous for its orchids) and at the junction of **JALAN MAHAKAM** and **JALAN MELAWAI** in Kebayoran Baru is a flower market that is cheap and refreshing, set among the trees of a small park. An array of flowers is also sold at the **JALAN SUMENEP** market in Menteng.

On the CULTURAL side Jakarta has really come of age in the last few years. No longer are Embassy information centres the only cultural watering holes in this vast city; it is unlikely in fact that they ever were. One of the many pleasurable things about Jakarta is that a night's hunt often yields unexpectedly rewarding insights into "cultural" life — in its broadest sense: interesting things are going on in the most unlikely of places.

Pride of place for strict *haute couture* goes to the **TAMAN ISMAEL MARZUKI** on Jalan

Ethnographic artifacts (left) and Hindu-Javanese antiquities (right) fill the Musium Pusat. English-language tours are conducted on Tuesdays, Wednesdays and the first Saturday of each month beginning at 9.30 a.m.

Shopping spree in a wide variety of boutiques, galleries and shops.

Cikini in Menteng. Nearly every night T.I.M. offers a solid programme: exhibitions of Indonesian painting, overseas jazz groups, Surabaya *ludruk* comedy troupes or the latest piece of Indonesia's vibrant and emerging theatre. Monthly programmes for T.I.M. are distributed in hotels and travel agencies, or a copy can be obtained directly from the T.I.M. office. Don't miss it. On another cultural level, Indonesia's best permanent exhibition of textiles and weaving is at the **TEXTILE MUSEUM** on Jalan Satsuit Tubun, open 9.00 a.m.-2.00 p.m. Tuesdays through Sundays.

Behind T.I.M., and forming part of an arts complex centred on T.I.M., is the **LEMBAGA PENDIDIKAN KESENIAN JAKARTA** (Jakarta Arts Education Institute), another achievement by the former Jakarta Governor, Ali Sadikin. Divided into five faculties (Music, Theatre, Cinematography, Dance and Fine Arts) the LPKJ offers the best arts training in the country. The staff and students are friendly so don't be shy: wander in and find out what's going on. Daytime activities include theatre rehearsals, film screenings and jazz concerts, depending on the mood of the moment.

Besides this mainstay of the Jakarta cultural scene, there are a number of other places where performances of living Indonesian culture (not just museum pieces) can be seen. One of these is the **SCHOOL OF FOLK ART** of the Universitas Nasional (National University) which is located in a small, unprepossessing complex on Jalan Bunga V, off Jalan Mataram Raya. Don't be deceived by appearances: there is an abundance of primarily West Javan artistic activity going on, from Cirebon-style gamelan to rehearsals of wayang golek.

Wayang wong is the Javanese word for live theatre using actors. Although developed long after the puppet *wayang* form, *wayang wong* has adapted the legends of the Ramayana and Mahabhrata, and mixed them up with a lot of indigenous Javanese lore. The result, even for the non-Javanese speaking, is enthralling, particularly the scenes of combat and courtly dance. The best place to see *wayang wong* in Jakarta is still at the **BHARATA,** a cinema-style building on Jalan Kalilio No 15, near Pasar Senen, that has a huge *kali* head over its front entrance. Performances begin at 8:00p.m. every night except Mondays and Thursdays. *Wayang* of the puppet variety can also be seen on the Taman Fatahillah courtyard on every third Saturday of each month, and at the Directorate General of Fine Arts office on Jalan Abdul Salim No. 80 each Thursday at 10.00 p.m. The Java Pavillion at the Taman Mini Indonesia has *wayang kulit* demonstrations every

Indonesian culture in an astonishing variety—even for those with little time.

other Sunday, beginning at 10:00 a.m. and lasting about five hours. Finally, the National Museum organises *wayang kulit* performances every other Saturday which last the whole evening. Literally.

Although Indonesian films are slowly devouring the market that once was dominated by live theatre, a bit of the old Betawi street theatre still lingers on at **TEATER MISS TJITJIH** (pronounced Miss Cheechee), located on Jalan Stasion, a small lane off Jalan Angker in a poorer part of the city, west of the Kota area. The Miss Tjitjih group once commanded a regal theatre in the Pasar Senen part of town, but the popularity of films has driven them to this obscure part of town. Yet what remains is a treasure: faithful spectators watch a variety of themes played out in the Sundanese language, and there is always a show, starting at about 8:00 p.m., every night. Miss Tjitjih is good Jakarta proletarian stuff and should not be missed.

The best foreign cultural centres are the German and Dutch institutes, located on Jl. Matraman Raya 23 and Jl. Menteng Raya 25, respectively. Printed monthly programmes are available on request, or from the respective embassies. To their credit these institutes help foster indigenous artistic expression by giving exhibition and stage space to local artists and performers.

To round off the cultural side of Jakarta are two Indonesian organisations. The first is *Lingkar Mitra Budaya Jakarta*, a group of well-heeled persons, mostly Indonesian, who are interested in the arts. A programme of the Lingkar's monthly activities can be obtained from its pleasant office and exhibition centre at Jalan Tanjung 34, in Menteng. The second group is the *Balai Budaya*, a group with an exhibition hall on Jalan Gereja Theresia 47 in Menteng, used almost exclusively for exhibitions of painting. Drop in and see what's happening.

If you find yourself attracted by some of the work of Indonesia's carvers and contemporary painters you may even consider purchasing a representative sample of their work. There are many studios of varying description and quality, many of which — as you might expect — sell little more than fast buck "Bali" paintings or forest-nymph type wood carvings. For peerless quality in paintings (and antiques) visit Alex Papadimitriou's home at Jalan Pasuruan 3. Nearby is the Srirupa shop (on Jalan Pekalongan 16) where there is literally the best collection of antique furniture you will see for sale in Jakarta.

Genuine treasures are hidden amongst the junk at Jalan Surabaya's 'flea market'.

A walk through Indonesia in a few hours, at Taman Mini.

Other shops are listed in the "City Guides" section of the Guidebook.

Jakarta, like any other city, is really more a matter of mood than a recitation of whistle stops. Many visitors do not sample the atmosphere of even one urban *kampung,* an oversight that robs them of a feel of the city as it is known by the great majority of its population. The Jakarta Municipality in recent years has worked hard to upgrade basic services and the result in many areas are closely settled but often very charming *kampungs* which are pleasurable to visit. One of the best examples of these Kampung Improvement Projects is in the Menteng Sukabumi Kampung on the southeast side of Menteng bordering a railway shuttle line. Any cabdriver knows the area, and a wander through will add an extra dimension to your memories of the city. Have no fear: The natives are especially friendly and it is easy to find your way in — and out.

Jakarta's mood is also captured in the following places: the **RAGUNAN ZOO** in south Jakarta; nightime food stalls along the entire length of Jalan Peconongan in the fascinating Kebon Kelapa area of town, just across a drainage canal from Bina Graha, the President's working office; the Glodok Chinese quarter sandwiched in between Jalan Gajah Mada and Jalan Mansyur just south of the old Kota area: the open book-stalls which spring up each night at about 5.30 p.m. in Pasar Senen; and not least the Tanjung Priok port area where first class sea food places, modest in appearance, rub shoulders with shadey night spots and ubiquitous billiard halls.

Jakarta is also filling in time a glass of plain tea at any one of the seemingly thousands of *warungs* — canvas topped street stalls that can (and often must) pick up and move at a moment's notice, just out of reach of a police sweep of "illegal" traders. Jakarta is also a visit to the home of Pak Sulaeman Prawiradilaga on Jalan Matraman Raya no. 32, to see how he makes *wayang golek* puppets. A stop at the Salemba Raya or the Rawamangun campuses of the University of Indonesia is an interesting way to spend a morning: curious students, anxious to practice their English, will show you around.

The permutations are endless: *becak* drivers tuned in to all-night gamelan broadcast as they curl up in their passenger seat at three in the morning is a special part of Jakarta; another and relatively pleasant way to get a feel for this conglomeration of seam-to-seam urban villages is to buy a seat on the *Jabotabek* commuter railway that can take you around the JAkarta-BOgor-

At Taman Mini, a cable car will give you a bird's-eye view of the all-Indonesia park.

A lavish reception hall and soon an all-Indonesia museum as well at Taman Mini.

TAnggerang-BEKasi conurbation. The best place to wait for the train, if you are in the Menteng area, is at the Jalan Pegangsaan station.

One very underrated (and occasionally overrated) attraction is Jakarta's **TAMAN MINI INDONESIA INDAH** ("Beautiful Indonesia in Miniature"), which is located on the southeast side of the city and is reached by taking the first turn-off from the new "Jagorawi" toll expressway. For all its obvious play for tourist dollars it does provide a good introduction to the country's variety and is well worth a visit.

Taman Mini is consciously designed to capture all of Indonesia's local culture in one single complex. Stretching over nearly 100 hectares the park provides the visitor without too much time in Indonesia with exciting insights into the complexity of this vast country. The twenty seven provinces of Indonesia (the most recent inclusion being East Timor) are each represented by a pavilion. Each of these buildings, constructed in the distinctive style of the various regions, presents inside the decorative skills and local art forms of each province, including textiles, carvings, metalwork, traditional dress and panoramas depicting scenes of everyday life. Each pavilion has its own programme of cultural performances, ceremonies and dances, all of which is noted in the monthly Taman Mini programme, available free from most hotels.

Equally impressive are the various special purpose buildings at Taman Mini such as the new museum (opened in 1980) and the superb performance centre facing the entranceway which is styled after the aristocratic Javanese *pendopo* form. There are also buildings following the distinctive architecture of each of Indonesia's five accepted religions: Islam, Protestant Christianity Hinduism, Buddhism and Catholic Christianty. There is even a wonderfully austere building with an exquisitely carved interior for the adherents of the various forms of *Kebatinan,* a form of mystically-inclined religious practice found chiefly in Java.

To cover the distances inside Taman Mini one can choose for transport horse-dawn carts, a mini-train, buses or a cable-car that crosses the park and the artificial lake that is carved in the shape of a gigantic map of the archipelago. There are restaurants and several shopping areas, and even a miniature Borobuddhur Temple.

All in all, even though Taman Mini is undoubtedly "touristy" it is undoubtedly also a superior attraction and well worth the visit.

If you look out the window when flying to

West Sumatran wedding dress, displayed in an adat *(traditional) house at Taman Mini.*

Tropical waters just outside of Jakarta.

Jakarta you will most often see a large number of coral islands lying off Java's north coast. These islands, known as **PULAU SERIBU,** are Jakarta's marine attraction. Pulau Seribu (the "thousand islands") actually consist of slightly over six hundred privately owned and uninhabited. Close to the Jakarta port the islands of Pulau Onrust and Pulau Air are popular for day outing, as both have coral shores that abound with shells. During the 18th century Onrust was an important ship-yard, and James Cook had the 'Endeavour' careened there in 1770: '... the bottom of the ship was thoroughly repaired, and much to Capt. Cook's satisfaction, who bestowed great encomiums on the officers and workmen at the Marine-yard; in his opinion there is not one in the world, where a ship can be laid down with more convenient speed and safety, nor repaired with more diligence and skill.' The island was later a fort, and a quarantine for *hajis* (pilgrims) returning from Mecca. Part of the island is now under cassaya cultivation, but its woods, shoreline, old ruins and foundations, and a cluster of vine-covered 18th and 19th tombstones, make it a relaxing spot. Onrust and Air can both be reached from Tanjung Priok (Jakarta's main port) in a fast boat.

Pulau Putri is the most developed island, replete with cottages, a restaurant, and live entertainment. Not surprisingly it is also expensive. Bookings need to be in advance through a travel agent or directly with the Pulau Putri Company on Jalan Thamrin 9 (in the Jakarta Theatre Building). Other islands popular with the snorkeling and diving set are Pulau Genting, with an outstanding coral reef on an off-shore channel and Pulau Opak Besar, where A-frame accommodation is available. Pulau Melinjo also belongs to the Putri company but is still "undeveloped". There are camper facilities, including most basic amenities and drinking water, and the cost is only about Rp 5000 per day. A trip to this island is most rewarding during the week — you will not likely be on your own — and transport is available free of charge from the company which takes you from Pulau Putri by boat. A special attraction of Pulau Melinjo are the four-foot lizards who wait patiently to eat whatever scraps you may leave behind.

To reach Pulau Seribu you can take a "Skyvan" flight which leaves every day from Kemayoran airport in Jakarta to a small strip near Pulau Putri, or you can hire a boat. Any travel agent in Jakarta will be able to give you details on accommodation, boat hire and flight.

The warm, limpid waters of Pulau Seribu, *the Thousand Islands, are a paradise for divers.*

WEST JAVA

In their haste to leave Jakarta many travellers make a bee-line for Yogyakarta, Bali and other points east. Apart from, perhaps, a cursory glance at Bogor or Bandung, Jakarta is their sum contact with West Java and Sunda.

West Java's recorded history begins with what is perhaps the earliest known written record found in the island: an inscribed stone, dating from around 415 A.D., which records the royal presence of Purnavarman, king of Taruma. The stone, *Batu Tulis*, can still be seen a little southeast of Bogor, *en route* to Puncak.

Taruma has left little more than a few inscriptions. There are no temples, no palace remains. The Sanskrit inscription suggests an Indianized ruler, one of the first in Indonesia, but there is a yawning gap in West Java's recorded history for the next thousand years. The empires and kingdoms of Srivijaya, Sailendra, Mataram, Kediri, Singosari and Mojopahit rose and fell in South Sumatra and Central and East Java. Then, as the Islamic city ports gained control of the northern coast, from Pasuruan in the east to Banten in the west, Pajajaran emerged for a brief moment in history's spotlight.

The kingdom of Pajajaran was located in the hills around Bogor, with a secondary town and port at Sunda Kelapa. It is believed that the rulers of Pajajaran were Sivaistic, and were forced inland by the growth of the Muslim coastal states during the 15th century. Within a hundred years the kingdom was destroyed, overrun by the forces of the Banten sultanate. It is possible (though unlikely) that the survivors of Pajajaran sought refuge in the rugged, hilly country south of Rangkasbitung, and were the forebears of the Badui, an isolated people still living in the area.

Near Bandung (previous pages), West Java offers the peaks of Careme (left) and Slamet (right), Java's second highest peak at 3,400 metres.

To the west and south of Jakarta, Banten resisted the onslaughts of Mataram, only to succumb to the Dutch in 1684. To the east, Cirebon was eventually brought to heel by Mataram, and in 1705 became a fief of Batavia.

Despite the continual depredations of sporadic warfare in Sunda, a vigorous culture stayed alive. Bandung, and the area around Cirebon, are still a rich source of dance, *wayang golek*, *angklung* music and *wayang topeng*. In the south, around Tasikmalaya, a flourishing weaving industry supplies a constant demand for its fine products. Cirebon and Tasikmalaya are also important *batik centres*.

For lovers of the great outdoors, the west coast along the Sunda Strait offers some fine beaches; the southern coast, though dangerous for swimming, is scenically magnificent; the hill resorts of Puncak and the Bandung area are a cool change from the Jakarta plain; and at Ujung Kulon (known to mariners as 'Java Head') in the far southwest corner of Sunda, is one of Java's greatest wildlife and nature reserves.

In the following pages, the area of West Java is divided into three parts. 'Banten And The West Coast' (pages 133 to 143) describes the region west of Jakarta, the historical remains of the 16th and 17th centuries, and the shores of the Sunda Strait lying between Java and Sumatra. 'Bogor, Puncak And The South' (pages 144 to 149) covers trips from Jakarta heading directly south, via Bogor, to the Indian Ocean at Pelabuhan Ratu, as well as via the Puncak Pass on the road to Bandung. The third part, 'Bandung "Paris of Java"' (pages 150–157), presents the city of Bandung, the various ways of getting there and its splendid surroundings that can be exlored using Bandung as a base. Even if you see no more of Java than Sunda, you'll have found many rewards.

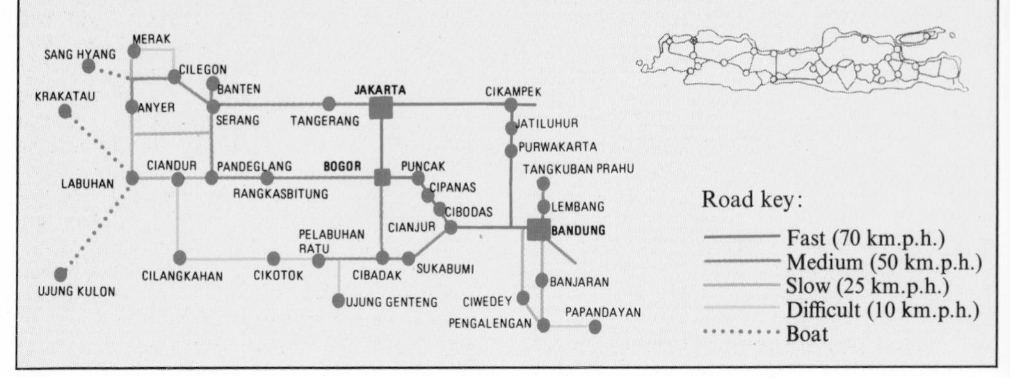

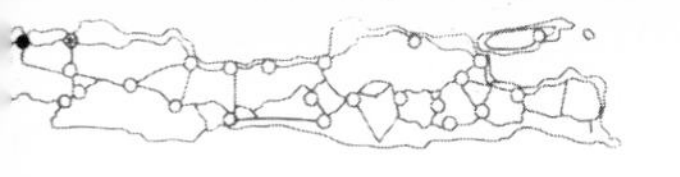

BANTEN AND THE WEST COAST

Banten, some time in the 1690s: *Your name is Johannes Oosterman. A reluctant soldier of fortune, plucked from your portside tavern with the help of a lead-weighted blackjack, awakening with a foul mouth and bleary eyes to find yourself somewhere south of Brittany on the way down towards the west coast of Africa and the Cape. Now, twelve months later, your eyes are sunken in their sockets, your skin is like yellow parchment, your body racked with fits of shivering. Malaria, the decimating plague of the Indies, freezes you to the marrow of your bones while you stand before the triangular loophole under the shallow dome of the watchtower, gaspingly hot and fetid in your rotting knee-boots and salt-rusted breastplate of heavy steel, your flintlock arquebus propped against the stone wall (hopefully primed with damp black powder). Three metres beneath your feet, in narrow barrel-vaulted passageways, prisoners or slaves or recalcitrant soldiers struggle with stinking casks of dried fish and weevil-infested grain. And you wait to die in this rotten heat, to be laid beneath Banten's rank soil in the European graveyard some 300 metres to the east of where you stand, where mangrove spikes and sword-grass will be your lilies of the valley, your forget-me-nots, your violets.*

Four hundred years ago **BANTEN** was a princely state of great wealth and splendour. Banten town was an energetic maritime city; and the countryside it controlled (also known as Banten) embraced a huge slice of Sundanese territory, from the Java Sea to the Indian Ocean, and eastwards from the Sunda Strait to the borders of Sunda Kelapa in the north and the bay of Pelabuhan Ratu in the south.

The name still covers that great area, but the glory has long faded. The present day town of Banten, far from being a splendid city, is now little more than a few picturesque ruins, masses of coconut palms and strings of shabby, tiny villages lining tidal creeks and canals. As a crowning indignity, the popular farmyard cockerel known to the English-speaking world as a bantam does not come from 'Bantam' (the European name for Banten) but from Japan.

The Portuguese were the first Europeans to visit Banten, arriving early in the 16th century when the great Javanese commander Falatehan, at the behest of the sultan of Demak, was completing his conquest of the area. Banten rapidly grew in importance, defeating and finally dispersing the Hindu forces of Pajajaran who sought refuge from Islam in the rugged hills and mountains to the southwest of Bogor, and around the port of Sunda Kelapa.

Banten's grip on the entrepôt pepper trade was the source of its wealth. Some of the pepper grew within Banten, but most came from Sumatra, and by the middle of the 16th century, when the Portuguese were granted limited trading rights, more than 1,500 tonnes of the precious spice were leaving Banten every year in ships bound for India and China.

This was Banten's hour of glory, its brief century-long strut upon the boards of history.

The year 1596 proved to be fateful for Banten, and ultimately for the entire archipelago. On 22 June four Dutch ships, commanded by Cornelis de Houtman, dropped anchor in Banten's roadsteads after a voyage which had lasted fourteen months and cost the lives of almost half the fleet's complement of 250 men. The survivors were the first 'Hollanders' to set foot on Indonesian soil.

Their mission was trade, and their initial impressions were highly favourable, as the ship's records show:

'There came (on board) such a multitude of Javanese and other nations as Turks, Chinese, Bengalis, Arabs, Persians, Gujarati, and others that one could hardly move . . . so abundantly that each nation took a spot on the ships where they displayed their goods . . . Of which the Chinese brought all sorts of silk, woven and unwoven, twined and untwined, with beautiful earthenware and other strange things more. The Javanese brought chickens, eggs, ducks, and many kinds of fruits. Arabs, Moors, Turks, and other nations of people each brought everything one might imagine.'

The walled city housed the ruler and his nobles, and also the wealthy Chinese merchants and some of the more powerful Indian entrepreneurs. The market-place was outside the city walls, and there (as the historian van Leur described it) could be found 'all sorts of foodstuffs . . . pots, pans, pepper bags, spices, Gujarati and Bengali with painted articles and trinkets, Persians and

Banten: 17th-century ruins of interest to the historian.

Arabs with jewels, rows of Chinese shops . . . with all their expensive goods: damask, velvet, satin, silk, gold thread, cloth of gold, porcelain, lacquered work, copperwork, woodwork, medicinal products, and the like . . . the international Asian trade of the stapling point Bantam . . . the meeting place of merchant gentlemen and ships' captains.'

The Dutch were soon followed by the English, and by Danish and French traders. The tiny English community, about fourteen men at any one time, fought and brawled in the streets with the 'Flemings', but loved them nonetheless for they were all brothers in an alien environment.

The fortunes of the invaders, and of Banten itself, waxed and waned. Plot followed plot, blockade followed blockade, and one sea skirmish led to another as men fought and died in a constant struggle for economic hegemony. In 1638 one of Banten's princes made the holy pilgrimage to Mecca and formally received from the Caliph of the Turkish Ottoman Empire the right to bear the religious title of *sultan*. But by 1684 the Dutch had, more by accident than design, assumed control of Banten from their base in Batavia and had embarked on the construction of a massive fortress, Fort Speelwijk, to protect their interests. Banten's role as an independent sultanate thus was finally eclipsed.

Despite the depredations of time and events there is still enough left in Banten, around the site of the old city, to excite the imagination and evoke the past. It can be a fascinating voyage of discovery.

At Serang, 90 km due west of Jakarta, a good surfaced road leads 10 km north to Banten. About 2 km short of your destination, on the right-hand side of the road, is the tomb of Maulana Yusup, the third ruler, who died in 1580. Nearer the present village, on the left-hand side, are the remains of *Istana Kaibon*, a palace built for one of Banten's princes, lived in by the mother (and guardian) of another prince, and destroyed in 1832. Even as a ruin, the massive walls and archways, and the stark silhouette of a great gateway, make this an impressive and sombre place.

Across a narrow river, and a little to the north-west, is the sprawling one-hectare site of the so-called 'Portuguese Fort', *Pakuwonan*, the high-walled and heavily fortified palace compound which was built, wrecked in a bloody civil war and rebuilt, all during the reign of Sultan Abulfatah Agung (1651–83). Its final destruction, ordered by the Dutch about 1810, was carried out reluctantly over a period of 30 years, but grass-covered mounds and hillocks mark the sites of storerooms, dwellings and casements, and shrub-crowded holes lead down into intriguing passageways now blocked by debris. The great walls, still three to four metres high, look good for another thousand years.

On the northern side of Pakuwonan lie the grassy plain of the *medan* and the imposing white *menara* (reputedly designed by a Chinese Muslim) built by Maulana Mohammed in the closing decades of the 16th century. A narrow, simply ornamented doorway leads to a spiral staircase, the steps of which, worn and rutted by tens of thousands of feet, follow a tight, shoulder-wide

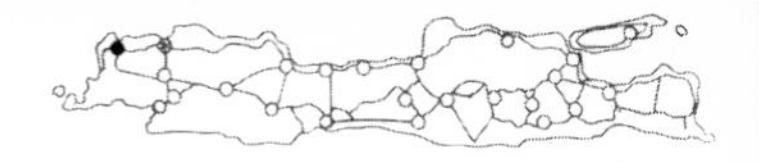

ircuit up through the walls of the tower to two ɪigh balconies offering superb views of the *ɪedan*, the mosque (with its pool and adjacent emeteries), Pakuwonan and the flat coastline to he north.

Legend claims that the small two-storeyed ɪuilding standing next to the mosque was the econd *Masjid Agung* ('Great Mosque') built in 3anten, designed in 1559 by a Dutch Muslim ɪamed Cardeel. More than a century later there *vas* a Cardeel: a renegade from the Dutch East ndia Company (VOC), he had become a Muslim, ɪnd maintained friendly links with his former mployers, helping design and build Fort speelwijk in 1685 after having planned the econstruction of the sultan's palace in 1681. Certainly the two-storeyed building is European n style, and a European may have designed and ɪuilt it some time during the 17th century.

It now contains an interesting little museum, where the treasures include beautifully carved ivory kris-hilts (in the traditional 'bird-man' form), old bottles and clay pipes, an assortment of weapons, and strange iron instruments (long spikes with a sort of Tibetan prayer-wheel device at the blunt end) which were plunged into the bodies of entranced mystics without drawing blood . . . such rites, in many extraordinary forms, can still be seen in the Banten area.

A kilometre away to the northwest are the ruins of Fort Speelwijk. The fortess, built in 1682, was extended in 1685 and in 1731, and finally abandoned by Governor-General Herman Willem Daendels at the beginning of the 19th century. It originally stood on the sea's edge, but is today separated from the sea by more than 200 metres of sand-silt marsh and coconut palms. A single watchtower stands high on the perimeter wall, its triangular loopholes offering a dispiriting vista of littoral marsh and, perhaps, in the distance the

On a long coastal strip, the beginning of a new seaside resort and an industrial area.

buff-coloured sails of solitary *prahus*. Fifty metres through the eastern gateway of the fort, in a bleak tangle of brambles, are the ravaged tombs of another era. One inscription remains: an ornately chiselled rectangle of slate embedded in the graveyard's largest mausoleum and celebrating the last resting place of Hugo Pieter Fauré who died in Banten in 1763, aged 44. The only other headstone now lies next to the Masjid Agung, tersely recording that 'Here lies the body of Captain Roger Bennett, commander of the Bombay Merchant, deceased on 3rd January 1677'.

More recent is a red and yellow Chinese temple opposite the entrance to Fort Speelwijk. It is probably 200 years old, with its symbols of Buddhism, its Taoist *yin* and *yang* designs: where you can hear the hypnotic rattle-and-swish of divinations sticks, and breathe in the pervading aroma of incense; where you can see the gleam of candlelight on polished brass and on altar cloths embroidered with metallic thread; and in the back courts a sacred chair, superbly carved and coloured, locked inside a glass cage.

Performed by pairs of devotees of certain Islamic mystical societies in this area is the *debus*, the Banten equivalent of Balinese *kris* stabbing. Accompanied by music and chant, one devotee holds a sharp spike against his stomach or chest, while the other strikes it with a large hammer. Yet there is no injury. These are occasional happenings, but the local hotels and travel agents may know of one taking place, so ask about them.

Banten can be reached from Jakarta by road or rail, and the railway continues on for a short distance to Merak (northwest) or Anyer (southwest). There is no casual accommodation in the tiny villages of 'Banten Town'; overnighters should head for nearby Serang, Cilegon or Merak.

Ruins, romantic or otherwise, are not everyone's favourite sport. Apart from Banten (the town), Banten (the area) still has much to offer, for along the shores of the Sunda Strait there are attractive resorts and beaches where the waters are generally calm, though during the monsoon season metre-high waves are not unusual. For ornithologists and nature lovers there's a worthwhile half-hour boat-ride from Banten to the island of Pulau Dua where between March and July an amazing variety of migratory birds arrive for a season of squabbling, mating and nesting.

The west coast is close enough to Jakarta for a long day's outing or for a satisfying few days of sun'n'sea, and once you escape the city limits and the traffic tangles the road is good and fast.

In Tangerang you may like to take a break and buy one of the finely woven 'panama' hats which are an important local industry. Between Tangerang and Serang the countryside is flat, patterned with *padi* fields and ground-hugging buildings of thatched palm-frond (*atap*) which are both factories and drying sheds for bricks and tiles. About 20 km northwest of Serang, at **CILEGON**, you can branch north to the hilly coastline around Merak and Pulau Rida (also known as Florida Beach) or south towards Anyer. Cilegon itself is dominated by the vast

A beautiful coastline around Anyer.

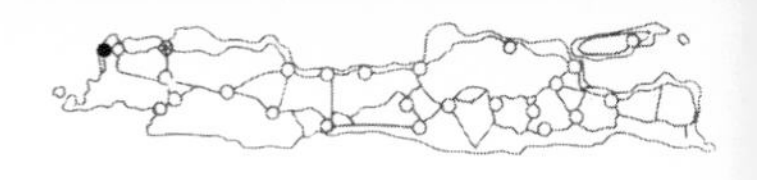

Krakatau Steel plant, begun in the early 1960s with Russian aid, partially dismantled after 1965, and now resurrected with backing from Pertamina. Spiral-welded pipes up to a metre in diameter are currently being produced, and plans include the construction of an iron-ore smelter and a rolling-mill for steel plate.

A happy side benefit of this giant enterprise has been the opening of the Krakatau Country Club and Guesthouse, a modern complex offering excellent accommodation and a first-rate 18-hole golf course. Although the guesthouse (a series of self-contained suites in a landscaped 'garden suburb' setting) and the golf club with its full 19th-hole facilities are privately owned, visitors are welcome. The Dayeuh Kuring restaurant, also part of the Krakatau Steel family, is across the road from the guesthouses, attractively sited overlooking ornamental lakes and bamboo bridges.

These and other facilities along the coast are a natural outcome of the rapid economic development, principally in secondary industry, which is taking place in the area. The standards are generally high. So too are the prices, which mostly seem tailored to suit the expense-account executive.

The coast is a difficult area for budget travellers, so if you are travelling penny-wise pack a picnic lunch and treat the western beaches as a day trip. If you're looking for a *losmen* or similar inexpensive accommodation, you'll invariably be told to try the 'Ramayana', another name for the modern, Jakarta-priced Merak Beach Hotel. Serang has some modest accommodation, but apart from its proximity to Banten town it is in the middle of nowhere.

One of the most popular spots is the area around **FLORIDA BEACH**, a small series of protected bays where the sea is flat and calm and the ripples barely tickle the sandy shore. For those who feel stout of heart, and have an even stouter car, there is some pretty coastal scenery to be explored and enjoyed on the narrow dirt road which traces an arc northwest and then north around the top of the Merak peninsula and finally links up again with the main road in Cilegon. This route is not recommended in the wet season.

South of Cilegon, running down the coast, there is a spate of activity in and around **ANYER**. There are pretty bays and long stretches of beach, but development plans suggest that this might become the Miami of West Java, with plenty of industry thrown in for good measure. The most comfortable place to stay is the new luxurious Anyer Beach Motel, formerly owned by Pertamina. Seven kilometres short of the Motel a red hill was bulldozed into the sea to make a breakwater and a barge wharf for a new off-shore rig-platform assembly plant. Other industry, including a ship-building yard, is also slated for the area.

If you're in the mood for a minor voyage of discovery the motel can arrange the rental of a boat with an outboard which can get you

Merak fishermen bring in their haul (right); Banten's imposing white menara *(left).*

Sang Hyang island: corals and decaying World War II fortifications.

across to **SANG HYANG** (Sangiang), a seldom-visited 700-hectare island an hour to the northwest of Anyer. It is almost deserted, and there is no accommodation available, but it's an exciting and rewarding experience.

At the island's southern tip, through a maze of swampy mangrove trails and coral-rock beach-heads, are the jungle-clad remains of two deeply entrenched Japanese shore batteries. The great 150-mm barrels, long ago wrenched from their mounts, still aim ominously seawards where their arc of fire once controlled the narrowest point of the Sunda Strait. Breastwork passageways of packed stone and concrete lead back through the hill to an old roadway which plunges steeply down through the jungle to the creeper-covered ruins of barracks and storehouses and the wreckage of an ancient staff-car.

Or you can chug slowly up a shallow inlet, coral branches and huge starfish less than a metre below, and above you mangrove branches swarming with brown monkeys. You break through the end of this sinuous, humid tunnel and out onto the glass-like waters of a still inland lagoon, and make your landfall under the shadow of an immense tree whose roots stretch out into the water. Then a short trek inland across the waist of the island through groves of coconut palms, passing an occasional *atap* shack and small plots of cassava; the pathway meanders through a field of sword-grass, across bleached coral rock and black basalt. You hear the roar of surf, and suddenly you burst through the last line of stunted shrubbery to find a crescent bay blocked to the north by a monstrous green cliff and to the south by a ragged, shattered bundle of volcanic rocks, coves, hollows and caves. The sea-front, pounded by irregular grey breakers, is littered with a sculptor's dream of driftwood, lava rocks and enough

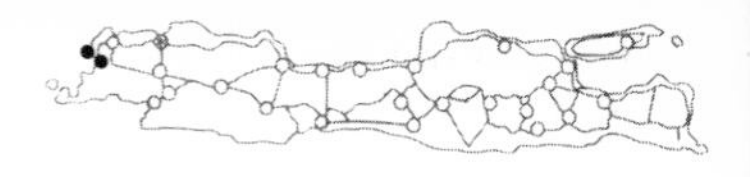

sea-rounded pumice stone to fill a thousand bathrooms; pumice, no doubt, from Krakatau, its high black cone visible across the restless sea.

The flat plain you have traversed was reputedly a Japanese airstrip. You think of the single-prop fighters of the Pacific War and hazard a guess that there might have been length enough for a take-off run, but scarcely enough for a safe landing . . . only to be told (fact or fiction?) that this was a *kamikaze* strip.

From memories of war to tangible beauty. The southeast coast offers a few small sandy beaches, with calm shallow water inside a reefline only 50 metres from the shore, but mostly the coast consists of strands and banks of shells and coral thrown up by the tides. Not all is white. Much of the dead coral retains its brilliant hues of vermilion, crimson and carmine, or pale blue darkening to indigo, its delicate honeycomb cells a masterpiece of organic engineering. There are shells by the hundreds of thousands, and even amongst the tide-wrack you can find excellent specimens which have not lost their porcelain sheen. But all that is on the rough, crumpled shore. Beneath the island's clear leeward waters are reefs of layer upon layer of fan coral, brain coral, coral trees and a treasure trove of cowries, volutes, turbans, cones, clams, spindles, murexes, conches . . . the world!

When you've had your fill of diving and snorkelling and exploration, you can satisfy the inner self with the superb mangoes, papayas and bananas which are part of Sang Hyang's abundance. One small warning: mosquitoes are also abundant, so be prepared.

Back on the mainland it's about a 6-km run south from the Anyer motel to **KARANG BOLONG**, a huge stand of rock which forms a natural archway from the land through to

A pleasant junket takes you to Hot Springs.

the sea. Some of the natural beauty around Karang Bolong has been lost with the erection of a chain-wire fence and a cluster of unattractive *warungs*, but it is nonetheless an imposing sight.

Beauty has also suffered at **BATUKUWUNG** Hot Springs, 21 km inland from the coast road (the turn-off is 3 km short of Karang Bolong). The drive is pretty, but the spring site was developed in 1965 and already has a feeling of concrete shabbiness. The spring water arrives at a temperature of 70°C, and is rich in sodium and calcium salts. Accommodation at varying prices is available and bookings are heavy during weekends and holidays. The complex, with its pools, tennis courts and recreational facilities, can also be reached inland through Serang, a drive of 30 km.

Besides the coastal road link between Anyer and **LABUHAN** (41 km long), the latter can also be reached by the inland route through Serang and Pandeglang, a 63-km drive. The attractive Labuhan coast offers launches for trips to Krakatau and the game reserve at Ujung Kulon.

For several centuries **KRAKATAU** (or Rakata), an unimportant and uninhabited volcanic island 40 km off the Sunda coast, had lain dormant. Then, in 1883, it achieved instant and lasting infamy. A series of cataclysmic explosions ripped the island and blew out so much ash (almost 16 cubic kilometres) that the earth's crust collapsed forming a monstrous 41-square-kilometre submarine caldera. The sea rushed in, and then tidal waves up to 30 metres high swept the coasts on a voyage of destruction that claimed

Dusk on the Sunda Strait, where gentle waves foam ashore on grey-gold sand (previous page); between Java and Sumatra, calamitous Krakatau (below) pushes steam skywards, its menacing plumes disturbing a tranquil line of clouds.

Slumbering Krakatau volcano and its smouldering offspring.

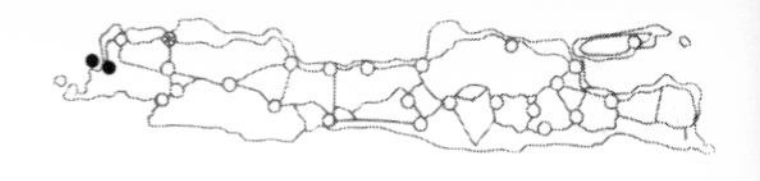

more than 35,000 lives. The explosion was heard more than 3,000 km away in Australia, and stygian blackness covered the land for 160 km around. Ash is believed to have drifted around the earth three times, producing spectacular sunsets as far away as England.

In the decades following the catastrophe, undersea volcanic activity continued, and a new cone with a gaping half-crater emerged from the drowned bed of the caldera: *Anak Krakatau*, 'Child of Krakatau', smouldering and steaming, a son following his father's habits.

Of the islands visible from the Anyer-Labuhan coast, Krakatau is the gently sloping cone lying farthest to the south, with *Krakatau Kecil* ('Little Krakatau') smoking away to the north and *anak* lying between and a little behind these two. The main island, on which meagre vegetation is once more gaining a foothold, can be visited in a long one-day launch trip from Labuhan Good travel agents in Jakarta can arrange the details for you, though it is possible to do-it-yourself in Labuhan. There are no regular launch services to Krakatau during the monsoon season, from the end of November through to the end of March.

Labuhan is also the take-off point for the

About 1512 A.D. the court of Portugal received a gift from the Indies, a one-horned rhinoceros. The first seen by Europeans (though Marco Polo claimed to have seen a horrendous 'unicorn' in Sumatra in 1292), it was sketched by a friend of Albrecht Durer, and became the subject of the artist's famous wood-cut.

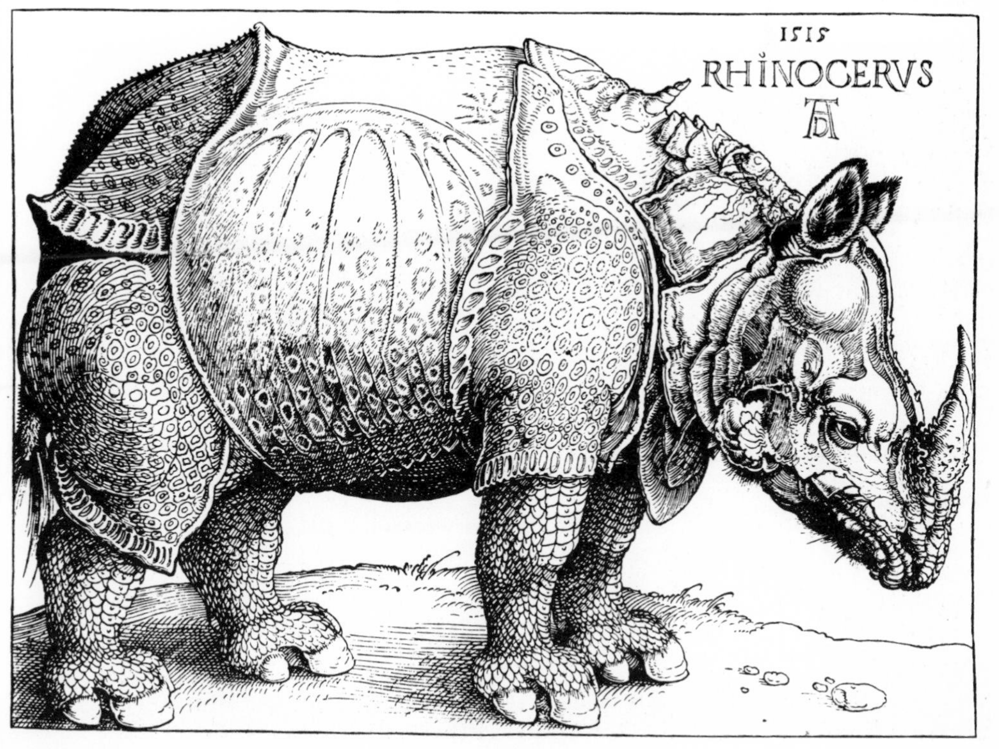

A nature reserve of rare beauty in Java's southwest corner.

long launch ride (more than 12 hours) to **UJUNG KULON**, an outstanding wildlife and nature reserve on the far southwest corner of Java.

Prior to 1883 Ujung Kulon was lushly enveloped in a thick mantle of jungle, impenetrable and economically unexploitable. What was left of the peninsula's growth after Krakatau's explosions and tidal waves was smothered under a blanket of volcanic ash and dust, and in the years that followed all that grew there was rough pampas grass and low, hardy scrub. The area became a paradise for the *banteng*, the fast and dangerous wild ox which still roams there. Now, almost a century later, the jungle is creeping back and the future of the *banteng* concerns naturalists and preservationists. Even greater concern is lavished on the one-horned rhinoceros, an increasingly rare beast found in few other countries, and in Indonesia limited to the 510 square kilometres of Ujung Kulon where it enjoys the protection and encouragement of the World Wildlife Fund.

Most of the reserve's other animals and birds can be seen in the other game parks in Java, but nowhere else is there such a concentrated array of different species: monkeys, crocodiles, tigers, pythons, peacocks, panthers, mouse deer, boars, bats and countless other denizens who crash, thump, whoop or glide through this untouched wilderness of swamp, grassland, forest and jungle, of plains, hills, valleys and estuarine shallows.

Ujung Kulon is accessible only by boat from Anyer or Labuhan, or by helicopter from Jakarta, for the narrow isthmus separating the peninsula from the mainland is a trackless marsh. A brief there-and-back visit will probably whet your appetite, and you should try to allow at least five days to make the most of your adventure. There is very limited accommodation in Peucang, where there is also a watchtower, but if you plan to move around take camping gear: lightweight tropical tent, insect-netting and repellants, groundsheet, jungle boots, machete or *parang*, a change of clothes, and enough food and drinking water. The sea bordering the peninsula is a delight for conchologists and coral-watchers: take snorkel or scuba gear if you can, or at the very least borrow a facemask.

Permission to enter the reserve must be obtained beforehand from the Forestry Department (Bagian Perhutanan), Jln. Juanda 9, Bogor. If you're arranging your trip through a good travel agent he should be able to look after these details.

An alternative route from Labuhan to Jakarta, or a straight-on route if you're planning to head east by road, is through Pandeglang, Rangkasbitung and Jasinga to Bogor. Another option, if time is no object and you enjoy rough but beautiful back-country journeying, is the route from Labuhan east to Ciandur, south to the coast at Cilangkahan, east again past the Cikotok goldmines to Pelabuhan Ratu (Samudra Beach), then north to Bogor or farther east to Bandung (see pages 144ff. for the Bogor-Pelabuhan Ratu area).

Half of the 100-km journey from Rangkasbitung takes you through a magnificent landscape or rubber trees, rolling hills and high ridges. Beyond Jasinga the country changes again as you plunge down onto rich river flats green with *padi*, dominated in the distance by the rugged peak of Gunung Salak.

Of special interest for the anthropologically-minded is the 'Badui territory' to the south of **RANGKASBITUNG**.

Most visitors, during their sojourn in Java, hear rumours, murmurs and tall tales about 'lost tribes' and 'mysterious people' who live locked away from the outside world in a mountain fastness where all kinds of strange things happen and where explorers disappear (never, of course, to be seen again . . . the most recent version tells of two Germans who ventured into this wilderness in 1967). Even educated Indonesians occasionally pass on the latest story about cannibalism and the eating of babies.

Most of the gossip is appallingly wrong.

A remote and isolated people does exist. They are the Badui, approximately 4,000 of whom live in 39 villages within the 51 square kilometres embraced by the boundaries of *desa* Kanekes. This territory lies a little more than 35 km south of Rangkasbitung in hilly country ranging from 300 or 400 metres in height to mountain passes, near Gunung Kendeng, which are crossed at 1,200 metres.

Land of the legendary and secluded Badui.

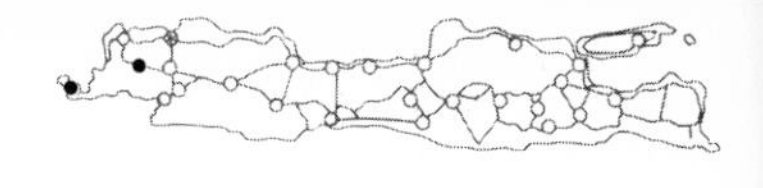

In one sense a 'lost tribe' also exists, for within the larger Badui community, near the southernmost boundary, are three villages inhabited by 400 Badui *Dalam* ('Inner' Badui people); they are completely surrounded by a protective buffer zone of Badui *Luar* ('Outer' Badui people), and deliberately shun all contact with the world beyond their group. Each of the three Badui Dalam villages is headed by a *puun*, a hereditary spiritual and temporal leader whose person is sacred (the notion of inherited leadership is unknown in most Javanese villages); the land within Badui Dalam territory is also regarded as sacred, and outsiders, including the Badui Luar, are forbidden to till its soil or settle there.

The Badui Dalam are not permitted to wear any cloth but the rough white homespun they weave themselves. They may not cultivate cash crops, use fertilisers, eat any four-legged animals, domesticate any livestock apart from chickens, or use any medicines except their own herbal preparations. Their agriculture is limited to *ladang*, 'shifting cultivation', which relies on the natural fertility of newly cleared ground and which is seldom productive for more than two seasons.

Taboos such as these, and the complete isolation of the inner communities, make an unhappy combination. Health is poor, life expectancy is short, and there is a high infant mortality rate. Nudged along by fantasy, these facts are easily misconstrued by the sophisticated outside world as 'cannibalism' (no *four*-legged animals) and 'infanticide'.

Similar taboos and restrictions apply to the larger group of Badui Luar, but are less rigidly observed. Although obliged to wear only their homespun blue-back cloth, and forbidden to wear trousers, some of the Luar people now proudly sport the colourful sarongs and shirts favoured by their Sundanese neighbours. Other elements of 'civilisation' (toys, money, batteries) are rapidly infiltrating, especially in the villages to the north, and it is no longer unusual for an outer Badui to make the journey to Jakarta, or even to work outside as a hired hand during the rice-planting and reaping seasons; some even work in big towns and cities like Jakarta, Bogor and Bandung. Animal meat is eaten in some of the outer villages where dogs are trained for hunting, though animal husbandry is still forbidden.

The origins of the Badui are obscure, though ethnically they appear to come from the same ancient stock as the Sundanese and Javanese. It has been suggested that they are remnants of the last Hindu kingdom in West Java, Pajajaran, but this fails to account for the unique nature of their religion, which shows no Hindu influence. Rather the religion is a strange blend of animism and certain Islamic elements, with some original ideas thrown in for good measure. The ultimate authority is vested in Gusti Nu Maha Suci, who originally sent *nabi* (prophet) Adam into the world to lead the life of a Badui, and *nabi* Mohammed to organise the world's religious affairs. The Badui's most hallowed ground lies on Gunung Kendeng in a place called Arca Domas, which is visited annually (and only) by the *puuns* of the inner communities.

The lives of the Badui are hardly idyllic, though the beauty of the country in which they live suggests another Shangri-la. Nevertheless, there is great vitality in their *angklung* music (the sound of rattled bamboo tubes is often accompanied by the deeper tones of goatskin drums) and in sonorous rhythms beaten out on hollow rice-pounding logs.

The Badui also have a formidable reputation as medicine men, and their herbal preparations are eagerly snapped up by country and city dwellers alike. Many itinerant *tukangs*, with the streets of Jakarta as their beat, claim to be genuine Badui (an important part of their sales pitch), though if the claims of the charlatans were to be believed the number of real Badui would probably double overnight.

If you are genuinely interested it is possible to visit some of the villages on the northern rim of the Badui area. The most easily accessible is *desa* Kaduketug, a good four-hour hike from Leuwidar (24 km south of Rangkasbitung). Do note that permission *must* be obtained beforehand from the *Kantor Kabupaten* ('District Office') in Rangkasbitung.

East of the misty rice-fields and hills of Badui country (see photograph page 40) are the taller and cooler slopes beyond Bogor.

BOGOR, PUNCAK AND THE SOUTH

The road to **BOGOR** leads slowly uphill through a tunnel of huge trees. At the top, an 18th-century landscape painting springs to life: beyond a pair of handsome wrought-iron gates can be seen an imposing, porticoed residence surrounded by sweeping lawns where herds of white-spotted deer graze. A sentry-box houses a smartly turned out 20th-century soldier, comfortably attached to an automatic rifle. This is the summer palace of the President of Indonesia.

Although only 290 metres above sea level, Bogor is appreciably cooler than Jakarta (54 km to the north), and it is easy to imagine the pleasure of Governor-General Baron Gustaaf van Imhoff when in 1744 he left Batavia's malarial plain and reached this spot. Nothing now remains of *Buitenzorg* ('Free of Care'), the country house he built, though the present palace was built on the same site in 1856, and from 1870 to 1942 was the official permanent residence of the Governors-General of the Dutch East Indies.

In the years following independence the palace and in particular a small pavilion within the palace grounds became a favourite haunt of the late President Sukarno. The palace still contains a large part of the huge art collection which he amassed, and can be visited if you make arrangements through a good travel agent.

Raffles lived there for some years, and fell in love with the place. He wrote in 1811 that 'I have now from my window a prospect of the most delightfully picturesque scenery . . . a valley filled with rice, with a romantic little village at the beginnings of a stream which rushes down by twenty torrents and roars booming over rocks innumerable; in the background a magnificent range of mountains, wooded to the top and capped in clouds.'

Pangrango and Gede, two 3,000-metre peaks in that 'magnificent range', still dominate the town. The stream, too, still runs clean and clear through the grounds of Bogor's world famous Botanical Gardens before coming to a sad end in the viscous black waters of a canal at Pasar Ikan.

Bogor's real glory is the Botanical Gardens, *Kebun Raya*, which virtually surround the palace. They are open every day, and on Sundays and public holidays become Bogor's playground, when brightly coloured clothing vies with flaming borders of canna lilies as hundreds of families picnic on the grass under the shade of trees up to 30 metres in height. Aspiring Rudy Hartono's sneak in a quick game of badminton (no net) beneath a cluster of palms; hordes of brown-and-white-uniformed schoolchildren on a class outing strip down to their knickers, or less, and gambol among the rocks and eddies of a swift-flowing stream; giant waterlily pads, improbably dubbed 'Victoria Regia', sit on tranquil ponds waiting for the Frog Prince; and 'Rafflesia', the world's largest flower, hailing from Sumatra, opens its metre-wide bloom in Bogor each October.

A cobbled pathway leads to a tiny cemetery locked in a thicket of wrist-thick bamboo. The names on the tombstones are mostly Dutch, though an English sea captain made his last landfall here in 1835 and was buried, 'much

Just south of Jakarta, Bogor's famous Botanical Gardens.

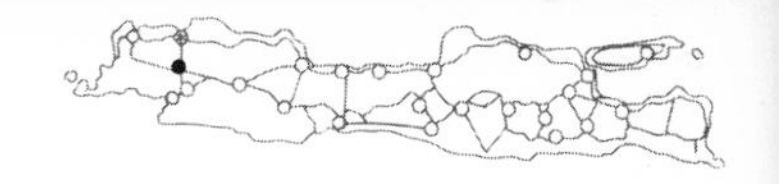

regretted by his relations & friends', only a few hundred metres from the back of the palace. On the placid surface of an ornamental pond are the shimmering reflections of elegant white columns, the façade of the palace rising above an expanse of immaculate lawn.

Close by is a small Grecian-style cenotaph in memory of Olivia Mariamne Raffles (who was in fact buried in Batavia). Her arrival in Java was marked by a conflict with the wives of many of the Dutch officials: she objected to their habit of wearing the *kebaya*, 'adorning themselves with vulgar jewellery and chewing *sirih*'. Happily, an amicable settlement was reached and the good ladies duly bowed to 'proper' English taste!

Raffles has often been credited with laying out the *Kebun Raya*, but the honour belongs to Prof. C.G.L. Reinwardt and his assistants from Kew Gardens, James Hoper and W. Kent. The gardens were officially opened as *'sLand Plantentuin* in 1817, and gained international repute during the 19th century for their range of botanical specimens and for research into such cash crops as tea, cassava, tobacco and cinchona; although oil palm was not developed commercially in Southeast Asia until this century, a small plaque identifies the oldest and probably the tallest oil palm in the region, brought from the west coast of Africa in 1848.

The gardens contain over 15,000 species of trees and plants (including 400 different types of palm) and more than 5,000 orchid varieties from Indonesia and abroad (the orchid houses are another Eden!). There is also an excellent zoological museum in the grounds. Students and visitors are welcome at the well-stocked *Biblioteca Bogoriensis* in Jalan Raya (a treasure house of botanical tomes), and the town is an important research and teaching centre with

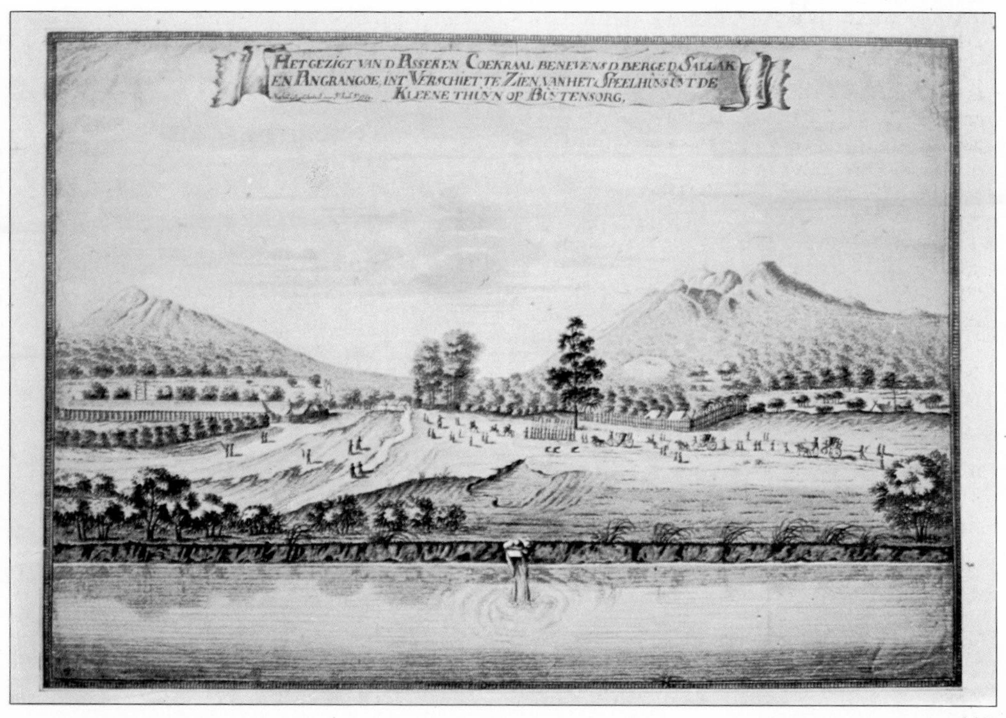
HET GEZIGT VAN D RSSEREN COEKRAAL BENEVENS D BERGE D SALLAK
EN PANGRANGOE INT VERSCHIET TE ZIEN VAN HET SPEELHUIS UIT DE
KLEENE THUYN OP BUITENSORG,

A winding road climbs Puncak Pass, to tea plantations and a multi-coloured lake.

university faculties in agriculture, forestry and veterinary science.

The road to Puncak climbs steadily from Bogor, winding its way through a manicured landscape of tea plantations. Beyond the top of the high pass the descent opens up a vista of pines and conifers on steep hillsides. Nestling amongst the trees on the more gentle slopes are dozens of hotels, guesthouses and 'week-enders', and the roadside is crowded with restaurants which cater for cool-climate appetites with (amongst other things) tasty *ikan mas* or golden freshwater carp.

While parts of Bogor display a stately elegance, the atmosphere of the hills around **PUNCAK** ('Summit') can be bucolic. A number of the scenic spots are easily accessible; others, including awesome craters and what little remains of triple-canopy jungle in Java, require more time and a love for hiking and the wilds. Guides are necessary for the more remote and densely forested mountains; enquire in Bogor at the *Lembaga Biologi Nasional* (LBN, the National Biological Institute).

Beyond Puncak, on the way down to Cibodas, the massive shattered rim of Gunung Gede juts almost 3,000 metres into the sky. Raffles climbed Gede in 1815, and carried a thermometer so as to judge the height of the volcano on the basis of the drop in temperature. His estimate of 7,000 feet was well short of the mark, but his description still holds: 'We had a most extensive prospect from the summit—Batavia roads [i.e. harbour], with the shipping so distinct that we could distinguish a ship from a brig on one side, and Wine Coops Bay [Pelabuhan Ratu] still more distinct on the other; the islands all around were quite distinct and we traced the sea beyond the southernmost point of Sumatra; the surf on the south coast was visible

From Bogor to Pelabuhan Ratu—a spectacular way to a seaside resort off the beaten track.

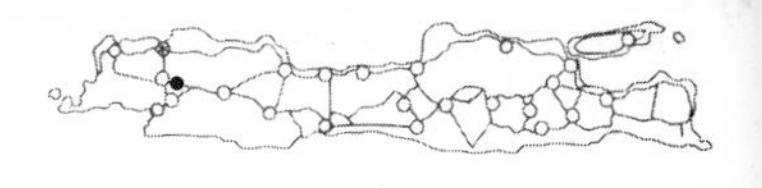

to the naked eye. To the eastward we included Indra Mayu point in the prospect, and Cheribon Hill rose high above the rest.'

The startling point for the day-long climb to Gunung Gede and back is 5 km south of Cibodas at the Cibodas Botanical Gardens (an extension of *Kebun Raya*, started in 1862 for temperate climate specimens, and well worth visiting in its own right). Less strenuous is the five-minute walk from the main road to *Telaga Warna* ('Lake of Many Colours'), just short of the pass.

Cipanas (literally 'Hot Water'), a little before Cibodas, is famous for its hot springs. Governor-General van Imhoff, that indefatigable traveller of the 1740s, commended the healing properties of its waters and established a health resort there that was heavily patronised despite the four days' bone-shaking ride from Batavia. On the outskirts of the town stands a quaint little 'palace' with elegant wrought-iron columns and deep, low-spreading eaves which marry the styles of a classical Javanese *pendopo* and a Victorian 'folly', Once part of the health resort, it is now a seldom-used country house for the President.

The southern coast of West Java, beautiful but dangerous, is also within easy reach of Bogor. The most accessible spot is **PELABUHAN RATU**, where the ragged, wind-lashed Indian Ocean foams and crashes onto black-sand beaches, grey-gold beaches, and onto rocks sculpted and hollowed by salt spray, rain and sun.

Pelabuhan Ratu is just 90 km from Bogor, 160 km from Jakarta (through Bogor), 155 km from Bogor through Puncak and Sukabumi, or 160 km from Bandung. If you're coming from Jakarta you can save time by flying: Pelita,

In the manicured tea plantations of Puncak one encounters unexpected beauty (below).

Samudra Beach Hotel, an island of modernity in unchanged surroundings.

the Pertamina airline, operates a light-aircraft service on Saturdays and Sundays at a little over Rp.10,000 for the return trip. The views on this hedge-hopping (or 'mountain-hopping') trip are superb, but scenically it is just as good on the road.

The road south from Bogor follows a winding route over the pass between Gunung Salak (2,211 metres) and Gunung Pangrango (3,022 metres), where the valleys and hillsides are a lush garden of rubber trees, tea plantations and terraced *padi*-fields. If you were to go no farther, you could say that you had seen Java in the proverbial nutshell, for this wonderfully varied landscape embraces most of what the island offers in scenic attractions and spectacular views. Even the minor distractions are a delight: yet another breed of *dokar* or horsecart, quite unique and resembling the back half of pre-war automobiles which have been neatly guillotined

Perhaps the most appealing of all are the unspoiled fishing villages along the coast. 'Unspoiled' is often a cliché designed to hide a multitude of unattractive sins, but at Pelabuhan Ratu there is real freshness and vitality in the village life. The fish market does a roaring trade in the mornings, with fish of every imaginable shape and size (some easily exceed a metre in length). The coastline itself, backed by steep hills, is raw and varied in its beauty.

From the village of Pelabuhan Ratu, past a series of small, pleasant weekend 'bungalow' hotels, the road follows the seashore through handsome natural forest to the site of the Samudra Beach Hotel, an island of modernity in otherwise unchanged surroundings. The hotel has long been popular with Jakarta's outdoor set (who like their comforts as well), and is generally heavily booked at weekends, but on weekdays it is quiet and restful. This is an internationa

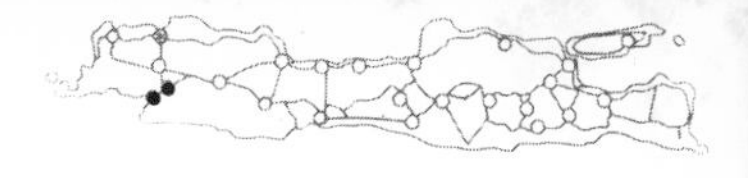

standard hotel and room rates are high.

The beach is pretty. The surf is treacherous and unpredictable. Many people, ignoring the admonitory legend of Dewi Loro Kidul (Queen of the Southern Ocean), have discovered to their cost that swimming in the ocean is dangerous, so it's better to enjoy the hotel pool.

About 5 km west of the hotel, at Karang Hawu, a towering cliff looks out over a tangled mass of rocky reefs. Farther west is the tiny fishing village of Cisolok where a hot spring gushes forth from a small riverbed.

For a breath of adventure, you can head on towards Cikotok where Java's most important gold and silver mine is operating. Cages plummet down into two 50-metre shafts, and you should be able to arrange with the management for an exciting descent into the netherworld.

The coast road beyond Cikotok is outstandingly beautiful and seldom used. It doesn't always stick to the coastline, but plunges inland at various points, scaling saddles and ridges through heavy forest before nosing back to the ocean front. With four-wheel drive, good weather and accurate information about road conditions it is possible and rewarding to make this gruelling trip, which will eventually land you back in 'civilisation' at Labuhan on the west coast of Sunda above the Ujung Kulon peninsula.

A less demanding four-wheel safari can take you south of Pelabuhan Ratu to Ujung Genteng, one of Java's less well known game reserves. It's advisable to check with the police or the hotel in Pelabuhan Ratu before setting out: the road is rough, and could be impassable.

Heading east from Pelabuhan Ratu in the direction of Bandung and Central Java, the best route goes through Sukabumi. The attractive drive winds through hilly country before linking up with the main highway at Cianjur.

BANDUNG 'PARIS OF JAVA'

From Puncak to **BANDUNG** it is only 120 km. Beyond Cipanas the country changes abruptly. The vistas of terraced hillsides, plains of *padi* and forests of pine give way to massive limestone outcrops creating phantasmagoric patterns, where clusters of lime kilns with roaring open-mouth furnaces bring Dante's *Inferno* to a weirdly untropical landscape. Basalt, the 'blue metal' of roadbuilders and construction engineers, is also a money-earner here. Its extraction and treatment are a familiar sight in Java: smooth river stones are collected in baskets and then slowly reduced by hand (hammer blow by hammer blow) to a fine grey sand which is moulded into tough, cement-like bricks; in other places large basalt rocks are levered and wrenched from their nests of red soil, broken down with hammers, and used as filling or for road surfaces.

Approaching Bandung from Jakarta there is an alternative route which avoids the hills around Puncak. By road or rail the route is almost the same. The *K.A. Parahyangan* express, with comfortable allocated seats and a restaurant service, does the three-hour trip four times a day (try to book a day ahead, and be at the station half an hour before departure time: Gambir Station, on the east side of Jakarta's Medan Merdeka, is the most convenient station). Views from the train are at times spectacular, especially when crossing slender steel bridges that span yawning ravines; below, stepped *padi*-terraces as little as a metre wide climb up and down almost vertical slopes and nestle alongside huge boulders strewing the riverbeds.

The road east from Jakarta can be hot. Very hot. The heat sits like a pale yellow mist over flat expanses of sugar-cane and rice-fields; heavy trucks churn up dust as they race east or west on errands of commerce; and the towns, green-shuttered in the early afternoon, seem tired and grumpy. Only the free-loading easy-riders who cling to the front of the boiler of a huge Krupp coal-burning locomotive, or who cluster like limpets over its tender, exhibit the peculiar *joie de vivre* which is so Sundanese; those in a hurry straddle the carriage roofs of diesel expresses.

East, then south, and the road begins to climb. At Jatiluhur is a huge hydro-electric and irrigation dam, completed in 1965, where calm waters are ideal for boating, water-skiing and fishing. Beyond Jatiluhur the foothills of Java's central mountain range are covered with teak forests which disperse the sunlight through gold-green leaves. The temperature grows cooler. In Purwakarta, where you can buy excellent local pottery (including big water jars with shiny black glazes and buff-coloured decoration), the air is refreshing after the heat of the plains. A little farther south, and slightly higher, carefully tended rubber plantations make leafy tunnels across the winding road. Soon you'll be in *becak* territory on the outskirts of Bandung.

One could be excused for thinking there are more *becaks* than people in Bandung: with the exception of a few *becak*-free zones in the centre of the city, most streets bristle with these three-wheeled pedi-cabs, amongst the most colourful and imaginatively decorated of their kind in the whole of Java. Their ranks were swelled in 1973 by a *becak* 'invasion' from Jakarta, where increasing limitations on the areas of *becak* operations caused many fleet owners to uproot their squadrons and move to greener pastures. Bandung, closer to Jakarta than other big cities, became the new haven for *becak* owners and drivers, and the result is a mind-boggling tangle of wheels, legs and brightly painted 'carriages' which swarm through the city's cycleable streets.

As Java's cities and towns go, Bandung

A pleasant commercial and educational centre that is a good base for excursions.

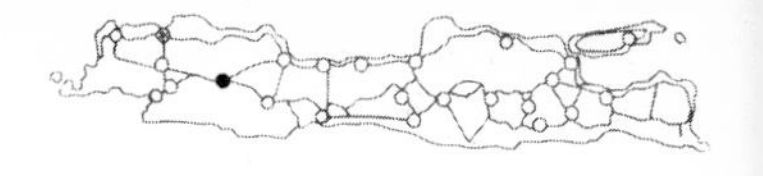

is comparatively new. It was established by the Dutch in the early years of this century in the northern foothills of the enormous Bandung plateau, enclosed by high ridges and peaks with magnificent views of pretty countryside. The city rapidly acquired importance as a commercial and educational centre (Sukarno received his engineering diploma from the famous Bandung Institute of Technology in 1926). Its attractive tree-lined streets on the hills north of the railroad cutting through its centre are the epitome of suburban respectability, and the pleasure of living there, in a mild upland climate, can be easily imagined. It is still a 'pilgrimage' point for nostalgic Dutch visitors, and seems to hold a spot far closer to Dutch hearts than most other towns in Java. It does have a certain polish and veneer of old-fashioned 'colonial' civilisation which somehow refuses to die; it is ironic that Bandung was the site of the first (and only) Afro-Asian Conference in 1955, a time when many of the participants were shrugging off the yoke of colonial masters.

Parts of the city today exude a somewhat jaded air, but the abiding impression is one of bustle and vitality, appropriate to Indonesia's third largest city. The population is now officially 1.5 million but it is almost certainly higher; as many as three million if the immediate Bandung environs are included.

Bandung is the centre of Sunda culture and the Sundanese and their lively language and style dominate the town. Bandung, also called **KOTA KEMBANG** (the flowering city), has often been described as the "Paris of Java", a wistful sobriquet which does justice to neither city.

There is little in the way of architecture that predates 1900 in Bandung, and in fact little of substance was built before a great residential expansion of Dutch people between 1920–1940. Some splendid examples of Art Deco survive: the Savoy Hotel — replete with furniture and fittings from the era — is the best monument of this transplanted art movement that can be found in Asia. Novel designs with stained glass and tile in the *art nouveau* style can also be found in some of the older Dutch housing. The relative newness of Bandung (established in the nineteenth century as a Dutch garrison town) contrasts oddly with the ancient Sunda culture which, regrettably, left little in the way of physical remains behind.

Apart from the main shopping area on Jalan

Shopping or just strolling for a taste of town life.

Braga there is a wealth of other possibilities in Bandung. The **CERAMIC RESEARCH CENTRE** is worth a visit. First class copies of classical Chinese porcelain are produced as well as a wide variety of other ceramic goods. The Centre makes pottery to order. Bandung's quinine factory, which is *the* major supplier of quinine to the world, is also a good stop. An intriguing spot is the Chinese Cemetery, about two kilometers off Jalan A. Yani, where there is some interesting tomb architecture. Several Chinese confucian temples are also found in Bandung, the best being on Jalan Kelenteng.

The Bandung Institute of Technology is Indonesia's equivalent to M.I.T and its students have a reputation for outspokenness and activism. The Institute ("ITB" is the Indonesian abbreviation) also boasts one of the country's best fine arts schools; many of Indonesia's prominent artists received their initial training here. The facilities are impressive and visitors are welcome to watch the current crop of students at work. The principal campus complex of ITB is architecturally the most pleasing of all Indonesia's centres of higher education, and a wander through the campus' spacious grounds and gardens is a relaxing experience.

Sundanese culture is less refined and epicene than the high court culture of Central Java, and it is characterised by an earthiness which is often lacking further east. Although the best place to experience Sunda dance and music is the hundreds of highland villages from Sukabumi east to Tasikmalaya, Bandung also presents many of these varied offerings.

Ketuk Tilu (the Sunda term for traditional dance and music) can be viewed in the evenings at Jalan Otto Iskandarinata 541A, and *wayang golek* (the *wayang* of the wooden puppets, a Sunda innovation) may be seen each Saturday night on Jalan Naripan No. 7. The **RUMENTANG SIANG,** on Jalan Baranang Siang No. 1 next to the Pasar Kisambi, offers regular productions of drama and music; timings of performances are noted on a monthly programme. In West Java *wayang golek* is preferred to the *wayang kulit* or 'shadow plays', although both forms feature well-known stories from the *Ramayana* and *Mahabharata* tales. The wooden puppets are larger and more vivid than those of Central Java, and quite apart from their function as

Bandung: Jalan Asia-Africa, green suburbia, and old themes recurring in a new design.

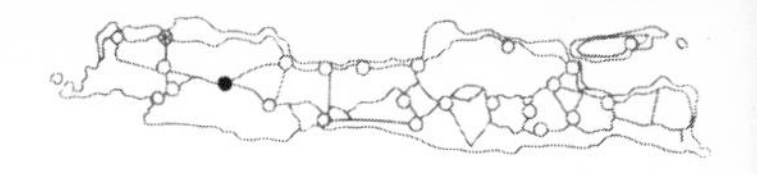

the 'actors' of a *wayang golek* performance, they are colourful complements to *wayang* puppets available in other parts of the country.

Angklung music may be heard in the confines of the **KONSERVATORI KERAWITAN,** located on Jalan Buah Batu 212, in south Bandung. The Konservatori is also home to a fascinating mixture of traditional Sunda arts instruction, and the students are always happy to receive visitors. The sound of the word *"angklung"* suggests something about the nature of this form of indigenous music: delicate hollow notes reverberating in bamboo tubes. Originally tuned to a five-note scale and played on ceremonial occasions only, the *angklung* is now more often heard in western octaves, but the effect in either scale — especially when the *angklung* is accompanied by the Sunda flute (the *suling*) — is hauntingly beautiful. Those who are captivated by this rich musical heritage will find all kinds of Sunda musical instruments (and those from Central Java as well) in the **TOKO MUSIK** on Gang ("alley") Suniaraja No. 3, off Jalan ABC. Another focus of artistic activity in Bandung is **PAK UJO'S SCHOOL,** on Jalan Padasaka No. 8, *Wayang golek* is performed nearly every afternoon, as is Sunda dancing. Traditional musical instruments are sold here as well.

Bandung is also famous for its **PASAR BUNGA** in the Wastukencana area. This is a fascinatingly diverse flower market and a visit, particularly in the cool early morning hours, is a refreshing way to begin the day. The bird and fish market at **PASAR WARINGEN** is another justifiably well-known "must" in Bandung, as it is a rival to Jakarta's **PASAR BURUNG** in virtually every respect.

There are several museums in Bandung, including a military one reserved for the history and exploits of the Siliwangi Division of the Indonesian Army (which is based in Bandung). A museum unique to Indonesia however is found in the massive old headquarters to the Dutch Geological Service, now the office of the Geological Survey of Indonesia. The Geological Museum is open from 8.00a.m. until 1.00p.m. every day except Sunday, and it displays an extraordinary array of fossils, rocks, maps and (of special interest in this geologically active, earthquake-prone area) some first class models of volcanoes. Incidentally, the Publications Department of the Geological Survey sells topographical and geological maps of all places in Indonesia. Maps

Nearby hill stations, such as Lembang.

of West Java are also available.

Travellers keen to catch up on local news will find branches of the Goethe Institut, the Alliance Francaise and the British Council in Bandung. These institutes are offering more Indonesian cultural selections than was the case in the past, it is worth the trouble to find out what their monthly programmes are.

The city is also ideal as a comfortable stopover point for jaunts into the nearby hills and mountains. Try **LEMBANG**.

You'll perhaps wake to the 'thwock' of tennis balls and the sight of lithe figures in blue tracksuits pounding around an asphalt court. Come breakfast, and bare-footed waiters pad silently to and fro from your table, bearing mounds of toast, marmalade, eggs, fruit juice and hot coffee: the coffee needs to be hot, for at a height of more than 1,400 metres the morning air can be quite cold.

Notwithstanding a busy programme of modernisation and expansion, the New Grand Hotel in Lembang still possesses a gentle, old-fashioned charm, and it seems only natural that at least one of the waiters has been there since the original Grand Hotel opened for business in 1926. Some of the family rooms are little less than suites: two bedrooms, bathroom, living room and (in the remaining old wing) the inevitable servants' room. The blankets are thick, and the beds are comfortable. The views, the cool-climate trees and shrubs, the masses of flowers and well-ordered gardens, and the marvellous fruit market just up the road in Lembang village all contribute to a feeling of profound peace.

The hotel (the only good one in Lembang) is half a kilometre from Lembang village and 16 km north of Bandung on the way to the Tangkuban Parahu craters. A couple of small local resthouses cater to the poorer traveller. Bandung is regarded as Jakarta's market garden, but the hills around Lembang are where the goodies grow: onions, cabbages, corn, Chinese cabbage, cauliflowers, carrots, avocados. Excellent bananas grow locally, but the delicious apples come from Tasmania.

From Lembang to **TANGKUBAN PARAHU**, the famous 'Upturned Boat' mountain and its three craters, is a steep, winding 16 km on a good but narrow road. Hardy Sundanese farmers traverse this road, and others, at a steady jog-trot, delicately balancing shoulder poles slung at each end with a 50-kilo basket of cabbages. Higher up the road, where vegetable plots vanish and tall pines reach for the sky, the baskets give way to rough-hewn wooden slings filled with lengths of sweet-smelling white pine and toted at the same heart-pounding pace.

Early morning is the best time to see the main and most accessible crater on Tangkuban Parahu, when the mist swirls around nearby peaks and ridges and a glancing ray of sun turns it to quicksilver. The vegetation is harsh and scrubby, complementing the dormant threat of the far-from-dead volcano.

On the Bandung plateau, life is cool, while Tangkuban Prahu's crater still simmers.

The 'Upturned Boat' volcano intermittently bubbles and steams.

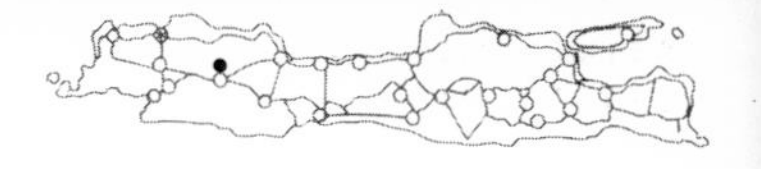

There is, of course, a legend. With Oedipal overtones.

Queen Dayang Sumbi had a son, Prince Sangkuriang. The inevitable generation gap led to words and finally to blows, and Sangkuriang skulked out of the palace with a scowl and a ferocious scar. Time passed, and he acquired both fame and fortune. He met a beautiful princess, and their love ran true until the day Dayang Sumbi (for it was she!) discovered the scar and her lover's real identity. *Quel horreur!* The answer to this awkward impasse, Dayang Sumbi thought, would be to set her lover an impossible task

The project involved the damming of the Citarum River and the building of a boat for crossing the resulting lake . . . and it had to be done in one night between sunset and sunrise. As it happened, Sangkuriang got a little help from his friends (gods and others in high places), and the job was almost finished when his mother awoke just before dawn and discovered the horrible truth. She in turn implored some other gods to get her out of the mess, and they obliged by bringing the sun up a few minutes earlier than usual. Sangkuriang knew when he was licked, but he was so mad that he kicked the *prahu* fair amidships, broached his dam, and generally behaved badly before storming off. The water drained away leaving the upturned boat, *Tangkuban Parahu,* firmly aground on the spot where it can be seen to this day.

Sangkuriang is apparently still simmering. The floor of the volcano's main crater, looking like a giant grey pancake, still squeaks and steams and bubbles, sending sulphurous odours up to the 1,830-metre rim. Souvenir sellers, occasionally engulfed in these noxious vapours, pluckily combat the fumes and the morning cold on the lip of the crater; they sell brilliant

Hot springs beside head-cracking ram fights.

yellow lumps of crystalline sulphur, and strange monkey-like objects which have been fashioned from tree-fern fibre. Depending on the crater's mood, guides may be able to take you down into the depths for some moonscape sightseeing; on the other side of the crater ridge they can also guide you to hot springs and sulphur holes.

Stomping around a cold mountain top can sharpen the desire for food and for a hot bath. The latter is well catered for at **CIATER**, where there's a choice of public or private hot pools, warm enough (though not scalding) to relax the most travel-weary limbs. Head back down the road from Tangkuban Parahu, turn left at the tollgate you passed on the way up, and you'll find Ciater about 7 km farther on.

Closer to Lembang are the **MARIBAYA HOT SPRINGS** (4 km east), tucked snugly into a high-walled, sun-trap valley. Trimly landscaped, its small park is a glory of hillocks, dells, copses, cascades, swings and slides, pools, streams and bridges . . . the perfect spot for family outings and family snapshots. A four-room *penginapan* in chalet style, with spring-fed bath houses beneath it, offers clean accommodation, and there's a restaurant just a few metres away. If you happen to be at Sukarandeg, within a kilometre of Maribaya on a Sunday, you might care to take time out to watch a ram fight:

A big black and white ram strains at his leash. Magnificent horns curl back from the crown of his skull and encircle his ears. His proud, heavy head looks out of place above his long, spindly shanks (a wrestler's torso on a cross-country runner's legs). His opponent, white and lighter horned, stands with his handlers on the far side of the ten-metre square. The leashes are dropped. For almost a second the two warriors glare at each other across the hard-packed earth. Then there's a mad blur of speed and a heart-rending

Pengalengan, south of Bandung, the home of Malabar tea.

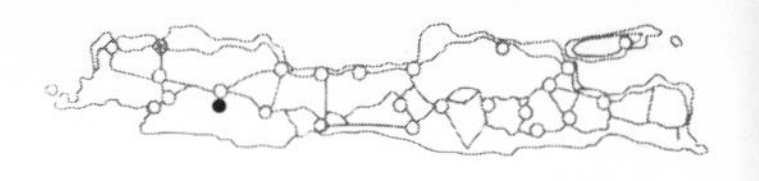

crack as two lumps of flesh and bone meet head-on. The force of the collision carries the black and white ram up and over the foreshoulders of his foe, who staggers and almost falls.

They back off with a slow, deliberate step, their gaze never faltering. They stop momentarily, and charge again. Crack! The white ram staggers, then drops to his knees. A tinge of pink stains his snowy crown. The handlers separate them and they return to their corners. The white ram, his Irish up, comes out like a berserk locomotive. Crack! They back off, pause, and strike again. This time it's black and white who falls. He half rises, and falls again.

It's a TKO in the fourth. The crowd roars (500 people can make quite a noise) and betting money changes hands as victor and vanquished are led away and tethered to a pair of stout bamboo poles. The first match of the day is over.

The spectacle takes place every Sunday morning, starting around 10 o'clock, in a small glade set among towering bamboo on the road between Lembang and Maribaya about one kilometre short of the springs. There are usually 20 matches, but only rarely is an encounter fatal. If you enjoy a coliseum bout, and are not a paid-up member of the RSPCA, you'll enjoy the ram fights. A *warung* across the road dispenses liquid refreshments.

Two southern trips may be of interest before you take the road to the east. At Ciwidey, 30 km to the southwest on the way to Gunung Patuha, you'll find cottage industry craftsmen working with iron and turning out a fascinating range of hand-forged knives and daggers with carved wooden hilts.

A reasonable good surfaced road links Ciwidey to **PANGALENGAN** which may also be reached by taking the road due south from Bandung through Banjaran. The attractive hilly country leading up to Pangalengan via both routes provides the usual picture of mixed crops, with bananas, rice and cassava fighting for space in a verdant jumble. This, however, hardly prepares you for the formal iron gateway and neatly clipped hedges like the entrance to a seigneurial estate, or the seemingly endless vista of rolling hills smothered under a mantle of tea bushes, or the ordered rows of spick and span houses clustering amongst the greenery, that greets you at Pengalengan.

A number of government controlled tea estates are located in this area, generally better known, broadly, as the Malabar Estate after the nearby 2,300-metre peak of Gunung Malabar. Farther to the southeast you can drive to within striking distance of Gunung Papandayan, which offers magnificent views if you're prepared for the long but not too arduous walk to the peak. Papandayan is an active three-sided crater, still boiling but safe, which blew out its fourth side in a catastrophic explosion in 1772 that killed more than 3,000 people.

In Banjaran, or at nearby Batu Karut, you may catch a performance of one of the unique regional dances that appear to have evolved from ancient trials of strength. Now formalised, like the martial art of *silat*, they are still powerfully masculine in feeling.

BORDERLINE INTERLUDE

Outstanding *batiks*, pig-shooting, wild windswept beaches, superbly situated mountain temples, wildlife reserves, steaming craters, triple-canopy jungle and exquisite picture-postcard landscapes are among the reasons for giving time to the countryside between Bandung and the cities of Central Java.

It is also a countryside which is all too often ignored as the time-is-precious tourist makes a mad dash from Jakarta to Yogyakarta and then on to Bali (or vice versa). But the rewards are many if you've time to spare. For the colour-film buff, the devotee of scenic beauty, the would-be archaeologist, the lover of folk arts, the explorer, the beachcomber, the historical romantic . . . for all of these, the border country can be an absorbing interlude.

The administrative line separating West Java from Central Java is, for the traveller or tourist, a fuzzy one. Although there are notable cultural and linguistic differences between the two provinces (Sundanese is spoken in the west, Javanese in the centre) there are no distinct geographical features or major towns demarcating the border, and one province blends imperceptibly into the other.

Gaily prowed fishing boats (previous pages) decorate a harbour near Cirebon, making this north coast port look like an amusement park.

Bandung, in round figures, is 150 km by road to the west of the border; east of the border, Semarang is 200 km away, and Yogyakarta 280 km. In describing routes between these cities it would be arbitrary to fix a cut-off point at the official provincial boundary just because it happens to be there. The following pages, therefore, cover a little of West Java and a little of Central Java in setting out a logical link in your travels from west to east, and offer three basic routes.

The 'north coast route' is the fastest and, in most respects, the least interesting: it runs through Bandung or Jatibarang to Cirebon, then on to Tegal, Semarang and down to Yogya.

The 'south coast route' is the slowest, but it offers many scenic compensations *en route* through Bandung, Tasikmalaya and Kebumen.

The 'middle route' is quite fast and (depending on where you choose to join it) is the most attractive. It begins with either the south coast or north coast route, and then blazes a new trail a little east of the border: you head south from Tegal or north from Buntu, and then in both cases swing east from Banyumas along the mountainous road through Wonosobo.

It is possible to drive straight through from Jakarta to Yogyakarta in as little as 14 hours but it's tiring whether you're driving or being driven, and a more leisurely pace is recommended. There are numerous variations on the three basic routes, though if you're planning to take any back roads be sure to check first on road conditions with the local police or military

'Borderline Interlude' is divided into descriptions of routes to Yogyakarta and Central Java. The first route is the most travelled and most picturesque, 'Southeast From Bandung To Yogya' (pages 161 to 164). This route leads to one of Java's more accessible game reserves at Pangandaran, and to the 'Dieng Plateau, Mists And Mysteries' (pages 165 to 168). The misty plateau, on which are found ancient temples dedicated to Siva, lies on what we call the 'second or middle route'; one may also divert south from the Cirebon route at Tegal and veer towards Dieng. The third route, 'Cirebon To Semarang And South To Yogya' (pages 169 to 177), lies along the flat north coast.

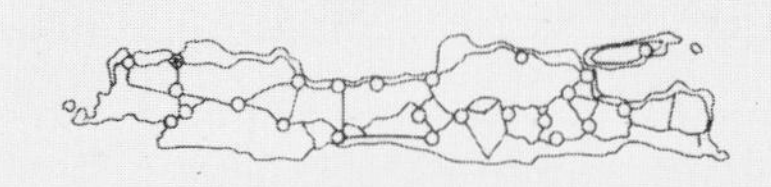

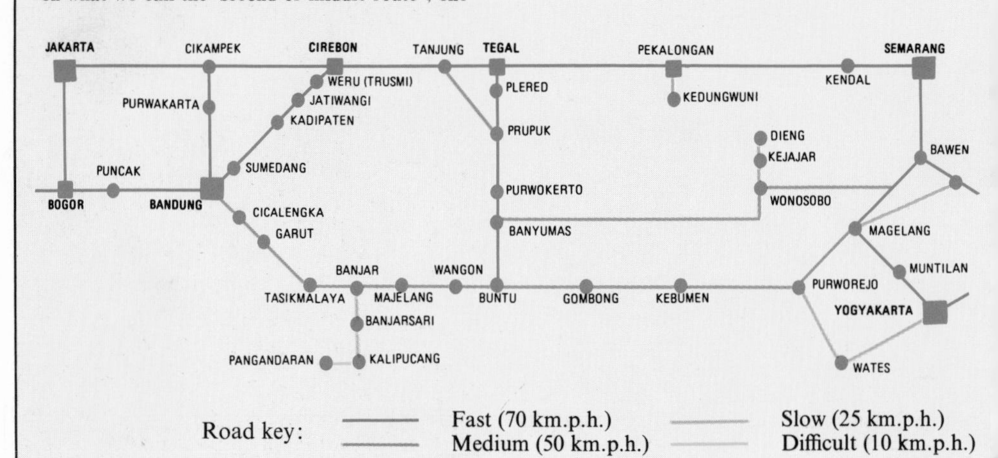

Road key: Fast (70 km.p.h.) Medium (50 km.p.h.) Slow (25 km.p.h.) Difficult (10 km.p.h.)

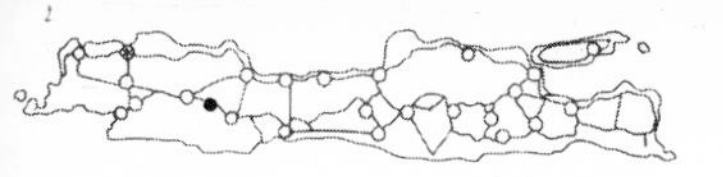

SOUTHEAST FROM BANDUNG TO YOGYA

This is the 'slow boat' route to Yogyakarta. Eight peaks over 2,000 metres high make the area south of Bandung a demi-paradise for nature-lovers, bush-walkers and amateur volcanologists, and there's some wonderful exploring to be done.

Nature's charms were less obvious to the Dutch and their Ambonese mercenaries when they first fought their way through this natural guerrilla terrain in the early 1680s and reached the shores of the Indian Ocean: their steel breastplates, sweltering buckskin jerkins, and moisture-prone black-powder flintlock muskets didn't make good jungle companions. Even today it is utterly believable that Parahyangan (Priangan or Preanger) was a no-man's land between Mataram and Banten.

Between Bandung and Garut almost every side-road leads to a mountain or crater or hot spring. One of the more spectacular mountains is Gunung Guntur: leave the main road at Cicalengka and go south through Majalaya and Paseh. Walking up to the mountain's steaming array of holes and gaping craters will take you through beautiful, sun-dappled forest. 'A deep silence reigns in this fairy wood where the huge old trees are clad with soft velvet-like mosses,' observed a travel writer some 50 years ago.

To nominate the 'picturesque' heart of Java is to play with fire, but if there had to be such a nomination, the long, winding stretch of country through Garut and on to Tasikmalaya could stake a claim. Although lacking the rugged majesty of Bromo or Dieng, it encompasses all of the gentle clichés of landscape, embroidered with deftly worked threads of green and gold, set up for viewing in a jolting, breathtaking package.

There are naked children lolling on the greasy wet backs of mud-bathed *kerbaus*, a hot sun burning down on a sea of ripening rice, and plumes of feathery bamboo dipping and nodding in an afternoon breeze like long-necked waterbirds.

There's a powder-pale sky, hinting at pink, reflected on the surface of a flooded, unplanted *padi*-field. A flash of sunlight transforms a column of water into a band of silver, dropping from one rice-terrace to another.

There are little towns, more spacious than those in the north. White dolls' houses, trimmed with curlicues of equally white icing, cool within deep, colonnaded verandahs. The *becaks* are cleaner and brighter and (if it's possible) more colourfully and lovingly decorated than anywhere else on the island. The ponies, bedecked in a jangle of polished silver 'horse brasses' and scarlet pompoms of Napoleonic regimental style, strut with a higher step. Their carriages (to call them carts is unkind) shine like cherished old walnut desks.

Even the presence of people, people and more people at every twist and turn of the road, is here less a reminder of precarious overcrowding than a symbol of warmth and bucolic vitality.

GARUT is the starting point for this idyll. Appropriately, the cone of nearby Gunung Cikura, a little off the main road to the southwest, is as perfect as a volcanic cone can be. Off to the

east, Gunung Telaga Bodas, also worth a visit, has a crater lake alive with sulphur which is 50% pure and easily extracted; the lake has become one of Indonesia's principal sources of this valuable element.

Beyond Garut, man-made volcanoes in the form of sky-spearing chimney-stacks mark the site of kilns where earthenware pipes and roofing tiles are churned out in hundreds of thousands. Tiles are another of Java's minor surprises. The tropics, and especially the idealised tranquil village, suggest a world of thatched roofs. But Java's houses (with the singular exception of some in the Banten area), from the mansions of Menteng to the tiniest plaited-bamboo dwelling, are carefully topped with tiles, a 19th-century innovation designed to eliminate plague-carrying rats that liked to bed and breed in the nooks and crannies of a sun-warmed palm-thatch roof.

TASIKMALAYA, 57 km east of Garut, is the centre of a prolific weaving trade in *rotan*, *pandan* leaf and bamboo, and its finest wares adorn the shelves and windows of souvenir shops throughout Java. Less well known is its smaller but exciting *batik* industry, where the local predilection for detail produces some of the most colourful and attractive floral motifs in the *batik* catalogue. An engaging memento of Tasik, combining the workmanship of both crafts, is a finely woven solar topee. Raj-style, covered with *batik* (wear it, if you dare!). For woven-on-the-premises purchases it is worth diverting about 12 km north to the village of Rajapolah where many of the weavers live and work. At Banjar, 42 km east, is the turn-off to Pangandaran (see page 164).

Almost all fertile land is cultivated, forcing much of Java's wildlife into remote sanctuaries. (Right) A typical midday jam—at Purworejo.

nto Java's bustling
and exciting heartland.

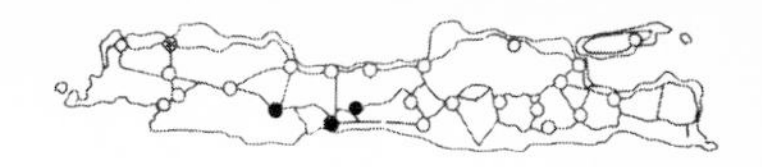

Back on the main road and heading east from Banjar there is little more of interest. Minor notes: huge panniers, filled with snow-white cassava chips, and spread out over dozens of sunny slopes; Majelang, where the *pasar* bulges with attractive pottery and basketware; Wangon, acclaimed as the cleanest and prettiest town in Central Java, and looking just that with its neat houses set well back from the road behind white-washed fences of split bamboo; Buntu, where a road junction can take you 9 km north to Banyumas and the start of the 'middle route' through Wonosobo; and looking south, on your way to Gombong, the knobbly hills of Karangbolong, bump after bump like a giant set of filed-down shark's teeth washed up on the coast, where limestone caves yield a valuable crop of edible swallows' nests for the famous birds'-nest soup.

Local transport, as ever, bespeaks regional differences. Here the *opelets* are battered Chevy ranchwagons; the woven-roofed bullock carts have a carved and fretted back panel not seen anywhere else; and in the pony-cart 'caravanserai' at Kutowingangun the harnesses are topped not with pompoms (as in Garut and Banjar) but with feathered plumes like those worn by a grenadier. One labour-intensive result of all these carts, gigs, wagons and carriages is a multitude of *tukangs* who earn their livings as wheelwrights, wainwrights and blacksmiths. Shoeing a horse is a skill still much in demand, though the humped oxen wear tie-on sandals made from old tyres.

At Purworejo, on the last leg of the journey, you have a choice of driving northeast to Magelang and then south again to Yogya; or you can head southeast through Wates which saves 40 km.

One of Java's more easily accessible game

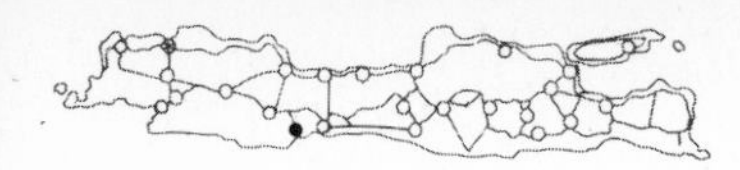

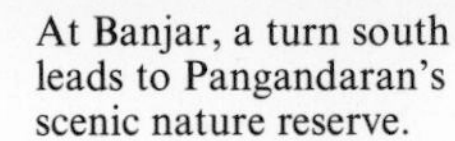

At Banjar, a turn south leads to Pangandaran's scenic nature reserve.

reserves, **PANGANDARAN**, is almost 60 km south of Banjar, through Banjarsari and Kalipucang.

Monkeys, *banteng*, tapir, small deer and powerful, bright-beaked hornbills abound in the heavy forest which clings to the slopes and hills of the Pangandaran peninsula and envelops three grassy upland clearings where the wild ox roam. The strangest sights along the narrow bush trails are the small bands of sweepers and hackers who keep the pathways free of leaves and trim at the edges. The narrow neck of land linking the reserve to the mainland is only a kilometre across, but seawards the peninsula breaks out and then closes back again like a flat onion. East along the coast, the water is calm within the shelter of Pangandaran Bay, where the nets of fishing traps hang lazily from their bamboo platforms, and where a few fishermen patiently work their seine-nets along the shore. The sheltered waters make this a good swimming beach. To the west is the flat sweep of surf-pounded grey sand which stretches 15 km to Batu Hiu and beyond. It could become great surfing territory.

There are two tollgates at Pangandaran. The first, at the village, allows you the privilege of enjoying the east and west coastlines. The second, at the barrier fence on the neck leading to the reserve, lets you into the game park. At weekends, and during holiday periods, a few portable *warungs* do brisk business near the entrance, but in-between times the peninsula is blessedly quiet and relaxing. Accommodation is simple, spartan, and inexpensive. A few enterprising souls are also running a lucrative souvenir trade which includes handsome shell necklaces and an amazing range of stuffed and mounted animals: the pairing of taxidermy and a wildlife reserve apparently holds no contradictions.

DIENG PLATEAU MISTS AND MYSTERIES

Roughly halfway between Cirebon and Semarang on the north coast route, or between Bandung and Yogyakarta on the southern route, you have the choice of branching off for an inland diversion through Banyumas to Wonosobo and farther on to either Semarang or Yogya.

Although the inland route is mountainous the road is good, and at Wonosobo you're only an hour's drive from the attractions of the Dieng Plateau. The plateau, its temples and lakes, and the surrounding mountains, are among Central Java's great scenic rewards: a landscape of constantly changing moods, swathed in mist at one moment, alive with sunshine the next.

On the north coast route, turn south at Tanjung or Tegal. The road runs through Prupuk and Bumiaju, under the shadow of Gunung Slamet (at 3,428 metres the highest mountain in the province), then on through Purwokerto to Banyumas.

On the southern route, beyond Wangon, there are a number of turn-offs to Banyumas; the fastest route leaves the main road at Buntu.

Banyumas, a small, well-scrubbed town, is worth a few minutes of your time. Its broad streets, trim white buildings and a turn-of-the-century atmosphere suggest a conservative bachelor suddenly on the lookout for a bride, his dress enhanced with a touch of the local *batik*.

The 85-km run from Banyumas through to Wonosobo follows (in reverse) the turbulent, rocky course of the Kali Serayu, a foaming river with stretches of rapids that look just right for shooting. The road, twisting and winding its way up the narrowing valley, hemmed in by high walls of hills, begins to anticipate some of the beauty that awaits you on the final stage to the **DIENG PLATEAU**.

There is only one sure way to get to Dieng, and that is to head north from Wonosobo. The

At Buntu, a turn north leads through Banyumas and Wonosobo to Dieng.

The 'abode of gods' could be in the Andes or a Nepalese fastness

scenery is magnificent. The country becomes more steep and rugged, and the people change with it. They're a hill breed, tough and stocky, and they tote vast loads of farm produce and firewood up slopes and tracks that would make a mountain goat think twice.

In Kejajar, 16 km from Wonosobo, the morning market is a festival of colour and (to the outsider) confusion: pale green cabbages the size of beach-balls, coconuts from the lowlands, cakes of boiled rice, saucer-sized pats of *gula Jawa* (brown sugar).

In the next 9 km the road climbs more than 700 metres. The terraces become ragged, groping for a foothold here, a toehold there, as they straggle up the precipitous slopes. Huge polished aluminium mirrors show you the other side of hairpin bends. The road noses upwards into what must be a dead-end gorge. Suddenly there's a narrow downhill defile, and there in an other worldly light, lies the plateau. Straight ahead, the cluster of ancient, weathered temples.

The existence of demons, spirits and wrathful giants seems not only plausible but probable as grey skeins of mist envelop the surrounding ridges of the Dieng Plateau. The noonday sun, so clean and bright only half an hour before, shrinks from sight behind black fingers of cloud. The cold rain falls, sarong-shrouded figures hurry through the gloom, and darkness covers the face of the earth.

Di Hyang, 'abode of the gods', should be somewhere in the Andes or locked away in a Nepalese fastness. Seven degrees south of the equator, on the Dieng Plateau, it seems like a blunder of geography. Its eerie strangeness, its proximity to the heavens, may have been among the reasons that men laboured there to erect the series of temples that still dominate the plateau.

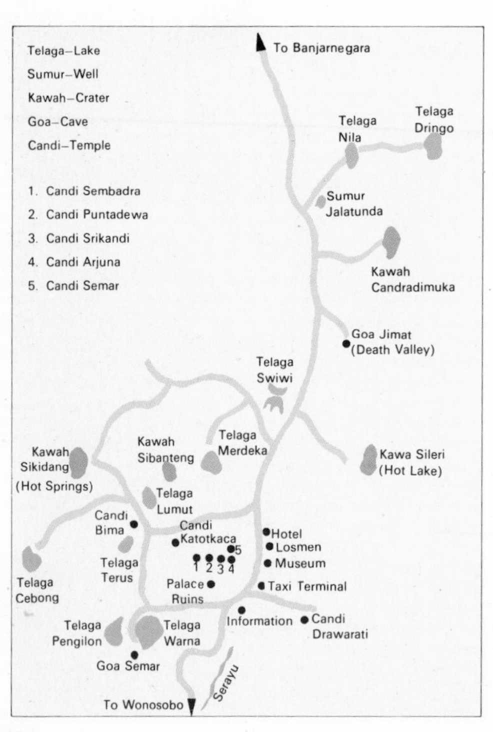

A weathered relief of Siva adorns one of the many temples atop the Dieng Plateau.

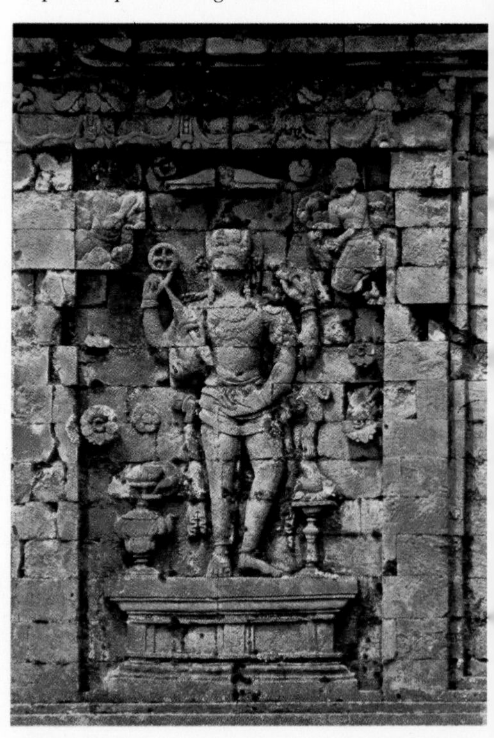

Intriguing temple ruins,
lakes and boiling mud.

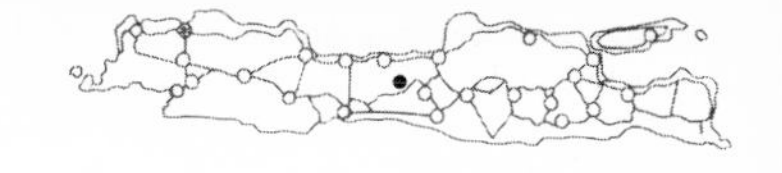

Built to honour Siva, and probably constructed in the early decades of the 9th century at about the same time as Borobudur was being laboriously pieced together down on the plains, the Dieng temples are remarkable for their simplicity and their spare sculptural ornament. Their severity contrasts strongly with the exuberance of the great complex, also dedicated to Siva, which was erected at Prambanan only a century later. Perhaps the majesty of their setting was ornament enough.

The main group of temples is named after heroes and heroines of the *Mahabharata*, though the names may have been given only a little more than a hundred years ago. Arjuna, Puntadewa, Srikandi and Sembadra stand in the centre of a flat field, accompanied by the squat, ungainly servant, Semar. The ground about them looks firm enough, but it's mostly deceptive marsh, and any attempt to reach the temples except by the raised causeway is a guarantee of black mud to the ankles or knees (lines of small raised dikes appear to intersect, but there's invariably more than a jump-sized gap between them). A millenium ago the marsh was drained by a complex series of tunnels; the remains can still be seen on the northwest corner of the field, but they no longer work.

Candi Gatokaca stands alone at the southern end of the plain, and farther south on a hill embraced by slender acacias is *Candi Bima* with its unique sculpted heads in horseshoe-shaped roof niches. Near the main group are the foundations and outlines of what may have been dwelling places for priests and pilgrims.

The plateau is not always wrapped in mists and mystery. When the sun shines, as it often does, it lights up a profusion of pansies, lupins, snapdragons, briar roses, marigolds and wild fuchsias, and glints on the curved plastic-sheeted

On the way to Yogya, two-wheeled pony traps and scores of cyclists.

roofs of the weird 'nissen huts' (like a deserted army camp) that house thousands upon thousands of mushrooms and their spore.

In the early morning, when the air is still cold, a walk along the wooded pathways encircling *Telaga Warna* ('Coloured Lake') and *Telaga Pengilon* ('Mirror Lake') is enchantingly peaceful and beautiful, and colours sing: orange lichens on tree trunks, translucent blood-red leaves, brilliant apple-green fern fronds, milky green water where drowned hot springs bubble to the surface. Knolls and dells, straight from a Chinese brush painting, hide small caves and grottos still popular as retreats for meditation. Beyond the lakes to the south, 2 km along a bumpy but passable track, a never-ending billow of steam marks a fissure where boiling mud plops and splutters in a scalding dance.

There are a couple of *losmen* along the two muddy roads that make up Dieng town, but the nights are so chilly and the flies so bad that a stop-over is not recommended. The drive up from Wonosobo can be done comfortably in an hour (a Dutch guidebook published in 1925 said two or three days by sedan chair), and an early start leaves plenty of time for casual exploring. Wonosobo is a pleasant enough town in which to spend the night before going up to the plateau, with a few adequate *losmen* and hotels at the southern end of the main street near the cinema.

Moving on from Wonosobo to Yogya there are impressive views of Gunung Sumbing (3,371 metres) on your right and Gunung Sundoro (3,135 metres) on your left, a handsome pair of sleeping volcanoes who haven't bothered anyone for years. Kledung, the pass between them, is crossed at almost 2,300 metres, and the views are beautiful.

Slumbering Sumbing, massive and spread-eagled, will claim a good percentage of your vision all the way through Secang to Magelang as the road traces an arc north, then east, then south. Magelang is big and bustling, with the unkempt look common to many towns in Java.

Below Magelang, 42 km from Yogya on the main north-south road, familiar signs of the coastal plain begin to appear: the terraces are less steep, the *padi*-fields are larger and coconut palms display their inimitable silhouette against the sky. Gunung Merbabu and Gunung Merapi are seen more often to the east as hills and trees diminish in height and number. Rushing mountain torrents (a source of river stones for the craftsmen around Muntilan who carve, amongst other things, good copies of ancient temple deities) open out into wide streams and rivers which meander seawards. The traditional Yogyanese men's dress makes its appearance: a tightly folded *batik* cap sprouting two tiny wings behind the ears, long-sleeved high-collared jackets in striped *lurik* with a *batik* sarong, or black jackets and matching knee breeches. Girls in almost mod gear flash past on small motor-cycles, heading for Yogya's campuses. Bicycles, eminently suited to the city's billiard table flatness (give or take a small rise or two), show up in pairs, then scores, then hundreds, dominating the quiet country roads.

CIREBON TO SEMARANG AND SOUTH TO YOGYA

The first port of call on the 'northern route' is the ancient sultanate of **CIREBON**, best approached from Bandung via a slower and more attractive route than the flat and sometimes boring coastal plain. The road meanders down through tree-clad slopes to Sumedang (depending on the time of day, stop for a snack or meal at Restaurant Tampomas Baru) and disgorges onto the plain at Kadipaten, a jumping-off point for wild boar hunting in the Ujungjaya area. Keep an eye open for crowds around an improvised stage in the villages, for you might catch a *wayang topeng* (masked dance) with Panji confronting his red-visaged adversary Klono. *Wayang topeng*, once famous around Cirebon, came close to extinction, but a grass-roots revival is gaining momentum. As a stranger you may become an impromptu player or a source of comic relief.

Rugged limestone hills, gouged and quarried, announce Jatiwangi. Huge lime kilns look like medieval battlements during a siege. Dusty figures carry rock-laden baskets up treacherously crumbling stairways to the lip of the furnace mouth. In the smoke-filled air they look like harried defenders shoring up a breach. Farther on, lovers of colonial architecture will find a cluster of tiny gems in the neat, compact town of Jambelang, all wide eaves and columns and big shutters. Near Weru there are *warungs* selling simple *rotan* furniture.

Cirebon, with Javanese, Sundanese and some Chinese elements in its culture, is an interesting potpourri. Crawfurd, in his famous *Descriptive Dictionary* of 1856 noted that 'perhaps its name (is) correctly Charuban, which in Javanese means mixture', and many people still speak a local dialect which blends Sundanese and Javanese. Its popular name, *Kota Udang* or 'Shrimp City', is a tribute to the local fishing, but does scant justice to Cirebon's turbulent past.

Warred over by Hindu Pajajaran and Muslim Demak in the 15th century, sandwiched between the kingdoms of Banten and Mataram in the 17th century, and conquered and re-conquered, Cirebon finally became a restless fief of Batavia in 1705, jointly administered by three sultans whose courts rivalled those of Central Java in opulence and splendour. The present sultan, deprived of his royal revenues in these democratic days, is appropriately a banker.

Two of the ancient *kratons*, Kesepuhan and Kanoman, are open to visitors. In the southeast corner of the city, adjoining a striking tiered-roof mosque, Kesepuhan, with its low-walled grassy forecourts, exudes the bewildered air of an Edwardian dowager deserted by her maids and butlers. Blue and white Delft tiles dot vertical white-washed surfaces like stamps in an old album with foliated borders. The small dusty museum (opened on request) has some marvellous but ill-kept treasures and curiosities, including a gilded coach that makes a griffin seem human: dragon's head, elephant's trunk, eagle's wings and bull's forelegs. The Chinese-influenced 'rocks and clouds' decoration on the chariot is a recurring motif in Cirebon's arts. The motif occurs in

The Kesepuhan kraton *of Cirebon contains a dusty museum with marvellous treasures.*

Cirebon still flourishes culturally and excells in the art of *batik* making.

woodcarving, plasterwork and *batik*, but for exuberant embellishment nothing matches the ruins of Candi Sunya Ragi (about 4 km out of town on the southeastern bypass). First built by a cirebon prince early in the eighteenth century, its present weird form was put together by a Chinese architect in 1852. It is a grotesque amalgam of plaster, red brick and concrete put together like a child's sand-drip castle and honeycombed with tunnels, grottos, secret chambers, doors for dwarfs and staircases leading nowhere.

Five kilometres north along the main Jakarta road, is the sacred tomb of Sunan Gunung Jati, one of the nine great *walis* who helped establish Islam in Java. Pilgrims burn incense and perfor their worship at the doorway leading to the inner sanctum, closed to everyone save the tomb's caretakers. A maze of courtyards filled with gravestones surround the holy tomb and cover the slopes of the small hill across the road.

Artistically, Cirebon may seem to be in a decline. This is more apparent than factual, as a glance at the activities board in the cultural centre, *Kantor Pembinaan Kebudayaan*, will quickly show. The office of the cultural centre is housed in a pillared, low-eaved building on one side of the city's *medan*, and here you can find an impressive list of regional acts and dances which take place in the surrounding area. There is no permanent performing arts venue in Cirebon itself. *Wayang topeng Cirebon* and a local version of the horse trance dançe are both popular in the district, and so too is *angklung*. The latter is hardly a new fad, for the *Java Gazette* described way back in 1813 'a native band which after playing some minutes on their different instruments entirely composed of bamboo tubes, and

Left to right: a grotto at Sunya Ragi; batik from Ibu Masina's studio; a peaked Cirebon prow.

A riot of colourful boats in Cirebon's harbour.

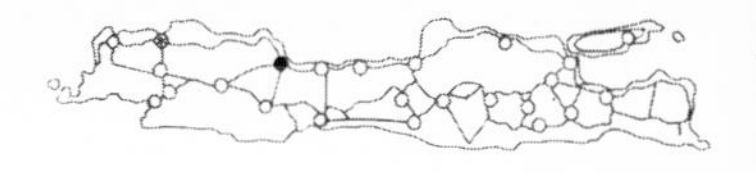

accompanying them with their voices, commenced a Malay dance'.

The local *batik* industry is flourishing, notwithstanding claims by some *batik* merchants in Central Java that Cirebon *batik*-making is in decline. It is true that the cream of the Cirebon crop ends up in cities like Jakarta, its price magnified as much as 400% by enterprising entrepreneurs, but in the numerous cooperatives around Cirebon, mostly within 5 km to the west near the village of Trusmi (Weru), you can find outstanding examples of the *batik*-maker's art.

For a view of the finest *batik*, pay a visit to Ibu Masina's studio. Almost opposite the office of the *kecamatan* in Weru is a signpost pointing south to 'Sumber 6 km'; take the opposite road north for one kilometre, and you'll find Ibu Masina's place along the edge of a narrow lane, housed in a long, low white building directly across from a grassy clearing. Depending on how much the good *ibu* has in stock (may of her *batiks* go to the GKBI institute in Jakarta), you'll have the chance to see some extraordinarily fine hand-drawn *batiks*, including superb blue and red bird designs and the handsome classical Cirebon motif of 'rocks and clouds' in magnificent tones of blue.

Farther east along the coast the prospect is generally dull. Occasionally there are small estuarine towns where colourful boats ride easily on the tide. High-peaked prows adorn the boats like painted dorsal fins; tall three-pronged rowlocks wait to receive the long rudder oars; and hulls are ablaze from stem to stern in a riot of colour. Rolled nets, stacked between the thwarts, shimmer in the bright sunlight like giant cocoons of raw silk. Downriver, homing craft with great sheets of squarish sail rigged to port and starboard look like butterflies gliding on their tails.

Pekalongan *batiks* for the true connoisseur.

Farther along the coast the market of a tiny village, devoted to small red onions, is doing a roaring trade. At the next whistlestop you might chance upon an afternoon performance of *wayang golek* celebrating a circumcision ritual: the puppets are magnificent, and the price of admission is cigarettes for the *dalang* and his musicians.

Across the fields of sugar-cane and *padi* to the south of Tanjung, shimmering in the heat, is the blurred outline of a range of hills. At the eastern end of the range the second highest mountain in Java, Gunung Slamet, thrusts its 3,428 metres in the sky.

Except as a road junction, and as a centre of fishing and mechanised weaving, **TEGAL** has little to recommend it, though pottery and handicrafts enthusiasts may be tempted by the excellent ochre-ware which includes teapots decorated with brass strap-work and paired with pierced-brass trays; roadside stalls about 10 km on the southern road out of Tegal are the best hunting ground.

What the north coast lacks in scenic beauty it makes up for in *batik*. **PEKALONGAN**, like Cirebon, is another famous *batik* centre. Quite apart from the retail stores along Jalan Hayam Wuruk, Pekalongan justifies its sobriquet as *Kota Batik* ('Batik City') with the presence of dozens of independent hawkers who will descend upon you the moment you set foot in town or enter a restaurant. Competition is fierce but good-natured, and you should be able to halve the initial asking-prices (or do even better) with a little care and some judicious bargaining.

There are *batiks* in Pekalongan, hand-waxed, stamp-waxed and even machine printed, which you won't easily find in other parts of Java. The pilgrimage point for the true connoisseur is the

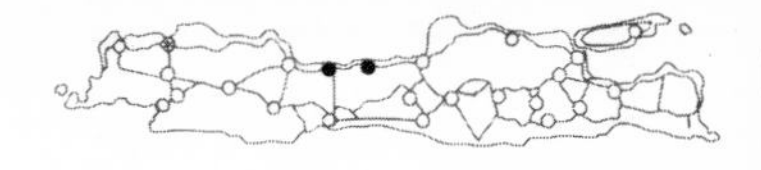

small workshop of Oey Soe Tjoen, the source of the most exquisitely wrought *batik* in the whole of Indonesia.

Take the road south from Pekalongan to the village of Kedungwuni, 9 km away. About 200 metres before the village police station (a reminder in case you miss the unpretentious house) is No. 104 Jalan Raya. This is where the cream of Jakarta's society comes for its *batik*. If the wives of ministers, generals and diplomats don't actually make the journey themselves, they make sure they see the wares somehow. They invariably buy the expensive pieces.

Each length (sarong or *kain*) takes around nine months to complete. Ibu Oey does the designing and *tulisan* waxing, with detail so intricate that it's hard to believe this is handworked (until you see a sheet of cloth in progress and can examine every dot and line of wax). The dyeing, in gentle tones of mustard-ochre, olive and corn-flower blue, pale rose pink, dull orange and mauve, is done by her son. It's a family business that still continues to produce bird, flower and butterfly designs of such finesse, and colours of such delicacy. In response to requests (especially by foreigners), Ibu also makes smaller pieces of batik which are ideally suited as wall hangings. Even if you're not buying, visit the workshop just to see what really fine batik is all about. It is customary in the Pekalongan area for batik workers to take their holiday on Fridays.

For half the distance between Pekalongan and Semarang the road runs fast and smooth through teak plantations, gently rolling hills, and villages of neat houses with wooden façades and shallow verandahs. Then there's rice and sugar-cane, and finally Semarang ... discussed in more detail on the following pages.

On the north coast route to Yogya, Central Java's capital city of Semarang.

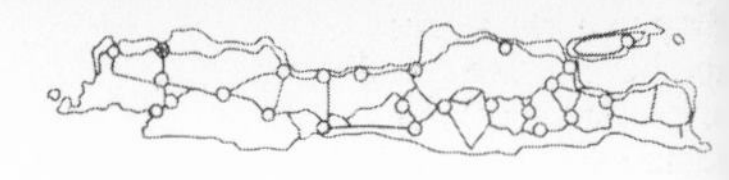

The decline of the great north coast ports, which reached its nadir during the turbulent course of the 17th century, was hastened by the growth of the inland state of Mataram, the Dutch control of coastal waters, and the slow flow of silt from land to sea which filled in harbours and made rivers unnavigable. Demak was once a port. So too was Pati, its vassal and salt centre. And less then 500 years ago a navigable channel separated Gunung Muria, northeast of Jepara, from the mainland. Today the channel is filled with *padi* and salt pans.

Deprived of their trade, the entrepôt ports had no money for men or for dredging. The mud thickened, and overcame.

So the fortunes of **SEMARANG** rose, in a sense, from the mud. Eclipsed as a port by its stronger and wealthier neighbours during the 16th and 17th centuries, it nevertheless offered a small, calm river-mouth; and, its roadsteads were sheltered enough to provide safe refuge for trading vessels which swung at anchor whilst bum-boats and barges ferried cargoes to and from the shore. In the course of the 18th century it rapidly gained ascendancy over the older, mud-choked ports. Today Semarang still flourishes as the capital city of the province of Central Java.

Modern Semarang has few relics of an illustrious past. Those remaining bear witness to the presence, in bygone days, of a large population of Dutch traders and officials, and a fair sprinkling of Chinese merchants: old buildings with exterior wrought-iron staircases, great warehouses, colourful temples and solid churches.

On Jln. Let. Jen. Suprapto, a little south of Stasiun Tawang (the main railway station) is Gereja Blenduk, a fine example of 18th-century church architecture: a shallow Greek-cross floor plan, a high drum and a huge copper-clad dome, pale green above the white-washed walls and the heavy columns of the porch. The church was consecrated in 1753, and is probably the oldest remaining Christian church in Java after the 'Portuguese Church' built in Jakarta around 1696 (the Gereja Tugu near Jakarta's Tanjung Priok was probably built in the 1760s). Semarang's church is still in use, and visitors are welcome. Inside, the baroque organ is a mad swirl of cream and gold angels, though its pipes no longer sing: a modern organ was installed behind the façade some seventy years ago.

The streets in the area are dotted with old balconied buildings of shabby charm. Closer towards the railway station are numerous bulky but shapely warehouses. There are also a number of old and not-so-old Chinese shop-houses, though unhappily, in many parts of the city, their sugar-icing frontages are being given a ravaging face-lift which destroys their character.

Heading farther north up the river towards the coast, through the old section of town and along Jln. Pekojan, you'll find Gang Lombok, a tiny lane full of excellent Chinese eating-houses, the shops of scrap-iron merchants and a small square enclosed on two sides by the buildings and halls of the large Klinteng Temple complex. The main temple, built in 1772, has beautifully carved beams on its high ceilings, and the interior is full of carved

Strong limbs a must to climb to beautifully sited Gedung Songo temples.

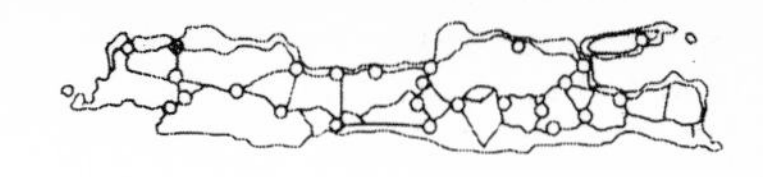

and painted gods, ritual objects, oil lamps, brassware and the pervasive aroma of incense. Unlike many more recently built Chinese temples, Klinteng is mercifully free from the garish gold paint usually applied with more vigour than artistry.

Although Semarang is not a *batik*-making centre, an excellent range of Pekalongan *batiks* and a smaller selection from Ceribon and Solo can be bought there. Two good shops are GKBI on Jln. Pemuda, and PPIP at B.12 Jurnatan shopping centre on Jln. Haji Agus Salim.

Farther west, on the main road to Kendal, is the large red and yellow Sam Po Kung temple, also known as *Gedung Batu*. It traces its history back to the middle of the 15th century when a small cave (the central and most holy shrine in the present complex) was dedicated to the memory of Sam Poo, a high-ranking envoy from the imperial court of the Ming dynasty, who visited Java in 1406 and again in 1416, when he landed at nearby Simongan. To reach the temple, turn left (south) at Jln. Salaman immediately after crossing the new bridge on the main west road, and follow the tar-sealed side-road for almost two kilometres.

A few kilometres farther along the west road is the well-kept cemetery honouring the many Dutch civilians who died in Japanese internment camps during the occupation.

On the lighter side, Semarang caters adequately for nightlife. There are a number of nightclubs and massage parlours. For Javanese theatre the best place is Ngesti Pandowo at Jln. Pemuda 116. *Wayang wong* is the main attraction, though *ketoprak* is performed once a week. At Sri Wanito, as the name *wanito* (*wanita*) suggests, all the roles are played by women.

Leaving Semarang, and taking the road south towards Yogya, you'll pass through Candi Baru, the 'new town' built on rising hills at the back of the old city. Many of the houses and gardens are beautiful, a pleasant change from the shabbiness of much of the city's central area. The views, as the road climbs higher, include superb panoramas of the harbour and the coast.

At Bawen, 35 km south of Semarang, a road junction breaks southwest through Ambarawa (the turn-off point for **BANDUNGAN** hill resort, and the site of an infamous Japanese internment camp) and Magelang, and southeast through Salatiga towards Kartasura and Solo on a good fast road.

There are three temple sites high on mountain slopes: Dieng (p. 165), Sukuh and Ceta on Gunung Lawu (p. 214) and the **GEDUNG SONGO** or 'Nine Buildings' group on the southern slopes of Gunung Ungaran above Bandungan. Sukuh, mysterious and forbidding, enjoys a reputation as Java's only explicitly erotic temple; Gedung Songo deserves a place as the most beautifully sited group.

You can have Gedung Songo three ways. With sunshine, with mist, or with a combination of both. The latter is a dream, for in the strange half-light the landscape takes on the sculptural quality of a naked body: smooth hills, shadowy valleys, dark clefts and long upland plains.

You've plodded uphill for close to half an hour, slipping sometimes on the hard-packed damp

A roaring ravine, green moss and hot springs.

dirt track, sweating through groves of bananas, maize, cassava, runner beans, plots of onions and cabbages, and masses of pink and white briar roses. Before you, the silhouette of the first temple, black against the dull green hillside and the wraiths of grey-white mist. You reach it. A small, simple structure, flat surfaces lightly ornamented with squares and triangles of ancient memory, roof corners picked out with little *dagobs*, exterior wall niches long since robbed of their statues.

You nose forward through the light mist, following a path above a steep winding gorge, with patches of greyish rubble in the bracken swathing the hillside. The ground underfoot, if you take to the ridges, is soft and spongy with peat moss. The pungent smell of sulphur, carried by mists from heights you know are there but cannot see, assails your nostrils. The light plays strange tricks, and you might feel you're suspended in a world of ethereal magic: a sudden updraft thins the mist, a flash of sunlight outlines moving figures on a ridge and reveals another shape softly etched against the skyline, another temple visible for seconds and then wrapped again in a shroud of shifting grey silk.

And so it goes. Mist, silver sunlight, temples, more silver, the shrill cries of mountain birds in gullies below you.

A temple complex. Three reasonably intact buildings in a sea of rubble. In three niches, battered but appealing statues of an eight-armed Durga, an Agastya, a Ganesa . . . and another childlike statue of the elephant god secreted away, below eye-level, in a base niche. Scattered around are finials and *linggas* and *yoni* pedestals.

A roaring ravine, high-walled and narrow with treacherous soft patches of grey-blue, grey-mauve mud, filled with little springs of water far too hot

A first glimpse of a Gedung Songo temple.

Countryside to be explored between Salatiga and Magelang.

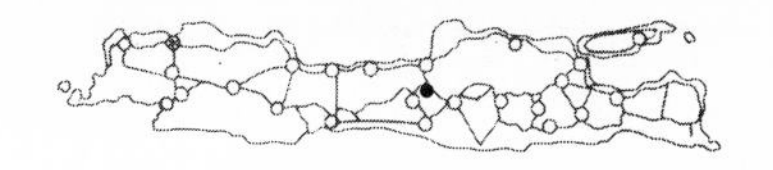

o touch. A hole, reaching back into the bowels of he earth, whistling and shrieking. Green moss, framing a tiny fissure which steams and hisses like an angry cat.

The mist may have cleared by the time you reach the final temple on the final ridge, a great breast of land thrusting into and above the broad plain where Salatiga's shallow lake lies under the shoulder of Merbabu and the hills and peaks to the south, the valley a patchwork quilt (yes!) of intricate *padi*-terracing and fallow land. To the west, under a cloud cap, the pillars of Sumbing and Sundoro, the gateway to Dieng. Behind you, to the north, trees and shrubs cling to a vertical rock that backs the gorge you've climbed and skirted. Around you, visible from the spur on which you stand, are the other temples on their small spurs, a ring of perfection, serene and enchanting.

The Siva temples of Gedung Songo were built about the same time as those on the Dieng Plateau (some 60 km westwards as the *garuda* flies) in the early years of the 9th century. Five of them are easily reached and explored in a two-hour hike, and even if you don't care for temples, the walk and the views are magnificent.

Gedung Songo is accessible from Ambarawa, a little beyond Bawen on the southwestern route to Magelang. In Ambarawa, take the clearly sign-posted 7-km road to Bandungan and turn left at the T-junction at the top of Bandungan's main street (marked by a mass of hoardings advertising local hotels and guesthouses). Turn right (north) up the new 5-km road from Bandungan to just below the first temple. Not so long ago the temples could only be reached after a solid half-hour climb. Following the gully trails beyond this point the best route is left (south) up a narrow ridge to the main temple, where you carry on with a circular route on clear but slippery paths past the sulphur gorge and back to where you started.

Lovers of ancient locomotives (as opposed to ancient temples) will find a windfall in Jambu, a few kilometres southwest of Ambarawa on the Magelang road, for this is the home of a unique engine: its driving power is transmitted through a ratchet-wheel which grips a notched centre-rail. This 1905 antique still makes odd sallies from Jambu to Bedono on a little used branch line. It is possible to arrange for a special outing through the State Railways (PJKA) office on Jln. Thamrin (behind the Pertamina office) in Semarang, or see the station-master at Ambarawa. A good tour operator should be able to look after details.

There is much beautiful country to be explored, by car or on foot, in the ragged hills and lower mountain slopes between Salatiga and Magelang. **KOPENG,** about 14 km from Salatiga, is a popular hill resort. There are outstanding veiws of Merbabu's huge slopes and in the surrounding area there are many smaller peaks which cry out to be climbed. Road junctions, mostly unmarked, lead off into a maze of pretty valleys and gorges before linking up with the small towns of Ngablak or Grabag and the main road to Magelang.

A time-worn statue of Agastya, Siva's Divine Teacher, at Gedung Songo.

CENTRAL JAVA

Central Java, including *Daerah Istimewa Yogyakarta*, the 'Special Area' of Yogyakarta, accounts for more than 25,000,000 people: 30 per cent of Java's population, 20 per cent of Indonesia's total.

The area also embraces a seemingly disproportionate number of attractions.

To the north are the ports of the once-powerful Muslim kingdoms. Along the southern coastline, the boom of surf counterpoints the liquid cadences of Central Java's *gamelan* music. The sequestered silence in the courtyards of its palaces can be found again, a thousand years older, at the sites of ancient Hindu and Buddhist temples. There are music and dance and ragged cliffs, manicured *padi*-fields and awesome craters and misty peaks, secluded sunlit back-streets and wonderfully boisterous markets.

Most of the high-points of Central Java are concentrated within and around the cities of Yogyakarta and Surakarta (Yogya and Solo), for it was on the lush, productive plains of the Progo, Opak and Solo rivers that the greatest of Java's early civilisations flourished. Buddhist Borobudur and the Sivaistic Prambanan complex testify to the wealth, power and artistry of the Sailendra and Mataram dynasties during the 9th and 10th centuries A.D., and there are dozens of other temple sites nearby. There are temples too on the high plateau of Dieng, and on the slopes of Gunung Ungaran below Semarang.

Solo palace guard, Prajurit Warengan, *in a portrait taken 50 years ago (previous pages).*

But Central Java's fame does not rest solely with its temples. Its role as a cultural centre has long been recognised, and its vast artistic wealth has been assiduously documented. As the late Claire Holt noted in her excellent *Art in Indonesia: Continuities and Change*, 'In most studies devoted to Indonesia, Java inevitably remains the centre of attention . . . Recent efforts to escape from historical "Javacentricity" have not been too successful.'

The renaissance of Central Java's political ascendancy began in the 16th century with the disintegration of the Mojopahit kingdom. Strong maritime Muslim states arose in the north, but their heyday was brief. To the south, Senopati was carving out a new Mataram empire. Demak fell to him in 1588, rebelled in 1602, and was put down again. In 1613 Senopati's grandson Nyokro Kusumo inherited the throne and his grandfather's vision of empire. Victory followed victory: Pasuruan (1616), Tuban (1619), Banjarmasin in Borneo (1622), Madura (1624) and Surabaya (1625). The conqueror assumed the title of *susuhunan*, 'he who is above others'. In 1629 he attacked the 10-year-old Dutch trading post and

The description of Central Java is divided as follows. 'The Gentle Pulse Of Yogyakarta' (pages 183 to 190) first describes the artforms and places of interest in the Yogya area, followed by 'Shopping In Yogya' (pages 190 to 194). Pages 194 to 199 cover 'Side-trips From Yogya', leading to the section 'To The Greater Glory Of the Gods' (pages 200 to 205), dedicated to the numerous temples and shrines of Central Java, which can be visited from Yogya. 'Surakarta, An Ancient Capital' (pages 206 to 209) describes Solo, including hints and tips for 'Shopping In Solo' (pages 210 to 212), along with 'Side-trips From Solo' (pages 214 to 219) for nearby explorations. The last two sections describe two routes to Surabaya: 'Solo To Surabaya' (pages 220 to 221), and Semarang To Surabaya' (pages 222 to 225) for those who might travel directly to East Java along the north coast.

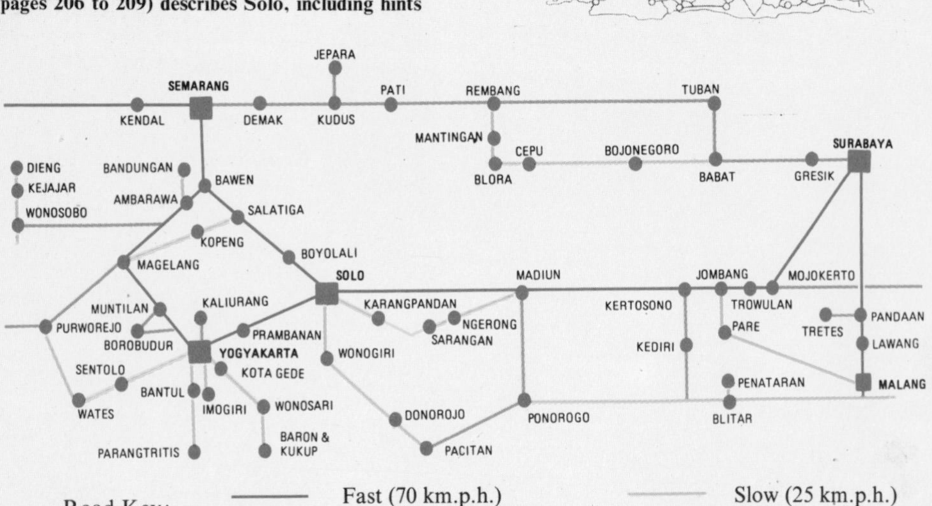

fortress of Batavia, and lost his only battle, though not his empire or his reputation. In 1638 he was granted the right to the Muslim title of *sultan*, and became known to history as Sultan Agung.

The 'Great Sultan' died in 1645. His successor, Hamangkurat I, was deposed by the Madurese prince, Trunajaya, in 1674, and the *kraton* was destroyed. Trunajaya was in turn trounced by the Dutch, and Hamangkurat II gained the throne but lost much of his power. His son, Hamangkurat III, was staunchly anti-Dutch. As a result his uncle, Pangeran Puger, was placed on the throne as Pakubuwono I ('Axis of the Universe') in 1705; Hamangkurat fought the decision, but was defeated in 1708 and exiled.

Another Madurese, Cakraningrat, demolished the forces of Pakubuwono II in 1740, but the 'emperor' was restored to his throne in 1743 and in 1745 the royal court moved to a new *kraton* at Surakarta. By 1755 internicine intrigues had reached their peak. The Dutch, firmly in control and rapidly losing patience, finally split Mataram. Pakubuwono III retained control of the Surakarta court, but had to accept the presence of his cousin, Mangkunegoro I, as a ruling prince within his kingdom; his uncle, Mangkubumi, became the first Sultan of Yogyakarta, Hamengkubuwono I.

The struggles ended, and energies once devoted to conquest and the maintenance of political hegemony were poured into artistic and cultural pursuits which still animate Central Java.

The peace was broken only three times in the next 200 years. In 1812 the English stormed and looted the *kraton* of Yogyakarta. In 1825 Prince Diponegoro rose against the Dutch and led a bloody five-year guerrilla war. And in 1948 the Dutch bombed and captured Yogya.

The 1812 campaign reflected little glory on either side. Thomas Stamford Raffles, in his first year as Lieutenant-Governor of Java, was arrayed against the forces of Hamengkubuwono II. The English, victorious, became looters. The Javanese, vastly superior in numbers, should not have been beaten.

'I should mention,' wrote Raffles in his report, 'that the Craton was a regular fortified position about three miles in circumference, surrounded by a wide and deep ditch, with a wall forty-five feet high, defended by well-constructed bastions . . . and the gates protected by drawbridges after the European model . . . it was calculated that there could not be less than 11,000 armed men within the Craton . . . The assault [20 June 1812] was made by escalade; we soon got possession of the ramparts, and turned their guns upon them . . . at nine o'clock the Craton was ours (and) the Sultan was taken in his strongest hold.'

The hapless sultan was exiled to Penang and a new sultan, Hamengkubuwono III, was installed. Paku Alaman, the fourth of Central Java's principalities, was also established; Prince Notokusomo, a son of the first sultan, was set on the throne as Paku Alam I, and part of the area of Yogyakarta was ceded to him.

The victors, 600 strong, shared booty worth around US$7,000,000. The sacred *pusakas* (royal heirlooms) were eventually recovered, and the *kraton* was returned to the new sultan in 1816. Many of the court's records eventually ended up in the British Museum, but micro-film copies are now held by the palace and the ancient texts are being meticulously reproduced by hand.

Over 130 years later the *kraton* was once again threatened. In 1946 Yogya had become the capital of the beleaguered Republic of Indonesia. In December 1948 the city was bombed, several Republican leaders were captured, and the Dutch advanced on the gates of the *kraton*. The Australian historian Ailsa Zainu'ddin records the famous sequel: 'When (the Dutch) attempted to negotiate with the Sultan . . . (he) retired into his *kraton* and refused to have any dealings with them at all until the Dutch threatened to force their way into the *kraton* by tank. Then the Sultan granted a ten minute interview but was prepared to discuss only one subject—the withdrawal of Dutch troops from Yogyakarta. At the end of the ten minutes he indicated that the audience was concluded and again withdrew to his residence inside the *kraton*.' The palace was spared and the Sultan, Hamengkubuwono IX, later served in several governmental posts.

Dancers wait for a lesson at Yogya's kraton.

THE GENTLE PULSE OF YOGYAKARTA

In Yogyakarta, more than in any other of Java's towns, the presence of an old and highly developed culture can be felt and heard. It is easy (and commonplace) to describe that culture as a hot-house flower, or a bloodless survivor from an aristocratic past with as much relevance to the present as a fly preserved in amber. Such judgements are trite and unfair.

Much of the city's culture owes a debt to the *kraton*. Less immediately obvious is the influence of a boisterous and sometimes coarse vitality from the village markets and the villagers themselves.

These two elements, patrician and peasant, meet and blend in Yogya: in its arts, life style, and being. And this, perhaps, is why most visitors fall in love with Yogya . . . a gentle fall, a red rose and a *billet-doux*:

One of the delights of this city is that things are always happening in a quiet and subtle way, and this can be most rewarding. You can spend hours relaxing around the markets. You can go to any dancing school, from the Kraton to the smaller schools around town, and see the kids practising. You can even wander past a house and see young children learning to play the gamelan orchestra in the garage (!) as we did in Kota Baru this morning. You can watch batik artists at work, go to the dalang school and see wayang golek or wayang kulit. All this is happening so much of the time in Yogya: the continual practising and perfecting of fine arts and other aspects of Javanese culture. Yogya is still very alive as a centre of culture, not just as a site where the remains of previous cultures can be seen. It is not just the shopping and the nearby temples. And there's always the presence of Merapi, the big volcano north of the town, weirdly companionable and ominous at the same time. This evening I stood against the railing of Gondalayu bridge, watching the volcano and enjoying the sunset . . . great free clouds tinged with red and orange and pink. The breeze was cool, and I felt a tremendous sense of freedom and serenity. I think this was partly because I didn't rush the experience here. I didn't try to scream through it as though there were no tomorrow. I adjusted myself to Yogya's pace. I feel sorry for people who can't give it more than a couple of days.

A sarong *has no pockets, so this is the novel solution by a Yogya dancer to the modern problem of carrying a watch at a dress rehearsal.*

Yogya does need time, for a first, fleeting impression can be dispiriting: the long hot summer of Jalan Malioboro, a feeling that you'll never find the many treasures that you know lie tucked away in a myriad side-streets, an apparent lack of vast and obvious cultural monuments in the manner of Rome or Athens. But give it time, and you'll begin to understand why Yogya has captured so many hearts. It is not *all* of Java, but it could claim to be the pulse.

GAMELAN music is the sound of that pulse. You'll hear its insinuating, liquid melodies floating over a white-washed wall in a quiet, sunlit street, or bursting forth from a transistor radio at a *warung*; you may hear it as you stroll through the yards and forecourts of a palace, or in the lobby of a hotel; and *gamelan* is an integral part of Javanese dance dramas and the ever-popular puppet shows.

The number of instruments in a *gamelan* orchestra may vary from as few as 13 to as many as 75. They are almost all percussion instruments, ranging from the large gongs, 'kettles' and resonating slabs of bronze to smaller pieces like the *genders* and the *gambang* or xylophone. A *rebab* (two-stringed viol), a *celempung* (a kind of zither) and occasionally a *suling* (flute) are the only string or wind instruments. The larger and more sonorous pieces carry melodies with long notes, whilst the smaller and lighter instruments carry melodies with shorter notes and (generally) a faster tempo. To foreign ears the most curious aspect of *gamelan* is the tuning, which normally combines a five-tone system (*slendro*) and a seven-tone system (*pelog*).

An appreciation of *gamelan* music is of course a very personal experience: people attuned to the vigorous Balinese form often find the Central Javanese version soporific; lovers of Central Java's style often decry West Java's as monotonous and unimaginative. Although describing music with words is a dangerous occupation, the following much-quoted quotation, cited by Jaap Kunst in his *Music of Java*, seems to sound the right chord: '(Gamelan) is comparable to only two things: moonlight and flowing water. It is

A multitude of traditional arts carried on at an unhurried pace.

pure and mysterious like moonlight and always changing like flowing water . . . it is a state of being, such as moonlight itself which lies poured out over the land.'

Visitors to the *kraton* are welcome to attend the *gamelan* rehearsals on Monday and Wednesday mornings; for a small fee you may tape the music. The smaller Pakualaman palace has adopted the soft, lilting style of Yogya's rival, Surakarta. Concerts are staged there every fifth Sunday on the date Minggu Pahing (ask, or check a Javanese calendar). Music begins at 10.00.

Of all Yogya's arts, **WAYANG KULIT** is probably closest to the hearts of its people. The bemused Westerner, lost in a welter of seemingly unidentifiable characters and a rapid flow of incomprehensible Javanese, may view *wayang kulit* as an ancient picture show, and leave it at that. In fact, the visual aspect, enchanting though it may be, is only a part of the *wayang kulit* performance, for the interplay of music and the amazingly varied character voices of the *dalang* are even more important to a Javanese audience.

The *dalang* is the key to the performance: a masterly producer, ventriloquist, conductor, puppeteer, historian, wise man, comedian and storyteller. The basic outlines of the stories, of the various episodes from the *Ramayana* or the *Mahabharata*, are familiar enough to the audience, but it is the *dalang* who breathes new life into each re-telling of these ancient tales, continually reaffirming the currency and relevance of the harmony of life, the balance between antagonist and protagonist, that is a central motif in Javanese philosophy; and he introduces the present in bawdy asides and outrageous satire that reduce the audience to helpless laughter.

The *dalang*'s voices, his story-telling ability, and his verbal humour are the reasons for *wayang kulit*'s popularity on Radio Indonesia's programmes. Ironically, the aural appeal of *wayang kulit* has given the *dalangs* some problems: their association claimed recently that the plethora of cassette recordings of *wayang kulit* performances was harming their livelihood, and they requested the government to impose restrictions on the sale of these tapes since 'the more such cassettes are available . . . the more people shun puppet players'.

Despite the *dalangs'* fears, *wayang kulit* flourishes in Yogya. Performances celebrating a *selamatan* are likely to occur at any time, and often in modest venues: it is not unusual to come across a *wayang kulit* show on the pillared back porch of a house, with a six-hour afternoon performance as a warm-up for the evening presentation which will start around 8 or 9 o'clock and run through till dawn.

There is a full eight-hour performance of *wayang kulit* on the second Saturday of every month at Sasono Hinggil Dwi Abad, south of the *kraton*. It starts at 9 o'clock in the evening, when the *dalang* introduces the characters and intones the outline of the story; the first hour or so is relatively static, but before long the action picks up and the shadows hasten back and forth in dramatic confrontations, furious fights and chases reminiscent of a Mack Sennett movie.

Short *wayang kulit* performances may be viewed at Ambar Budaya, across the street from the Ambarrukmo Sheraton Hotel on Mondays, Wednesdays & Saturdays from 9.30–10.30 a.m.; and at the Yayasan Kesenian Agastya (Agastya Art Institute, at Gedong Kiwa III/221, just off Jln. Bantul) on Sundays through Fridays from 15.00 to 17.00.

WAYANG GOLEK, in which life-like wooden puppets generally act out tales from the Arabic *Menak* stories, has never held the same appeal for the mystically inclined Javanese as the flickering, highly symbolic *wayang kulit*. However, many visitors prefer the vivid action and the astonishingly realistic movements of *wayang golek*. Performances are less common than those of *wayang kulit*.

The old master of *wayang golek* is Pak Widi who lives in Sentolo village, about 20 km west of Yogya. Now a wizened septuagenarian he very rarely performs but the younger *dalang wayang golek*, including one of Pak Widi's sons, have learned much from the old master's astonishing dexterity. To watch the puppets flick their *selendangs* in the manner of human dancers is to believe that the *dalang*'s hands can bring them alive; it is easy to lose yourself in this fantastic world of sword fights (the puppets clutch tiny leather krises), flying mortals, and extraordinary characters who change themselves

For many, the *Ramayana* epic is the best introduction to the performing arts of Java.

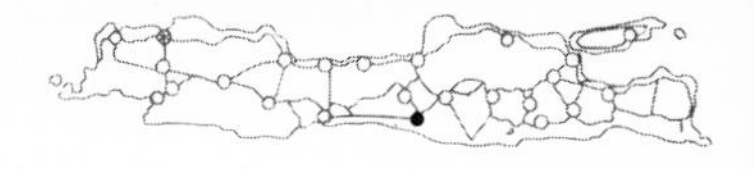

into other people, thus mystifying an audience unfamiliar with the tales.

There is a regular performance of *wayang golek* at the Yayasan Kesenian Agastya every Saturday from 15.00 to 17.00, and at the Nitour office (Jln. K.H. Ahmad Dahlan 71) every day (except Sunday) from 10.00–12.00. Lovers of crisp, inspired theater should sneak in a visit.

Yogya's indigenous form of dance theater, called **WAYANG WONG**, is infrequently performed, restricted nowadays to the anniversaries of the leading dance schools. Designed to be staged under the roof of an aristocratic *pendopo* by a vast corps of dancers drilled to recite set lines in archaic Javanese and to execute complicated mass maneuvers and battles amidst the teak pillars, it could never become a medium of nightly entertainment. In Solo, however, a different dramatic format set on a proscenium stage and consisting mostly of improvised, colloquial dialogue became a model for *wayang* troupes throughout Java. The dancing is only rudimentary, a pale shadow of the elaborate Yogyanese choreographies, but the level of stagecraft achieved is remarkable.

Wayang wong Solo-style and **KETOPRAK** (similar, but based on events and legends of Javanese history) draw regular crowds at THR, Yogya's engagingly seedy amusement park. The performances are woefully inferior, yet still colorful and amusing. The action starts around 9 o'clock.

DANCE is one of the highlights of Yogya's culture. Some dances are performed on special occasions, others are performed regularly; some are resolutely classical, some again are ancient in inspiration but modern in choreography and style. All of them enjoy a devoted following, and should you stumble on a rehearsal, a visit to one of the city's dancing schools might suggest that everyone between the ages of 5 and 15 is a dance student.

Classical court dancing, fluid yet superbly controlled, originated in the *kraton* and is still taught there. A practice session (Sunday mornings at 10 o'clock) is fascinating not just for the insights it gives on the subtleties of Javanese dance, but also for the delightful atmosphere of the *kraton* and the painstaking care with which the old dancing masters coax along their young charges.

Classical dance is also taught at Krido Bekso Wiromo (the first school to teach court dancing outside the *kraton*) and at Siswo Among Bekso. The most active schools of strict Yogyanese classical technique are Mardawa Budaya and Pamulangan Beksa Ngayugyakarta; classes are in the late afternoons and evenings.

The state dance academy (ASTI) combines all of Indonesia's traditional dance forms into its curriculum. Modern and modernized classical dances can be seen at Bagong Kussudiarjo's studio. Rehearsals take place every evening (except Fridays) from 16.00 to 18.00.

The full beauty of Javanese dance is best appreciated in an actual performance. Special make-up, glittering jewels and elaborate costumes transform young girls into ethereal nymphs from the Southern Ocean; young men don a *topeng* (mask) in the role of a lovesick prince preparing to meet his beloved; clowns tumble with athletic agility; and forbidding giants strut ominously. Several of the hotels in Yogya provide evenings of Javanese dance for their guests' enjoyment and, given notice, Bagong Kussudiarjo or the dance schools can arrange special performances.

For most visitors, however, the **RAMAYANA BALLET** is the perfect introduction to classical dance in all its mythical wonder and drama. Held at an outdoor theatre in Prambanan, 16 km east of Yogya on the road to Solo, with the magnificent Loro Jonggrang temple as a backdrop, the Ramayana Ballet presents a memorable enactment of one of mankind's greatest epics.

Unlike many dances in other countries which have lost much of their vitality and flavour in being commercially packaged and sold like soap powder, the Ramayana Ballet has stayed remarkably true to its origins in *wayang wong*. The static verbal encounters have been snipped out (even the Javanese often find these boring) and greater emphasis has been given to the dancing. The result is spectacular 'theatre': Rawana, high-stepping, angular, always menacing; Rama, smooth, couth, cool; and Sita, liquid grace, delicately tossing the trailing ends of her *selendang*. The engaging but slightly haphazard *corps de ballet* (variously demons, monkeys and fish), and the use of dramatic stage lighting are of course recent innovations, but they are effective.

For two hours, visual and aural delights at Prambanan's *Ramayana* festival.

It is said that the inspiration for the Ramayana Ballet came from a gentleman in the employ of Cook's Tours. He took his idea to the late President Sukarno, who said 'yes'. That was well over a decade ago, and the venture grows in reputation and appeal with every performance. The reasons are obvious: four clear nights on and around the full moon, each month from May through October; a large outdoor amphitheatre (concrete seats, so bring a cushion) and more than 100 assorted dancers and *gamelan* musicians; a shirt-sleeve tropical night, a thousand-year-old temple of inspiring beauty as part of the scenery; and a story of gods, giants, mortals, monkeys and beautiful women.

For two hours, from the moment the spotlights turn the temple to antique silver ('Ooooohhh!' gasps the audience) to the last deep-throated note of the gongs, you'll be enthralled by a succession of visual and aural delights. Brilliant costumes, dramatic confrontations, tumultuous battles, hypnotically sinuous music, extraordinary displays of acrobatic skill and dancing.

This version of the *Ramayana* epic, unfolding over four successive nights, leaves out many of the complex stories-within-stories found in the original tale. One example: early in the story Laksmana, Rama's brother, cuts off the nose of Rawana's sister . . . which explains the black triangle on her face when she appears in the ballet. Despite excisions, the ballet's plot is still involved. If you're in doubt about who is doing what to whom, and why, check with the local audience.

If you've only time to see one performance, try for the second night when all the leading characters have a chance to display their dancing skills before being killed off in that night's or later episodes. Highlights include a duel to the death between Rawana and the gallant but doomed Jatayu (whose last feeble wing-beats are astonishingly realistic and poignant); and Hanuman setting fire to Rawana's palace, a monstrous conflagration with real flames and real smoke that provide an exciting finale.

Suyudana, the ambitious and devious leader of the ninety-nine Korawa brothers, is a major character in wayang kulit *performances.*

The *kraton* palace,
hub of old and
new Yogyakarta.

'When a man is tired of London,' said the inimitable Dr. Johnson, 'he is tired of life.' The same can be said of Yogyakarta, for there is enough within the city and in the surrounding countryside to satisfy most tastes.

The palace, the hub of old and new Yogyakarta, is a good starting point for your peregrinations. From the bottom end of Jalan Malioboro take a straight line to the south. You'll reach a large grassy square, the *alun-alun lor*, dominated on the west by the Masjid Besar (Great Mosque). In the centre of the square are two *waringin* trees, between which white-robed plaintiffs once sat when they wished to make representations to the sultan. The trees should be the same size, but one was destroyed by fireworks during a Sekaten festival; its replacement lags behind its older twin.

At the southern end of the *alun-alun lor* lies the **KRATON**, the palace compound of the Sultans of Yogyakarta.

Karaton Ngayogyakarta-Hadiningrat, like most things Yogyanese, is a gentle experience, for behind its massive walls there is a single-storeyed world of grace and delicacy where elegant *pendopos* reign supreme.

Construction of the palace began in 1755, following the division of Mataram, and continued for almost forty years during the long reign of Hamengkubuwono I. The innermost group of buildings, *Proboyekso*, was completed in 1756, and is still the private domain of the sultan and his immediate family; it also houses the revered *pusakas* or sacred heirlooms. *Sitihinggil* and *Pagelaran*, the pavilions and buildings facing the *alun-alun lor* (and now used by several faculties of Gajah Mada University) were finished the following year. *Dono Pertopo* and *Kemagangan*, the two great gateways to the central courtyard, were completed in 1761–2; the Masjid Besar in 1773; and the *Beteng* or great wall in 1777. The glory of the *kraton*, the splendid reception hall known as the Golden Pavilion or *Bangsal Kencana*, was finished in 1792.

Structurally, very little has been altered in the intervening years. The closing decades of the reign of Hamengkubuwono VII and the accession of Hamengkubuwono VIII in 1921 saw a flurry of decorative activity. Half a century ago the gilt-framed mirrors, crystal chandeliers, cast-iron columns, stained glass, Italianate bronzes and marble floors were the last word in palatial décor. Resolutely European in taste, these items today strike a charming, anachronistic note, recalling the spirit of a gracious if somewhat artificial life.

It is not a feast of splendid oriental gaudiness. Somehow, these rococo fantasies sit well amongst the severe, classical proportions of the *pendopos*, the white-washed walls and the massive gateways; even a strange little bandstand rotunda, decorated with stained-glass images of musical instruments, has a patrician air about it.

Even the young guides who now help the courtly retainers handle visitors do not dispel the illusion that time has stood still within the palace walls. There is an unhurried grace and deference that evokes a feeling of calmness, reflecting the mood of the sunwashed well-swept courtyards.

In the *Sri Manganti* courtyard two *pendopos* hold a collection of carved and gilded palanquins and sedan chairs, and four sets of *gamelan* instruments: *Kyahi Gunturlaut* and *Kyahi Kebo-ganggang*, both dating from the Mojopahit period; *Kyahi Gunturmadu*, which once belonged to the 16th-century Demak sultanate; and *Kyahi Naga-wilaga*, an 18th-century copy of a second Demak set (the original is owned by the court of Solo). Beyond a gateway flanked by two silver-painted guardians is the *Pelataran Karaton* courtyard, the site of the magnificent Golden Pavilion. On the other side of the courtyard a passage-way leads through to the museum, filled with fascinating paraphernalia: gilt-metal copies of the sacred *pusakas*, royal portraits by Raden Saleh, a superb saddle richly ornamented in velvet and gold and silver thread, gifts given by European monarchs and the titled elite. In a nearby *pendopo* is a bed decorated with pink and blue Murano glasswork and mirrors.

Kraton festivals highlight the Yogya year, the largest being the three *Garebeg* ceremonies—*Maulud, Sawal* and *Besar* (check with a tourist office for exact dates). Royal dragoons and guards in traditional uniforms escort the *gunungans*,

Private apartments at Taman Sari, reached by a long tunnel, line the circular corridor above the dry fountain and pool.

Extensive restoration and fresh paint faithfully reproduce the past at the playful 'Water Castle'.

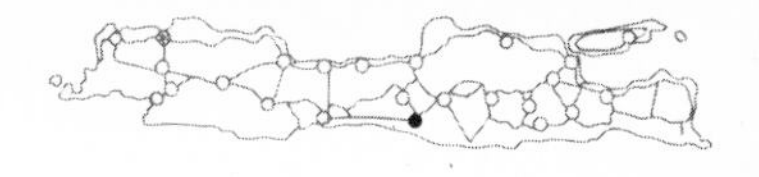

mounds of rice, from the *kraton* to the mosque. Crowds are huge and boisterous on these days.

The streets and lanes outside the *kraton* walls should be explored slowly, in a *becak* or on foot. To the west especially they hide unexpected pleasures, for this in days gone by was the equivalent of an address in Mayfair or the East Sixties, and there are still many beautiful old buildings and *pendopos* where court-sponsored *wayang* performances are sometimes held.

Staying with things royal, the recently restored *pendopo* in the grounds of the Ambarrukmo Palace Hotel is another entrancing link with the past. The palace was built in the 1890s by Hamengkubuwono VII as a country retreat, and the hotel stands on what was once the palace orchard.

The evocative ruins of **TAMAN SARI**, the 'Water Castle', lying a little to the west of the *kraton*, would have gladdened the hearts of those romantically inclined 18th-century gentry who erected crumbling 'Gothick' towers wrapt about with moss and creeping tendrils. This huge and once magnificent pleasure park was begun in 1758. One popular story says it was built by Spanish slaves, though research suggests that the faintly Iberian flavour was injected by an architect of Portuguese descent who lived in Batavia.

The vicissitudes of time, climate and temporal powers, helped along by an earthquake in 1865, have reduced much of Taman Sari to an intriguing collection of roofless halls, eerie underground passageways and shattered arches. Birds-and-flowers stucco ornamentation, weathered *kala* gargoyles, and a gilded stone screen can be found amongst the lush growth. Bananas, bamboo and papayas surround the dozens of *kampung* houses that have sprung up along once-royal pathways and against equally regal walls. Small *batik tulis* workshops flourish in this labyrinth of

tropical foliage and ancient glory, a wonderful place to browse and buy.

Close to the *kraton*, in the northwest corner of the *alun-alun lor*, is the **SONO BUDOYO MUSEUM**. This should be compulsory viewing for anyone interested in Central Java's rich artistic heritage. Informative labels are sadly lacking, but there is nevertheless a wealth of delights: an 18-carat gold Buddha unearthed in a rice-field in 1956; another Buddha, slightly larger, with gold-inlaid lips; a superb array of household goods fashioned from bronze and brass; an exuberantly worked *gamelan* set from Cirebon; and some excellent *wayang kulit* figures. Try to spare at least an hour.

Birds swing and sing in high cages at the Pasar Ngasem bird market, just north of the Taman Sari 'Water Castle'.

The city fathers of Yogya have given a modest boost to man's age-old quest to beat the world's swords into plowshares. After forming an Arts Council, they proceeded to commandeer Vredegurg, an old Dutch garrison on Jln. Malioboro near the Post Office. The planners envisage a national cultural center on this historic site, where so much bitter tragedy was enacted.

Restoration began in 1980, and the various exhibits will take up residence as space becomes available. Eventually, the fort's powder rooms and barracks will house museums, galleries, workshops, and concert halls. The new name is **BENTENG BUDAYA NASIONAL**; for current activities, check the sign board that faces onto the street.

Yogya is a treasure-house of attractions for the curious, probing shopper, and its fascinations are almost endless. Silver, *batik*, antiques, curios and *wayang kulit* will be at the top of most shopping lists, though once you hit the browsing and buying trail you'll find plenty more, from the sublime to the vulgar, to excite your fancy.

Kota Gede is the centre of the **SILVER** industry. There are two major workshops and a handful of smaller ones where (buying or not) you can pass an intriguing half hour watching the hammering, beating, heating, cleaning and polishing of the metal. Deft fingers create spider-web filigree; anvils clang till your head rings; gentle hammer-blows tap out elegant repousse work. The temptations are enormous, and even if a superb miniature of Yogya's royal coach is beyond your means, there's a wide range of rings, bracelets and pendants, coffee sets, ash-trays, flatware and occasional pieces of modern jewellery to choose from, at more moderate prices. At Tom's Silver (Pandean Kota Gede 3–1A) visitors are welcome to watch one of Yogya's larger workshops process and design high-quality silver.

Back in town, at Jln. Mas Sangaji 2 (just north of the Tugu monument), there's a house and workshop of Tan Jam An where good copies of modern silver designs are made. Prices for silver-work and for combinations of stones set in silver are reasonable; they will even retrieve your stone and melt down the silver and start again if you're not happy with the design. An unusual sideline is

The home of Affandi, grand master of modern painting.

…he sale of old *kebayas*, once worn by Java's older generation of Chinese women but now seldom seen. Made of fine lawn or muslin, with hand-worked lace and embroidery, the *kebayas* are showpieces of Javanese traditional handicraft.

BATIK is one of Yogya's great drawcards. Unless you class yourself with the connoisseurs, it's a good idea to begin at *Balai Penelitian Batik dan Kerajinan* (Batik and Handicraft Research Centre) in Jln. Kusumanegara, east of the main post office, for a comprehensive and well-displayed introduction to the staggering variety of patterns and colours to be found throughout Java. An individual guided tour costs nothing, and in the course of it you'll see every step of the *batik*-making process: designing, *canting*- and *cap*-waxing, dyeing, cleaning. It is essentially a research centre though part of what is made there is for sale, including sample cloths showing the different designs.

Stall food is a cheap and delicious way to keep up your energy during a shopping spree.

Batik cloth is sold all over Yogya. There are several shops on Jln. Malioboro (besides the market) that offer the usual range of ready-made *batik* clothes and traditional *batik* lengths. Terang Bulan, with fixed prices (*harga pas*), will give you a good idea of what is available. The several large and well-appointed shops along Jln. Tirtodipuran offer every possible item that can be batiked, plus clothing and *batik* lengths, both modern and traditional that come in various sizes (remember this when buying). Good modern *batik* and such popular style clothing as T-shirts and singlets can be found at Batik Ardiyanto and Tobal Batik. Dressier (and pricier) clothes are designed and displayed at several famous art galleries.

Many of the city's better-known artists, and a number of aspiring ones, also produce *lukisan batik*, paintings made in the usual wax-and-dye manner but specifically designed for framing and hanging. You'll quickly notice a preference for the rather repetitive Hanuman-visiting-Sita-in-the-garden themes (though some classically inspired work is fresh and exciting) or the more vital and certainly more varied essays in abstract impressionism and pure abstraction. Try Gallery Amri, Bambang Oetoro, and Sapto Hudoyo and the smaller galleries in Taman Sari.

The art of **PAINTING** is fairly active in Yogya, though standards, themes and techniques vary considerably. During the revolutionary and immediate post-revolutionary years Indonesian painting was strong and vigorous; sometimes crudely executed, these works nevertheless projected an almost explosive vitality. Today, much of that groping, grass-roots urgency has disappeared. Many painters seem more interested in technique, and in the interplay of form, colour and texture. The result is attractive, if somewhat derivative, work which owes much to Western norms, and it is difficult to find painting which could be described as specifically Indonesian in feeling: rather, Yogya painting is 'international', sometimes in the case of figurative and semi-figurative painting overlaid with a veneer of

Strong legacies from the past turn up gems for the antique lover.

Indonesian subject matter. It is therefore fair to make value judgements (in terms of dollars and cents) against the price of comparable work in other world markets.

Affandi, Indonesia's 'grand old man' of contemporary painting, has a large studio-cum-gallery overlooking the river on Jln. Solo, close to the Ambarrukmo Palace Hotel. Fame has brought fortune in its wake: the starting price for an original is US$800, which you may consider a bargain by international standards. In 1973 Affandi acquired the status of 'painter laureate' when his gallery received the blessing of the government as a permanent museum (the first of its kind in Indonesia), though unhappily for the collector, most of his earlier and finer work is not for sale. The works of other artists, including Affandi's daughter Kartika, are also displayed.

To see where the up-and-coming generation is moving in painting, sculpture and handicrafts, you'll be very welcome at ASRI (Academy of Fine Arts) in Gampingan, opposite Gallery Amri.

For **ANTIQUES AND CURIOS** the hunting grounds include the many shops that line Jln Malioboro, and one more across the tracks on Jln Mangkubumi, the streets to the south and west of the *kraton*, a handful of small shops near the Ambarrukmo Palace Hotel, and Pasar Beringharjo for cheap handicrafts.

Among the things that may catch your eye are carved and gilded chests for herbal medicines, or a pair of polychrome *Loro Blunyo* wedding figures; a handful of copper coins with the Dutch East India Company's cipher, VOC, or thin silver pieces from Zeeland, Friesland and other provinces; an ornately carved, roofed and 'walled' bed, or the gilded panels of birds and flowers that once adorned these huge pieces of furniture. There are *naga*-wreathed stands for *gamelan* gongs; bronze statuettes of Durga, Nandi, Siva,

Attractive leathergoods at reasonable prices.

Ganesa and Agastya, of Buddha and innumerable bodhisattvas; crude *wayang klitik* figures, delicately lacquered boxes; and porcelain from Annam and China.

Highly concentrated perfume and fruit essences may take your fancy. *Beknamol* is flowery; *antol oli* has a sandalwood fragrance. Make your choice at Pantja Karya, Jln. Jen. Achmed Yani 72; or at Apotik Sanitas, Jln. Jen Achmed Yani 4 (both located at the 'bottom' of Jln. Malioboro).

The southern end of Jln. Malioboro also introduces Pasar Beringharjo. One of Java's biggest markets, it will assail you with sensual pleasures: golden arrays of brass pots, pans and pestles; narrow passageways filled with stalls of *batik* and antiquated sewing-machines (have a sarong run up in half a minute); hanks of rope and strands of string ideal for macramé work; herbs and spices and odiferous roots destined for a *jamu* concoction; earthenware pots and sets of miniature terracotta cooking ware (children's toys); and always the busy and often raucous clamour of Yogya's women doing their shopping.

Farther west, in the quieter streets of Pasar Ngasem, are dozens of small shops selling biscuit-coloured charcoal braziers, water-jars, pottery moneyboxes (often brightly painted), and handsome leather moneybelts and pouches. Nearby is the fascinating bird market, the cages swinging on high poles.

Yogya's **LEATHERGOODS** are attractive. Buff-coloured hand-tooled leather, decorated with floral motifs and sometimes with *wayang* figures, is available in a wide range of suitcases, overnight bags, briefcases, pocketbooks, sandals, belts and money pouches. Leather ages to light mahogany color. Check stitching and hardware closely; weak fastenings fail long before leather does. BS and Kusuma in the Ngasem area stock the best quality, strongest constructed goods in this style.

Leather is also the starting point for **WAYANG KULIT** figures (though the thin, semi-translucent buffalo hide or *kulit* should properly be called 'parchment'). The finest pieces, as delicately worked as guipure lace and as finely coloured as a butterfly's wing, are indisputably examples of craftsmanship becoming art. Prices vary, depending on the quality of the parchment, the standard of the gold paint (there are three grades used), and the complexity of the figure. An outstanding *gunungan* (mountain) incorporating the tree of life will take at least a month to make. and will cost around Rp 100,000 many good and less complex figures can be had, ready-made, for about Rp 15–20,000.

The *wayang kulit* puppeteers, the *dalangs*, are still the main buyers of the best figures. Nevertheless, superb pieces are occasionally made for display rather than for use.

There are quite a few *wayang kulit* workshops in and around Yogya, though some are hard to find. The best places to watch puppets being made, and to see a good range of high quality work, are Ledjar's (near Malioboro street) and Moeljosoehardjo's (Jln. Taman Sari 37 B).

A modern batik *painting by Marsudi, and a colonial antique from a Yogya treasure-trove.*

MASKS and **WOODEN PUPPETS** for use in *topeng* dances and in *wayang golek* performances are also good buys. Many pieces are hastily put together for the tourist trade, and their quality is dubious. For the finest work, made by one of the few remaining craftsmen who still carves for the actors and *dalangs*, rather than for casual visitors, visit Pak Warno Waskito.

Pak Warno is a shy, gentle old man who's been plying his craft for more than 50 years. He never went to school, and taught himself to use the keenly honed knives and chisels that litter his workbench. Around him, unpainted heads sit in rows above a shoulder-high wall like headhunters' trophies; a sharp-nosed Panji mask regards the world with a permanent half smile, wooden lips parted over wooden teeth; and in dim corners you may find ancient puppets of unknown vintage, perhaps a little battered and scarred by time and use, but Pak can perform miracles of rejuvenation if you ask him to restore a piece. He accepts special orders, but doesn't speak English.

To reach Pak Warno's secluded hideaway, take the Bantul road south from Yogya, turn right at the 7.6 km marker, walk about 300 metres, turn left, and stop at the first house on your right. Signposts will guide you.

You can combine a visit to Pak Warno with a call at *desa* Kasongan for cottage industry **POTTERY**. On your way back to Yogya, turn left at the 6.5 km post (a sugar-cane trolley track crosses the road at this point) and follow the side-road for about a kilometre. If you've admired the jauntily coloured moneyboxes in the form of elephants, roosters, mythical beasts and mounted cavalry which can be found in Yogya, especially around Pasar Ngasem, Kasongan is where you can see them being modelled by hand, fired in an open blaze of roots and palm leaves, and then painted with a verve and panache that's almost Mexican in feeling. Kasongan sprawls, and there is no real centre to the village, but almost every household you come to will have a potter. It is possible to have items made to order; allow up to a week or 10 days for a 'special'. If you prefer unpainted pieces, remember that the lovely ochre ware has been fired only once, and is fragile; double-firing gives a more durable result, but the colour will be grey-black.

Six kilometres away to the southeast is the town of **KOTA GEDE**, famous for its silver workshops. It is a compact little town, its main street lined by an honour guard of shop-houses which give way near the river, to a shambly array of once-stately architectural fantasies: columns where columns don't make sense, strange lead-glass windows, outbursts of coloured tiles, and gateways that seem to lead nowhere.

Kota Gede was founded in 1579 by Senopati, also the illustrious founder of the second Mataram dynasty, who now lies buried in a small moss covered graveyard only half a kilometre from the town's central market. A broad pathway and two enormous *waringin* trees herald a secluded courtyard through which a narrow pathway leads on to an ancient mosque and a maze of lesser courtyards and decorated doorways. In the midst

Pottery moneyboxes—a speciality at Kasongan

Kota Gede's famous silver workshops.

Excursion to Imogiri and a famous grave.

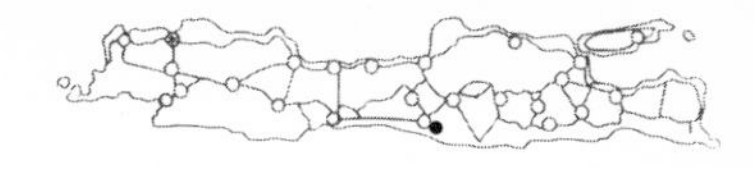

of this serene labyrinth lies the tiny, high-walled cemetery. Offerings of flowers, petals, incense and cigars strew the worn stone steps in front of the large, weather-grained wooden door leading to Senopati's tomb.

Senopati's original *kraton* is believed to have stood a kilometre farther on. The site is now occupied by a beautiful garden cemetery established by Hamengkubuwono VIII. The main gateway, small and unobtrusive, is inscribed *Hasta Renggo* (Eight Founded). Beyond a second and more ornate gate is a lovely walled garden, filled with roses, jerberas and small frangipani trees, and the well-kept graves of many members of Yogya's royal house.

In the square outside the cemetery is housed a lump of polished black rock, the size of a double bed. It is variously described as an executioner's block, or as Senopati's throne. Next to it are three large balls of yellow stone, ranging in size from a shot-putt to a volley ball, and reputedly used for juggling.

Another and more splendid link with Yogya's past is at **IMOGIRI**, 20 km to the south along a narrow road linked with others (to Parangtritis, 26 km, and Bantul, 12 km) by even narrower lanes that crackle across the landscape like the fine fractured-wax lines on a piece of *batik*. Occasionally you may have to stop as a stumpy yellow diesel engine, or a little black coal-burner with a Casey Jones smoke-stack, rattles and sways across the roadway on its narrow-gauge track, dragging behind it an unsteady train of cane-trucks.

Imogiri has an ancient, sturdy air about it. Close-packed houses made of fired brick are roofed with S-profile terracotta tiles; tall wooden shutters covering the shopfronts are unpainted or faded, adding to a pervading feeling of sun-drenched cleanliness. A little beyond the village the road ends in a tiny square containing a single *warung* and an old *pendopo*. Ahead, a broad pathway leads off through an avenue of trees, the starting point for the climb to the royal tombs.

The famous Sultan Agung was the first of his line to be buried there, interred in 1645 on the top of a small rocky outcrop that springs from the plain roughly halfway between Yogya and the sea. Since then almost every prince of the house of Mataram, and of the succeeding royal families of Yogyakarta and Surakarta, has been laid to rest at Imogiri.

A visit to this venerated site takes on the air of a pilgrimage (which indeed it is for many Javanese), for the 345 shallow-tread steps of the wide, formal stairway will exact considerable penance. Happily, even at midday the steps are shaded for most of the way, and there's a touch of magic as shafts of sunlight drop through the overhanging trees and catch eddies of smoke from burning leaves, or the bright colours of a *kebaya*.

The tombs lie within three major courtyards at the top of the stairway: in front are those of Mataram; to the left, those of the *Susuhunans* of Solo; to the right, those of the Sultans of Yogya. Each great courtyard encloses smaller courts

If you need exercise, try the 345-step stairway to the Imogiri tombs, or run wild and free on the grey-black dunes at Parangtritis (following page).

An expanse of black sand dunes at Parangtritis.

containing the memorials and tombs of the princes. Entry into the smaller courts, and viewing of the tombs, is permitted briefly only on Mondays and Fridays after noontime prayers, and you must wear formal Javanese court costume to visit them. This is less demanding than it may sound, and the necessary garments can be hired on the spot for a low fee.

Although the forecourts and inner courts are closed at other times, the long, high-walled walks along the front of each complex are always open, and their tranquil and relaxing atmosphere, like that of a medieval cloister (with tropical sunshine and shade), makes the climb worthwhile. At each end of the front gallery an archway leads through the walls to a pathway which reaches the real summit of the hill. It's an uneven but easy ten-minute walk to circle the complex, and the views are magnificent: Yogya and Gunung Merapi to the north, an agricultural kaleidoscope to the west, and to the southeast a low rim of ragged, treeless hills which suddenly plunge seawards to Parangtritis.

The shore at **PARANGTRITIS** is linked with an ancient tradition which may have flourished in pre-Hindu times as a fertility cult, and which was later observed symbolically by Sultan Agung and his successors. Legends claim that Senopati, or perhaps Sultan Agung, was married in fact (not fantasy) to Raden Loro Kidul, the 'Queen of the Southern Ocean' whose domain, also known as the region of death, is beneath the waters of the Indian Ocean. Ritual observances of the marriage are still performed in the Central Javanese courts: a special dance, the *Bedoyo Ketawang*, takes place in Solo on the anniversary of the *susuhunan*'s accession, and until recently could be witnessed only by the *susuhunan* and the closest of his nobles, for the dance symbolises his marriage to Raden Loro Kidul. In Yogya, on the

The rugged coast on the Indian Ocean at Baron and Kukup.

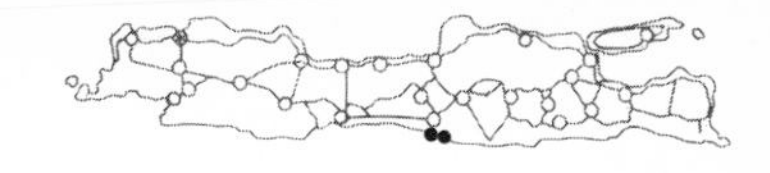

occasion of the sultan's birthday, a special *Labuhan* ceremony involves the distribution of sacred nail- and hair-clippings, together with *melati* flowers which have been offered during the year to the royal *pusakas*, at rituals held on the slopes of Gunung Merapi and Gunung Lawu, and on the shore at Parangtritis.

Raden Loro Kidul, 'Queen of the Southern Ocean', may be the consort of kings, but she has a malevolent disposition. Swimming on her rough southern coast is tantamount to entering her territory without a permit, and offenders frequently drown. She has a special predilection for young men dressed in green (her colour).

Legend or no, the rips and violent currents, and a heavy surf, make swimming dangerous on most of Java's southern coast. At Parangtritis this seascape is backed by a forbidding shoreline of jagged cliffs and great dunes of shifting, iron-grey sand. Desolate, angry, weirdly beautiful.

The road south from Yogya, through Bantul, ends abruptly at Kretek where the Opak River glides down to the sea. The flat grey river-bed stretches almost 500 metres from bank to bank, and there is no bridge. During the dry season the river is easily fordable on foot, or you can take one of the shallow-draught ferry-boats; on the other side hire a bicycle or a *dokar* horse-cart (prices negotiable) for the remaining four kilometres to Parangtritis.

The spell closes in. Extraordinary twists and curls and subtleties of masses of dunes; clearly defined yet melting divisions between black and grey on huge sand-slopes. The dunes won't be the same tomorrow; they'll even change today, sand moving and shifting. Black, grey, another grey, black. An intricate harmony of patterns like taffeta or watered steel.

Its expressions change. Black sand, a heavy sky waiting to fall, a pewter sea. On the ridges a sudden eye-opener as late light catches a solitary figure on the way from nowhere to nowhere. Even in the brightest sunlight, when the heat is scorching underfoot and the sky is cool blue above, the sand retains its stunning black menace.

Farther afield are the twin beaches of **BARON** and **KUKUP**. Baron is a narrow, long bay hemmed in by modest cliffs and small coves which can be reached from the main beach along pathways traversing the intervening ridges. Kukup, a kilometre to the east, is more open, with an exciting mixture of rocky islets, a couple of caves and stretches of weed-slicked limestone shallows jutting out into the surf. Both are a little safer for swimming than Parangtritis, though caution is still essential.

The route to Baron will take you 55 km southeast of Yogya on a good though narrow road. Turn south off Jalan Solo at the 'Solo 60 km' post, and turn south again at Wonosari for the last 22 km through country which is both pretty and rugged: rock-fringed hillocks of the 'Thousand Mountains', *Gunung Seribu*, jut up from the limestone landscape, with black cavemouths grinning from scrub-strewn slopes.

A limestone shelf at Kukup is fun for paddlers, but the drop is sharp and dangerous on the edge where the surf rages ashore in a mass of foam.

Comfortable Kaliurang hill station on the slopes of restless Merapi volcano.

Less attractive than Baron, Kukup or Parangtritis is **SAMAS** (variously Somas or Somos), but it has the advantage of being closer to Yogya. The road is good, small chalets and eating places are shooting up, but there's little more to be said. The surf, spectacular to look at, is dangerous because the beach shelves abruptly; the treeless dunes and reed-fringed inland lagoons are bleakly attractive, but the black sand underfoot can get very, very hot. It's no tropic isle, though for landscape watchers it is magnificent on a stormy day.

The beauty of most of the coastline south of Yogya is well matched, and more, by the mountains crowding in from the north, where you can choose between the cool and peaceful relaxation of a hill station like Kaliurang, or lace on your stoutest shoes or climbing boots for a tough volcano trek.

KALIURANG, 23 km due north of Yogya, offers plenty of guesthouses, two swimming pools, a tiny herd of deer from Bogor and a beautiful 2.5-km lung-exercising walk to 'Overseer Point'. The weather can be unpredictable: even if Merapi is crystal clear from the lowlands it may be shrouded in cloud by the time you reach the lookout at Plawangan (1,275 metres).

Near the summit of Plawangan the path traverses a narrow ridge where tree-clad slopes fall away steeply on both sides, splashed with fiery red and yellow lantana blossom. Normally there is nothing to be heard but the sound of birds, though if the mist comes down you'd swear the spirits of the volcano were abroad: softly swirling vapours creep through the trees, and through the silvery grey light floats the eerie sound of *gamelan*, the disembodied wailing chorus sounding like the denizens of the crater itself.

On a clear day **GUNUNG MERAPI** can be seen in all its glory. Watching it is a full-time job at the Plawangan seismological station where the volcanologists, armed with binoculars and seismographs, work in month-long shifts before moving on to Gunung Kelud or Ijen or wherever else Java's crust is growing restless. Merapi is the most volatile of the island's volcanic tribe, and tops the dangerous list: the closing months of 1973 were marked by a series of minor lava flows and the ensuing (and more damaging) *lahar* streams of water, mud and ash; the last serious eruption occurred in 1954.

Another good observation point is to the west of the mountain. A small side-road, well signposted in English, branches off the main route to Muntilan at 23 km from Yogya and creeps slowly through tunnels of bamboo and tall stands of pine before revealing the ravaged western slope of the volcano, scarred and twisted by a continuing series of lava flows. At night, dull red globs of molten rock can be seen through the darkness, oozing slowly over the rim like monstrous science-fiction slugs, sometimes accompanied by bursts of sparks and flaming cinders. By day, when clouds and mist swirl around the crater's pinnacled rim, huge boulders flung from the core bounce and bound down a steep, grey gulch, raising plumes of ash and smoke as they strafe the slope.

That is one view of Merapi. There is another, from the rim itself.

To stand on the rim of Merapi, gazing down on the world from a height of 2,900 metres, and down into the Dantean crater as well, is probably the most exciting mountain experience in all of Java. Bromo, in East Java, is usually given more attention for it is easier to get to. At Bromo, you walk. At Merapi, you climb.

Although the climb is heart-pounding, the starting point is easily reached. Head east from Yogya to Kartasura (just 8 km short of Solo), take the northwest junction to Boyolali and turn off there at Jalan Merbabu (*not* at Jalan Merapi). The road leads to the great saddle which links Merbabu and Merapi, and on to the little village of Selo where another volcanology post is located. The men on duty will let you rest there, and can arrange for your guides. Spare mattresses are generally available. A reasonable payment must be made to the guides, and a donation to the professional volcano-watchers will be greatly appreciated.

Merapi can be a daylight trip, but it is best to start the adventure at 2 o'clock in the morning with a full moon. Snug-fitting boots or shoes are essential, and you should take warm clothing, a good torch and a supply of water and energy foods in case you get hungry. You may feel hot

Clouds, mist, steam and smouldering rubble on Merapi's western slopes.

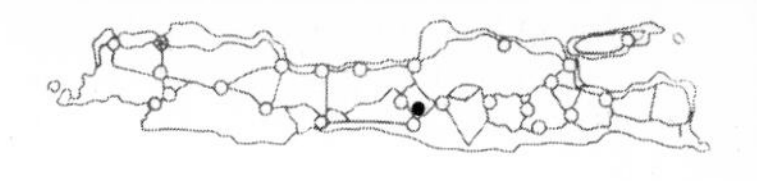

to start with, but up near the rim it's tooth-clacking cold.

The trek from the volcanology post to the crater rim and back will take roughly seven hours. With one exception the climb is steep all the way. It starts through pretty, grassy country dotted with cassias; snakes upwards through a realm of flowers, wild raspberries and stunted bushes; and finally inches onto slopes which are bare of vegetation. Here, on a small plateau, you can make your peace with the world.

In the clear, clean dawn light this is paradise indeed. To the west, the peaks of Sumbing and Sundoro, Dieng's guardians, and beyond them the crown of Slamet, 140 km from where you stand; eastwards, Lawu and farther again to Wilis; the Java Sea to the north, the Indian Ocean to the south; and below you, a million black and silver mirrors, the glass of *padi*-fields trapped in the sky's first light, as cold and shining as tear-drops scattered upon the pristine Earth.

For the sure-footed there is one more goal: the crater rim. The guides mutter 'berani', and follow you as far as they dare (*berani* usually means 'brave', but in the context of where you're going it translates more aptly as 'crazy'). Don't try to fight the mist if it comes down: less than a metre's visibility, with instant cremation lurking somewhere in the gloom, is not to be toyed with.

The slow climb takes you over razor-sharp rocks, warm rocks, hot rocks. Sulphurous vapours swirl around your ankles. And there, a death's fall below you, under treacherous ledges and jutting rocks, is the devil's well where all the trouble starts: plunging cliffs, a terrifying roar of steam, and a stomach-churning sense of ferocity and power which (you might feel) must be an answer to the world's energy problems. It's time to scuttle back to the safe white walls of Yogya's *kraton*.

TO THE GREATER GLORY OF THE GODS

BOROBUDUR, one of the world's greatest Buddhist monuments, was built some time between 778 and 842 A.D. during the Sailendra dynasty: three hundred years before Cambodia's Angkor Wat, four hundred years before work had begun on the great European cathedrals of Amiens, Köln, Lincoln, Chartres and Rheims. Ironically (though in perfect accord with the Buddhist doctrine of ephemerality) the centre of power had, by 1100 A.D., shifted to the eastern end of Java and Borobudur was being engulfed by vegetation.

Raffles visited Borobudur in 1815, and ordered that the site be cleared of undergrowth and then thoroughly surveyed. The work was carried out, but it was not until 1907, when Dr. Th. van Erp began a massive five-year restoration project, that real progress was made. It was then found that the structure of Borobudur was not in fact solid, but merely a casing of un-mortared stone enclosing a natural hillock. Although the original builders had incorporated many spouts to carry off rainwater, and despite van Erp's great care, seepage within the newly exposed monument became a serious problem. Soil and rubble from the inner hillock were gradually washed down against the retaining walls of each terrace, building up enormous pressure which threatened to burst the whole structure like a fermented orange. Chemical salts, too, were slowly eroding the reliefs and carvings.

Experts convened, and a frantic SOS went out to the world: 'Borobudur must be saved!' With UNESCO helping to raise money, almost US$23 million, the gigantic task of rescuing Borobudur was launched in August 1973. Work was completed in ten years and President Suharto officially reopened Borobudur on February 23, 1983.

Borobudur must be
aved!'

Stone Buddhas
ccumulating virtue for
ll eternity.

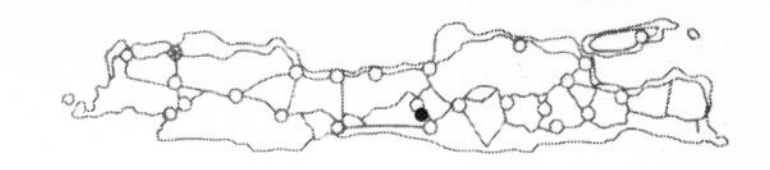

Borobudur is only 41 km northwest of Yogya: 31 km will take you a little north of Muntilan, where a sign-posted side road leads to the site; if you're coming from the north, there is another turn-off 7 km south of Magelang.

Borobudur, as a classical *stupa*, is both a *meru* (mountain) inhabited by the gods, and a replica of the three divisons of the Mahayana Buddhist universe: *khamadhatu*, the lower sphere of the everyday world; *rupadhatu*, the middle sphere of 'form', spiritually superior to the world of the flesh; and *arupadhatu*, the higher sphere of total abstraction and detachment from the world.

There were originally ten levels at Borobudur, each falling within one or other of the three spheres. At the bottom, now only partly visible, was a level with bas-reliefs depicting the delights and damnations of *khamadhatu*, the physical world; this level was probably covered even before the completion of the temple, possibly to buttress the monument, possibly because the unholy realities of earthly lusts had no relevance to a pilgrim.

The next five levels (the outer processional path and the four square terraces) show, in their reliefs, the life of Prince Siddharta on his way to becoming the Gautama Buddha, his previous incarnations, and episodes from the life of the bodhisattva Sudhana. These are within the sphere of *rupadhatu*, and are the most absorbing and delightful of the Borobudur sculptures: ships, family life, musicians, dancing girls, saints and heavenly throngs.

The square terraces end. Above, three circular terraces support 72 latticed *dagobs* (miniature *stupas*), most of which are still whole. Most contain a statue of a *dhyani* Buddha, but one *dhyani* stands alone, bereft of his shell, gazing out towards the strange mountain range of Menoreh which seems to echo the silhouette of Borobudur . . . and where one series of lumps and knobs is said to be the profile of Gunadharma, traditionally the temple's architect.

These three terraces are a transitional step between *rupadhatu* and the tenth and highest level, the topmost *dagob*: the sphere of *arupadhatu*, of formlessness and total abstraction. This crowning *dagob* contains two pyramidal chambers. The movement upwards from the material world to the realm of Sublime Reality would suggest that the two chambers were originally empty, the ultimate symbol of absorption into the supreme spirit, yet a kris and an uncompleted Buddha statue were found in the lower and large chamber during the 19th century when there was a gaping hole (since sealed) in the side of the *dagob*. Had the statue been there for a thousand years? The kris could not have been, but who had placed it there, and why? There are not yet answers.

Borobudur was probably erected for the glorification of the Ultimate Reality, the Lord Buddha, and as a tangible, tactile lesson for priests and pilgrims, a textbook on the path to enlightenment. Even now, when windows in the *dagobs* are stuffed with shoes and clothes of workers, there is a cleansing sense of freedom, especially on the upper sphere of the monument which opens up to the sky and mountains.

Aesop's-fable panels at nearby Candi Mendut.

The original paintwork has long gone, dissolved by a thousand years of monsoons and humidity. The stonework is blotched with moss and lichens, or coloured a dull sandy yellow where erosion has pitted the surface like a roughly broken loaf of rye bread. Yet once a year, on Waicak Day (the celebration of the Lord Buddha's birth and death), the temple relives some of its past splendour as thousands of saffron-robed Buddhist priests perform a grand processional by the light of the full moon, offering flowers, incense and prayers in a timeless gesture of humility. Even non-Buddhists revere the statues of the *dhyani* Buddhas, silently shrouded within their latticed *dagobs*, and good fortune is assured if you can touch a figure through one of the square or diamond shaped holes.

Experiences of Borobudur can vary. Most visitors are impressed by its size, and delighted by the reliefs. Others find the immense scale a little too much to cope with. More personal, but scarcely less powerful, is **CANDI MENDUT**, 3 km back towards Muntilan.

Candi Mendut was built about the same time as Borobudur, but it is not a *stupa*. It resembles most Central Javanese temples with its broad base, a high central body and a steep pyramidal roof once crowned by a large *dagob* and a series of smaller ones. The superbly carved panels on the outer walls depict various bodhisattvas and Buddhist goddesses, and are the largest in Indonesia. On the outside of the staircase balustrade small panels relate charming folktales, many of which, in the manner of Aesop's fables, are about animals. The walls of the passageway to the antechamber and the interior of the temple are also decorated with fine reliefs of the tree of heaven surrounded by pots of money and *kinnaras* (half bird, half man), and with two beautiful panels of a man and a woman amidst swarms of playful children. It is thought that these represent a *yaksa* and a *yaksini*, child-eating ogres who converted to Buddhism and became protectors instead of devourers.

The Mendut panels are delightful in their artistry and detail, but they hardly prepare you for the stunning impact of the temple interior and three of the finest statues to be found in the Buddhist world: a magnificent 3-metre high figure of Buddha as Sakyamuni flanked on the left and right (of the viewer) by the bodhisattvas Lokesvara and Vajrapani. This is, as Bernet Kempers says, 'one of the greatest manifestations of Buddhist spiritual thought and art . . . For many visitors to Mendut a silent sojourn in the interior must (be) one of their most impressive contacts with a higher world.'

Many people respond with an equal or greater joy to **PRAMBANAN**, a temple complex (16 km east of Yogya) named after the village which thrusts up to the southern boundary of the temple group. Prambanan is best seen shortly after dawn or in the late afternoon when slanting sunlight picks out details with a rounding, golden touch. But it is still beautiful at any time.

Borobudur's welter of niches, stairs and reliefs are overwhelming, and not truly inspiring, until one reaches the upper sphere beneath the sky.

Siva's 'Slender Virgin' at Prambanan.

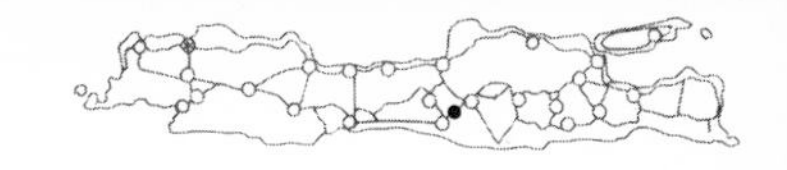

Prambanan was completed about 900 A. D. It was deserted within a hundred years, and collapsed about 1600. Preparations for the restoration of the central temple began in 1918; work started 19 years later, and was completed in 1953.

The highest courtyard contains the remains or reconstructions of eight buildings. Entering from the south you pass a small 'court temple'. On your left (west) are three larger temples: the first was dedicated to Brahma, the second and largest to Siva, and the third to Visnu. Opposite these are three smaller temples which contained the 'vehicles' of the gods: the gander (*hamsa*) of Brahma; Siva's bull (*nandi*), a monolithic, amazingly relaxed beast carved with consummate skill, and unfortunately the only 'vehicle' remaining; and the sun-bird (*garuda*) of Visnu. At the far north is a second 'court temple'. Beyond the central courtyard, at a lower level, there were once 224 minor shrines or temples, almost all of which are still in ruins.

The largest temple, the masterpiece dedicated to Siva, is also known as *Loro Jonggrang* ('Slender Virgin'), a name sometimes given to the whole Prambanan temple complex. As legend tells it, Loro Jonggrang was the daughter of Ratu Boko (Eternal Lord). Wooed by an unwanted suitor, she demanded that the man build a temple in one night, and then frustrated his almost successful effort by pounding the rice-logs in a premature announcement of dawn. Enraged, he turned the maiden to stone. She remains at Prambanan as Siva's consort, Durga, a statue in the northern chamber of the main temple. Other major statues include Agastya, the 'Divine Teacher', in the main temple's southern chamber; Ganesa, Siva's elephant-headed son, in the western chamber; and an outstanding 3-metre figure of Siva in the central chamber. There is also a multi-faced

Brahma in the roofless Brahma temple.

One aspect of Loro Jonggrang's appeal is its glorious symmetry and grace. Another is its wealth of sculptural detail: on the base of the main terrace, the so-called 'Prambanan motif' in which little lions in niches are flanked by trees of life and a lively menagerie of *kinnaras*, hares, geese, birds, deer and a host of other endearing creatures; on the outer balustrade of the terrace, animated groups of singers and dancers, and panels of relaxed, beautiful celestial beings; on the main wall of the temple, the regents of the heavenly quarters; and finally, on the inner wall of the balustrade, the wonderfully vital and utterly engrossing *Ramayana* episodes which end (on the Siva temple) with the arrival at Langka of Hanuman and his ape army.

The positioning of the reliefs is formal. The movement within each panel is free-flowing, filled with fascinating detail. Even the most tumultous scenes include lovingly rendered touches: monkeys in a fruit tree, birds robbing a grain bin, kitchen scenes. Prambanan's beauty and variety demand more than one visit.

CANDI SEWU and **CANDI PLAOSAN** are within 2 km of Prambanan. Take the road behind the temple and then head east through fields of *padi* and sugar-cane; or follow the main road towards Solo and watch for small signposts on the north (left) side.

Sewu, the 'Thousand Temples', was built about 850 A.D., with a central temple surrounded by 240 minor shrines (some have been restored, work progresses on others, but the main temple cannot be completely rebuilt). It is a very romantic site, and a delight to explore. The central temple has an unusual closed gallery with remains of 'Moorish' niches and archways, and the walls of the smaller temples reveal a tantalising array of Buddhist deities.

Plaosan, about 1 km east of Sewu, originally consisted of two large, rectangular temples. Both were two-storeyed, three-roomed buildings, bounded by a multitude of little shrines and solid *stupas*. One major temple has been restored, and a good reason for visiting Plaosan is to see restoration work in progress on the other: a painstaking task where stones are stripped from the ruins of the old site and fitted together like a monstrous jigsaw puzzle before being reassembled as a whole. The restored temple contains a number of beautiful small Buddhas and bodhisattvas, very fine *kala* heads above the windows (an unusual feature), and reliefs which perhaps depict donors who helped finance the building.

CANDI SARI, prettily set amongst banana and coconut groves (200 metres north of the 14.4 km post from Yogya), is similar to the Plaosan temples, with two storeys, windows, internal cuttings for wooden joists supporting the floors, and superb external reliefs of heavenly beings. Temples like Sari and Plaosan were probably also monasteries where priests, votaries and pil-

One of many Buddhas seated in the two-storeyed chambers at Candi Plaosan, near Prambanan. Early morning or late afternoon are the best times to visit Central Java's temples.

Watching Sambisari temple emerge from the soil, you wonder how many others are still hidden.

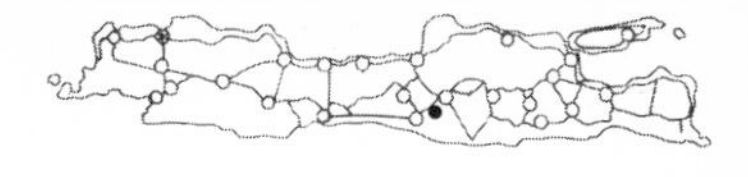

grims lived above the sanctuaries. Some of Candi Sari's relief statues show traces of 'diamond plaster', hard and stone-like, which helped preserve the carvings, enabled sculptors to add fine detail, and provided a base for the bright paintwork that once lit up these temples like immense, multi-faceted gems.

Remnants of fine, yellowed plasterwork can also be seen at **CANDI KALASAN**, 50 metres off the main road at the 14 km post. An ancient inscription dates Kalasan at 778 A. D., but the existing structure is probably a century younger. The outstanding feature is a huge, ornate *kala*-head above the southern doorway. If you can stand the sweet-ammonia stench of bat droppings, the inner chamber of Kalasan reveals the overlapping blocks of an extraordinarily high and steep pyramidal structure; it once housed a huge bronze statue of Buddha.

The area around Prambanan (the temple, the village) is the most prolific site of temples in Central Java: more than thirty lie within half an hour's walk. Some are just foundations. Some are just magnificent. And there is also *Kraton Ratu Boko* (or *Baka*), the 'Palace of the Eternal Lord'.

For those who love, within the mind's eye, to reconstruct history, **RATU BOKO** is a dream. The main site is on a small plateau 1.6 km south of Prambanan village. A steep, rocky pathway to the plateau starts opposite a 'Yogya 18 km' post. The trek is best done at dawn or in the late afternoon when the views from the plateau's ridge are most beautiful.

Ratu Boko was probably a fortified palace built by the Buddhist Sailendras and later taken over by Hindu Mataram. Little remains apart from a huge, sparsely ornamented gateway and a series of foundations and bathing places, but the atmosphere is enchanting. A few hundred metres to the south on another small plateau (linked with the first, but difficult to find) is a large stone platform with decorated waterspouts and staircases surrounded by an empty moat; a little below the platform, through *kala*-head gateways, is a group of tranquil green pools, one of which is still used by the villagers.

To see a discovery-in-progress, visit **CANDI SAMBISARI**, where the remains of a small temple, discovered in 1966, are being excavated. The floor of the temple lies four to five metres below the surface of the surrounding *padi*-fields, and ancient walls, doorways and altars have been finely preserved under centuries-old layers of volcanic ash and dust. Parts of the temple have been tentatively reassembled on the edge of the dig, but there is still much more to be done. To find Sambisari, turn north just beyond the 10.2 km post (from Yogya) and bump along a pretty country lane for another 2.2 km. Watching Sambisari emerge from the soil, you'll wonder how many more temples are hidden in the heart of Central Java.

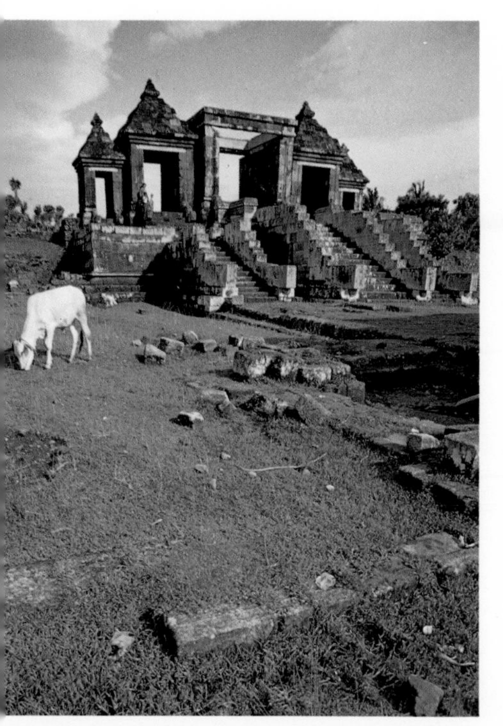

The brooding gateway at Ratu Boko dominates a mysterious and little-known site on a plateau above Prambanan. A trek at dawn up the steep pathway is rewarded with magnificent vistas.

SURAKARTA AN ANCIENT CAPITAL

Surakarta, or **SOLO** as it is better known, is an easy one-hour drive from Yogya. The countryside between the two cities is a glorious patchwork of agricultural endeavour and small towns. Prambanan, with a view of Loro Jonggrang rising above river-side trees; at Klaten, a fast by-pass through rich tobacco fields and counter-balanced well buckets standing like storks in a field; at Gondang, a huge factory dated 1860, a remnant of Java's early industrial revolution; before and beyond, 100-metre thatched 'long-houses' for drying tobacco; Delanggu (or Jalanggu), famous for its woodcarvers, but more immediately notable for the masses of *tukang gigi* signs (a *tukang gigi* is less a dentist than a maker of false teeth: the signs are a dream for the collector of pop art); Kartasura, once known as Wanakarta, and for six decades the capital of Mataram, where only a crumbling brick wall recalls former glories; then a final 8 km to Solo's main street.

Solo is a city loved by students and scholars of Central Javanese culture, for it was here that royal patronage brought that culture to its greatest flowering. Although at first glance the flat, sprawling city seems even less a royal capital than Yogya, Solo rewards patience. As the artist and writer Iwan Tirtaamidjaja has noted, the *susuhunan* of Solo 'was the only Javanese to whom the Dutch paid full respect. His palace . . . was an enclave where absolute deference was awarded to ancient Javanese laws and traditions.' That deference (even if politically inspired) led to the cultivation and preservation of arts which can still be enjoyed.

The early years of the 1740s were tumultuous ones for the island of Java. A massacre of Chinese merchants and traders in Batavia sparked off a frightening chain of events, bewildering in their complexity and repercussions. Chinese and Javanese combined forces, seized some of the

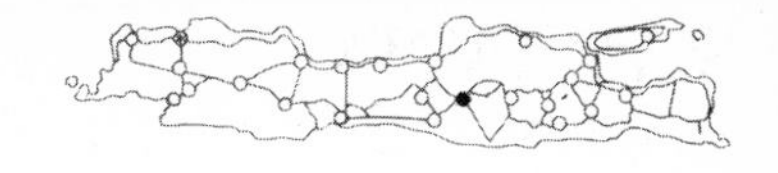

fortified port cities in the east, laid siege to others, and annihilated the Dutch garrison in Kartasura, the seat of the Mataram dynasty. The Madurese prince Cakraningrat, nominally a vassal of Mataram, sided with the Dutch in putting down the revolts. The *kraton* at Kartasura was reduced to ruins, Pakubuwono II was deposed, and a pretender was placed on the throne as Hamangkurat V. In an ironic twist of fate, the pretender's reign lasted a mere six months and Pakubuwono was returned to his throne in 1743 under the aegis of the Dutch. Cakraningrat received nothing for his loyalty.

Kartasura had been the capital of Mataram for only 63 years before the destruction of the *kraton*. The *susuhunan*, Pakubuwono II, nevertheless decided to move his capital. A new site, hopefully more auspicious, was selected eight kilometres farther east on marshy ground along the banks of the *Bengawan Solo*, the Solo River. Two years of preparation followed, and on 17 February 1745 a wondrous day-long procession followed a flower- and banner-bedecked route from Kartasura to the new capital of Surakarta.

Leading the procession were the royal *waringin* trees, wrapped in silk and destined for the northern square (*alun-alun lor*) in front of the new palace. There followed the *Bangsal Pangrawit*, a special audience chamber which would be ready to receive the 'emperor' (as the *susuhunan* was called by the Dutch) on his arrival. Next came the emperor's elephants and horses, the first group of officials, the court artisans (goldsmiths, tailors, armourers, coppersmiths), the keeper of the royal seal, a group of ministers, five troops of soldiers, the crown prince and his retinue (including Major van Hogendorp, representing the Governor-General), regalia bearers, religious officials, mounted relatives of the emperor, the royal guard, more bearers of regalia, and then the *susuhunan* himself.

'Just then came the king, dressed as a bridegroom in the royal wagon Kyahi Grudo accompanied by high-ranking officials and other regalia carriers. The soldiers of the Tamtama (royal bodyguard) were on the left and righthand side of the king, 200 men on each side. In the rear were the officials Martalulut and Singanagoro carrying the wadungs (knives) of the king, called Kyahi Pangarab-arab and Kyahi Buta Mancak, wrapped in silk.'

There was more. The royal ladies, wives and relatives; the emperor's *pusakas* and his library, carried on palanquins; the cooks and utensils for creating the royal meals; the two *waringin* trees for the southern square (*alun-alun kidul*); the *gamelan* sets; and finally the wealthy traders and merchants, the animals belonging to the royal family, the official hunters and fisherman, and a huge crowd of people from the northern coastal districts who helped carry the emperor's cannons.

The emperor arrived at his new palace. The portable audience chamber had been set up, the queen and the court ladies were despatched to their quarters, and Kandjeng Susuhunan Pakubuwono addressed his people:

A plush coach at Solo's Mangkunegaran Palace, and the royal crest at Sitinggil pavilion.

The Kraton of Solo and its museum of well-kept memorabilia.

Adipati Pringgoloyo, Sindurejo and all my subjects. Hear and obey that this day I have the wish to change the name and status of the village of Sala and make it into the capital city of my kingdom with the name . . . Surakarta Hadiningrat. May it be spread to all the people of the whole country of Java.

The promise of that magical journey was short-lived. Within twelve years the Empire of Mataram was in a terminal death throe. Pakubuwono II was dead. In 1755 his son and successor, Pakubuwono III, could only watch helplessly as his domains were fragmented: his uncle, Mangkubumi, became the first Sultan Hamengkubuwono of Yogyakarta; his cousin became Mangkunegoro I, controlling a small domain within Solo's remaining territory; and politically, the Dutch held the reins.

The famous 'Division of Mataram' was also a blessing in disguise, at least for posterity and today's traveller. The *susuhunan*, although politically emasculated, was still permitted to receive revenues from his lands. Art flourished in the court of Surakarta as it had not done for a hundred years in Mataram. With incoming revenues no longer destined for their war coffers, the *susuhunans* gave their gold to the development of dance, *wayang kulit*, *gamelan* music, kris-making and *batik*. It was perhaps an aristocratic hot-house culture, but the culture (if not the power and the glory) survives even now.

The **KRATON** of Solo, *Karaton Surakarta Hadiningrat*, lies just to the south of the eastern end of the city's main street, Jalan Slamet Ryadi a new Protestant church under construction marks the corner). The road south runs a short distance to the *alun-alun lor*, down between the two royal *waringin* trees, and stops in front of the pale blue *Pagelaran* pavilion with its shining expanse of cool marble tiles and the glassed-in audience chamber, *Bangsal Pangrawit*, from which Pakubuwono II addressed his subjects in 1745.

At the back of the *Pagelaran* a broad flight of steps, guarded on each side by iron railings and old cannons, leads up to the *Sitinggil* pavilion which originally faced onto the *alun-alun lor*. The great *pendopo* now contains a sacred cannon, *Nyai Setomi*, once part of the Portuguese defences in 16th-century Malacca and later captured by the Dutch.

Since 1976, the *Pagelaran* has been converted to offices for a major Surakarta university.

The main body of the *kraton* is enclosed in a series of courtyards behind the immense gate-house of *Kori Kamandungan Lor*. Here, shaded by groves of leafy trees, between which flit the bare-shouldered *abdidalem*, the female attendants, is the large audience hall of the *susuhunans*. The columns supporting the roof are richly carved and gilded, but are hung with protective drapes which are removed only on special occasions. Crystal chandeliers hang from the rafters, marble statues line the walkways, wrought-iron columns and ornately glazed Chinese flowerpots vie for one's attention. A superb stained-glass screen bears the arms of Pakubuwono X who, during a

Under Pakubuwono X the court of Solo flourished, developing the arts and winning Dutch respect.

he Solo River
–Java's longest.

Nightly performance; of *wayang wong* by the Sriwedari troupe.

6-year reign (1893 to 1939) was responsible for he main decorative elements that now delight he eye in every corner of the *kraton* complex.

The museum associated with the *kraton* was stablished in 1963 and is one of the better nuseums in Java. Its treasures are well displayed nd cared for. The collections of ancient Hindu-avanese bronzes and Chinese pottery and orcelain are excellent; there are good krises nd pikes; a violent diorama of Prince Diponegoro ighting the Dutch; and three marvellous coaches. The oldest, a lumbering, deep-bodied carriage uilt about 1740, was a gift from the Dutch ast India Company (VOC) to Pakubuwono II nd carried the emperor in his grand procession rom Kartasura to Surakarta in 1745; named *Kyahi Grudo*, the coach was displayed for 40 days n the *alun-alun lor*. much to the mixed delight nd alarm of the citizenry. The museum also isplays some remarkable figure-heads from the oyal barges, including the huge-nosed visage of *Kyahi Rojomolo*, a giant of surpassing ugliness who decorated the prow of the *susuhunans'* private barge.

The Solo River is the longest in Java. From n unpromising beginning in the harsh limestone nills near Donorojo it traces a tortuous course north and northeast for more than 350 kilometres, before breaking into a number of estuaries on he Surabaya Strait. As a navigable link between he rich, rice-growing heart of Central Java and he coastal trading ports (Gresik, Sedayu, Surabaya) it played a vital role in Java's recorded nistory.

Of all the vessels that made the long voyage rom Solo to the north coast, *Kyahi Rojomolo* was he most splendid. Over 35 metres long, with a 7-metre beam, it contained four rooms and a dining hall that could seat thirty people. It began ts service during the reign of Pakubuwono IV (1788–1820), made the return voyage to Gresik three times, collected the Madurese bride of Pakubuwono VII (1830–1858) from Bojonegoro, and was finally retired from service towards the end of the 19th century.

The *kraton* and museum are open daily 9.00 to 12.30 (Fridays, 9.00 to 11.30).

There is a different but equally absorbing museum in the **MANGKUNEGARAN PALACE**, north of Jalan Slamet Riyadi at the top end of Jalan Diponegoro.

At the palace only the museum and the huge front *pendopo*, built for Mangkunegoro IV early in the 19th century, are open to visitors. The *pendopo*, with its dark green columns, their bevelled edges picked out in gold, displays three *gamelan* sets and a fine group of 19th-century coaches and carriages: the lamps are magnificent.

The museum is in the main hall of the palace building, immediately behind the *pendopo*. A regal flight of steps leads past an array of daisies and gilded statues into the hall (open from 9.00 to 12.00 daily, except Sundays; entry Rp.300, or Rp.150 for nationals).

The collection recalls that of an 18th-century gentleman, the sort of inspired amateur who filled his 'cabinets' with a *pot-pourri* of fancies. There are gold-plated dance ornaments, pieces of miniature furniture in filigree gold and coloured enamels, a *sirih*-set in silver-mounted agate; there are dozens of Hindu-Javanese bronzes (mirrors, bracelets, bangles), cases of gold jewellery and superb rings, and amongst a group of tiny bronze statuettes a small dog which must be the prototype of Charlie Brown's Snoopy! The palace also has a fine collection of *wayang topeng* masks, but special permission is needed to see them as they are kept in Mangkunegoro's private quarters.

At Sriwedari Park, on Jln. Slamet Riyadi, is the Radyapustaka Museum with a good though not outstanding collection. It is open from 8.00 to 12.30. The preservation of traditional culture in Solo owes much to the interest of Raden Tumenggung Hardjonagoro who welcomes visitors at his home at Jln. Kratonan 101.

The Sriwedari Park boasts the most accomplished *wayang wong* group in Java. There is a performance every night from 20.00 to 24.00. Dance rehearsals and occasional performances may be seen at the Akademi Seni Karawitan Indonesia (ASKI) and the Pusat Kebudayaan Jawa Tengah, both near the main *kraton*.

The two *kratons* hold important yearly festivals whose exact dates must be checked with a travel agent or hotel, because the Javanese year follows a lunar calendar. Most important are the *Sunan* ceremony, *Sekaten* (with its month-long night market) and the *Garebeg Maulud* festival.

SHOPPING IN SOLO

Solo is a place for the unhurried shopper who likes to explore hidden-away corners in the hope of finding an unexpected treasure . . . and there are treasures to be found which will satisfy most tastes and inclinations. As a starting point, the markets of Solo are worth a few hours of your time.

Halfway between Jln. Slamet Riyadi and the Mangkunegaran Palace, on the righthand side of Jln. Diponegoro, is **PASAR TRIWINDU** (Pasar Windu Jenar), Solo's 'flea market'.

For the devotee of bric-à-brac, curiosities and honest junk, this is paradise indeed. Five minutes' browsing will whet your appetite. Fifteen minutes of plunging from one stall to the next will have you in rhapsodies over stoneware bottles, Japanese teacups, glit-brass uniform buttons with the ciphers of Solo's royal houses, *naga*-buckles inlaid with brass, garnets and brilliants (or at least passable pastes), lovely old bell-jars with cut-glass finials and etched 'MN' initials, brass *sirih* sets, charcoal-heated irons, and a wonderful selection of refurbished hanging oil lamps.

Pasar Trewindu's supply of lamps, of varied ornateness and size, seems to be the best in Java, and apparently limitless. The source must, of course, dry up eventually and prices are therefore rising. Early in 1978 a small hanging lamp in good working order, including the paraffin-bowl and wick, the chain-and-counterweight and the opaque white-glass shade, was fetching upwards of Rp. 10,000–15,000 depending on the ornamentation: 'flowers and baskets' were at the lower end of the scale, but 'lions and palm trees' and similarly extravagant motifs were more expensive; larger lamps, some with as many as six branches, were of course more highly priced. If you're considering buying a lamp in Java (most visitors are entranced by them) don't forget that the metal counterweight will add a good five to ten kilos to your baggage.

Lamps aside, there are possibilities for decorating a dozen houses in fond remembrance of the 1920s, another dozen in nostalgic 1930s style, and a handful with a regretful salute to the last days of Europe's gilt-and-candelabra era *circa* 1910: there are plates, cups, incomplete dinner services, tiles, glasses, goblets, statuettes, baignoires, chafing dishes, silver-plated cruet sets, vases, lamp-bases, inkwells, ash-trays, teapots, salvers and rolling-pins.

There's also plenty of out-and-out junk (empty plasma bottles, chipped enamel bedpans), but even amongst the debris you might find quaintly labelled tins that once contained dubious nostrums, old medicine bottles in startling green glass, or an ornate temperature-gauge which in 1913 decorated the bonnet of a long forgotten automobile.

Prices at Pasar Trewindu depend a lot on one's bargaining expertise, though it is the kind of place where you may feel that whatever you buy is a bargain.

Another off-beat shopping event is the **TOY MARKET**, open daily in the front grounds of the Radyapustaka Museum (Sunday is best). Simple materials, cut, hammered, sawn and brightly painted, are turned into simple toys which mostly clatter, clank, clunk and click when pulled along

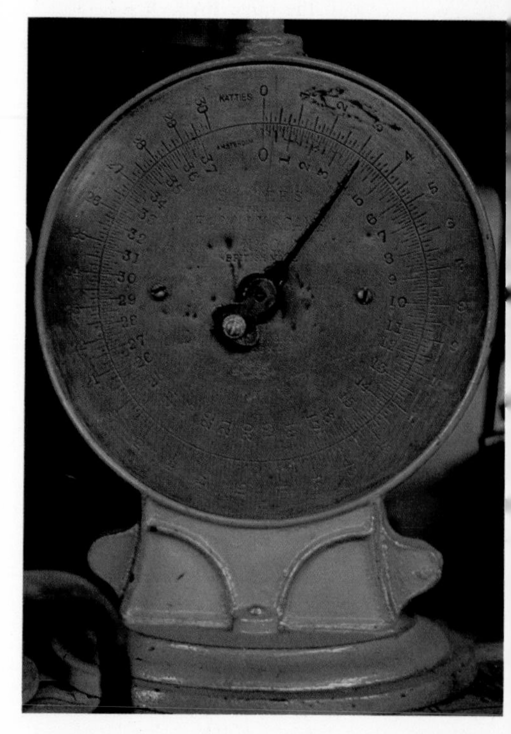

hopping starts
t Solo's 'flea market',
asar Trewindu.

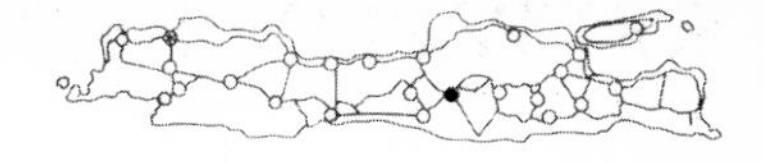

t the end of a string. Their lifespan is predictably rief, but they're a delightful change from plastic, sychologist-approved toys at three or four times he price. Longer lasting are pieces of old-ashioned wooden dolls' house furniture, and olourful metal tea-sets prettied up with flowers nd painted posies. If your taste runs to the rotesque you could buy a very inexpensive ottery doll (crudely coloured in orange, black nd silver), or a cardboard *wayang kulit* figure ung together with paper staples. They're non-ense, but fun. More practical, and delightful oys for both adults and children, are miniature *amelan* xylophone sets whose eleven silver-ainted keys, set between painted wooden ends, re perfectly tuned to the strange intervals of lassical *gamelan* music.

Solo has long enjoyed a reputation as one of ava's most important *batik* centres, and calls tself the City of Batik. To discover vhy, pay a visit to the huge **PASAR KLEWER** t the eastern end of Jln. Secoyudan, under the hadow of the west gate to the *alun-alun lor*. The entire market is devoted to fabrics, with undreds of neat stalls jammed together along arrow passageways on two floors. *Batik* is verwhelmingly predominant, though some stalls pecialise in *lurik* of various grades and a few ffer *kain ikat* and other materials.

But *batik* is the life blood of Pasar Klewer, and he whole enormous complex is more like a vholesale clearing house than a retail outlet. This can be confusing, for it is difficult to be ure about who is selling to whom: *batik* makers r their agents sell their wares to a stallholder vho in turn sells it to another middleman (or voman) who sells it to a retailer; sometimes the tallholder is the maker; or the stallholder might e the wholesaler and the maker and the retailer. Not that it matters. The result is a bewildering rray of choice *batiks*.

The only caution is this. The market is a place vhere professionals do business with other rofessionals (in a broad sense, 'professional' lso includes the *desa* housewife shopping for a sarong, for she too has spent her life in a world of *batik*). The lengths of cloth, whether sarong or *kain* or *selendang*, are seldom displayed in full, and it is difficult for the casual visitor to judge the merits of a design when all that can be seen is a couple of centimetres sandwiched between a mass of other patterns, or when a small cellophane window reveals only a segment of a tantalising design.

Despite rising prices, Pasar Trewindu is still a narvellous place for bargain hunting . . . or just for browsing.

Still, if you do your homework at some of the good display centres in Yogyakarta (see page 190), and if you know what you like and what you're looking for, the Solo *batik* market is exhilirating and rewarding. The bargaining is tough, and you need to have a good idea of prices. Much of the *batik* is in the muted Central Javanese style (colours of indigo, brown and cream pre-dominate), though some traditional designs are available in brighter colours. There is also a fair selection of the more colourful north coast patterns from such areas as Pekalongan, though you won't find any of the 'boutique' or contemporary designs and colours that are being produced by the new breed of *batik* makers.

Amongst all the *batiks* you may come across stalls festooned with long strips of velvet (black, green, blue, turquoise, rose) edged with gold or silver braid, and wider lengths of plain material ranging in colour from salmon pink to vermilion: these make up the traditional belt-and-sash still worn by Solonese men with their 'court dress'. The sash or wrap-around cummerbund keeps the meeting point of shirt and sarong-top firmly in place, and also (more importantly) holds the kris and scabbard that are tucked into the back of the sash. The colourful braided belts are fastened with buckles which are often finely wrought. Pre-shaped and folded *batik* headdresses in traditional style are also on sale. Beside Pasar Klewer there are a number of well-known *batik* shops and factories.

To the northeast of Pasar Klewer, across the river at the bottom end of Jln. Urip Sumoharjo, is **PASAR BESAR**, the general market with much the same merchandise as Yogya's Pasar Beringharjo. Its chief attraction is the market building itself, two-storeyed with outside balconies and an inner gallery overlooking the main body of the market. On street level, outside, there's a coffee merchant's shop where the aroma of roasted beans and freshly ground coffee, in many blends and varieties, will drive a coffee-nut crazy.

Across the road from the back of the market, on the corner of Jln. Wetan Pasar Besar, is Be Thian Kiem, a goldsmith's shop where silver-plated trophies gather cobwebs and a gigantic 'watch' without any hands glowers at the passing parade. Under a glass-topped counter a score of small saucers hold the glittering residue of a long-lost era: lozenges of shimmering black jet, straight out of the '30s; miniature cameos (a dancing girl in a Ginger Rogers ballgown) and metallic clusters of faceted marcasite; and a hoard of agate, chrysoprase, jasper, moonstone, amethyst, coral, jade, topaz, garnet, turquoise, tourmaline and pale sapphire. Not exactly a king's ransom, but if you're looking for cut or cabochon stones for a ring or cufflinks, for a pendant or bracelet, this is a happy hunting ground and prices are reasonable.

At Jln. Urip Sumoharjo 117, on the left-hand side (west) is Toko Singowidodo. Amongst an extraordinarily varied range of **ANTIQUES AND CURIOS**, including hundreds of fossils and cabinets full of all kinds of surprises, you'll find a good range of large chunks of semi-precious rocks: uncut, unpolished, but a flourishing mine for the amateur lapidary.

There is a good choice of antiques at Toko Parto Art in Jln. Slamet Riyadi, where fine reproductions of furniture (mostly cabinets and chairs) are of particular interest. Pak Partosuwarno, the owner, employs a number of skilled woodcarvers from Jalanggu, and their work is amongst the finest in Java. If you'd like to see real artisans at work, surrounded by a treasure trove of ancient chests and cabinets which are scheduled for restoration, Pak welcomes visitors at his home workshop at Kusumoyudan Timur RT 3B. This is one case where owning a reproduction can be as rewarding as owning the original.

Another source of outstanding reproduction furniture is Mirah Delima in Jln. Kemasan RT XI, where the specialty is chairs with superbly carved and bowed backs and legs. The works are not antiques, though the excellent finishes suggest they might be.

On the trail of exotica you can indulge yourself in **DANCERS' REQUISITES** at Toko Serimp on the corner of Jln. Hayam Wuruk and Jln Ronggo Warsito, or across the road at Toko Bedoyo (both shops are owned by the same family). These are theatrical suppliers' retail outlets, not souvenir shops, but of course you are welcome to inspect and buy a glorious range of anything and everything connected with the dressing of *wayang wong* and classical dance.

There are costumes, monkey masks with moveable lower jaws for Hanuman and the ape army, spangled golden head-dresses, the checked cloths worn by the clownish *panakawans*, gilded bracelets and armbands, painted or unpainted *topeng* masks, coloured gloves and matching tights worn by the various monkey regiments and stage krises of menacing realism. There are even a few old-fashioned buckles, though most items are new.

A two-stringed *rebab*, with a beautifully turned neck and delicate tuning-screws, can be bought or made to order at the **GAMELAN ASSEMBLY** workshop in Jln. Gambuhan 30, quite close to the *kraton*. A *rebab*, complete with its bow and ready for playing, will cost around Rp 35,000; a carrying case is extra. There is also a big selection of the various kinds of percussion instruments that make up the rest of the *gamelan* orchestra.

Many kinds of Javanese music, *gamelan* music with or without vocal accompaniment, and the music which accompanies the many forms of *wayang* (from puppets to people), are now available on pre-recorded cassette tapes. If you like browsing and strolling, a walk down Jln. Secoyudan, the goldsmiths' street, can be entertaining: not just for the dozens of *toko mas* with their golden baubles, but also for some of the names ('King Kong' sits uneasily as the name of a jeweller's shop).

For liquid refreshment in between shopping forays, try the delicious iced drinks at Seger Ayam at Jln. Secoyudan 16; *es sirsak* (iced soursop) is particularly good. For a meal or a snack, there is a row of small warungs on Jln. Diponegoro near the entrance to Pasar Triwindu, which also serve iced fruit drinks in any combination.

Amidst a treasure-trove of antiques and curios a stallholder waits for a customer.

Directly to the east of Solo lies the 3,265-metre bulk of Gunung Lawu, its gently rolling foothills smothered with *padi* and peanuts, its higher slopes clad with pine forests, virgin bushland and, frequently, swathes of dense white mist. The main road eastwards to Madiun and Surabaya skirts the northern edge of the mountain, but there are two reasons for travelling up or even over Lawu: the first is for a glimpse of one of Java's most mysterious temples; the second is for some inspiring scenery.

CANDI SUKUH, 910 metres up on Lawu's western flank, is sometimes billed as 'Java's only example of erotic temple carving'. If erotic means the explicit presentation of a stone penis or two, then the description fits, though don't expect the convoluted couplings found in some Nepalese and Indian art. Sukuh's appeal lies in its blend of mystery, of dark disarray, of almost satanic majesty, presented in a superb setting. It is utterly different in mood and in structure from temples elsewhere in Java, and this alone makes it worth seeing.

Five kilometres east of Solo take a right fork off the main road towards Karangpandan and Tawangmangu. Just through Karangpandan, a few metres beyond the 'TAW-12' kilometre post there is a side-road to the village of Kemuning. Follow this road for 5 km and turn off at the Candi Sukuh signpost for the steep climb up to the temple. The road is surfaced all the way. If you do not have your own transport, take the bus to Karangpandan, and then a *bemo* to the Candi Sukuh signpost. You will have to walk the final kilometer or two; or you can charter a *bemo* at Karangpandan to take you there and bring you back. There is a small charge to enter the temple grounds.

Built in the middle of the 15th century during the twilight years of glorious Mojopahit, on a

A trek to Candi Sukuh,
Java's 'erotic' temple.

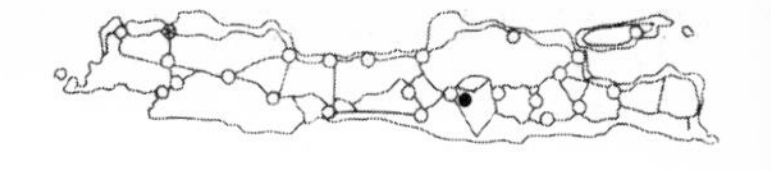

site which may once have been occupied by a temple dedicated to ancestor worship, Sukuh strikes a disquieting, alien chord with its flat-topped 'Egyptian' step-pyramid and its 'Mayan calendar' carvings. Only after a while do the familiar *panakawan* clowns, carved in the distorted *wayang kulit* style found in East Java, emerge intelligibly from the crude reliefs, weird and shocking after the sculptural finesse of Loro Jonggrang. A fertility cult may have been the *raison d'être* for Sukuh; certainly, it is a priapic paradise.

Although some of the carving at Candi Sukuh, on Gunung Lawu, is explicitly phallic it can hardly be called erotic or obscene, for it sings the praises of fertility with exuberance and exaggeration, and even with humour; only a puritan could fail to be impressed by the temple's mystery and grandeur.

At the top of the first stairway leading through a split gateway you'll tread on (or over) a large phallus aimed at a plump *yoni* and surrounded by browning rose petals left by previous supplicants.

Farther up the grassy terraces, at the edge of the main temple complex, a well-endowed boar (once part of a splendid high-relief frieze) gazes stonily down his snout at an even grander elephant. Under the shadow of the central temple and its guardian trees a headless gentleman clutches a club in one hand and his own bell-bedecked penis in the other.

Not all is phallic.

In its setting of steep, pine-clad hills, Sukuh possesses an impressive grandeur. In the main courtyard are interesting sculptures, enhanced by the eclectic styles.

Three enormous flat-backed tortoises stand like sacrificial altars on a stone-flagged courtyard. A roughly hewn demon glares balefully at the

Wild, primeval and magnificent—the road to Sarangan.

world, a sharp-beaked *garuda* is a hovering angel of death one one side of an obelisk, an anthropomorphic elephant is the proud proprietor of a blacksmith's shop hung with krises and swords. Figures crowd one another within the stylised outline of a womb. The unadorned pyramid squats heavily, four-square on the ground.

Sukuh poses many questions that remain unanswered. Were its builders religious refugees from East Java? Were they the locally-born, mountain-dwelling inheritors of an ancient faith? Were they, perhaps, the survivors of the great Central Javanese kingdoms of the 9th and 10th centuries? What were the origins of their diverse and seemingly unrelated sculptural styles?

We don't know, though that hardly matters, for not knowing enhances Sukuh's spell.

The surrounding landscape, steep and pine-clad, is the perfect complement to Sukuh's allure. There are a number of trails which begin close to the temple and lead high up the forested slopes of Lawu. Just to the right of the temple grounds there is a small, clean *pondok* which will sleep four people, and which makes an ideal 'base camp' for exploratory walks. There is no fixed price for accommodation; a nominal fee is asked.

Candi Ceta, with its Bima figures and numerous terraces, was built about the same time as Sukuh, but is less interesting. It lies beyond Kemuning, some 600 metres higher up the mountain than Sukuh, reached by a bad track.

Back at Karangpandan the road climbs up towards Tawangmangu, a pretty hill town which seems to be filled with white-painted guesthouses. To go farther you'll need a car with plenty of heart: the grades are alarmingly steep, and some of the bends are real 'hairpins'. Neat terraces give way to counterpane plots of cabbages and corn that dip and roll with the hillsides, tended by farmers in black jackets and half-trews, or in sarongs of deepest indigo.

Cultivation disappears. The road gropes ever upward through groves of wild acacias and banks of wildflowers into a sea of mist and dense forest where strands of pale green lichen drip from the trees. In places the road's paving stones are covered with layers of moss, or grown through with stubbly grass.

It's wild, primeval and magnificent. The road eventually crawls over a ridge and winds through the grey light. Woodcutters, ghost-like in the mist as they trim freshly cut logs and pare sticks for their charcoal kilns, may perhaps encroach on the solitude. Soon market gardens appear. The road drops sharply, twisting around sharp bends, and finally reaches **SARANGAN**, a popular cool-climate weekend resort for people from Madiun and the surrounding area. A couple of dozen *losmen*, hotels and guesthouses cluster at the northern edge of Telaga Sarangan, many of them offering superb views across the small lake with its background of soaring wooded peaks. Boating, riding, bush-walking and working up an appetite in the crisp mountain air are the main diversions in Sarangan, which is easily

Children, carrying loads their own weight, trot nonchalantly up and down a track that leaves most visitors gasping and wheezing.

Try extending your trip to the coast near Pacitan, past cup-cake hills.

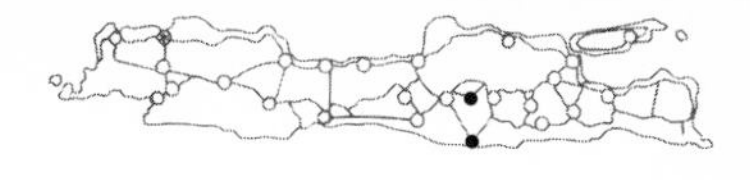

approached from Madiun if you prefer to avoid the low-gear route over Lawu from Solo.

Only five kilometres below Sarangan the little village of **NGERONG** nestles at the head of a pretty valley. There are a few *losmen*, though you may like to stay at the small, modern guesthouse run by Ibu E.M. Anugrah Damajhanty behind the *rumah makan* Anyar. Ibu's back garden is a masterpiece of terracing, and is filled with roses, pumpkins, jerberas, orchids, bonfire salvia, fresh young lettuces (in window-boxes) and a natural stream that tumbles through a steep gully almost straight beneath your breakfast patio.

Before or after breakfast, take one of the tough local ponies ('tough' sometimes means 'stubborn') and explore the local trails through forests and vegetable gardens, meandering from one cobble-stoned village to the next. The experience is one facet of heaven on earth, and the hire of a pony is quite cheap.

With two or preferably three days to spare, your jaunt to Candi Sukuh, Tawangmangu and Sarangan or Ngerong can be extended to include a surfing beach, harshly beautiful landscapes, a *gamelan* 'orchestra' with limestone stalactites for instruments, and a hundred hills looking like giant cup-cakes.

The destination is **PACITAN**, across the border in East Java on an estuarine plain where the Kali Grindulu runs into the sea and meets long lines of rollers sweeping into the broad bay.

With Solo as your point of departure and return there are several possible routes. You can go east around Gunung Lawu to Madiun, or across Lawu to Sarangan; in both cases you then head south to Ponorogo and on to Pacitan, and complete the circuit by coming back through Wonogiri for a total of roughly 300 km. An alternative is the southern route direct from Solo through Wonogiri to Pacitan, and back the same way, but a punishing 30-km stretch of pot-holed road beyond Wonogiri is bearable only once, not twice.

The road from Ponorogo follows a tortuous, tough course along the corkscrew turns of the Grindulu valley, riding high along cliff-tops and sheer hillsides, crawling under rocky overhangs, plunging into tight gullies crowded with teak or plots of corn. Ragged terraces of cassava scramble to the tops of blunted hills; a landslide has exposed a great red scar of earth and rock; seams of blue-grey clay are scoured for lodes of abrasive pumice; and immense boulders cling precariously to weathered hillsides, others lie like devil's marbles where they have come to rest on the valley floor. This is a spare, dry, handsome beauty.

A rapid series of bridges, a widening valley, then the plain, then Pacitan. Check with the *bupati* (the *kantor kabupaten* is one of a group of buildings backing the grassy square at the southern end of town), and you may be able to stay the night at the *pasanggrahan*, a kind of lodge, seven kilometres beyond Pacitan on the southwestern side of the bay. The cost is quite reasonable and the two-bedroomed cottage can sleep four comfortably and six at a pinch; take your own food. Fifty metres away is a large, clean public swimming pool which is usually deserted on weekdays. If the *pasanggrahan* is unavailable, there are clean *losmen*-style rooms on one side of the bus station in Pacitan.

The cottage, though a mite jaded, can be enjoyable, with a constant roar of crashing surf and a tree-framed view of a long crescent of grey-gold sand, white foam and dull green waves. The beach is accessible down a side-road about two kilometres back towards Pacitan, or can be walked and waded to from the cottage. The surf, which breaks heavily some distance from the shore, is quite safe closer to the beach. On the sand above the high-tide mark salt-bleached outriggers, looking utterly unseaworthy, huddle in a semblance of shipwreck.

On the way from Pacitan to the cottage, in a wilderness of windswept grass and odd sticks of cactus, is a Greek temple. Severe, classical, unbelievable. At the south end the pediment is inscribed 'R.I.P.'; at the north end, *Gegaan maar niet vergeten*, 'Gone but not forgotten'. A coffin-shaped sarcophagus lies amid the fluted columns, its long, well-chiselled inscription still unscarred, still legible, and utterly incomprehensible: it is in code from start to finish.

The most imposing view of the coastline is from a rubble-strewn ridge about 15 km out of Pacitan on the 105-km route to Wonogiri. The road soon loses itself in a crazy jumble of low, rounded

Nature music played on stalactites at Gua Tabuhan.

hills, terraced with rock walls right to their summits, sometimes blistered with exposed faces of limestone, sometimes blackened by the jagged mouths of caves which have, over a thousand years of history, sheltered kings, guerrillas, rebels and revolutionaries.

GUA TABUHAN, one of the finest caves, is said to have provided refuge for Prince Diponegoro during his five-year war against the Dutch. Purely as a cavern, hung with grey-white columns of quilted, rippled limestone (some of them still dripping, still growing) it is impressive. The vast antechamber, spattered with brilliant moss, seems to end abruptly in a dark dank corner until the flickering yellow light of bamboo torches reveals a small opening leading to another 50 metres of eerie, shiny-wet tunnel where hordes of little boys, acting as guides and guardians, will make you feel like Snow White making a royal progress through the Seven Dwarfs' mine. The tunnel floor is uneven and slippery, and the ceiling is skull-cracking low in some places.

The big event at Gua Tabuhan is the 'orchestral' performance in the main chamber. There is one small double-ended drum, with drummer. He sets the beat. There is one old man and six young boys, all clutching hard lumps of rock, and almost hidden behind an organ-pipe cluster of hefty stalactites; three of the smaller boys are wedged into crevices two or three metres above the floor, and only their feet can be seen. Then the music starts. Pure *gamelan* melodies clinking and resonating in perfect pitch as rock strikes rock, each stalactite vibrating and booming and singing like a monstrous tuning fork. The old man has the pick of the instruments: two blows, struck a handspan apart on the same column, produce two notes in perfect harmony. Ten minutes, three melodies. This is no free concert so do a little friendly bargaining

The last *dalang* of *wayang beber* at Donorojo.

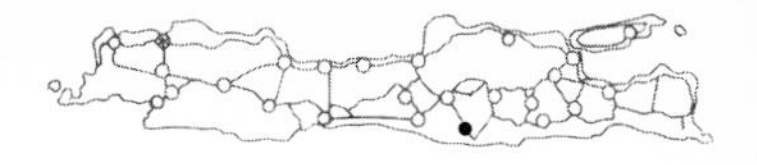

beforehand. Other boys, perhaps less accomplished as musicians, sell souvenirs: fist-sized lumps of hard, brilliant white quartz. Broken down into wearable chunks, the quartz is attractive set in silver as a ring or pendant, or some other item of jewellery.

The road leading to Gua Tabuhan is a *desa* track in much better condition than the main road. The turn-off is well sign-posted: approaching from Pacitan it is three kilometres beyond Punung; from Wonogiri, it is 2.7 km beyond Donorojo. The track runs one kilometre in from the main road, and another signpost guides you left for the last 1.5 km to the cave entrance.

DONOROJO is famous for two things: agate and *wayang beber*. Agates are found in the gullies and river-beds of the surrounding area, and a thriving cottage industry cuts and polishes the stones. They are for sale.

Wayang beber is an ancient and almost extinct form of storytelling in which the tale literally unwinds on a series of painted scrolls. The last remaining practitioner of this art, the *dalang* 'Pak Sarnen, lives in a village near Donorojo and performs about seven times a year. His scrolls carry episodes from the *Panji* tales, and the responsibility for their care is shared by families in the area. Experts agree that the scrolls are extremely old. Although it is impossible to date them conclusively, there may be some truth in the local belief that the scrolls once belonged to the royal dynasty of Mojopahit, and were given for safekeeping to 'Pak Sarnen's ancestors when Muslim Demak was rising to power in the north.

The co-operative care of the scrolls means they are not always in the same place, and they may take some tracking down. If you speak to the *camat* (head of the sub-district or *kecamatan*) at his office on the main road in Donorojo, you may be able to see the scrolls; finding them will probably take a couple of hours. You might even be lucky enough to see a performance.

A little beyond Donorojo, still in the hills and heading towards Wonogiri, the road crosses the border between East and Central Java. In case you miss the boundary maker, a large painted emblem of the Diponegoro Division ('Central Java's Own') will tell you where you are. This is the northern edge of the coastal range. Below you, the road winds down onto the plains and into a familiar landscape of *padi* and palms. Shortly before Wonogiri there's a seemingly precarious ride across a long railway bridge: the 'roadway' timbers on either side of the railway lines are splintered, cracked and even missing, but the prospect becomes less nerve-racking when you realise that fully-laden freight trains make the crossing.

If you're still in the mood for scenic vistas and an energy-consuming climb, a high pinnacle of rock, at the back of Wonogiri, offers superb views across the plains to Merapi, Merbabu, Lawu and the hills to the south.

A detail (left) from one of the ancient wayang beber *scrolls, at least three centuries old, which are preserved near Donorojo and still used a few times each year.*

SOLO TO SURABAYA

Skirting Gunung Lawu, with its temples, hill resorts and lake, the main road east from Solo is a fast 118 km to Madiun, the focal point of Java's abortive communist uprising in 1948. Fomented by pessimists and opportunists who thought the infant Republic, besieged by the Dutch, was doomed, the brief but bloody insurrection was put down by the famous Siliwangi Division commanded by General Nasution.

Madiun's place in history is assured, but it is otherwise a hot, sprawling, hazy town, simmering in a broad valley between two major peaks, and with little charm. However, railway buffs should note that it is the major repair and maintenance centre for Java's locomotives, which are serviced at the *Balai Yasa P.J. Kereta-api;* there, too, can be found the oldest working locomotive on the island, an ancient veteran that took to the rails in 1881 and which still makes short runs.

East of Madiun the road traverses harsh, straggly country towards Nganjuk and joins the broad valley of the Brantas River at Kertosono opening up a smooth, fast run to Trowulan.

TROWULAN, 17 km beyond Jombang, is little more than the main road, a handful of houses, and the museum. Unless you're careful you can be through it in a minute and not even know it. The museum is worth stopping for.

Justly famous for its Mojopahit terracotta statuary, the museum sits splendidly in a large garden crowded with frangipani trees and brick-bordered garden beds filled not with flowers but with thousands of archaeological rejects: lumps of ornamented terracotta, weather-ravaged stone carvings and countless shards of celadon-glaze and blue-and-white pottery.

Inside the museum, the collection consists mainly of articles made from fired clay. There are dozens of small portrait heads, many unmistakably Chinese in mien; a figure wears what looks like a European frockcoat; and one delightful fragment shows a dog biting the heel of a fleeing person. There is a big, roughly modelled, but expressive, headless torso of a heavily pregnant woman; there are dozens of miniature step-roofed *candis* with intricate incised designs, which may have been builders' or architects' models; and there are water vessels in the form of cockerels, or shaped like a mythical half-fish, half-frog. There is also some good stone sculpture, a collection of bronze statuettes and domestic artifacts (a marvellous beaker with *wayang kulit* ornament), a mixed bag of silver coins and Chinese porcelain, and a few fascinating pieces of woodcarving (dry rot is unhappily claiming some of them). Unfortunately there is the usual dearth of informative labels, and identifying pieces (date, origin, purpose) is left to one's knowledge or imagination.

Everything in the Trowulan museum has reputedly been found within a ten-kilometre radius, an area which was probably the seat of Mojopahit power. A detailed table-top map on the porch of the museum is a useful guide to nearby sites and remains, including *Wringin Lawang*, a gateway which may have led to the residence of Gajah Mada, the kingdom's famous prime minister.

Two of the more interesting remains are **CANDI TIKUS** and **CANDI BAJANG RATU.** The pretty country lane that leads to them is lined with trees and white brick fences with temple-roof gateposts; behind the fences are small, neat, white-washed and mostly windowless plaited-bamboo houses, their verandahs stone-paved, their verandah posts of unhewn wood, their doors often providing a colourful splash of yellow and green.

Neither Candi Tikus nor Candi Bajang Ratu is in fact a *candi* in the sense of being a temple. Tikus is an ancient bathing place, once resplendent with three water-filled pools (now dry) which were fed through a series of stone *kala*-head spouts. Bajang Ratu, about 500 metres from Tikus, is a fine, tall red-brick gateway with striking terracotta *kala* heads; long-nailed fingers on either side of the heads seem to anticipate today's 'peace' sign. The gateway, one of the best preserved in Java, is cared for by an elderly man who will probably try to sell you a 'Mojopahit kris', and is surrounded by a lush growth of papaya trees, shaded by an ancient *waringin* tree, and backed by white frangipanis and a blaze of scarlet hibiscus which bloom in a small Muslim cemetery.

Another cemetery of far greater historical importance is located at Troloyo (or Tralaja),

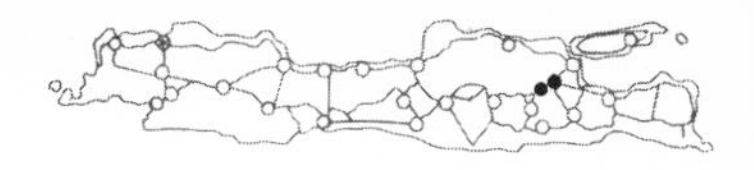

roughly two kilometres south of Trowulan. Here, in a summery setting of coconut palms and banana trees where pigeons coo and grass-hoppers clack in the dry grass, are the gravestones of some of the later members of the Mojopahit dynasty. Recent research shows that the oldest headstone dates from 1376 (1298 according to the ancient Javanese *saka* calendar); it is thought to be Muslim and, if so, would deprive the tomb of Maulana Malik Ibrahim (1419 A.D.) in Gresik of its claim to be the oldest Muslim grave in Java.

Back on the main road, and heading east out of Trowulan, a further 10 km will bring you to **MOJOKERTO.** The town straddles yet another arm of the mighty Brantas River, and offers a number of pleasures: in the old quarter, west of the main street, are charming traffic-free alleys (or *gangs*) lined with miniature canals; there are many imposing columned houses from 'the Dutch time'; and on Jln. Jen. Achmed Yani there is an excellent museum of Mojopahit stone carving and sculpture.

The finest work, however, is probably a thousand years old: a magnificient 'portrait statue' of King Airlangga as Visnu mounted on a huge and formidable *garuda*, once the centre-piece of a sculptural group which decorated the Belahan bathing place in the foothills above Pandaan.

There are other pleasures and treasures in the Mojokerto museum: a 'figure-head' water-spout of a slender, nubile young lady of astonish-ing sexiness; a pair of princes casually holding hands; and a series of stylised landscape panels, from Trowulan, filled with rivers, fields, forests, rice-terraces and animals. In a side gallery is a fragment of a giant fish (the head measures one metre across), and a superbly detailed *raksasa* moulded in terracotta and almost alive.

The museum opens every morning at 7 o'clock. It closes at 12.00 on Sundays, 13.00 on Fridays, and 14.00 on other days. Admission is by donation. To get there, take the main street through town (heading towards the bridge across the Brantas), and turn right into Jln. Jen. Achmed Yani where the main road breaks into a large square.

Surabaya is 42 km beyond Mojokerto. The road is quite good.

SEMARANG TO SURABAYA

For many travellers the journey from Semarang to Surabaya is likely to be more satisfying as a voyage of the spirit than as a physical encounter. There is little to see that *must* be seen, and a lot of dross between the few small nuggets.

With Semarang as your base, one-day return trips to Demak, Kudus and Jepara can be done comfortably. These towns can also be visited if you're travelling straight through to Surabaya, a route which runs through Demak, Rembang, Tuban, Babat and Gresik on a road that is generally wide, tar-sealed and often appallingly corrugated. The optional route from Rembang through Blora and Bojonegoro to Babat is shattering in more ways than one, and is not recommended; the stretch from Blora to Cepu on the border of East Java has some attractive, heavily timbered teak forests, but at both ends of both routes (and at the Gresik end in particular) the vistas are relentlessly boring: flat and mostly treeless rice plains, desolate salt pans, and scarred and quarried limestone ridges. This is not the stuff that dreams are made on!

Yet dream a wild dream of oriental riches. Let your imagination run riot through the aromas and perfumes of anice, aloes, benzoin, camphor, cinnamon, cloves, frankincense, mace, musk, naphtha, nutmeg, pepper and rose water; savour the weight and texture of carved woodwork, cherrywood, ebony, iron, ivory, lacquered wood, porcelain, salt, sandalwood, sapanwood, silver, sulphur and tin; taste the brandy, dates, preserved peaches, rhubarb, rice and sugar; listen to the calls of cassowaries, parrots and peacocks; clap your eyes on areca nuts, beeswax, Chinese copper coins, cotton cloth, elephants' tusks, glass bottles, hornbills' head-feathers, indigo, resin, rhinoceros horn, silk, tortoise-shell and white monkeys; dazzle your senses with visions of beads, carnelian, coral, crystal rings, diamonds, gold and pearls.

A dream? Perhaps so. But from the first to the 17th centuries these items, and more, were recorded on the bills of lading of the great junks, galliots, *prahus* and other vessels that traded, careened, chandlered and vittled at Java's ports, their holds brim-full and their deck-space jammed with treasures carried from the ports of Cambay, Calicut and Coromandel, from Canton and Tonkin, from Siam, Malacca, Jambi, Ambon, Borneo, the Moluccas.

Banten and Cirebon, away to the west, enjoyed a small slice of this trade during the 16th century, but it was the ports east of Semarang that revelled in the largesse for more than a thousand years: Jepara, Rembang (with its ship-building industry), Tuban (Mojopahit's sea-link with the world until about 1400), Brondong, Gresik, Jaratan (slightly east of Gresik) and Surabaya.

During the 15th and 16th centuries the men who ruled these ports, and the towns of Demak and Kudus, were for the most part native Javanese of wealth and power who had been born to (or converted to) Islam, and many came from noble families. Nine of these shrewd, tough, capable men have been suitably immortalised as the *Wali Songo* or 'Nine Saints' to whom the effective establishment of Islam in Java is attributed. Eight of them were in time given the epithet of *sunan* or 'prince'; the ninth, Malik Ibrahim, became known by the honorific *maulana* or 'great teacher'. With the exception of Sunan Gunung Jati, who was buried near Cirebon, the *walis* now lie in hallowed graves between Demak and Surabaya, and their tombs are pilgrimage points.

For more than fifty years **DEMAK** was the undisputed nonpareil amongst the coastal states, conquering Cirebon in 1475, and Palembang and Jambi shortly afterwards; it became a Muslim sultanate under Raden Patah in 1511, its forces had destroyed the feeble and shadowy successors of Mojopahit by 1520, and in 1526 Falatehan (also known as Sunan Gunung Jati, and perhaps Demak's most illustrious son) established the sultanate of Banten before capturing Sunda Kelapa, the site of modern Jakarta, in 1527.

The end came in 1546 when Demak succumbed to its once quiescent vassal and rice port, Jepara. Its vast *alun-alun* is today dominated by a mosque with a three-tiered roof; the mosque is said to have been founded jointly by the *Wali Songo*. Legend and history aside, the interior is cool, lofty and disappointingly bland.

In **KUDUS**, 24 km to the east, the past is more tangible. The oldest part of the town, Kauman, lies a little west of the river on the

)emak and Kudus,
nce great ports in
ava's maritime history.

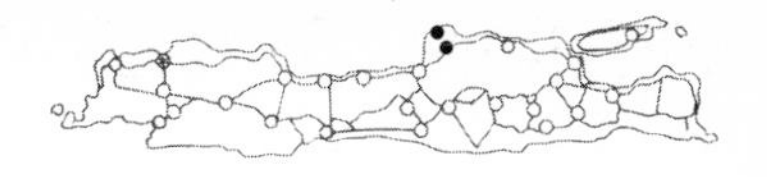

oad to Jepara and is the site of a mosque founded y Ja'far Shadiq (Sunan Kudus). The tall red-rick minaret, its third level marked by a orizontal line of Chinese export porcelain dishes nd its roof capped by a more recent pillared avilion and an anachronistic clock from Arabia, ates from the early 16th century and may nce have been part of a Hindu-Javanese temple tructure.

Behind the *menara* (minaret), through a maze f walls, tiny doorways and secluded corners, the tomb of the *sunan*, surrounded by the any graves of his descendants. Even today ere are townsfolk of humble means who roudly carry the title of *raden*, denoting their lood ties with the great *wali*. His mausoleum hung with a fine curtain of lace which all ut obscures the delicate lattice-work carving n honey-coloured stone walls; a small doorway, ilfully carved and chiselled, and hung about with gold embroidered cloth, leads through one wall to an inner chamber and the grave.

The name Kudus comes from the Arabic *al kuds* (holy), and the town is the only one in Indonesia with an Arabic name. This 'holy' title, coupled with the style of the ancient minaret, suggests that Kudus may have been an important religious centre before the coming of Islam; there is also a tradition decreeing that cows should never be slaughtered in the town, and this may be a misty legacy of a Hindu past. Nevertheless the character of the narrow streets around the old mosque is unabashedly Muslim and even Middle Eastern in feeling. Certainly it is not the Java of bamboo-walled *desa* dwellings. Here the houses stand tight and tall, often hidden behind high stone walls, white and blind to the outside world; many of them are imposing

Jepara, home of woodcarving artisans.

Finely carved teak and ebony chess sets, too, at Jepara.

structures with prettily ornamented eaves and broad areas of carved, unpainted wood.

Kudus is also *Kota Kretek* ('Cigarette City'). More than one hundred businesses, large and small, help account for roughly a quarter of Indonesia's annual production of clove-flavoured *kretek* cigarettes. The noxious weed is known as *sigaret kretek* when wrapped in white paper; in a wrapping of maize-sheath it becomes simply *kretek* or *klobot*; generally the one word, *kretek*, covers both types.

The cigarette industry explains two unusual things that you may notice in Kudus. Carts, wallowing like galleons in a gale, and laden fearsomely high with straw-coloured bundles, are carrying maize-sheaths. And buxom young women, streaming through a gateway as though hell-bent on a Women's Lib demonstration, are nothing more alarming than *kretek*-wrapping factory girls making the most of a work break.

From Kudus, a reasonable side-road can take you 33 km to **JEPARA**, long famous for the skill of its woodcarvers. Although many of Jepara's artisans have been drawn to the bigger cities, and bigger money, this small town is still an active carving centre. Faithful copies of antique chairs and tables are still dowelled, slotted, tongued and joined without a nail to be seen, and there is apparently a heavy demand for extremely detailed and finely worked decorative panels depicting scenes from Javanese mythology and legend.

Most of Jepara's portable products, especially boxes of various sizes, are available in curio-cum-souvenir stores in the larger towns and cities. Less well known are the handsome teak and ebony chess sets: the inlaid board doubles as a carrying case; and every pawn, every piece is carved by hand and has a unique and delightful character. Prices keep rising, but even so the value

Princess Kartini, a modern heroine who espoused emancipation.

In halcyon days, Rembang's wharves and shipwrights were unexcelled.

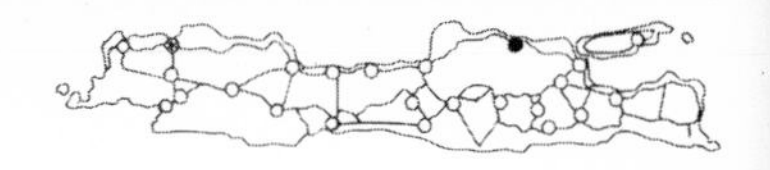

of Jepara's carved wood is outstanding.

Two of the town's daughters have achieved enduring fame. The queen of Jepara, Ratu Kali Nyamat, widowed about the time Jepara overthrew the Demak sultanate, laid siege to Portugal's Malacca stronghold in 1551 and again in 1574 with doubtful support first from Johore and then from Aceh. Although unsuccessful in both campaigns, she scared the Portuguese witless.

Raden Ajeng Kartini belongs to modern Indonesia's pantheon of heroes, a place earned through her spirited espousal of emancipation and freedom. Her writings, published as *Letters of a Javanese Princess,* are famous throughout the country: 'Conditions both in my own surroundings and in those of others around me broke my heart, and made me long with a nameless sorrow for the awakening of my country.' Born in 1879 in Mayong, a small *desa* outside of Jepara, Kartini was the daughter of the regent of Jepara. She married the progressive regent of Rembang, and died at the age of 25 shortly after bearing a son.

Both Kartini and Ratu Kali Nyamat are buried in the grounds of the old mosque at Mantingan, about 19 km south of Rembang on the road to Blora. The original mosque was built at the instigation of Ratu Kali Nyamat, and some of its finely carved reliefs were preserved during reconstruction in 1927.

Around Jepara, and farther east towards **REMBANG**, the roof-ridges of many houses are stunningly ornamented with black glazed finials, inlaid with what looks like mother-of-pearl, and sometimes shaped like a *fleur-de-lys*. The same delight in glitter and mirrorwork can be seen in the rigging of fishing boats drawn up on the beach at Rembang, where coloured fringes and tassels, and strangely curved rigging poles, evoke ancient sailing glory.

EAST JAVA

It is true that East Java suffers in some respects from comparisons with other parts of the island. Its many temples do not quite match the majesty and grandeur of Borobudur or Loro Jonggrang. Its kingdoms (Kediri, Singosari, Mojopahit) are preserved in a few pieces of ancient bronze and terracotta but not as extensive living palaces like the 18th-century *kratons* of Mataram's descendants. The vestiges of East Java's great cultural wealth are also less well preserved than those of West and Central Java, and the mighty coastal cities, once amongst the finest ports of Asia, have little to show of their former glory.

But what East Java does have is raw, natural beauty of peerless variety. Exciting, bewildering, surprising. It is a mass of contrasts and extremes, with desolate salt marshes and perfect southern seacoasts; it is the grand gesture, given without compromise, with sweeps of thorn-tree veld plucked from Africa, steep jungle trails brilliant with butterflies, and sulky smouldering volcanoes. It is a place for the walker, the explorer . . . though it does have its quieter and more restful moments. It is more demanding, physically, than the other provinces, and that too is part of the appeal of East Java.

Moonrise over Mt. Batok (previous pages).

A frequent corollary to outstanding scenery is a lack of accessibility and creature comforts. Though the Regional Tourist Development Board (BAPPARDA Jawa Timur), an active and energetic body, has done and is doing much to improve accommodation facilities, access roads and the like, what is worth seeing in East Java is often hard to get to. By building a bull-racing stadium at Bangkalan on the west coast of Madura and by encouraging *reog* and *kuda kepang* dance groups in Surabaya, BAPPARDA has brought these three attractions closer to the tourist. But even Mohammed had to go to the mountain, and if you want East Java to reveal its charms you'll have to do a lot of the footwork yourself.

There are so many possible routes, day-trips, circuits and voyages of exploration through the hinterland of East Java that a categorical statement on where to go and what to see would be presumptuous. With that qualification in mind, and with up to 4 or 5 days to spare, you'll find an interesting choice of tour bases between 55 and 90 km south of Surabaya. Beyond this point, heading east or west, 'mod cons' virtually disappear and road conditions vary from reasonable to appalling: 40 km on your map, anticipated as an hour's journey at most, may well turn into a 2-hour spine jolter.

Of all Java, this is the one place where (if you don't already have your own car or jeep) you should hang the expense and hire one.

East Java in the following pages is divided firstly into descriptions of 'Surabaya, City Of Heroes' (pages 229 to 232), and then the surrounding main attractions, nearby hill stations, the neighbouring towns of Gresik and Giri, and a visit to the island of Madura in 'Side-trips from Surabaya' (pages 232–237). The second section, entitled 'Temples And Things' (pages 238 to 247), covers the areas that can be reached using Malang or Lawang as a base for explorations of the little-known temples and sights of East Java. 'Byroads To Bali' (pages 248 to 253) suggests three routes to Bali. Probably the most adventuresome and breathtaking nature experiences in Java are described in the last two sections: 'On The Trail' (pages 254 to 259) and 'Bromo, Between Heaven And Hell' (pages 260 to 263). Regular tours take in some of East Java, but to really see this part of the island you should strike out on your own. Along unpaved trails and mountain roads and bush tracks, East Java sheds the last veil.

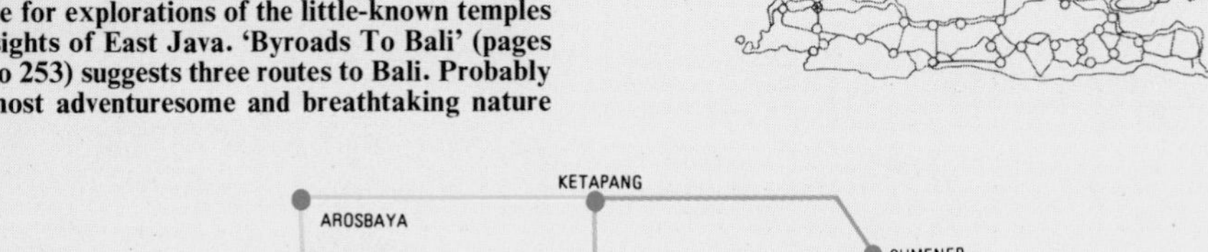

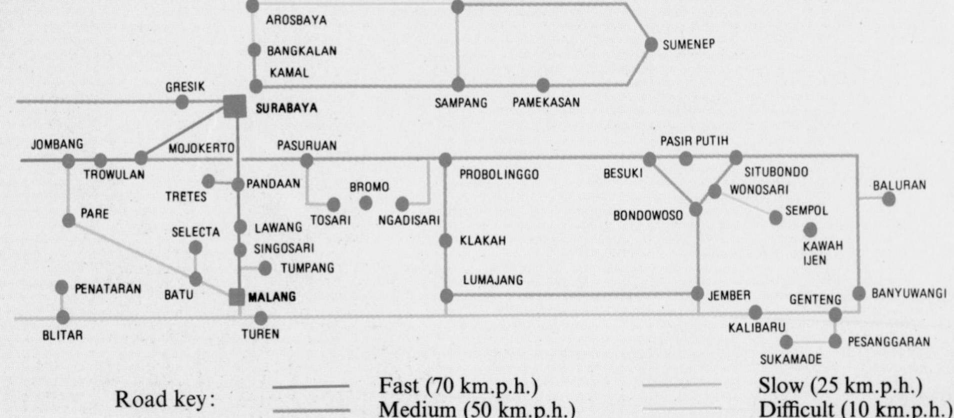

SURABAYA CITY OF HEROES

Surabaya is one of the few places in Java which, as a mere name to the outsider, is likely to evoke Conradian visions: square-riggers in full sail and lusty, brawling seamen drawing knives over a bag of gold or a handful of black pearls; the smells of spices and sandalwood, the reek of caulking pitch and sea-drenched hemp hawsers and copra drying in the sun; dusky maidens and peg-legged, eye-patched skippers; and legendary Surabaya Sue (who really existed).

Today's reality is mundane: Java's and Indonesia's number two city with a port second only to Jakarta's Tanjung Priok in size and importance; capital of East Java, and a vital, progressive centre for trade and manufacturing. Almost nothing remains of the colourful past, though an early-morning stroll along the wharves at Kali Mas (Golden River) at the far north of the city, the world of black-sail Macassar schooners, will whisk you back to the closing decades of the 16th century when Surabaya (once known as Ampel or Ngampel) was master of Sedayu, Gresik, Jaratan, Pasuruan, Panarukan and Blambangan before bowing to the onslaught of Mataram.

It was impossible to forestall the inevitable, and in 1625 Surabaya fell to Mataram's superior numbers after a prolonged and gallant defence, echoed 320 years later in some of the most savage fighting ever seen on Java's soil.

The 'Battle of Surabaya' began on 10 November 1945, less than three months after the Proclamation of Independence had been read in Jakarta:

We the people of Indonesia hereby declare Indonesia's independence. Matters concerning the transfer of power, and other matters will be executed in an orderly manner and in the shortest possible time.
In the name of the Indonesian people:
Soekarno/Hatta

The transfer of power meant one thing to the Indonesian leaders and quite another thing to the British troops who landed in Surabaya in September with the ostensible purpose of disarming the Japanese occupation forces (which the Indonesians had already achieved) and repatriating them, releasing Allied prisoners-of-war, and assuming a caretaker role until the Dutch could reclaim their estate. The result was a confusing and frightening tragedy of errors which led to the murder of the British commander, Brigadier-General Mallaby, in October and to reprisal bombing raids and finally a full-scale British invasion.

The Indonesian forces, hastily assembled, hastily armed, hardly trained (if at all) rallied to the cry *merdeka atau mati*—freedom or death! The British police action became a war of attrition, punctuated by atrocities on both sides, until the invaders' tanks overwhelmed the defenders' rifles and the Surabaya 'rebels' were driven from the city into the hills. The British phlegmatically acknowledged the tenacity of resistance; the outside world, hauling itself out of the wreckage of a disastrous war, was also impressed; and the Indonesians themselves were a little surprised and more than a

Sails are still a familiar sight in Surabaya, where schooners have traded for hundreds of years.

A proud heroes' monument in the city square.

little proud: *merdeka* could be, and would be, fought for.

The Tenth of November is now celebrated nationally as Heroes' Day, and Surabaya is honoured as 'The City of Heroes', with a tall commemorative monument standing aloof and proud in the centre of the main city square.

The city's ancient reputation as a major trading port is still upheld. It enjoyed preeminence during the Dutch regime, and only since independence has Tanjung Priok in Jakarta taken the lead. It is unfair to say that Surabaya is bereft of cultural compensations, but no doubt the last few hundred years of merchant mentality have given the arts little encouragement.

Surabaya's cultural diversions are mainly related to dance, and mostly to forms of dance which are deeply rooted in traditional folklore. The oldest of these is probably *reog Ponorogo*, named after the town lying to the south of Madiun where the dance was once most often performed, though its origins are obscure. There may be a grain of truth in the *reog* adherents' claim that the venerable Balinese *barong* dance was derived from *reog* following the dispersal of Java's Hindu powers in the 16th century (a suggestion hotly disputed by the Balinese), but this of course begs the question of its real origins. Both *reog* and *barong* perhaps owe something to the celebrated Chinese lion dance, but even this is conjecture.

The most striking aspect of *reog Ponorogo* is the huge and ponderously heavy head-dress worn by the main dancer: a tiger mask of ferocious mien surmounted by a magnificent fan of peacock tail-feathers. The mask weighs between 40 and 50 kilos and is mainly supported by a mouth-strap clenched in the dancer's teeth (it is said that a *reog* dancer can be identified by an outstanding muscular neck). Other participants include a small group of *kuda kepang* (bamboo horse) dancers and

At Candra Wilwatikta, a six-month season of East Javanese dance.

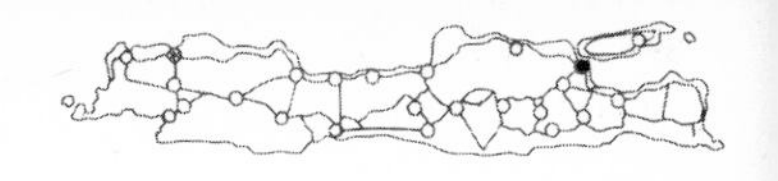

sometimes a trance dancer who does the usual grass-and-glass eating act. *Kuda kepang* can also be seen as a separate dance.

Both dances were and still are traditional town and *desa* activities of considerable ritual significance, but waiting in a remote village for a performance *au naturel* is generally only a little less frustrating than waiting for Godot. However, a number of *reog* and *kuda kepang* dance groups are on permanent call in Surabaya, and special performances can be organised, but try to give a few days notice if possible. The East Javanese Regional Tourist Development Board (BAPPARDA Jawa Timur) at Jln. Yos Sudarso 3 (near the City Hall) will be happy to help you with the details, or ask a travel agent or hotel. One *reog* group, that of Pak Amari Hamzah, is at Jln. Pucang Anom 53.

Although the *Ramayana* and *Mahabharata* have become the common cultural property of the whole of Java, the eastern province may properly claim two of the most popular *Mahabharata* episodes as its own: *Arjuna Wiwaha*, in which Arjuna is tempted by seven delectable nymphs, was composed in the Old Javanese language during the reign of King Airlangga in the 11th century; and the tumultuous *Bharatayuddha* (when the Pandawa brothers and the Korawa family finally stop talking and start fighting) was the work of another Kediri court poet some hundred years later.

Both of the great classics are regular fare at the *wayang wong* theatre in THR (People's Park), leavened with offerings of stories based on East Java's own historical and legendary sagas: *Damar Wulan* (a hero of Mojopahit days), *Menak Jinggo* (the sworn adversary of Damar Wulan, villainous enough to warrant stories in his own right), *Sawunggaling* (a 19th-century freedom fighter). *Ketropak* and *hudruk* are also performed.

Classical dance versions of these tales are also on the programme of the six-month season of East Javanese 'ballet' staged at the open-air **CANDRA WILWATIKTA** amphitheatre at Pandaan, 45 km south of Surabaya on the road to Malang.

Candra Wilwatikta, with the almost-perfect cone of Gunung Penanggungan in the background, was opened in September 1971 as the venue for the First International Ramayana Festival in which a number of dance groups from Asian countries performed national versions of the ancient epic. The theatre has since then been the site of a regular ballet festival held on the first and third Saturday nights of the months May through October.

Comparisons between the Pandaan and Prambanan (Yogyakarta) ballet festivals are largely irrelevant. The latter is exclusively devoted to one version of the *Ramayana* story as it unfolds on the panels of the Prambanan temples, and is performed serially over four consecutive nights. The Pandaan season includes performances of a shorter, one-night version of the *Ramayana* based

Surabaya, Indonesia's second biggest city, is resolutely modern and her main streets all business, but traditional memories surface in the masks of a National Day Parade.

SIDE-TRIPS FROM SURABAYA

on a series of reliefs found on the main temple at Penataran (in East Java), but more than half of the annual programme consists of dances based on East Java's indigenous tales.

Theatre apart, Surabaya has little to hold the visitor. The Arab and Chinese quarters are worth exploring. The zoo (*Kebun Binatang*) in the southeast corner of the city is well stocked and offers the famous 'Komodo Dragon', the world's largest lizard which grows to more than three metres in length. The shopping along Tunjungan is good (some electrical goods are cheaper here than in Singapore). There's water-skiing and boating at PORAS (Surabaya Watersport Club) near the harbour, or you can rent a *prahu* at Kenjeran. You might even make a call on *Joko Dolog*, the statue sculpted at the close of the 13th century to commemorate Prabu Kertonegoro, king of Singosari, and which now stands in front of Government House (*Joko Dolog* translates regally enough as 'guardian of young teak', though many Surabayans irreverently but affectionately refer to the statue as 'fat boy').

There are also some interesting **SIDE-TRIPS** to be made: Gresik and Giri, a short distance to the north-west; the museums at Mojokerto and Trowulan on a good road to the west (see pages 220 and 221), the island of Madura and its famous bull-races, and Tretes in the hills to the south.

Only 55 km south of Surabaya, **TRETES** is one of the prettiest and most pleasing of Java's mountain resorts. The air is fresh, the nights are cool, and the views of mountains and walks through the hillside tracks are very beautiful. There's a range of *losmen*, guesthouses and hotels to suit every pocket, from the cheap to the expensive (which offer all meals, modern private bathrooms with hot water). It is the sort of place for horse-riding in the morning

Tretes, one of Java's most pleasing hill stations.

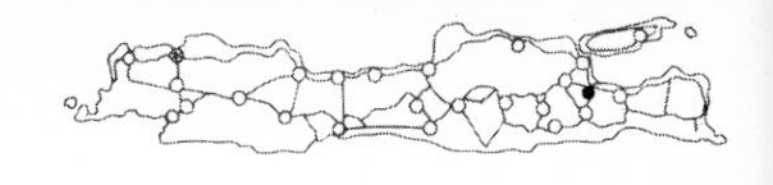

(perhaps to one of the three lovely waterfalls within easy riding distance), a nap after lunch, a huge pot of tea or coffee enveloped in a well-padded tea-cosy at four in the afternoon, and a general feeling of well-being after the heat of the plains.

If you enjoy the motley and the bizarre, drop in at *Iboe Djaja* (Ibu Jaya) about half way between Tretes and Pandaan, an extraordinary house-and-garden crammed with treasures and kitsch: classical stone carvings, bottled snakes, embroidered Chinese wedding robes, fossils, grotesque statuary and precious Ming platters. Room after room of aesthetic disasters and collector's delights. The latter include some beautiful goose-and-gander couples in carved, polychromed wood, once common in the homes of wealthy East Javanese but now seldom seen outside of antique shops.

The geese of the carvings, the legend goes, were once human, once man and wife. The husband unbeknown to his spouse, was *au fait* with the language of animals. Somehow (this is not explained) she caught on to his mysterious power, and demanded to know what two *cicaks* (house lizards) were saying as they chattered in the rafters. The reluctant husband ignored her pleas, but when his good wife threatened to kill herself, the husband capitulated. The *cicaks*, he said, were exchanging words of love. At which point husband and wife became gander and goose. End of story.

'Temple Territory' is covered more extensively on pages 241 to 247, but Candi Jawi, 7 km downhill from Tretes on the Pandaan road, is worth a quick visit. It was built about 1300, after the death of Prabu Kertonegoro, and sometime later (possibly after the earthquake of 1331) a Buddhist stupa was added to the top level of what was basically a Sivaistic structure. The story behind the attractive reliefs on the temple base is still a riddle.

There are also a number of terraced temple sites to be found on the slopes of Gunung Penanggunan (in fact, something like 81 sanctuaries at heights of 750 to 1,500 metres dating variously from 977 to 1511). They are difficult to track down, though the hunt is an excellent excuse for horse-riding and hiking, and some of the horse guides know a few of the sites. The most striking are the remains of 'Airlangga's Bathing Place' at Belahan, approached from about 5 km north of Pandaan on the road to Surabaya. It was from here that the superb and controversial 'portrait' statue of Airlangga as Visnu-on-Garuda (now a brilliant gem in the collection of the Mojokerto Museum) was taken in the early 19th century, but there are still two interesting 'spout' figures identified as Sri and Laksmi, Visnu's wives.

It is safe to assume that within East Java the decline of Hinduism and the rise of Islam were not marked by bloodshed. Certainly, there were wars, but these were political rather than religious, and no *jihad* (holy war) seems to have been waged in the early days of Islam's establishment in the northern coastal ports.

In the cool hill and mountain resorts south of Surabaya, waterfalls, fresh fruits, temples and horse-riding are major attractions.

Gresik and Giri on the sea roads of the past.

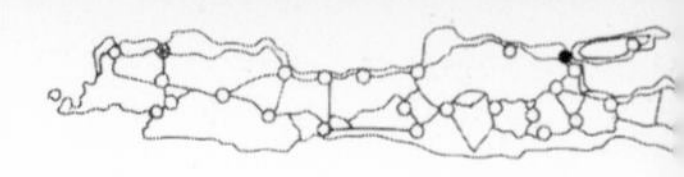

Tomé Pires, a peripatetic Portugese who lived in Malacca between 1513 and 1517, described **GRESIK** as 'the jewel of Java in trading ports where the ships at anchor are safe from the winds, with their bowsprits touching the houses . . . it is called the rich people's port (where) many foreign merchants have settled'. The great trading vessels have long since gone, but in the narrow streets of the old town, where houses with iron-barred windows stand tightly packed and women in white head shawls flit silently by on their way to the *masjid*, it is not difficult to recall Gresik's ancient role as a frontier post of Islam. Maulana Malik Ibrahim (or Magribi), one of the great *walis*, lies buried in Gresik, alongside his wife and children. His tomb, dated 1419, is generally regarded as the oldest Muslim gravestone in Java (a claim is made for one of the modest stones in the ancient cemetery at Troloyo which reputedly dates from 1376).

At **GIRI**, 2 km to the south of Gresik, is the tomb of *wali* Sunan Giri who, like most of his brethren, combined spiritual and temporal powers. He was the founder of a long-lived dynasty (referred to by visiting Europeans as 'the Popes of Grise') which survived as a *desa perdikan* or holy tax-exempt village until overwhelmed by Mataram in 1680, long after the other coastal states had fallen.

The 18 km route to Gresik and Giri is bleak and desolate, a seemingly endless sweep of ugly but economically important grey-and-white salt pans. Their harvesting has a long history, and more than 300 years ago foreign traders noted that 'on these sea roads come also the junks which come from the Molucca Islands and take in some salt until they have a full cargo . . . for there are many salts pans everywhere'.

Muslim schoolgirls, Madurese racing bulls.

Madura, home of bull racing.

Stampeding fury in 600 kilos of rippling muscle.

There is salt, too, on the neighbouring island of **MADURA**. But Madura is also the home of *kerapan sapi* . . .

Ten-thirty in the morning. A pair of big tan bulls, coats sleek and smooth, eye-whites flashing in spasms of fear and excitement. Nostrils snort and tug at nose-ropes and the dry ground soaks up a stream of creamy saliva. A shoulder heaves and a cloven hoof paws the white line. Ten strong men, sinews popping, thrust back against 600 kilos of taut, anxious flesh. A burning sun glints on a sequined head-dress, lights up the pale green shafts of the trailing sled and the crimson satin of the rider's hunched, half-crucified figure, spreadeagled between the rippling tonne of stud stock. The red flag falls. Whips crack.

In roughly 10 seconds two pairs of bulls, their sleds and riders bucketing and swaying, cover 130 metres and drive a foaming wedge of muscled fury into the crowd bunched behind the finishing line. Somehow nobody is killed. Miraculously nobody is injured. This time.

It's a strange sport, this *kerapan sapi*. As the Madurese tell it, it began long ago when plough-team was pitted against plough-team over the length of a rice-field. Part work, part play. Today, stud-bull breeding is big business on an island where the land is too wretched and poor for any more than the scantiest agriculture, and the races, with progressively bigger and better prizes offered by local government, have become a real incentive for stock improvement. Only bulls of a certain standard (condition, weight, colour) can be entered: from August onwards heats are held at district and regency level until the cream of the crop fight it out for the crown, the cups and the money at the grand final in Pamekasan, the island's capital.

Nine in the morning. The bulls parade before the throng as courtiers before Louis XIV, a-jangle

Madura is a spirited and rugged island.

with colours and finery, accompanied by fife and gong; hawkers set up their stands (a riot of rainbow potables); the crowd surges in a mass of purple and yellow, pink and green, ochre and orange; sellers of *pandan* hats slice their wares into shapes-to-order (take a conical hat like an ancient Portuguese helmet and apply a razor-sharp knife: the tightly bound pandanus fronds spring into new, bizarre shapes).

Ten in the morning. The bulls, stripped of their parade regalia, wait calmly behind the scenes with their handlers and supporters. When their moment comes they'll tense like steel springs. Now, they placidly blink their big, bovine eyes and look pretty in their sparkling headbands. Soon, the tornado.

Bull-racing is very partisan. Though it lacks the rattle-and-scarf crew of English soccer and the baton-twirling beauties of college football, it's district against district, regency against regency (even *desa* against *desa*) as far as the adoring crowd is concerned. This home grown enthusiasm can obscure the fact that one race is pretty much like any other, a flat-out straight-down-the-track contest. But it's superbly colourful.

The final bull-race meeting held at Pamekasan is the biggest and most colourful event, but races can also be seen during August and September in Pamekasan and at nearby Sampang. An impressive new bull-racing stadium has recently been completed on the outskirts of Bangkalan, at the far western end of the island only 16 km from the ferry terminal at Kamal, and races will be held there on the first Sunday of every month.

A regular car and passenger ferry service operates from the L.C.M. dock (Jln. Kalimas Baru) at Tanjung Perak, Surabaya's harbour: Rp.125 per person, Rp.1350 for a car, and 25 minutes will get you across the narrow strait to Kamal on Madura.

The Madurese have long enjoyed a reputation for toughness, and the mere sight of black-moustachioed Madurese sailors was once enough to strike terror into the hearts of the mainlanders.

The independent spirit of its people (whose language is quite distinct from Javanese and Sundanese) meant that Madura never took kindly to invaders and overlords. It was a fractious ally and (later) a vassal of Mojopahit. It was conquered by Sultan Agung's forces in 1624, when the puppet Raja of Sumpang was put on his throne, but under Prince Trunajaya during the 1670s it was a thorn in the side of both Mataram and the VOC (Dutch East India Company). A divided state after 1705, when the Dutch controlled the eastern half of the island, Madura became an ally and later a sworn enemy of Batavia under Cakraningrat in the 1740s, and was a supporter of Prince Diponegoro in his heroic but futile 'rebellion' of 1825. Together with Surabaya and Pasuruan it harboured an enduring hatred for Sultan Agung and all his successors, and was partly responsible for the eventual division of Mataram in 1755.

The harshness of Madura's rubbly, limestone terrain may account for the resilience of the Madurese.

Inland, ragged cores of rock thrust up between spindly clusters of trees in an inhospitable landscape. Crops struggle for a foothold on the poor, stony soil; straw and *pandan* leaf stacked in tree boles are like huge nests. Many houses, often little bigger than a double-bed, are still being built 'colonial style' with high hipped roofs and thick white columns that should survive Armageddon. Women carry everything on their heads (mostly in green and white enamel wash-basins or, in the north, on white enamel trays) unlike their sisters in Central Java who tote their baskets in a back-slung shawl or *selendang*; Madurese women walk with a comely grace, and many are extraordinarily beautiful.

Along the southern coast the fishing villages exude a solid but slightly jaded Mediterranean air. Fishing boats lie gunwale to gunwale in narrow estuaries, logs in a seemingly irreparable log-jam. Salt-water marshes are reaped of their only possible harvest: money-earning salt, dried on vast pans of blinding whiteness, then packed into bright blue sacks. At Tanjung the *prahus* carry huge triangular sails, wide-striped in orange and dusty brown, brick red and yellow ochre. Hulls rival Joseph's famous coat. White twin-outrigger dugout canoes sit on trestles above the sand-flats like ready squadrons of giant seagulls.

At Camplong there's a swimming beach at the end of a long avenue of graceful casuarinas. Far across the smooth water cottonwool clouds

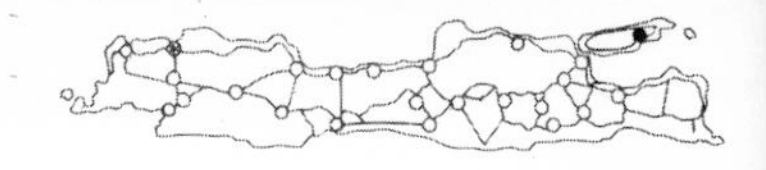

surround the invisible mainland peaks of Arjuna, the Tengger group and the mass of Ijen.

(A note for bed-watchers. At Sumenep there is an outstanding Chinese-style bed, reputedly 300 years old, amongst an otherwise small and motley collection of regal memorabilia in the tiny museum opposite the *kraton*. The deep, high-relief gilded carving is masterly: figures of a warlike Rama in *wayang kulit* style, *raksasa* heads in profile, *garudas* sculpted almost in the round.)

The northern corner of the island is pretty with coconut groves, sandhills and real golden beaches. Pasongsongan and Pasean are photogenic fishing villages: colourful *prahus* (but plain sails); dried fish, husked corn, cucumbers and mauve and purple *kue* in the market. From Sotaba to Ketapang the desolate hinterland encroaches.

In Sumenep, at the eastern end of Madura, old houses resemble lines of Roman temples.

Beyond Ketapang you can continue round the coast via Arosbaya on a dirt road, or cut through the centre to Sampang.

Impressions: goats, cactus (the ruinous 'prickly pear'), Muslim graveyards perched on rocky outcrops, green plaited-bamboo *tempat kue* for carrying *selamatan* offerings, horsecarts with immense two-metre wheels, a few thatched-roof houses, white face-powder turning women's faces mortuary grey, white cranes standing in rare fields of green *padi*.

At Arosbaya, 11 km short of Bangkalan on the northwest coast, ask the *bupati* for permission to visit the tombs at Air Mata (4 km inland). The main attraction is the large, ornately carved *gunungan* headstone on the grave of Kanjeng Ratu Ibu, consort of Cakraningrat I (1546–1569), though the whole setting on a terraced hilltop, with beautiful views across tiny valleys and a feeling of cloistered peace, is worthwhile in itself.

TEMPLES AND THINGS

A quest for temples can be one of the great joys of East Java. Ranging south from Surabaya it is possible to see the best of them in one day by tracing a long and tiring circuit through Malang, Blitar, Kediri, Mojokerto and back to base, but a more leisurely journey is recommended.

Even if old stones leave you cold you'll be well on the trail to some of the most beautiful country in East Java as you follow remote *desa* tracks, tiny back lanes overhung with forests of bamboo, roads where there's ne'er a bus to be seen.

Malang, 90 km south of Surabaya, is a perfect base for 'temple tripping': a charming, clean, attractive town with a mild climate. You may however be tempted by the surprisingly named Hotel Niagara in **LAWANG**, 18 km north of Malang on the main road.

In the years just before the Great War of 1914–18 a wealthy Chinese exporter of *kayu jati* (teak), Lim Siang Yew, hired a Brazilian architect by the name of Senhor Pinitu. Together they conceived and built a stately five-storey house on the outskirts of Lawang, nestling in the gentle foothills at a cool 491 metres under the eastern shoulder of Gunung Arjuna. Into this mansion with its five-metre ceilings went a sizeable fortune in teak, red brick, brass handrails, wrought-iron balustrades and a cage-like electric elevator. Wall tiles, terrazzo floors and stained glass transom lights display the sinuous *art nouveau.*

In 1963 the Lim family sold their inheritance. It became the Hotel Niagara, furnished throughout with *meubel antik Jepara*; the elevator, grudgingly, still works but pauses between floors; there is a swimming pool; fresh white and yellow arum lilies, perfect partners to the stained glass, sit on the tables in the bar ('sorry mister, no whiskey, only Black & White'); incense is still burned before Buddha and his attendants who huddle inside glassed-in niches on the flat rooftop

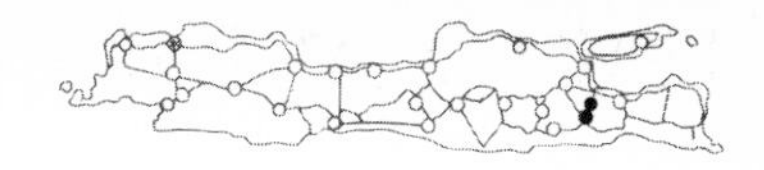

ʌn *art nouveau* otel at Lawang.

Ǝod's chosen' are osted to Malang.

ɹith its magnificent views of Gunung Arjuna; and ıere is a story of three female ghosts who haunt ne of the rooms.

It's not a Hilton. It's not a *losmen*. But it's the ind of place you could fall in love with. The nly blemish is a new but mercifully small ddition on the road frontage: modern, no oubt necessary, but fortunately begun well fter Senhor Pinitu paid a brief return visit in 971 at the age of 97.

MALANG has often been described as the most ttractive town in Java (a missionary, on learning ecently that a *confrère* had been posted to Ⅎalang, was heard to remark with a touch of ıost unmissionary-like jealousy, 'Ah, he is indeed ne of God's chosen'). The town's fortunes ate from the closing years of the 18th century 'hen coffee was successfully established as a cash rop; today, tobacco and an important cigarette ıdustry also add to its prosperity.

Its attractions are obvious. Unlike many Javanese towns which lie dead straight along a dreary, shuttered, down-at-heel main street, Malang sweeps and winds over gentle ridges and gullies along the banks of the Brantas River, offering unexpected views and quite backwaters that demand to be explored. It is kempt and clean, with a strong feeling of civic pride: neat houses and an attractive town centre, and even the canary-yellow *becaks*, all have a fresh-scrubbed look about them. There is also one of the most modern and well-cared-for museums in Java, the *Musium Brawijaya* at the southern end of Jln. Besar Ijen. Named after the kings of the Mojopahit dynasty, it houses mementoes, weapons, colours, documents, photographs, battle plans and other memorabilia associated with the VIII Brawijaya Division, the third of Java's KODAM or Military Area Commands.

A couple of blocks to the south of the main

Malang can be your base for exploring the area.

square is *Pasar Besar*, the huge new central market. It is full of exciting corners (including a clothing section where light filtering down through glass skylights evokes the feeling of a Middle Eastern bazaar). At the southern end, amongst an enthralling jumble of second-hand goods (*barang bekas*) you can unearth old Dutch china, brass curtain rails, Chinese incense burners, finely etched *sirih* sets, *wayang klitik* puppets and dozens of other minor treasures. The fruit section (depending on the season) is full of locally-grown apples and grapes, and masses of cheap avocados.

Still shopping, you might be tempted by the varied delights of a small *toko tembakau* or shop for smokers' requisites across the road and about 200 metres down from the YMCA Hotel in Jln. J.A. Suprapto (the main road north to Surabaya). Apart from an astonishing range of *kretek*, virginia cigarettes and vast bundles of tobacco for every conceivable purpose (shag, black navy-cut, twist, wad, curly), there are the Po Art phantasies of the *jamu* packets. *Jamu* is a all-purpose herbal preparation which apparentl cures most ailments known to man. The in dividual ingredients are available throughou Java, haggled over by housewives in every *pasar* but it also comes as a powder in a flat little sache somewhat smaller than a packet of instan chicken-noodle soup, and revels in brand names The selection at Malang's little tobacco shop i breathtaking, every one of its different packs perhaps a range of 50 in all, featuring a unique multi-coloured 1950s comic label.

Malang's YMCA is anything but the hoste one might imagine. It is one of the best an most modern hotels in town, others being th Splendid Inn and Hotel Pelangi. A important side-note; YMCA is pronounce 'Imka'. For food, European style, the best spo

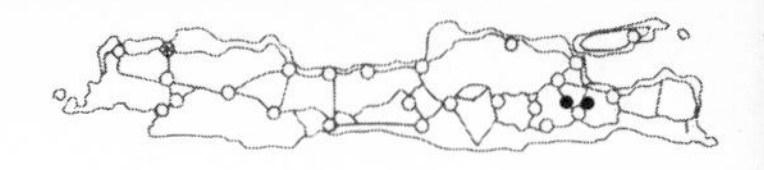

Another popular hill resort at Selecta.

Singosari temples and monstrous stone figures.

is *Toko Oen* in Jln. Jen. Basuki Rachmat (opposite the big new Sarinah shopping complex). It's a charming anachronistic survivor from colonial times, and amongst other delicacies it serves good wienerschnitzel, *broodjes* and *uitsmijter* (Dutch variations on a sandwich), and home-made ice-creams. Nikmat Lezat (Chinese food) and Minang Jaya (Indonesian food) are both good.

Another good base for temple-tripping is **SELECTA**, a popular town-sized hill resort set high on the southern side of Gunung Arjuna (5 km north of Batu, 20 km west of Malang). The climate is pleasantly cool, the apples excellent, and there are good swimming facilities. Above Selecta, through a world of wild orchids, huge trees and damp clouds, the tiny mountain village of Sumber Brantas sits astride the source of the huge Brantas River.

Selecta: a manicured hill resort.

The course of the Brantas, as it flows southeast, south, west, north, northeast and finally east into the Madura Strait, is also the course to follow in pursuit of East Java's ancient kingdoms, for its fertile valleys and its great delta were well able to support the sizeable populations that must have built the many temples in the area, many of which are extant and worthwhile visiting.

To reach **CANDI SINGOSARI**, look for the Garuda Bioskop on the northern outskirts of the town of Singosari between Malang and Lawang; turn left (west) at the *bioskop* (cinema) and another 600 metres will bring you to the temple.

Candi Singosari was one of the last religious-cum-commemorative monuments erected by the blood-spattered Singosari dynasty, and was built about 1300 shortly after the violent death of its last king, Kertonegoro. The main structure of the temple was completed, but the sculptors and masons responsible for the decoration (working

Over back roads to the temples of East Java.

downwards from the roof, as was the custom) never finished their task, due perhaps to civil strife and the dissension over royal succession. The stark, bald strength of the undecorated bulging-eyed *kala* heads above the doorways of the gods' chambers is more powerful and threatening than the finely carved *kalas* on many other temples. Of the statues which once inhabited the temple's chambers only one remains: Agastya, the 'Divine Teacher' and mentor of Siva.

About 200 metres beyond the temple is a pretty sweep of close-cropped grass and huge shade trees, a rural village green, unremarkable were it not for two monstrous carved figures of *raksasas* or *dwarapalas*, the club-clutching guardians stationed at the entrance to a town or temple. One seems to be resting languidly under a giant *waringin* tree, his hand raised in a half-threatening *noli-me-tangere* attitude. The other, a short distance away, lies buried to the navel in hard-packed soil, leaning slightly askew as though struggling to hoist himself from his ancient grave. Although only three metres high, the terrible twins with their fangs and clusters of skulls seem twice as large, especially when smothered under an ant-like swarm of village children. It has been suggested that they once guarded the main gateway of the Singosari kingdom, but there is a lack of decisive archaeological evidence.

CANDI JAGO (or Jajagu) offers a fair share of conundrums. It also has some marvellous reliefs in the two-dimensional *wayang kulit* style which is characteristic of much East Javanese temple carving, and includes some of the earliest known representations of the *panakawans* or servants (variously grotesque, obese, deformed, dwarflike) who, as Semar, Petruk, Gareng and Bagong, are still amongst the most popular of all Java's *wayang* characters.

Candi Kidal summarises the best in Singosari temple art.

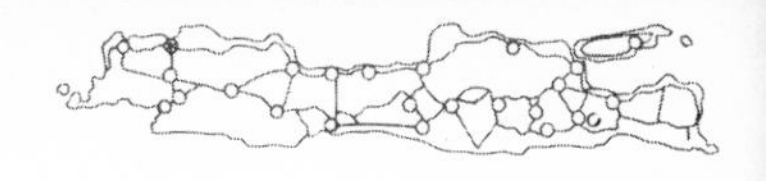

From the village of Blimbing, now virtually a northern suburb of Malang, take the sign-posted road east to Tumpang. Just 100 metres short of the Tumpang market (dominated by huge trees and dozens of horse traps) a small road to the left leads straight to the temple. There, for a small tip, the caretaker will escort you anti-clockwise through the five fascinating levels of reliefs which decorate the retaining walls of the three terraces and the temple itself: the immortal sagas of the Pandawas and Korawas, of Arjuna's meditation and temptations, of Krisna.

It's easy to spend hours there, unravelling the complexities of who is doing what to whom (and why), or delighting in the homely delineations of everyday life which crowd the panels. Between episodes the guide will regale you with the terrible tale (true enough) of an archaeological official who stole into the temple grounds in the dead of night and disappeared with seven of the finest free-standing statues of various Buddhist and Sivaistic deities. The culprit was apprehended but the statues have not yet been replaced.

Candi Jago was started in 1268 as a memorial to another Singosari king, Vishnuvardhana (the only one who died of natural causes). Changes and additions may have been made until as late as 1343, and further confusion is encountered in the form of Indian influences: Pala sculptural styles and the Nagari script.

A little over 5 km to the southeast of Tumpang is **CANDI KIDAL**, honouring yet another of Singosari's bloodily deposed monarchs, Anushapati, and completed around 1260. The route to Kidal is picture-postcard pretty, and the temple, in contrast to the history of the king it honours, sits like a gem amid banana trees and coconut palms: utterly serene, utterly perfect. It is not large, but for many people it summarises in

Candi Penataran, with a wonderland of carving, is a 'sleeper' among temples.

miniature all that is best in Singosari temple art: the tall, slender profile and stepped roof with its ornate carving, the bold, outstanding *kala* heads above the niches; the bas-relief medallions and especially the portraits of Garuda on three sides of the base.

The 80 km south and then west from Malang to Blitar and **CANDI PENATARAN** (11 km north of Blitar) will take a good two hours by car. Between Kepanjen and Wlingi the road twists and turns through teak plantations, passes the massive vertical slab of the Karangkates dam (watersports facilities are under construction on the shore of the huge artificial lake), and zooms through small towns and villages where the gateway of every house is identically moulded and painted in the form of a large '1945' and where the women's woven hats have a flattened top to make basket-carrying easier (the carry-all *selendang* of Central Java loses out in the east to the more stately, straight-backed goods-on-the-head technique). The turn-off to Penataran is clearly sign-posted at the eastern entrance to Blitar.

The Candi Penataran complex is, in Broadway's patois, a sleeper. It gathers momentum slowly, gradually dissolving the feeling of anticlimax which is a typical first reaction: it has no soaring Loro Jonggrang pinnacle, no stupendous mass like Borobudur, and its steel fence and iron-roofed entrance pavilion elicit about as much fervour as an amusement park on a wet day.

The gradually rising terraces cover long distances, flattening one's sense of perspective. Draw closer, and the individual delights and distractions begin to take shape. A broad, seemingly bare platform suddenly reveals its sculptured comic-strip saga, filled with wit and vitality as it unfolds the story of the fat and thin ascetics, Bubukshah and Gagang Aking. Farther

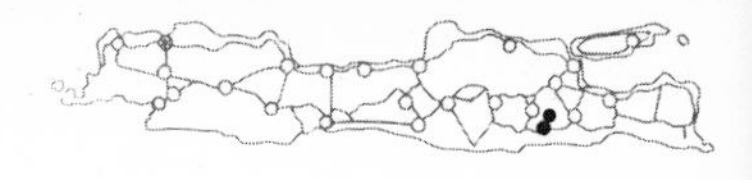

on, the finely detailed carving on the roof of the perfect little Dated Temple reveals itself. On the next level the heavy, sinuous snakes of the Naga Temple envelop the squat, square structure with the palpability of living pythons. Another level, and the magnificent boldness and bravura of the main temple commands the vision. And then there are the enthralling *Ramayana* reliefs.

Suddenly it all fits. The flat vista of the beginning becomes a wonderland of new details, new discoveries.

Penataran's stones were cut and carved and assembled over a period of some 250 years (between 1200 and 1450) though most of the important surviving buildings date from the great years of Mojopahit during the 1300s: the Dated Temple of 1369 (now the emblem of the VIII Brawijaya Division), the main sanctuary with its guardians dated 1347, and the decorated platform of 1375. The somewhat random arrangement of the whole complex is similar to many Balinese temple sites today, and it is assumed that most of the structures were roofed with wood and thatch (perishable materials which have not of course survived) which would have made a great difference to the existing skyline; the actual body of the main temple, which originally topped the three terraces, has been reconstructed at ground level and now sits alongside its three-tiered base.

The superb reliefs on the base of the sanctuary tell only part of the Ramayana story, but happily a part which is filled with action and excitement: followed anticlockwise the panels (interspersed with medallions of birds and animals) unfold the drama of Hanuman's secret mission to Rawana's palace on the island of Langka (yesterday's Ceylon, today's Sri Lanka), his capture, his escape, and finally the ferocious battle in which the death of the giant Kumbhakarna anticipates the eventual demise of Rawana on the sharp end of one of Rama's magic arrows. (This is the excerpt from the *Ramayana* danced with all its fury and derring-do at Pandaan's *Candra Wilwatikta*).

The bold, formalised *wayang* style of the *Ramayana* panels is quite different from the more naturalistic style of the Krisna stories on the second terrace, where more realistic people topple headlong from war chariots and soldiers do battle with dagger-like weapons which are the first known visualisations of the famous kris.

A hundred metres or so to the rear of the temple there's a small bathing place which ought to be filled with naked nymphs. Steps lead down to cool, inviting water, and the walls of the pool are lushly carved with birds, beasts and flowers. It bears the date 1415, which probably makes it the oldest still-used bathtub in Java.

A short way outside of Blitar, on the right-hand side of the road leading to Penataran, is a small, well-tended cemetery for heroes and patriots

Less immediately arresting than the temples of Central Java, Penataran nevertheless reveals a wonderland of detail and variety. On the base of the main temple, decorative roundels share wall space with stories carved in stone. In the background, the Dated Temple (1369 A.D.).

Near Blitar, Sukarno's unnamed grave.

(*Taman Makam Pahlawan*), one of many such cemeteries in Java. The small white headstones briefly record name, rank, number and unit, and only the dates link these quiet tombs with celebrated military actions writ large on Indonesia's battle colours.

Amongst the blood-red jerberas and flowering shrubs one grave stands slightly apart from the others on a raised terrace of brushed sand. There is no inscription on the two plain stone markers, but a triple-tiered umbrella (traditionally an accoutrement of royalty) shades the last resting place of Ir. Dr. Raden Sukarno, the graduate in civil engineering who, as President of Indonesia, led his people from August 1945 until March 1967. He was, in his time, a charismatic nation builder, an erector of grandiose monuments and a subject of almost religious adulation. Nevertheless, it was Sukarno's wish to be buried in an unmarked grave at Blitar, next to his mother. He was laid to rest there in June 1970, and was accorded full State honours.

Musings on the ironies of life could well lead you to Tulungagung and the cave hermitage of **SELAMANGLENG**. Hacked and hewn almost a thousand years ago out of solid rock, the square-cut cave looks over a small, lush valley dominated on the far side by an immense slab of eye-tooth rock (a landmark visible for miles, and the best guide to the cave site). If you turn your back on the view, you'll find the walls of the retreat decorated with a charming selection of episodes from the *Arjuna Wiwaha*: celestial nymphs, enticing and delectable creatures, are sent at Indra's behest to tempt the untemptable Arjuna who is wrapt in penance and ascetic devotionals on Mount Indrakila (a suitable subject for a hermit's home, though the unknown sculptor was lighthearted and human enough to depict one of the nymphs relieving herself in a handy stream).

Tulungagung is 33 km west of Blitar through a land of cane-fields and coconut plantations. From here you can dash north to Kediri, or continue westward towards Ponorogo on a bumpy, meandering route where back-lane exploring has some minor rewards: small, cool waterfalls in narrow, tight-ended valleys; a bamboo ferry being hauled across a river by rope and muscle-power, the shallow deck awash with muddy water which wets the feet but not the spirits of its passengers; and everywhere the local hat, shaped like a lampshade or inverted flowerpot, and invariably painted dull green with odd traces of blue and yellow decoration. In Ponorogo, if you check first with the *bupati* at the *kantor kabupaten* on the west side of town, you may be lucky enough to catch a performance of *reog Ponorogo* in its original environment.

Although Kediri has figured largely in Java's history and legend (in particular as the inevitable, implacable foe of nascent dynasties) the present town has nothing to offer and need only serve as a whistle-stop *en route* to **PARE** and the nearby

In a patriot's cemetery near Blitar, a triple-tiered umbrella marks the last resting place of President Sukarno. At Candi Tegowangi, two partially carved heads, an unsolved riddle.

Pare, immortalized in a classic study of religion in Java.

East of Pare to Malang, a landscape to turn you on.

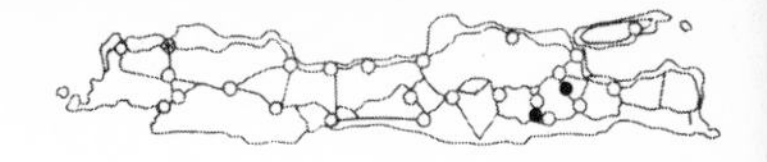

temples of Tegowangi and Surowono (Pare's immortality has been assured by its pseudonymous role as 'Mojokuto', the town so thoroughly analysed by Clifford Geertz in his classic study *The Religion of Java*).

The temples of **CANDI TEGOWANGI** and **CANDI SUROWONO** were both founded in the late 14th century by relatives of Hayam Wuruk, the last king of Mojopahit before the beginning of its rapid decline and dissolution. Only their square base-platforms remain, but in both cases these are divertingly decorated with animated and amusing reliefs. Tegowangi is unfinished on one side, and on another a broad flat pilaster carries the beginnings of two sculpted heads (one male, one female) which seem totally unrelated to the rest of the structure; on some of the panels there are superb landscape views of temples in a heavy tropical setting. Surowono has some appealing vignettes: a boar hunt, an assortment of gross *panakawans*, a lady by the name of Sri Tanjung astride a huge fish, and a motley assembly of fornicating animals.

If you've not already seen the Mojopahit museums and remains at Trowulan and Mojokerto (see page 220) a reasonably fast road will get you from Pare to Jombang and the main route to Surabaya. If you're heading back to Malang, there is a beautiful but at times very rough road running east from Pare. The 75-km route encompasses most of Java's landscapes: a varied kaleidoscope of rice-fields, dense forest, mountain peaks, waterfalls, high passes, rocky riverbeds, uncertain bridges, even worse roads, and a selection of visual delights that will mean at least a couple of rolls of film. Monkeys, pine forest, apple orchards, huge watermelons, orchid farms, more of those '1945' gateways, a swimming pool and *losmen* tucked into an idyllic corner. If landscapes turn you on, this is a trip to take.

Below Surabaya, along the southern shores of the Madura Strait, the wrist and bunched fist of East Java thrust out towards Bali. Of all the province's territory this is in turn the most desolate and forbidding, the most ravishingly beautiful, the most haunting, the most rewarding.

Here, in the 200 crow-flown kilometres between Malang and the warm waters of the Bali Strait, are more than a dozen of Java's mightiest peaks (six of them over 3,000 metres high) capped by the splendour of Gunung Mahameru, the 'cosmic mountain'.

You can fly over them; there's a daily 30-minute flight from Surabaya's Juanda Airport to Denpasar. You can skirt them by train; the Mutiara Express makes two journeys daily from Surabaya to Banyuwangi and the Bali ferry. You can even avoid them by taking the northern road through Pasuruan and Pasir Putih, a rather bleak and dispiriting route which should only be taken if you're really in a hurry.

But this exciting hinterland should be explored (by car, on horseback, by foot . . . or by a combination of all three). The rewards are those of free, untrammelled natural beauty, not those of tangible human history: there are no visible remains of the many incursions and invasions that wracked ancient Blambangan, the old name that once embraced the land from Malang to the east coast, but which now defines only the remote peninsula probing thumb-like into the sea in the far southeast corner.

It was amongst the peaks and high valleys of Blambangan that Hindu Java fought a stubborn rearguard action against Muslim Mataram, and it must have seemed that all was lost in 1639 when Sultan Agung's troops swept through to the coast and even subjugated part of Bali . . . which bounced back as though nothing had happened, pushed the invaders into the sea, and regained much of Blambangan as well. For the next hundred years the area was a favourite haunt of rebellious vassals who constantly harassed and harried a waning Mataram: Prince Trunajaya of Madura in 1674 (who sacked the *kraton* and drove Hamangkurat I into exile), the Balinese ex-slave Surapati in 1705 (curiously allied with Hamangkurat III against the VOC), and a mass of predatory Balinese who once again overran Blambangan during the shaky reign of Pakubuwono I in the early years of the 18th century. As late as 1715 Surapati's sons were busy building themselves a little kingdom where Malang now stands, and it was not until well past 1750 that the Dutch finally cleared the area and enforced the peace in a drastically depopulated land.

Outside of the rich river valleys and large towns like Bondowoso, Jember, Probolinggo and Pasuruan, the population is still sparse (at least by Javanese standards), and even along the busy north coast road there's one strip of 20 km with not a house or a *desa* to be seen. Seeing the country, you'll understand why.

THE NORTH COAST is very sparing in its favours, and about as visually charming as an empty parking lot. Pasuruan offers a few gems

Pearls for sale at Pasir Putih.

A fine seaside resort on the north coast at Pasir Putih.

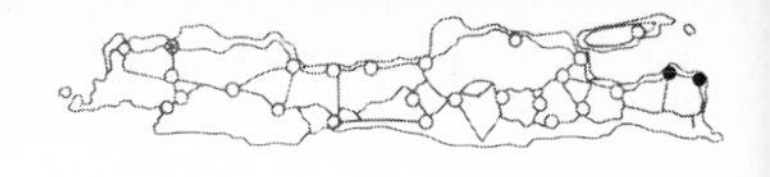

of colonial architecture; a monstrous, turreted, gabled edifice (a perfect setting for an operetta *circa* 1910) now used by Palang Merah, the Red Cross; and an interesting *pasar* where you might find Madurese silver anklets. Probolinggo's contribution is the turn-off to Bromo (see page 260). There are patches of mangroves and occasional outrigger *prahus*. Then suddenly, with a sigh of relief, you're in **PASIR PUTIH**.

The sand is more grey than white, but the string of clean, comfortable hotels squeezed along the beach-front between the five fingers of Gunung Ringgit and the sea are a mecca for Surabaya's weekend sun'n'sand worshippers (the big city is only 175 km away). If you stay overnight, the following day should start with breakfast on your balcony.

Fish from the first-light haul, charcoal grilled; hot, sweet tea with a hint of cardamom; the sun catching the loose sails of outriggers swinging gently on top of the tide, ornately carved and coloured helmsmen's backrests mounted slightly to port of the stern (the boats are for hire); farther out to sea large fishing *prahus*, five pairs of long oars driving them easily over the smooth water as the net drops away behind (images of an armed galley, bristling with hostile pirates bent on booty . . . you're glad of your swivel-mounted brass eight-pounder, packed with grapeshot and good dry powder); a swim, time out to float over the top of the luminous coral gardens, and a doze in the sun. Why move?

Then on through a flat parched land and vistas of sugar-cane. Situbondo with its neat little stone-fronted houses, four sturdy stone columns and a deep verandah black with shade, dolls' houses built to last forever. Asembagus, wooden-panelled porch balustrades neatly carved and fretted. A brief stretch of green, green *padi*, a last gasp of emerald before you're engulfed in a wilderness of stunted scrub and a colour spectrum that shifts from dun to drab olive to dun and back again. It's time to pull out your Stewart Granger safari hat with the zebra-hide band in readiness for the **BALURAN GAME RESERVE**.

Feet swish and crackle through the dry, flattened tussocks. A brace of quail, startled, sweep into the air from a grassy hollow almost under your step. A small herd of deer, barely visible through the shimmering heat haze, moves across a rise, the antlers of the big buck still visible after the fine heads and ear tips of his does have disappeared. Under a thorn tree, far out on the plain, a mob of wild water buffalo jostle sluggishly in the shade. Two hawks circle lazily, one beat of their wings catching an updraft as they call to each other in shrill two-note cries. Close to the shoreline, where mangroves embrace small yellow beaches, and hermit crabs and mud-skippers go about their business in the sun-bleached tide-wrack, monkeys shift uneasily then settle back to their eating and chattering and nit-picking.

The dried-out water courses would not be out of place in Africa or the Australian bush; the gnarled savannah growth and sweeping stretches of straw-coloured grassland are a far cry from the *padi* of Central Java and the humid

Deer, wild buffalo and banteng ox at your doorstep.

jungles of Papandayan; the mists of Tangkuban Prahu and Dieng Plateau belong to a different world.

The entrance to the game reserve is at Wonorejo village, 55 km east of Situbondo, and 37 km north of Banyuwangi. At Wonorejo, 2.2 km from the main road, contact the Game Reserve officials (Pengawas Pelindungan Alam) for permission to enter. About 12 km within the reserve, on Bekol Hill, there is a small guest house, a lookout tower, and a number of well-plied tracks that will enable you to see the wildlife but keep you clear of the fast, dangerous *banteng* or wild ox. August to November are best, for in these dry months, the animals must stay near the permanent water holes.

Baluran's physical aspect is exciting in itself: hot, thorny, and dry. Deer, buffalo and *banteng* are easily seen, especially at first light as they amble slowly away from the wells near the watchtower and drift across the pampas seeking solitude and shade. For birdwatchers it's another paradise: peacocks, tiny finches, golden-breasted honey-eaters, masses of wood pigeons, black and white fantails, parrots the colour of young rice shoots. It's the sort of place where binoculars and long lenses are essential, though it's possible (through stealth and a kind wind) to get within 100 metres of a herd of deer.

It's an absorbing diversion by day, but as the animals are best seen (or at least more easily seen) at dusk or at dawn it's a good idea to spend the night there if you don't mind roughing it.

Banyuwangi is less than an hour away to the south on a road dominated by coconut groves, coarse rocky outcrops and the looming 2,800 metres of Gunung Merapi, the extreme eastern shoulder of the Ijen plateau. The Bali ferry actually departs from Sukawidi, 7 km north of Banyuwangi. It leaves hourly (arrive an hour early if you're travelling by car); the cost for

A southern route from Surabaya to Bali.

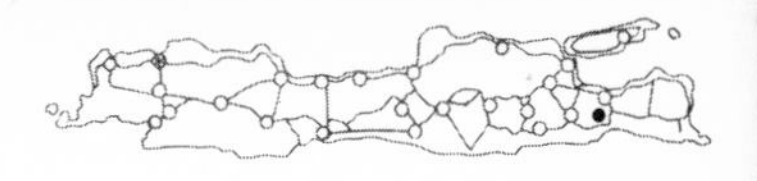

A sudden burst of palm trees and flowers before the magic mountain.

the half-hour journey is Rp.30 per person and Rp.1,250 for a car.

The **SOUTHERN ROUTE** from Surabaya to Banyuwangi, 375 km, is longer and slower than the northern option. Yet the beautiful country makes this an excellent route for those going on to Bali.

Below Malang the road traces a long arc southeast then east through Turen and Dampit, gathering up small ridges and then hills and then mini-mountains as it goes. The vegetation is as lushly tropical and varied as you could wish for. In between wondering whether or not the road will really succeed in tieing itself into a modern Gordian knot you can take in Kodachrome views at every bend and corner: coffee trees, dark ripple-edged leaves with a rich sheen; coconut palms against a vertical hillside splashed with impossible terraces of *padi*, magic staircases tumbling to the bottom of the valley: a sudden blaze of canna lilies, hibiscus with the spread of a dinner plate, and giant yellow daisies.

The ingredients of this landscape are familiar, but here, somehow, it's almost as though every corner, every gully, every hint of a hillock, has given of its best for the world's most spectacular Barnum and Bailey horticultural display. Or it may all be a tribute to **GUNUNG MAHAMERU**, the abode of the gods, the source of life-giving streams, the magic mountain.

For a while it's a game of hide-and-seek. Around one bend, and there's the enormous slope of the western shoulder, striped with grey-black,

A herd of skittish deer in Baluran Game Reserve freeze at the approaching footballs of a visitor. The reserve's savannah seems to come from another world, while 400 km away a symbolic vista of Java unfolds: the island's highest peak, abode of gods, Mahameru overseers paddy and plantation.

purple-black seams like a half-opened umbrella. The next corner, a brief glimpse of the peak. Another bend, and where the peak should be there's a mass of cloud. Then suddenly (about 65 km from Malang) you're running along the top of a cresent-shaped ridge, the rim of a broken rice bowl, and there to the north, clear, cloudless, unobstructed and less than 15 km away, is the whole majestic heap.

Gunung Mahameru ('Great Meru', variously Sumeru, Smeru, Meru) is, at 3,676 metres, the highest mountain in Java. Although it tops its nearest rival, Gunung Slamet in Central Java, by a mere 250 metres it was obviously considerably higher in its more youthful days.

As the ancient legends spin the story, it appears that the gods were in need of a suitable abode in Java, and arrangements were made to transfer Mahameru from the Himalayas and deposit it in West Java. Unfortunately, the gods, with their usual touch of almost human fallibility, had underestimated the enormous weight of the mountain. Java was thrown off balance, and a hasty decision was made to shift the new arrival farther towards the east. Speed overrode caution, and on the way Mahameru was the victim of 'damage in transit': large chunks broke off from the base, and when finally put down on its unsteady footing Mahameru teetered and slipped to one side and lost its top as well. The top is Penanggunan (the beautiful small cone near Tretes); the base fragments, running east to west, became Welirang, Kawi, Kelud, Wilis and Lawu.

Despite these tribulations the old peak has aged well, and there's a certain jaunty air to the plumes of white smoke that spasmodically billow forth from the crater. On a calm day these puffs

An innocent puff from Java's highest mountain.

A golden dance of wildflowers on the way to Ijen and Merapi.

A middle route to Bali through Klakah and Jember.

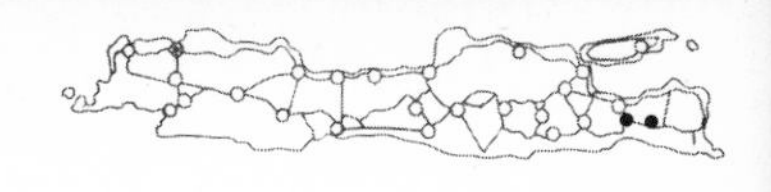

have all the awesome perfection of an atomic mushroom: dense white clouds rising with extraordinary languor then hanging suspended in space, seemingly motionless but imperceptibly spreading and softening and finally disappearing like a wraith.

Towards dusk the runnels and fissures and deep seams fill with blackness, hard and sharp against the pale eggshell blue sky. The immense sweep of the western slope moves from grey to mauve to purple, a line of gold shimmers briefly on a ridge cap, the black furrows blend with the coming night.

Out of the darkness come crimson fireflies dancing an Irish jig on a trampoline. You think about getting your eyes checked. Darkness again. A glob of red light appears in the distance and expands like a balloon of fiery bubblegum. It pops. The mountainside, black against a black sky, explodes in a cascade of scarlet stars as the lava oozes over the crater rim and plunges down.

The less exciting remainder of the trip passes tobacco plantations near Jember, crops of cassava and coffee, teak forests, a lovely road to Kalibaru and rubber plantations.

The **MIDDLE WAY** is more a bundle of suggestions than a fixed itinerary. You can leave the soulless north road at Probolinggo and head south through teak forest to Klakah, a green-belt of corn and tobacco, and a flat but pleasant run along the dike-top of a huge irrigation canal to Jember. Staying on the Klakah road as far south as Lumajang you'll enjoy some superb views of Mahameru (though not as exciting as the backdoor surprises from Malang). Just beyond Besuki, on the way to Pasir Putih, there's a good road south which wriggles upwards through rugged, handsome country to the agriculturally rich Bondowoso plateau and then through to Jember.

There are two side-trips off the Surabaya-Banyuwangi-Malang circuit which demand jolt-proof bones, a taste for the wilds and a modestly adventurous spirit. The first, **IJEN PLATEAU**, is highly recommended to mountain buffs and hikers; the second, Sukamade, is grist for coast-watchers. Both are spectacular, and about the only thing they have in common is coffee.

The Ijen Plateau can be reached through Bondowoso from either the northern or southern coast: the former is faster, the latter more attractive, and in both cases it's wise to make an overnight stop nearby in readiness for an early start and a full day (try Pasir Putih or Jember for reasonable accommodation; Bondowoso has clean *losmen*).

Sukamade is possible but gruelling as a one-day venture, and really needs at least two days. Your arrival time is not important, so you could spend the previous night in Banyuwangi to the northeast, or in Lumajang (after Mahameru) or Jember to the west.

Not so long ago (geologically speaking) Ijen Plateau was an active crater complex of gigantic proportions: 134 square kilometres of fire and fury, the easternmost chimney in Java's long chain of volcanoes. Today the bowl is home to 7,400 people who earn a living on the coffee estates that cover most of the valley floor. The ubiquitous acacia or *cassia*, coffee's parasol, is almost outnumbered by huge trees of Falstaffian girth which climb up and over the plateau's steep lip and drop away as deep, silent forests on the outer slopes of the ancient volcano: wild, rugged and utterly magnificent country which doesn't quite fit the usual image of Java. It's the Black Forest; it's where the spirit of Paul Bunyan walks abroad.

Ijen is dormant, not dead. In the far southwest corner of the plateau, Gunung Raung (3,332 metres) rumbles and frets; on the northeastern edge, 20 km away and less than 500 metres below the 2,800 metre peak of Gunung Merapi, the **KAWAH IJEN** crater lake broods with menace and malice afore-thought: to boil or not to boil?

From Sempol (a coffee estate village in the heart of Ijen) to Kawah Ijen and back is a solid walk of 4½ to 5 hours, plus another 20 minutes or so at each end for road transport from the village to the start of the trekking point. A guide is essential and the estate *kepala* (headman) can arrange this for you.

With luck (which means an absence of fallen trees blocking the track) you'll be able to drive as far as a small bridge. Then it's feet, feet, feet. The trail twists and winds and climbs through groves of casuarinas, across rocky streams, through thigh-high sword-grass and masses of purple morning-glories. From a small grassy clearing you'll catch sight of a white building high on a hill, half an hour away up V-shaped pathways filled with slippery grit. The 'house', an old *pondok*, is a 2,200-metre home for 30 or 40 men and boys who carry shoulder baskets of pure sulphur from a 'quarry' on the lake's edge under the shadow of the sheer walls of the crater. The labour, and the living conditions, are pure Dickens.

Beyond the *pondok* the track forks: to the right the trail is well defined, stamped hard by the hundreds of bare feet padding up and down its twisting length from dawn till dark; to the left it becomes a seldom-used pathway of rough grass strewn with fallen pine branches.

The right-hand trail is the easier of the two, despite a few wooden ladders that have to be ascended with caution. The left route is better suited to a mountain goat, for after lurching around bluff after bluff of pines and bracken it suddenly reveals not just a shattered, jagged, hell-fire landscape but also the semblance of a path-way: the trail inches its way across gaping crevices and frightening glissades, traversing almost vertical sheets of loose rubble, bouncing over one-plank 'bridges' no more than 20 centimetres wide. Underfoot, the ground has turned to ball-bearings.

Ten minutes. A lifetime. It all feels the same.

Then, at 2,400 metres, the southwestern rim of the crater. And the crater itself. A sheer-walled chasm of grey and mauve and red, scarred and harrowed, plunging into a lake of pale green milk; a line of yellowish sulphur scum above the waterline like the high-tide mark on a dirty bathtub; in a remote corner an evil mingling of smoke and steam, scalding out from beneath a precipitous overhang; and in the air the pungent stench of sulphur.

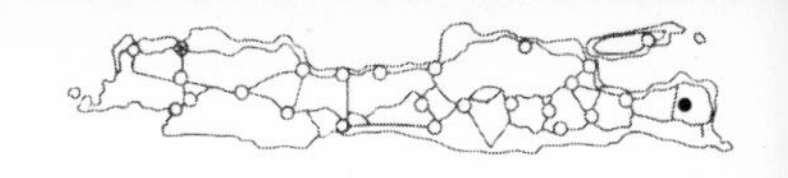

'he Black Forest
ınd Paul Bunyan
ıre up at Ijen.

ʌ killing road to the
jen crater and a
nagnificent hike to
he sulphur lake.

It is appalling, terrifying, stupendous. Weirdly ›eautiful.

If your nerves hold out you can totter 75 metres lown the crumbling remains of a concrete-and-teel stairway to the lake's edge where a safety-'alve dam has been built. Despite the hot fumes ınd smoke wafting across from the other side of he lake, the water is cool, and along the foreshore ›n the inner side of the dam's wall there are strange labs of compressed sulphur mud and pockets of rystals embedded in rust-coloured rock.

Below the dam the land drops away in a umultuous cascade of rock and rubble into the ops of a pine forest, the start of a yellow-coloured ›ut otherwise clear stream which is crossed a ouple of times, in its lower reaches, by the trail ›ack to Sempol.

The right-hand route is less alarming, but ›resents its own set of difficulties at the far end n the form of noxious white fogs of sulphur dioxide which billow forth from gaping slits and holes. A deep breath, taken at the wrong time, will have you wishing for a gas mask.

Vapours or not, the trek is rewarding, for this is where the sulphur comes from, oozing out of the cracks and fissures at the lake's edge in turgid red streams which soon harden into solid yellow shapes of exquisite sunny brightness.

The heavier lumps, broken with a hammer, are the daily bread of the *pondok* people. Although sulphur is extracted from the crater lake at *Telaga Bodas* near Garut (West Java) in far greater quantities, the mineral at Kawah Ijen is purer and is worth commercial exploitation despite the horrendous labour involved: Java's 'home-grown' sulphur is a natural source of sulphuric acid, in great demand in the oil-refining business and in the production of fertilisers.

The lighter pieces of sulphur sometimes come in the shape of beautiful drops, stalactites and

other curious formations. If you have a shapely stick handy you can make 'instant' coral branches in vivid yellow: dip your stick in a pool of molten sulphur (try not to asphyxiate yourself in the process), bring it out, let it cool, and there you have it. Don't wrap your treasure in any good sweater or natural-fibre material for protection on the long journey back, or a day or so later your equally precious clothing will look as though it's been invaded by an army of hungry moths.

The road to Sempol, and on to Kawah Ijen, leads off the main Bondowoso-Situbondo route, 2 km north of the little market town of Wonosari. The 48 km will take close to two hours over a surface which is, in parts, unbelievably punishing and strewn with great lumps of axle-cracking volcanic rock; it's almost as though some netherworld demon, with a grim sense of humour had sprinkled the route with handfuls of granit tetrapods. Excluding bumps, the high fores country is quite beautiful.

A sea of sword-grass on the way to Kawah Ijen.
A stretch of rugged coast near Sukamade.

Depending on what time you reach Sempol the jaunt up to the crater and its lake can be don easily in a day's outing, though if you like early morning starts limited accommodation is availabl in the village. The *pasanggrahan* or guesthouse ca be used if prior arrangements have been made wit the *Direksi Perkebunan* (Estate Management) i Jember, 41 km south of Wonosari. This is the onl official accommodation, but for around Rp.50 per person it's possible to stay in the village at th *Asrama Polisi*, the police hostel a few hundre metres beyond the estate checkpoint. Very basi accommodation can also be found, within a hour's walk of the crater rim, on a small platea which is the first staging post for the loads o sulphur on their way down from the *pondok*; th 'sulphur road', plied by pack horses and reall little better than a footpath heads down to th southeast over the outer rim of the Ijen caldera If you enjoy toting a back-pack this is a toug but interesting exit route which takes around si hours before reaching the nearest roadhead nea Licin, roughly 10 km to the west of Banyuwangi

Bondowoso and Situbondo are both well know for bull-fighting (bull against bull, not bul against man), and it's worthwhile checking i either town in case your trip coincides with fight. More peaceable, and fun, is an exploratio of the colourful animal market in Wonosari jam-packed with bulls, goats, sheep and ever villager from miles around. The covered sectio of the *pasar* has an astonishing array of good (it is, after all, the village 'supermarket' an general store combined). If you enjoy squattin in the dust and haggling for a quarter of an hou or so you could wind up with a couple of colourfu plaited rope *sapi* whips for a very reasonable price.

If you still feel rugged enough, you might lik to change from craters to crashing surf.

The **SUKAMADE BARU** estate was founded in 1927. Today it covers (in round figures) 1,10 hectares of which 310 hectares are planted with coffee, 350 with rubber and 100 with coconu palms for copra; what remains is river beds, the

Jungle-clad hills, some of the most attractive coastline and Om David.

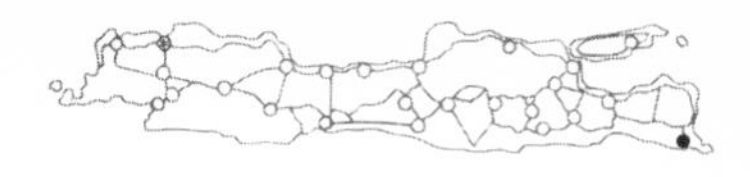

estate compound, a village, a bunch of almost inaccessible jungle-clad hills, and a stretch of some of the most attractive coastline in Java.

To get there you turn south at Genteng on the main road between Jember and Banyuwangi, but you'll need some preparation for the next 67 km, for on most maps Sukamade doesn't exist.

Borrow, hire or otherwise commandeer transport with a high clearance and preferably four-wheel drive; pack a couple of changes of clothing, swimming gear, a 'cold bag' and plenty of colour film; then head due south.

For the first 32 km to Pesanggaran you spin happily along a pretty canal-side road lined with banana trees, coconut palms, contented villagers bathing *au naturel* and other picture-postcard scenes. Pesanggaran itself boasts several of the finest old Fords in captivity: they started running in 1929 and still carry goods and people: the fact that they still work is not so remarkable: that they should stay alive on the roads they ply is astounding.

The next 35 km west to Sukamade takes a good two hours over potholes, narrow bridges, river fords, a minor hill through a rubber plantation, a major hill through towering natural jungle (broken occasionally by views of the jagged coastline) and finally a 50-metre ford across the Sukamade River just 5 km short of the estate compound. (About 24 km out of Pesanggaran the road nudges the back edge of a long, sweeping beach of fine grey lava sand; the surf runs heavy and uneven, but it's safe for swimming if you don't venture out too far, and deliciously refreshing. On a busy day you might see one or two fishermen, but most of the time it's deserted.)

At the estate you will be made welcome by members of the managerial staff of the company, who know at least a little English. Then at the

The last of Java's unique breed of tiger.

estate's *pasanggrahan* (no official prices yet, though there will be a charge), the surprises start. You'll be shown to a clean, spacious room (albeit spartan) with sheets top and bottom. The bathrooms are big and hygienic, and when you have cleaned up you will be offered a *bir yang dingin sekali* (ice-cold beer). There are many things to do and see on the estate, which bustles with activity: 1,600 people live in the estate village, 750 of them active workers earning low wages plus rice and helping produce 235 tons of rubber and 325 tons of coffee beans annually.

There are also, according to a World Wildlife Fund expert, the only six remaining Java tigers (*harimau macan jawa*), a breed unique to the island. They live in a steep valley on the eastern boundary of the estate which has been set aside as a tiger breeding ground, and their roaring can be heard at night. It is possible to see them, the estate staff will tell you, but only if you have plenty of time and plenty of patience, as well as a taste for nights in the alien world of the jungle

Smaller cats abound. The *macan tutul*, or spotted panther, and a number of sleek, long-bodied wild cats which take scant notice of headlights as they saunter saucily across the rough tracks.

And there are turtles. Big, heavy ladies, tipping the scales at around 200 kilos, who emerge wet and glistening from the pounding surf and chug laboriously up the beach-head as they seek a 'nesting' place beyond the high water mark. A few of their leathery ping-pong ball eggs are collected by the estate workers for food, but for the most part they are left to hatch (the 'nesting' site marked like a Christian grave with a small cross), for Sukamade values its reputation as an important wildlife reserve.

At night, after a gargantuan meal in the finest Javanese 'home cooking' tradition it's a jeep-trip

Big, heavy ladies at 'Turtle Beach' come ashore to lay their eggs.

to turtle territory, patrolling the beach in search of the tell-tale 'tank tracks' while you side-step skirmishing attacks from armies of crabs who roam the sand.

The next morning you can have your cold bag filled with beer or soft drinks from the refrigerator before heading off with one of the estate's jeeps, a driver and a 'porter' or two for Green Bay, a tiny landlocked cove backed by jungle where 200 metres of pale yellow sand sweep down into a surf which is an impossible, unbelievable green. *En route* over the mountain road you'll see families of the Black Monkey with their strange 'granny bonnet' fringes of grey hair, or groups of kingfishers in startling combinations of green, turquoise and yellow, or grey and white lace-wing butterflies by the hundreds.

The 20-minute walk from the jeep track to the beach is a jungle jaunt through an array of vines, lianas, and the whole spectrum of tropical growth (*Rafflesia*, giant among flowers, grows in the area). The trail is narrow, steep and slippery, but your goal is breathtakingly beautiful, and the swimming superb though do be careful of the undertow at high tide.

Back at the ford you can explore the sandbanks for the pugmarks of panthers and the footprints of monkeys. The estate has on record a 20-centimetre tiger pad, which is big for a mere cat. Keep your eyes open too for giant hornbills which flap slowly past like incoming B52s.

One last point. The estate can accommodate 30 people, and its policy is to care for visitors as though they were personal friends.

Sukamade Baru Estate, near a beautiful stretch of coastline, bustles with coffee production.
Evening light glints on Angel's Wing shells, at Sukamade's 3-km-long 'Turtle Beach'. At the east end are story-book pirate coves.

BROMO BETWEEN HEAVEN AND HELL

The ride is slow and black through air heavy with the fragrance of pine and acacia blossom, accompanied by the soft clop of unshod hooves on unseen earth, the creak of saddle leather, and a feeling of riding into eternity. You pause, shivering, on the precipitous heights of the Munggal Pass as the landscape comes to life for another day: the bare sweep of the Sand Sea, a misty olive and grey surf of tussock, a ribbon of silver first-light catching the shifting sand of a dried-out watercourse; a sudden daub of luminous yellow ochre splashing the face of Batok, the black walls of the Tengger basin against a cold salmon sky, the ominous mass of **GUNUNG BROMO**.

Or you might be huddled in your blanket on Bromo's rim. On one side the hiss and rumble from the volcano's core. Later, when light spills into the crater and catches the smoke and steam with the brilliance of a magnesium flare, a shift of wind exposes a monstrous circular shaft, plummeting downwards, a gaping elevator-well, express to the netherworld . . . where, as the Tenggerese know, departed souls take the swift underground route to Mahameru, 'the highest temple'. On the other side, a faint jangle of harness as horses move restlessly down where the mud of ancient lava-flows has been racked by wind and rain into a labyrinth of Wild West gulches and cliffs.

It's a place where colours take on a new bloom, a new depth which suggests that three dimensions just aren't enough. If you time your trek to coincide with the last days of the full moon you'll even find the old goddess, in all her luminous glory, sliding down the flank of Batok: a moonscape within a moonscape.

Below the guide, Bromo's vertical shaft descends to its fiery cauldron. Like cowboys (right) riders cross the lava gulch on the Sea of Sand.

Try magnificent Bromo, if nothing else.

The sunrise can be seen from two vantage points, both spectacular, both quite different: the first is the crater rim of Bromo itself (approached from **NGADISARI** to the northeast), the second is the 2,340-metre Munggal Pass (approached from **TOSARI** to the west).

Both mean getting up in the very early hours of the morning. From Ngadisari to Bromo across the Sand Sea and back again takes roughly four hours by horse or on foot. It's possible to take a jeep as far as the edge of the Sand Sea, though the grades on both sides of the pass from Ngadisari are very steep.

There are now a couple of good modern hotels in the Ngadisari area, as well as a cheaper one at Sukapura, the village before Ngadisari. In Ngadisari itself there is the Wisma UCIK, and above the village near the edge of the Sand Sea, the Hotel Bromo Permai. If you leave from Ngadisari expect to pay about U.S.$10 for a horse and guide for the four-hour round journey to Bromo.

The trek from Tosari is more strenuous, taking about 8 hours for the round-trip. Even with a horse (and you will surely need a guide) you'll have to walk down the steep slope of the Munggal Pass on your way to the Sand Sea (and stagger up on your way back). There are a couple of modest *losmen* in Tosari where you'll feel like members of the family, drinking coffee and hearing tales of the strange man who reputedly runs around the mountains in little more than a loincloth, living on bread and finding ancient Hindu bronzes (everyone knows where he lives, but he's never at home when anyone calls).

The circular trip, which involves a lot more walking, is thoroughly worthwhile. You can start from Ngadisari, sit on Bromo's rim and watch the sun come up, then take the horses as far as the foot of the Munggal Pass and hike back through the hills and forest to Tosari. There a cabbage truck can carry you back to 'civilisation' (with a car and driver you can naturally forget about the cabbage truck). The circular trip in reverse can be done, but is less exciting.

There is another outstanding view of the crater complex, with Mahameru glowering in the background, from Gunung Penanjàan (2,770 metres) on the north side of the Sand Sea. The best approach is from Ngadisari.

The Tosari turn-off is just south of Pasuruan on the road to Malang. The Ngadisari turn-off is 1.5 km short of Probolinggo (34 km east of Pasuruan) on the main north coast road. Both are well sign-posted.

Gunung Bromo, relative to its surroundings, is not high. It looks, in naked daylight, like a wrinkled, crabby, preposterous toad, reluctantly squatting on the edge of its pond, reaching out for the lotus-bud of Batok. Veined and tired, it has often been the victim of mistaken identity, and it is not unusual for visitors to greet their first view of Batok with the cry 'There's Bromo, folks!'

Statistically, too, it is unimpressive. A crater within a crater, standing a fraction more than 2,300 metres above sea-level at the highest point

Bromo's naked, haunted, tortured landscape—forbidding power.

of its narrow rim. Next to it is Gunung Batok, an almost perfect cone with a cut-off top and neatly seamed slopes. Both lie on the southern shore of the Sand Sea, a flat expanse of iron-grey sand and patches of scrubby grass, almost 2,200 metres high and enclosed by high-walled ridges which were once the rim of an ancient and enormous volcano (now dead) on the northern slope of the Tengger massif. To the south, hills stretch away to become the slopes of Gunung Mahameru, also part of the Tengger range (virtually another country, the highland home of 300,000 Tenggerese).

And yet, in that long hour before the sun comes up, when the chill morning light has killed the stars and your fingers are blue with cold, Bromo's naked, haunted, tortured landscape is enchanting; later, in full sunlight, it glowers with a forbidding power in which beauty and ugliness become inseparable.

The story of the creation of Bromo, Batok and the Sand Sea is similar to other mountain-origin tales in Java: a smitten lover, an unwilling princess, a task to be performed between sunset and sunrise, the crowing of rudely awakened roosters signalling a false dawn, and the frustrated suitor slinking off into the darkness. The princess in Bromo's case decreed that a great inland sea should be dug around the volcano's mouth. The tool used was the hard half-shell of a coconut which, flung away at the dawning hour, became Gunung Batok. The broad trench became the Sand Sea.

There is also the legend of the onions. Kyai Dadaputih, ancestor of all the Tengger people, lived with his wife in abject poverty, barely eking a livelihood from the soil. The gods, from their seat on Gunung Mahameru, promised him an everlasting abundance of food, in the form of red and white onions, if he sacrificed his youngest child in the crater of Bromo. The new vegetables flourished, but Dadaputih and his spouse (sometimes identified as the princess of the Batok tale) were naturally reluctant to meet their side of the pledge; then the gods threatened total catastrophe, and their twenty-fifth child was duly flung into the chasm (one version of the story says that this son was plucked from the cauldron and taken to live with the gods).

This also explains, in non-agricultural terms, why there is no *padi* in Tengger, and why the hills around and above every Tenggerese village are a huge market garden: onions, cabbages, maize, carrots, leeks, potatoes, cauliflowers.

Terrace upon terrace, plot after plot, creep up steep slopes, encircling compact villages of brown-black tin roofs where permanently burning brick hearths warm the kitchens and dry the vegetables hanging from the rafters. Clumps of liquorice-smelling fennel spring up along the mountain pathways, wild edible berries hang in luscious clumps, racks of corn-cobs (bleached by the sun) hold their seed for the next planting.

There's a strong element of Shangri-la in Tengger, a tangible sense of bucolic bliss. It would be naive to suggest that everything is perfect, though many people, anthropologists amongst them, have commented on the apparent contentment of the Tenggerese. Their life is hard and frugal. Religion, a curious blend of animism and Hindu beliefs, is simple. A flat smooth rock and two large overhanging trees are a shrine, and ritual gifts of vegetables and chickens are offered annually to the gods of the crater at the midnight ceremony held on Bromo's rim on the 14th day of *kesodo* (or *kesada*), the last month of the Tenggerese year. A primitive gesture of appeasement, perhaps, but hillside cuttings reveal layer after layer of ancient volcanic ash sandwiched between even shallower layers of soil. Bromo is not always quiescent.

The trek to Bromo is an intensely personal experience. Sunrise over its savagely beautiful landscape is part of it. So too is the same blistered wilderness in the full light of day. It is the releasing, joyous solitude of the Sand Sea, the sunlight discovery of gardens and enchanting pathways you passed in darkness. It is saddling-up before dawn . . . and wondering, on windswept ridges, if you'll ever feel warm again (gloves and a genuinely windproof jacket are recommended). It is an unheralded white plume from Mahameru's distant crater, turning pink in the dawn light. Strange, enduring, exhilarating. Another aspect of what Java is all about.

Dried streams of volcanic mud, the eastern shoulder of Batok and the cliffs enclosing the Sand Sea dwarf trail riders 200 metres below Bromo's rim.

Lobby bar
6:30
welcome

First

There are 7107 islands in the Philippines. So many, some have no names and even more are uninhabited. An impressive number have first class beach hotels.

Enjoy activities such as windsurfing, scuba diving, tennis, golf, horse back riding or just sun bathing on magnificent fine sand beaches.

As an added bonus, once in the Philippines we will give you a 50% discount on our domestic airfares to any c our Paradise Islands. We call it our 1000 Island Fare and a Philippine Airlines international ticket* holder can have it.

Experience the Philippines warm and friendly service on board our wide bodied aircraft to our 7000 island paradise. We will guarantee you'll have an affair to remember.

For your first affair in the Philippines, contact us or your travel agent.

Philippine Airline

Asia's first airline.

Amsterdam Athens Bahrain Bangkok Brisbane Canton Dhahran I
Kuwait London Los Angeles Manila Melbourne Paris Peking Port Mo

*Adult fare only.

affair.

o our island paradise.

urt Hong Kong Honolulu Jakarta Karachi Kuala Lumpur
San Francisco Seoul Singapore Sydney Taipei Tokyo Zurich

Guide in Brief

Traveling to Java

By Air

Coming from outside the Indonesian archipelago you have two main options: through Jakarta's international airport at Halim, soon to be replaced in 1985 by a new airport at Cengkareng 20 kilometers west of Jakarta or through Ngurah Rai Airport near Denpasar on the neighboring island of Bali with connecting flights to Yogyakarta, Surabaya and Jakarta. A majority of visitors arrive in Jakarta from Singapore. Garuda and Singapore Airlines have 5–8 flights daily from Singapore to Jakarta, each costing about US $170–$190 for round-trip, one month excursion fares. A one month excursion fare is available from Singapore to Bali with stops in Jakarta and Yogyakarta for approximately US$300. Many of the major international airlines of Europe, Asia and Australia serve Jakarta, Medan and Bali. Airlines with fewer flights, such as Thai International and Japan Air Lines may offer cheaper tickets. As a rule, discounted tickets are not sold directly by the airlines so inquire through a travel agent. A list of international airways serving Indonesia is provided in the appendix.

Many domestic flights connect cities within Indonesia. Garuda, whose fleet is now one of the biggest in Asia, has a near monopoly on domestic air traffic, but several small Indonesian operators offer less expensive flights. The most heavily traveled flights by foreign visitors to and from Java are Jakarta-Yogyakarta-Denpasar and Jakarta-Denpasar. Flights between Bali or Yogyakarta and Jakarta use the Halim International Airport. All other domestic flights pass through the Kemayoran Airport. (*see* Transportation)

By Sea

If you're one of the lucky ones with plenty of time (and money), an ocean cruise to Java should not be missed. Luxury cruise lines offer fly/cruise arrangements which allow you to fly to Bali and other ports where you can play in the sun, then catch your ship on the way home or vice versa. For those seeking elegance, three ships offer cruises to Indonesia and the number may increase. The *Princess Mahsuri* sailing for the Straits Steamship Company leaves from Singapore bound for Bali, Ambon and Sydney returning every six months. Contact Mansfield Travel, Ocean Building Shopping Centre, Singapore (tel. 93071) for details. The *Pearl of Scandinavia*, run by Harpers Travel (UIC Building Singapore, tel. 2202200), offers a 14 day Indonesian Islands cruise, which begins and ends in Singapore, to Penang, Belawan, Sibolga, Nias, Jakarta, Padang Bay-Bali and Surabaya. Harpers also handles the *Coral Princess* which sails out of Hong Kong during the winter months to Bali, Jakarta, Penang and Phuket. There are many discount fares when three or more people travel and you won't just be spending long hours staring at your friends; interesting scholars, artists, writers, historians and diplomats have been scheduled as guest lecturers and sailing companions.

If you like to travel with the footloose budget travelers, you can hop on a motor launch leaving Finger Pier, Prince Edward Road in Singapore for Tanjong Pinang where you can catch the *KM Tampomas*, flagship for the Indonesian National Pelni Lines who runs weekly sailings to Medan or Jakarta. There are many motor launches to Tanjong Pinang; one at 8:30 a.m. but none later than noon. Check at Finger Pier in the morning for schedules and tickets. The 5–6 hour ride costs S$65 (US$30) but a S$75 (US$35) fast boat is available. Intra Express Pte. Ltd next to the Garuda ticketing office in Goldhill Shopping Centre (tel. 7378403) also sells tickets. It is advisable to leave Singapore two days before the *Tampomas* departs and spend time on Tanjong Pinang. *Tampomas* leaves for Jakarta every Saturday at 5 p.m. local time. It costs the same amount of money to buy a package fare from German Asian Travels in the Straits Trading Building, 14th floor, 9 Battery Road, Singapore (tel. 915116) which includes the boat ride from Singapore, the transfer from Tanjong Pinang to the *KM Tampomas* by sampan and accommodations on board according to the class booked. Food and drinks can be purchased on board but may be costly. You might want to pack your own food. It is an 'unforgettable' two-day trip across the Java Sea aboard a crowded ship with primitive sanitation facilities and it's recommended only for the hardy. The ship arrives in Port Tanjong Priok, Jakarta on Monday at 5 a.m. and turns around to head back ready for embarkation at 6 a.m. Cabins must be booked one to two weeks in advance. Deck class can be obtained at short notice. (*See* Travel Advisories for custom and health formalities).

Several other big shipping companies run ships, both big and small, in and out of the hundreds of ports of Indonesia. However, most of them carry cargo with limited space for passengers and are less accommodating than the *KM Tampomas*. Check with the harbormaster for prices. It's often cheaper to go direct to the captain himself and pay for your fare.

Travel Advisories

Visa Regulations

Visitors from the ASEAN countries (comprising Singapore, Malaysia, the Philippines, Thailand as well as Indonesia), all West European countries, Australia, New Zealand, Canada and the United States will be automatically issued a two month visa. Transit passengers with onward bookings do not require visas if they wish to stop and sightsee.

An airport tax of Rp.3000 per person is required on international departures from Jakarta, Medan and Denpasar. Charges for domestic flights remain unchanged at Rp.1,200.

Surat Jalan: A *surat jalan* is a letter from the police permitting the bearer to go to certain places. It is advisable to carry one when traveling in some of the outer islands, but in Java only in such out-of-the-way places as the Ijen plateau. If in doubt check with a good travel agent. In Jakarta a *surat jalan* may be obtained in an hour or two at Police Headquarters

(Markas Besar Kepolisian Republik Indonesia) in Jalan Trunojoyo (Kebayoran Baru).

Health Precautions

Be sure to have valid inoculations against smallpox and cholera, and an International Health Certificate to prove it. Yellow fever vaccination is required if you arrive within 6 days of leaving or passing through an infected area. It is also advisable to be vaccinated against typhoid and paratyphoid.

If you intend staying in Java for some time, particularly outside of the big cities, gammaglobulin injections are recommended; they won't stop hepatitis, but many physicians believe that the risk of infection is greatly reduced. Diarrhea may be a problem: it can be prevented by a daily dose of Doxycycline, an antibiotic used to prevent 'traveler diarrhea.' Obtain this from your doctor at home. At the first signs of stomach discomfort, try a diet of hot tea and a little patience. Stomach reactions are often a reaction to a change in food and environment. Proprietary brands of tablets such as Lomotil and Imodium are invaluable cures. A supply of malaria-suppressant tablets is also highly recommended. Make sure the suppressants are effective against all the strains of malaria. It was recently discovered that a malaria strain in Java was resistant to the usual malarial prophylactic (chloroquine). Consult your physician.

Imported pharmaceuticals are expensive. Many international drug firms are now manufacturing in Java, but you may wish to bring some of these: a tube of antihistamine cream for the relief of itches (especially mosquito bites), an ointment for fungoid skin infections, a good prickly-heat powder and soap, a cold-suppressant such as Coricidin for the relief of colds and sniffles caused by abrupt changes of temperature, some form of insect repellant, and your favorite brand of aspirin.

All water, including well water, municipal water and water used for making ice, MUST be made safe before consumption. Bringing water to a rolling boil for 10 minutes is an effective method. Iodine (Globoline) and chlorine (Halazone) may also be used to make water potable. All fruit should be carefully peeled before eaten and no raw vegetables should be eaten. By practicing good hygiene and good preventive medicine you can be reasonably assured of a healthful tour. Watch what and where you eat and wash your hands frequently.

Last but not least, protect yourself against the sun. Tanning oils and creams are expensive in Java, so bring your own.

Customs

On entry, customs allow a maximum of two liters of alcoholic beverages, 200 cigarettes (50 cigars or 100 grams of tobacco) and a reasonable amount of perfume per adult. Weapons, ammunition, narcotics and pornography are prohibited. Cars, photographic equipment, typewriters and radios are admitted provided they are taken out on departure. They must be declared; a customs declaration form must be completed before arrival. There is no restriction on the import or export of foreign currencies and travelers checks so long as amounts in excess of US $500 are declared on arrival. However, the import and export of Indonesian currency exceeding Rp.50,000 is prohibited. Upon leaving limited quantities of duty-free purchases and souvenirs are exempted from taxes, but the export of 'national treasures' is severely frowned upon. (*see* Shopping)

Currency and Exchange

The *rupiah* is the basic unit, normally abbreviated to 'Rp.,' followed by the value.

Smaller denominations, Rp.5, 10, 25, 50 and 100, are in the form of coins, and larger ones, Rp.100, 500, 1000, 5000, 10,000, in the form of notes. The Rp.1000 note carries a portrait of Diponegoro, the famous 19th-century freedom fighter, and a watermark 'portrait' of Gajah Mada.

Values below Rp.50 are rarely seen on the hotel circuit, but are common in the markets and street stalls.

Change or *uang kembali* for high-value notes is often unavailable in smaller shops and stalls, and you may be offered tiny goods-in-kind in lieu of cash. It's a good idea to carry a handful of coins (also useful for tipping).

The exchange rate for a US $1 was about Rp.970 in early 1983. It is advisable not to exchange large sums of money if you plan to be in Indonesia for more than a month.

Changing Money: Foreign currency, in banknotes and travelers checks, is best exchanged at major banks or leading hotels (though hotel rates are slightly less favorable than bank rates). There are also limited numbers of registered money changers, but avoid unauthorised changers who operate illegally. Banks in many smaller towns are not necessarily conversant with all foreign banknotes, so it is advisable to change most currencies in the cities; always be sure to keep your exchange receipts. Your *rupiah* may be converted to foreign currencies when you are leaving the country.

Travelers checks are a mixed blessing. Major hotels, banks and some shops will accept them, but even in the cities it can take a long time to collect your money (in small towns, it is impossible). The US dollar is recommended for travelers checks. Credit cards are usable if you stay in the big hotels. International airline offices, a few big city restaurants and art shops will accept them, but they are useless elsewhere.

Getting Acquainted

Government

The basic ideology of the state is set out in the five fundamental principles known as *Pancasila*, an all-encompassing belief in "one just and civilized supreme God, humanity, unity of Indonesia, democracy and social justice." Understanding how these five principles of the national philosophy are implemented will help in understanding the complex make-up of the Indonesian society.

Readopted two decades ago, the 1945 constitution

vests the highest authority in the People's Consultative Assembly and provides for three independent Supreme State Organs and one Parliament body. According to the constitution, elections for the two highest legislative bodies, the Parliament and the People's Consultative Assembly, are to take place every five years although since 1945 general elections for these offices have been held only four times.

Bringing Indonesia together under one political entity has not yet been accomplished. Simplification of the multi-party structure has fused parties into three main organizations; the ruling Functional Group or GOLKAR, the Moslem United Development Party and the Indonesian Democractic Party, although there is no simple way to understand their administration.

In the day-to-day execution of the administration at the lowest levels, the ones with which the majority of the population deals most of the time, the pattern finds its basis in the country's own traditions. Supervising and coordinating the civic functions at the lowest level are the "block community organizations," next up on the administrative ladder are the "neighborhoods," followed by the district organization of Kecamatan or subdistricts and finally the city-level units of administration. This system manages to maintain much of the indigenous Indonesian pattern of *gotong-royang*, a kind of village socialism which is actually the real basis of political rule in which the community as a collective unit has the responsibility of looking after its members. *Gotong-royang* is increasingly being exposed to modern pressures and influences. It has been expanded and reinterpreted to function at the state and national level, each administrator of each administrative subdivision enjoying considerable autonomy.

As the Head of State, the President has the right to declare war, make peace, grant pardon, make statutes and conclude treaties with other states but action on all these matters must be ratified by the House and the President must remain responsible to the assembly. Suharto was voted into his third term as President in March, 1983, a fourth term lasting until 1989.

Economy

Indonesia is a country rich in natural resources. But she emerged as an indepedent nation in 1949 in a weaker position than most other colonized countries. The 1949 through 1966 period was devoted largely to nation building, foreign adventures, and ideological interests to the detriment of economic development. At the end of the Sukarno era, Indonesia had practically no industry. Years of solid economic growth under President Suharto have changed that. Today Indonesia is self-sufficient in textiles, cement and most kinds of fertilizers. Rich volcanic soils have resulted in widespread development of agriculture on the islands of Sumatra, Java and Bali. Thirty five percent of all arable land is devoted to cultivation and agriculture constitutes about half of the GNP. Smallholder agriculture, consisting mainly of food crops for domestic consumption and production of export produce, employs 60 percent of the labor force. The main crops are rice, corn, cassava, coconut, soyabean and spices. Rubber, tobacco, sugar, copra, hard fiber, coffee and tea are of national importance economically.

Tin has historically been the country's primary mineral export although the importance of oil has increased greatly in recent years. International investment is taking place in the industries of tin, oil, bauxite, nickel, copper and timber, many of which benefit the Western investors and deplete the Indonesian revenues hence contributing to the poverty of the people and plundering of the land.

The poverty and problems of Indonesia, like the country itself, are immense and complex. Because two-thirds of the population is involved in agricultural pursuits, poverty in Indonesia is primarily a rural phenomenon characterized by a high infant mortality rate of 100–150 per 1000, malnutrition affecting about seven million people under the age of five, 70 million people living below the poverty level, an illiteracy rate of 35 percent and a 40 percent unemployment rate.

Indonesia's leaders recognize that their economic development efforts have been far from perfect. They are aware of the problems and shortcomings and see the dimensions of the challenge to bring the country into the modern world.

Climate

If you spend most of your time in air-conditioning, or come from a temperate or cold climate, you'll find it hot; if you live elsewhere along the equator, you'll find it agreeably mild. There is no such thing as a European summer and winter. The only seasonal differences, as the historian Ailsa Zainu'ddin has noted, are that 'the hot season is slightly hotter and not quite so wet as the wet season, while the wet season is slightly wetter and not quite so hot as the hot season.' It is light at 5 a.m. in the morning and dark at 6 p.m. in the evening; this varies less than half an hour either way throughout the year.

Cities on the northern coastal plains average 26°C (78°F) all year round, though the temperature can reach 34°C (94°F) during the day in the drier months between May and September (the best time to visit Java). It is slightly cooler during the wet season between October and the end of April. Relative humidity for the island averages a high 75 percent; this can vary considerably from district to district, but it is seldom oppressive. Towns and cities nearer the south coast are generally a few degrees cooler than those in the north.

Nights are nearly always several degrees cooler. In hill and mountain districts more dramatic changes occur, and in some places the mercury can drop below freezing point.

The rain (most afternoons during the wet season, and intermittently at other times of the year) comes as a tropical downpour, but the clouds normally empty fast and depart as quickly.

Clothing

The accent is on simplicity and comfort. Sports shirts and light washable slacks for men are a basic day-to-day requirement: safari suits with short sleeves and plenty of capacious pockets are eminently suitable. Wear a tie if you're making business calls. Jackets are rarely required, and dinner suits or tuxedos almost never, though a lightweight suit can ward off the chill in air-conditioned hotel dining-rooms and nightclubs. Casual *batik* shirts are popular.

Women's clothing follows a similar pattern: lightweight, simple, washable and casual. Halter-necks and sundresses are sensible, but minis and shorts (except at beach resorts) may offend some people. Pants-suits are fine in the bigger hotels in the evenings, and a simple full-length cotton dress will also come in handy. Bikinis, increasingly worn by young Indonesian women, are fine for hotel pools and beaches. A stole or wrap is recommended for use in air-conditioned restaurants.

For both men and women, easily laundered clothes are a must, as you'll probably want to change at least once during the day; natural fibers such as cotton are far more comfortable than synthetics. Shoes should be 'sensible' if you're planning any walking; sandals are cool, comfortable and recommended. Don't bother about a raincoat: it will heat you up like a jockey's sweatbox, especially if it's plastic. Much better by far is to buy a cheap oiled-paper bamboo-frame umbrella.

Once you get above 300 meters, the nights and mornings start to get cool. A view of the sunrise from the crater rim of Gunung Bromo in East Java, one of the island's most spectacular sights, definitely demands cold-weather clothing and (though it may sound ridiculous at only 8° below the equator) gloves or mittens are advisable as well. Mountain resort towns like Tretes, Selecta, Sarangan, Kaliurang and Lembang all promise cool mornings and evenings.

Batik will certainly catch your eye. One easily-sewn seam turns a length into a *sarong* that's ideal for evening relaxation in your room, for quick flits to the bathroom, for sleeping in, or as a light covering in small hotels where a top sheet is a rarity.

The last word in casual attire usually belongs to the young dollar-a-day group. While Indonesians may look askance at some of the gear, they take exception only to immodesty and lack of cleanliness (being clean, modest people themselves). Neatness is important. So too is dressing in a respectful manner for temples and palaces which have a strong religious significance for the people of Java; T-shirts are not appreciated in the *kratons* (palaces) of Central Java.

Time Zones

There are three time-zones in Indonesia. Java and the neighboring islands of Madura, Sumatra and Bali are 7 hours ahead of Greenwich Mean Time (GMT plus 7). Central Indonesian Standard Time is GMT plus 8 hours and East Indonesian Standard Time is GMT plus 9 hours.

Indonesians usually regard the dark hours before midnight as belonging to the next day, though the calendar date does not change. For example, the Western Saturday night is, for Indonesians, *Malam Minggu* (literally the 'night of Sunday'). For an evening appointment, be sure to specify the date as well as the day. Many religious festivals adhere to the Islamic calendar, and a Javanese calendar with a five-day week is still used (side-by-side with the Gregorian calendar) in Central and East Java.

Etiquette

The people of Java combine natural friendliness with an exceptional degree of courtesy. Although different ethnic groups within Java have their own customs, the basic aim is to make life harmonious and pleasant for everybody. Naturally, foreigners are not expected to be aware of the many subtleties of etiquette, but a general knowledge of local manners will help make your stay more rewarding.

Generally, Indonesians dislike being conspicuous and are basically conformist at heart. To be different is embarrassing. It is essential to avoid shaming people (making them *malu*), particularly in front of others. No matter how hot or tired or frustrated you get, try not to shout or show anger.

Since the Javanese dislike saying unpleasant things to another person, they avoid doing so directly and will often say what they think the listener wants to hear; an outright 'no' is seldom heard (be prepared for 'perhaps' or 'maybe next week').

The majority of people in Java are Muslim (at least nominally), and certain Muslim customs are widely observed. The major ones relate to the left hand, which is used for private bodily cleansing and is therefore unclean. Giving or receiving anything with the left hand is strictly avoided (you may notice Javanese clasping their right forearm with their left hand as they give you food or money). When you eat without a spoon (for example, when tackling fried chicken) use only the right hand.

There are other courtesies regarding eating and drinking. When given food or drink, never start until actually asked to do so. Most people like their tea or coffee much cooler than Westerners, so you may have to watch your drink get progressively cooler until your host says *silahkan minum* (please drink). Don't empty your glass completely unless you want a refill; leave a small amount in the bottom. When eating, help yourself to only a small portion of food initially, and take more when invited.

Although it is sometimes hard to remember, pointing with your finger (especially at people) is considered ill-mannered, so use your thumb with your fingers tucked lightly underneath. If you're beckoning someone, don't rake the air with a crooked finger — it's more acceptable to use a downward wave of the hand (almost 'camp' but not quite). Putting your hand or hands on your hips is interpreted as definance or arrogance, and this social gaffe is compounded if you stand with your legs akimbo, gun-slinger style.

Indonesia's long history of exposure to a variety of faiths and beliefs, and its people's pragmatic approach in accepting what has seemed relevant (and discarding what has seemed irrelevant), are reflected in the generally tolerant attitudes of the various religious groups. Islam is the dominant religion (95 percent of Indonesians are nominally Muslim), but the churches and assembly halls of many Christian denominations can be found all over Java, along with the shrines and temples of other faiths.

Tipping: Tipping, with its attendant abuses, is increasing in Java but has not reached epidemic proportions. Unfortunately, in some hotels tips are increasingly expected for shoddy service, and foreigners with more money than finesse are partly to blame for this (though the compulsory 10 percent 'service' charge in many major hotels is a contributing factor). You'll generally find that the people of Java provide service with a smile, and that a tip for special service is money well spent. There is no firm rule, but Rp100 is fair for bellboys, barbers, bar attendants and waiters in big cities; in smaller cities and towns tips are not normally expected in restaurants and eating places.

Airport and hotel porters expect Rp.200–300 for each bag (of average size). Tips are not required with metered taxis, Rp.100 for special service is fair, and taxis hired by the hour may merit Rp.100.

Sometimes, somewhere in Java, you will be importuned by beggars. Looking through them or ignoring them won't make them go away: whether you're down to your last *rupiah* or not, they *know* that all foreigners are rich. The answer is simple: one or two very small coins, given with grace.

Air-conditioning

This is something you'll have to learn to live without if you depart from the big or higher-priced hotels. Many people regard it's absence as nothing more than a minor inconvenience, for nights in Java are nearly always pleasantly mild, and cooling breezes sweep through most towns at the close of day. Most places of public entertainment also lack air-conditioning, so a fan is a good idea (woven pandanus-leaf, tortoise-shell, *kulit* (leather), or aromatic root).

Electricity

In most places, it is 220–240 volts since a massive city-wide change-over. Major towns in Java are well supplied with electricity but if you get off the beaten track, your source of light may be kerosene or paraffin lamps.

Weights and Measures

The Indonesian measuring system is based on the European metric system.

Banking

The stabilization of the *rupiah*, the growth of foreign investment and joint ventures, and the opening up of oil-search concessions have brought many foreign banks to Indonesia in recent years. There are now more than 45 international banks with offices of representations in Java. Bank Indonesia is the Republic's central bank, and (among other things) is responsible for the issuing of bank notes and coinage; Bank Negara Indonesia has branches throughout the country and offers full banking facilities for both local and foreign currencies. Banking hours vary, but the bank of your choice will always be open between 8 a.m. and noon Monday through Friday, and between 8 a.m. and 10.30 a.m. on Saturdays. Banks are closed on Sundays and public holidays. (*see* appendix for a list of international and domestic banks)

Business hours

Java gets up with the sun and goes to work soon afterwards.To make the most of your time, start early and try to get your shopping and business calls done before midday. Hours of business vary from city to city, and from one business to another.

Indonesians schedule appointments on *jam karet* or rubber time, where time can be stretched to fit the occasion. Business meetings and appointments rarely start at the scheduled hour. It is in Indonesia where one learns that patience is a virtue.

It is impossible to specify times in detail, but the following guide should help:

Government offices are open from 8 a.m. to 3 p.m. on Monday through Thursday, from 8 a.m. to 11 a.m. on Fridays and to 1 p.m. on Saturdays. They are closed on Sundays and public holidays.

Trading firms and travel agents start by 8 a.m., have an hour off for lunch between noon and 1 p.m., and close at 4 p.m. Monday through Friday, with a half-day on Saturdays.

Department stores and supermarkets in the bigger cities are open 6 days a week (the closing day varies) from 9.30 a.m. until 7 p.m., but the majority of shops and many eating places are open only from 9 a.m. till 2 p.m. and again from around 5 p.m. to 8 p.m. or a little later. In many small towns, restaurants and eating places close a couple of hours after sunset.

Public Holidays

Religion is a way of life in Indonesia, and throughout the entire archipelago people enjoy and celebrate Buddhist, Hindu, Moslem and Christian holidays. The first national holiday is **New Year's Day** observed throughout the country. Although celebrations vary from area to area, it is often celebrated with street carnivals, fireworks, special entertainment and shows. **Chinese New Year's,** timed on the lunar calendar, continues for 15 days until the night of *Cap Go Meh*. In contrast, the Javanese New Year **Suro** is celebrated very quietly. The Balinese New Year **Nyepi** (Day of Silence) is also a national holiday timed to the Wuku Calendar which divides the year into 210 days. It is a Hindu holiday of retreat and spiritual purification.

The most important Moslem celebration is **Idul Fitri** (Grebeg Sjawal) on the first day of the 10th month (Sjawwal) of the Islamic calendar symbolizing the end of the fasting month of Ramadan. All over the country mass prayers are held in mosques and town squares and everyone wears new clothes and visits relatives seeking forgiveness for past transgressions. It is a two-day public holiday. Also on the Islamic calendar is **Maulud Nabi** (or Grebeg Mulud) in commemoration of the birthday of the Prophet Mohammed preceeded by the Sekaten festival (*see Festivals*). The day of the **Ascension of the Prophet Mohammed** falls on the 27th day of the seventh month on the Islamic calendar and **Idul Adah** (Grebeg Besar) on the 10th day of the 11th Islamic month is the Moslem day of sacrifice where goats and cattle are slaughtered and meat is given to the poor and needy.

Good Friday in March is a national holiday as is the **Ascension of Christ** (Kenaikan Isa Almasih), the 14th day after the resurection.

April 21 is **Kartini Day,** a national holiday commemorating the birthday of the late Raden Ajeng Kartini, the pioneer for the emancipation of Indonesian women at the turn of the century. Everywhere women appear in national dress.

More recently the impressive Buddhist ceremony on **Waicak Day** (*see* Festivals) became a national holiday. It is commemorated at the Borobudur in May.

August 17 is Indonesian national **Independence Day** (Hari Proklamasi) celebrated throughout the country with organized sports events, puppet and shadow plays, traditional cultural performances, carnivals and festivals. Jakarta usually has the biggest celebrations of all.

October 5 is **Armed Forces Day,** the anniversary of the founding of the Indonesian Armed Forces with military parades and demonstrations of the latest achievements of the army, navy, air force and police.

Christmas Eve is celebrated by Christians throughout Indonesia with church services and mass. A joyous national public holiday, **Christmas** is celebrated with candlelight gatherings and religious ceremonies.

Be sure to check the schedules for holidays during the period of your visit: the lunar, Islamic and Hindu holidays fall on different days each year of the solar or western calendar. For a list of other colorful events, see the section on Festivals.

Transportation

Domestic Air Travel

Indonesia has several domestic airlines which offer services within Java. Garuda, the nation's flag carrier, and Merpati offer the most regular services to be followed by Bouraq, Pelita and Mandala. Among them, they fly to Jakarta, Bandung, Semarang, Yogyakarta, Surakarta and Surabaya. All domestic flights take off from the Jakarta Kemayoran Airport. (*see* appendix for domestic airlines listing)

Garuda, in addition, offers Jakarta-Surabaya and Jakarta-Semarang shuttle services. Reservations cannot be booked for these flights, so it's good idea to arrive an hour or more before the scheduled departure. During holiday seasons, the flights are more crowded.

Buses

This is the cheapest, most easily accessible but terribly crowded means of getting around the bigger cities. A single fare rate prevails no matter how far you are going. Route maps for Jakarta can be bought at roadside stands and bookstores.

For intercity buses, the advantages are low cost and frequency of service. The buses used on the fast night-express runs between big towns are large, modern and comfortable. Many are air-conditioned. Next to flying, this is the preferred method of travel for the majority of Indonesians, not only from the standpoint of comfort but they are faster and cheaper than first-class trains. Buses link Jakarta with all the main cities of Java.

Colts, the trade name of the Mitsubishi minibus, link the major towns too. They are slightly more expensive and, without doubt, the most dangerous form of public transportation.

Bus company offices are usually centrally located, but bus and Colt stations, due to a building craze in recent years, are quite often on the edge of a town or city.

Railways

The main trunk lines are from Jakarta through Yogyakarta and Solo to Surabaya, or along the north coast through Cirebon and Semarang. Frequent trains from Jakarta to Bandung link up with east-bound regional services. At the top end of the scale is the air-conditioned *Bima* night express from Jakarta through Yogyakarta to Surabaya; the 1,300-kilometer journey takes 16 hours, the first-class cabins have two berths and wash basins, while the second class cabins have three berths (fares are Rp.28,000 and Rp.22,500 respectively).

You will unfortunately have to expect organizational inefficiency if you travel by rail. Exact departure times are not easily available and tickets can only be bought when the locket at the station opens, usually a couple of hours before the train leaves, and collection is usually chaotic. For a small administrative fee the agent will get the ticket (which saves a lot of bother) but again you can only pick it up a few hours before departure time. In Jakarta the best agency is Carnation Travel Service at Jalan Menteng Raya No. 24, Jakarta Pusat (tel. 344027) and at Jalan Kiyai Maja No. 53, Kebayoran Baru, Jakarta Selatan (tel. 713943). It is virtually impossible to book a ticket from a town you have not yet reached: if you are in Yogya, and want to make an onward booking from Bandung, forget it!

One good thing about train stations is that they are centrally located, with *losmens* nearby. Jakarta and Surabaya have more than one train station and different routes leave from different stations, so make sure you are at the right place.

Waterways

Island hopping is still possible on small ferries but these vessels are not particularly attractive to tourists as accommodations and sanitary facilities are primitive. The ferry services come in three classes and fares vary accordingly. The ferry charge from Ketapang to Gilimanuk in Bali, for example, ranges from Rp.375 for a first class to Rp.125 for a third.

Public Transportation

Taxis: Taxis are more expensive than other forms of transport, but are more convenient for distances over two kilometers. 'Cruising cabs' with meters are found only in Jakarta and Surabaya. Radio-controlled metered cabs are available in Jakarta. The meter starts at Rp.250 for the first kilometer and ticks up at Rp.125 for each additional kilometer.

Unmetered taxis are still common in Jakarta, and abound in other towns and cities where they cluster around airport, train and bus terminals. Many are private cars, and you should be able to negotiate a price of around Rp.1,000 for most journeys within a radius of two or three kilometers. Many taxis also operate as 'hire cars' and charge by the hour at a minimum of two hours (and sometimes three hours). In Jakarta the rate is around Rp.3,000 to Rp.4,000 for two hours (it is best to make arrangements through your hotel); outside of Jakarta the rate is around Rp.1,500–Rp.2,000 per hour.

Some drivers of metered taxis will offer you a flat rate for the journey (always higher than the meter would show), or claim that the meter is broken. Try for another cab with a working meter, or strike a price of no more than Rp.1,000 for a reasonable distance.

Opelets and Bemos: Operating in the suburbs and on the outskirts of big cities like Jakarta are small vans holding from six to 10 passengers (there always seems room for one more). The smallest is the three-wheeled *bemo,* basically a motorscooter with an enclosed driver's cabin up front and a six-man passenger compartment behind. An *opelet* is a four-wheeled vehicle, of various makes and vintages, the older models gradually being replaced by new Japanese passenger vans. Different cities occasionally have different names for these vehicles. Usually they ply fixed routes at Rp.50 or 100 per person, irrespective of distance. In Jakarta *opelets* generally have fixed routes though *bemos* are free to move anywhere only within a specific zone of the city.

The term *opelet* (variously Colt, *bemo,* taxi) also describes the extraordinary range of cars and vans which run between towns and villages all over the island. The ubiquitous Colts, modern but already showing signs of mistreatment are backed up in many places by American sedans of dubious vintage, from 1929 Fords to Plymouths, Mercurys, Dodges and De Sotos of the mid-40s to the early 50s (including a few forlorn examples of the classic back-to-front Studebaker).

The Becak: This is a three-wheeled pedi-cab with room for two adults or six tiny school children. The character of the *becak* varies from town to town, and the aspiring connoisseur will quickly note the difference between (for example) the Yogyakarta model, with a low seat-back and bulbous mud-guards, and the Jakarta version with its high seat-back and narrow mudguards. Even more striking are the regional variations in decoration, for a great deal of care and imagination are lavished on these mobile picture shows. The student of *becak* iconography will fall in love with those in Bandung and Garut, smothered with gaily painted episodes from the *Ramayana* or scenes of placid lakes and alpine peaks; or the names, in wrought and welded iron, which bedeck the *becaks* in East Java: 'Radio,' 'Norton,' 'Luxor,' 'Honda,' 'Manis' (sweet), 'Datsun,' 'Timun' (cucumber).

Becak drivers, working long hours for little money, have a reputation as one of society's unruly elements. They're a pretty tough breed (and they need to be), but are amicable towards visitors: they'll try to charge too much, but once you know the going rate in a town or city (and this varies) you should have no trouble striking a reasonable price. Be sure to do your bargaining before and not after your journey. Fares range from Rp.200 to Rp.300. In such cities as Jakarta, Semarang and Surabaya, *becaks* are banned from certain major streets during specific hours.

The Dokar: The 'dog car' is a two-wheeled covered pony-cart found in most parts of the island. Like the *becak* it offers fascinating regional variations: handsome silver-ornamented harnesses and scarlet head-dresses around the southeast of West Java; dark green carts with wide-apart brass-tipped shafts in the south of Central Java: solid maroon colors along the central north coast; high-wheeled versions with strange box-like structures on the top, their rear windows fretted with a sunray design, near Jepara and Demak; huge crude carts with two-meter wheels in an isolated stretch of Madura's northwest coast. Packed with brightly garbed village ladies on their way to market, the *dokars* are a delight to the eye and a natural candidate for cameras.

The Andong: A four-wheeled horse-cart found mainly around Yogyakarta and Solo. What it lacks in decorative qualities is more than made up for in size and the amount of people and goods it can carry. It's like being jolted back to the 1890s to watch the stately progress of an *andong* laden down with four good housewives and enough market produce for an agricultural fair. It is also a delightful way to travel: if you're in Yogya, take an *andong* ride to Kota Gede's silver workshops. In Bogor there are four-wheeled horse-carts known as *delman;* they carry three passengers inside, and one next to the driver. Determine the price beforehand.

Car and Motorcycle Rentals

Car hire service is offered by a few of the larger travel agents and some private operators. Cars almost invariably come with a driver. Buses and mini-buses are available for group travel, but can normally be arranged only in the bigger cities or through bus companies with branches in most parts of Java. You can save yourself a lot of time and trouble by going straight to a good travel agent or hotel for details.

Drive-yourself service is still in its infancy in Java and, if anything, discouraged. To emphasize the point, very few car hire companies of individuals are willing to lease a car without their own drivers to take you around in safety.

Motoring Advisories

Driving yourself is not a good idea. Few rent-a-car companies will allow you to anyway, but if you have brought your own car or borrowed one to make a few trips the following pointers and suggestions should help.

Indonesia drives on the left. The majority of cars are therefore equipped with steering wheels on the righthand side, though a few American-made cars have not been converted. Non-verbal road signs indicating grades, railway crossings, one-way streets and so on follow accepted international codes, though you will notice some unusual ones prohibiting the entry of *becaks,* bullock-carts or pony-carts. Of the verbal signs, the most important

The deluge of magazines includes many devoted to the private lives of film stars and pop-culture heroes, but the weekly news magazine *Tempo* (shamelessly similar in format to the *Time*) is excellent value as a summary of what has happened, why, and to whom, in the previous week around the world and at home in Indonesia. Large hotels and big bookstore chains are the best source of international newspapers and magazines, but prices are steep; weeklies like *Time* and *Newsweek* are easy to find.

Radio and TV

Radio is a vital force in the dissemination of *Bahasa Indonesia* and a vehicle for aural aspects of Indonesia's diverse cultural traditions. Besides the government radio (RRI) there are small commercial networks in larger cities. There are also a great source of pop music. For the foreign visitor the chief appeal of television might be reruns of ancient serials from the West. On the main television network (TVRI) there is a nightly American show at 10.30 p.m. after the news.

Health and Emergencies

Pharmacies

Proprietary brands of drugs and medicines are available through hotel drugstores and *apotik* (pharmacies) in larger towns; physicians' prescriptions will be filled at an *apotik*.

Hospitals and Doctors

Good in the big cities, but in rural and provincial areas doctors are often hard to find. Major hotels normally have a resident house physician, or a regular physician on call in case of emergencies. General practitioners (*Praktek Umum*) are normally open for surgery calls between 4 p.m. and 6 p.m. (*see* the appendix for listings of pharmacies and hospitals).

Security and Crime

Indonesians borrow things and forget to return them, although they rarely borrow from each other. Be sure, when you choose a room, that the windows and doors can be securely locked and that you are the only one with the key. Thieves can even enter your room and steal your purse, your camera or your satchel while you sleep. Security in the more expensive hotels is better. Even in the streets your bags could be stolen off your body by a passing motorcyclist or slit by thieves with razors on the bus or the sidewalk. A pack, a purse or a shoulder bag can disappear through an open window of a train, a restaurant and even from your own car. Moneybelts worn inside your clothes are good idea. Jewelry and watches which can be stolen right off your body should be removed and cameras should never dangle around your neck in public. When it's gone, there's no use going to the police. At the very most, they will console you and more often than not they will ask you to pay them to look for your lost article. It's best to carry your passport, air tickets, important documents and money with you at all times.

Dining Out

Centuries of contact with other great civilisations have left their mark on the wonderfully varied cuisine of Indonesia. Indian and Arab traders brought not only merchandise, Hinduism and Islam, but new spices such as ginger, cardamom and turmeric. Later the Chinese and (to a lesser extent) the Dutch added their own distinctive touch to the cooking pot. The result is a happy blend of the best of each culinary tradition.

Spices abound in Javanese cooking, and are usually partnered by coconut milk (made by squeezing the grated flesh of the nut) which adds a rich flavor and creamy texture to dishes containing intriguing tropical vegetables, poultry, meat and fish. Happily for the unaccustomed foreign palate, Javanese cooks are light-handed with both spices and chilies (unlike their Sumatran counterparts). They are fond of using sugar as well as fragrant roots and leaves, and the result is food which is both subtle and sophisticated.

The basis of an Indonesian meal is rice (the word of rice and meal is the same: *nasi*). Each person treats himself to a helping of steaming white rice and then to a little of the three or four dishes of vegetables or meat (known as *lauk*) which are placed in the center of the table for all to share. Indonesians do not swamp their plates with food on the first round, but help themselves to a little more of their fancy as the meal progresses. A side dish or *sambal,* made with red-hot chilies grounded with dried shrimp paste and other seasonings such as lime juice, should be approached with caution (if you ever scorch your mouth or throat with chilies don't rush for the nearest glass of water to quench the flames; water aggravates the problem, and cold beer or other fizzy drinks are worse: the quickest relief comes from plain boiled rice, bread, cucumber or a banana). Common side dishes are *tempe,* a protein-rich savory cake of fermented soya-beans, and small crisp cookies (*rempeyek*) made of peanuts. Both are delicious.

The Dutch word *rijsttafel* (rice table) is sometimes associated with Indonesian food. The name was originally given to gargantuan banquets of rice and countless dishes of vegetables and meats accompanied by savory offerings such as *krupuk* (fried prawn or fish crisps), *acar* (cucumber pickles), sliced banana, peanuts, chilies, and anything else capable of adding fragrance and flavor to the whole mountainous spread. Full-scale extravaganzas are seldom witnessed (let alone eaten!) these days, although a few hotels make a modest attempt at imitation, and all of the individual dishes of the old *rijsttafel* can still be found and enjoyed. For the most traditional *rijsttafel* feast, try **The Oasis** restaurant on Jalan Raden Saleh in Jakarta. But go prepared for a big bill.

National favorites include *gado-gado,* a lightly cooked vegetable salad which includes beansprouts, cabbage and potatoes covered with a rich peanut sauce; *Padang* food from Central Sumatra is robust and fiery (a wide range of dishes is placed on the table, and you pay only for those you eat . . . the beef *rendang* and *otak* or brains are particularly good); *sate*, sometimes regarded as Indonesia's national dish, is a tempting assortment of meat, chicken or seafood grilled on skewers over a charcoal fire and served with a spicy sauce.

A tasty, substantial soup known as *soto* is found everywhere. Try *soto Madura*, a rich coconut-milk soup delicately spiced and chock full of noodles, chicken, beansprouts and other vegetables, or *soto Bandung* made from tripe.

Chinese influenced noodle dishes such as *mie goreng* (fried wheat-flour noodles) and *bakmi* (rice-flour noodles, either fried or in soup) are also common. *Capcai* (previously *tjap tjai*) is very popular and tastes much better than its Western name 'chop suey' would suggest.

Javanese vegetables dishes are excellent. The slightly sour *sayur asam* (especially around Jakarta) is well worth trying. Other Jakarta specialties, are *martabak* (an Indian stuffed pancake) and *gulai kambing*, a thin mutton curry with a taste of turmeric.

Central Javanese delicacies include *gudeg*, made from young jackfruit cooked in coconut milk and *ayam goreng* (fried chicken). The variation known around Yogya as *mBok Berek*, is superb: the chicken is simmered in spiced coconut milk before being fried. Move over, Colonel Sanders!

You will, of course, find *nasi goreng* (fried rice) everywhere; topped with a fried egg, it makes a good breakfast. *Nasi rames*, white rice served with a small helping of savory meat and vegetables is very good.

Some restaurants offer *bistiek*, so-called European food with chips, tinned peas and all. It's frightful!

Like all Indonesians, Javanese are very fond of snacks. Wherever you go, you'll find someone selling sticky cakes, crunchy peanut biscuits, strange salted nuts and lentils, steamed sweetmeats wrapped in banana leaf, and a host of other extraordinary but thoroughly delicious goodies. Although ice-creams and other iced confections are sold in most places, it's wise (for health reasons) to avoid those sold by street vendors.

The tropical fruits of Indonesia are excellent: pineapples, bananas (ranging from tiny finger-sized *pisang mas* up to the foot-long *pisang raja*), papayas and mangoes are joined by even more unusual seasonal fruits. Some of the most outstanding are rambutans (hairy red skins enclosing sweet white meat), mangosteens (purplish black skins with a very sweet juicy white fruit inside) and *jeruk Bali* (pomelos). The huge spiky durian has (to most people) a revolting rotten smell, but its buttery-rich fruit is adored by local people and a few adventurous visitors.

Thirst Quenchers

Most familiar Western drinks are available in Java, though some of them take on an exciting new dimension. Javanese tea is usually very fragrant, and similar to Chinese tea in flavor. Served hot or cold, *manis* (with sugar) or *pahit* (without), it is delicate and refreshing. Javanese coffee is a delight to real coffee lovers, being served almost Turkish-style with a few grounds floating around (known as *kopi tobruk*). Locally manufactured beer (Anker and Bintang) is similar to European lager beer. It's moderately priced and available everywhere, but as it is seldom kept chilled, you may be faced with the choice of warm beer, beer *pakai es* (with ice) or no beer at all.

Fresh fruit juices are popular. *Air jeruk*, as orange juice is called, is served either hot or cold: be sure to specify what you want. There are also juices made from pineapple, apple and other common fruits. Westerners accustomed to regarding avocado as a vegetable will probably be amazed at the *apokat* drink, but it's worth trying: avocado, rum or coffee essence, palm sugar and tinned milk are blended to make a thick, rich liquid that leaves most milkshakes for dead.

Cordials are known as *stroop:* among the best are *zirzak*, made from soursop and *markisa*, made from passionfruit. *Es kopyor* is favorite concoction of rose syrup, ice and scoops of jelly-like flesh from the inside of the *kopyor* coconut. *Es campur*, mixture of shaved ice with fruits and jelly (also known as *cendol*), *es tape* and *dawet santen* are all absolutely delicious.

Where to Eat

Eating places in Java range from expensive Western restaurants in the first class hotels to large Chinese restaurants, medium to small sized eating shops with limited menus, '*warungs*' (street stalls) with their wooden benches or stools right down to itinerant food vendors who carry their kitchens on bamboo shoulder poles.

The large Chinese restaurants are generally clean and serve fairly good Chinese food. They're the only places in Java where you can find pork, which is forbidden to Muslims. Many smaller eating shops sell inexpensive noodle dishes, or specialize in one type of food such as *Padang* cuisine. *Warungs* also specialize, often in *soto* or similar dishes, while much of the best *sate* comes from the street hawkers. In Jakarta it is generally advisable to avoid *warungs* since the standard of cleanliness is often dubious. Outside of Jakarta, provided you use your own judgement and eat in places that seem clean, you need not worry about suffering unpleasant after-effects. (*See* the appendix for a listing of suggested eating places in the major cities.)

Shopping

There are basically two kinds of shopping in Java: situations in which you pay a fixed price *(harga pas)*, and situations in which you bargain.

A fixed price is a fixed price, and that's it. You may strike off a few *rupiah* on shop-soiled goods, or get a slight reduction on a superseded model, but in supermarkets, department stores and in shops run along Western lines the price tag generally means what it says.

Within the overall shopping scene in Java, however, such places are rare. Outside of the biggest cities and towns they seldom (if ever) exist, and you will find that most shopping transactions will involve bargaining: the first price asked is never the price finally paid, and even a modicum of bargaining skill can save money.

There are some peculiarities. Sales pressure is generally low (compared with Singapore's famous Change Alley, it doesn't exist). Even more striking, especially if you've experienced the bazaars of the Middle East or Central Asia, is an apparent reluctance to sell, the lack of a sense of urgency to make a sale. The old ploy of stalking out the door in feigned disinterest is pretty much a waste of time, especially in Central and East Java, even if the seller's best price is demonstrably outrageous. You won't be called back. If he doesn't sell now, maybe he'll sell tomorrow, or perhaps next year. Perhaps never. It doesn't seem to matter.

On the other hand, don't play with bargaining. If you have offered *your* rock-bottom price and if your offer has been accepted (even if it seems absurdly low to you), you should honor the negotiations by buying.

Determining the real price in a bargaining situation is largely a matter of experience, knowledge, judgement and (sometimes) sheer luck. It is predictable that as a foreigner, floundering through the complexities of a *pasar* (market), you'll be asked to pay too much for fruit, or for a woven hat that appeals to you. As a general rule, if you don't know the going rate for such things, try not to pay more than 50 percent or at most 70 percent of the starting price.

In the realm of handicrafts and souvenirs just about anything can happen. Prices are on the up and up, especially in the case of antiques and old curios where the source of supply must eventually dry up. Oil lamps, *wayang klitik* figures, decorated buckles and gilt-and-red wood-carvings, as a few examples, are becoming increasingly expensive. Handicraft and artisan items like *batik* lengths and *wayang kulit* figures are also rising in price, though many handsome pieces are still bargains.

In most of the larger antique-cum-curio shops, and especially those in the big hotels, bargaining is a tough business. Prices are normally inflated to start with (a fairly natural outcome of the supply and demand cycle), and getting a reduction of even 10 or 15 percent can be quite an achievement. Some places can't be bothered with bargaining, though these are rare; others seem to enjoy the challenge.

Apart from *not* paying the first price asked, there can be no hard and fast rules about bargaining in Java. It exists, it's widespread, and is fun, though obviously on small items there's little point in quibbling over a mere hundred *rupiah* or so, unless you enjoy the spirit of the transaction. Values are of course relative: even if you get something for a tenth of the price you'd pay something for a tenth of the price you'd pay for the same item in New York, London or Amsterdam you may still be paying too much by Java's standards. Nevertheless, the value that *you* place on something is always a good guide on how much you should spend (even if your friends think you're crazy).

An excellent place of basic training is **Jalan Surabaya** in Jakarta, the local version of every big city's flea market where all kinds of tantalizing bric-à-brac, curiosities and occasional treasures can be found. The **Pasar Trewindu** market in Solo and the **Malang market** also have a good range of quaint bits and pieces ranging from fine antiques to outrageous but delightful junk.

Antiques and works of art deserve their own set of cautions, and are discussed in greater detail below. Prices are rising steadily as the demand for irreplaceable pieces increases. Last year's bargain brought home by a friend may since have gone up three or four times in value, though you can still be lucky if you know your chosen field well and don't mind shopping around.

A general caution when you venture into markets and similar crowded shopping areas: keep a tight rein on your wallet or purse, and try to avoid flashing high-value bank notes when you're making an inexpensive purchase. Even the Javanese will warn you about pickpockets. Also keep an eye on any small parcels or bags that you may be carrying with you, especially if you put them down for a moment while you look at a possible purchase.

What to Buy

The most that can be done at this point is to whet your appetite. The longer you stay and the farther you travel through Java the more you'll find things, big and small, old and new, that take your fancy.

Batik: This is the name of a traditional Indonesian process of dyeing cloth: the area to be left free of dye is coated with a thin layer of wax, the cloth is dyed, the wax is then removed, and the process is repeated again with more wax, more dyeing (this time another color) until the required design has been achieved. This scarcely begins to suggest the complexities and subtleties of *batik* production, and does not even hint at the kaleidoscopic variety of patterns and colors: there are geometric batiks, flowery batiks, batiks incorporating ancient motifs, vibrant modern batiks — you'll see them in their multitudinous array all over Java. The magnificient artistry of the finest hand-drawn cloths commands and deserves very high prices, but even mass-produced batiks possess a unique charm. Many excellent batiks are available ready-made as clothes, and a long simple batik skirt is an elegant addition to milady's evening wardrobe. There are also batik shirts, fans, hats, shoes, slippers, ties and handbags. It is even possible to buy partly-finished batik; in the early stages of the process, the brown wax on a cream cloth with one or two dyes applied is striking to look at, and makes an unusual memento.

Other Materials: *Kain ikat* is a kind of cloth, widespread in Indonesia, in which the individual warp threads (and, on rare occasions, the weft threads as well) are dyed to a predetermined pattern *before* the cloth is woven. Prices for good pieces are high but the finished materials are minor works of art. Machine woven *kain ikat*, known as *tenunan*, is also sold in Java and it is less expensive than the hand-made materials. A little *kain ikat* is made in Java.

Several beautiful handwoven cloths from Sumatra, Sulawesi and Maluku are sold in Java. *Kain songket*, a Sumatran material heavily embroidered with thick gold thread complementing rich ochres, oranges and other 'autumn' tones; the antique cloths, which are particularly attractive, were worn as a sarong on formal or ceremonial occasions. Sulawesi silk is fine and delicate, and available in a brilliant range of colors (the width of a single piece is only 70cm. but wider pieces more suitable for dressmaking are becoming available.) Art shops often stock *kain ikat* from Nusatenggara Timur, the best known being *Kain Sumba* with its fine animal figures and rich red color. A popular inexpensive material is '*lurik*,' rather like a 'homespun' in weight and texture; it is a durable and attractive material in checks, stripes and 'tartans!'

Furniture: Locally made furniture using materials like bamboo and *rotan* (rattan), or teak, beautifully carved with traditional motifs, is very attractive and serviceable. Much of its has a strong 'Eastern' flavor which is the perfect compliment to other smaller souvenirs. Jakarta has a large number of shops where furniture can be made to your specifications or designs (even an old advertizement or photograph will do as a starting point), but obviously you'll need time if you're having furniture made to order; 'old' cured wood is generally used, though ask for a money back guarantee against splitting if you're taking your treasures to a less humid climate (air-conditioning or central heating can quickly split and warp wood which has been cut and cured in the tropics).

Woodcarving: A profile output of carved wooden figures, heads, dancing girls and bare-breasted peasant maidens adorns every art and curio shop through the length and breadth of Java. Their link with traditional Javanese culture is tenuous, and the curious elongated figures from Bali that are happily snapped up as pieces of 'folk art' are hapless (and highly profitable) variations on Brancusi-like themes that found their way to the island during the 1930s: they're as traditional as 'acid rock,' though the skill of the carver is often outstanding. There are also many tasteful, classically-styled heads with ornamental crowns and tiaras, and there are excellent boxes in teak and sandalwood to choose from as well. The quality of the craftsmanship and the wood itself (which also includes mahogany, ironwood and striped ebony) vary considerably, as do the prices. Many shops offer small pieces of lacquered and gilded carving, often of mixed Chinese and Javanese inspiration, which in days gone by, adorned wedding beds and other large pieces of furniture. Much of this carving is very fine, with birds, flowers and plant motifs rendered in loving detail. Similar carving can be found on old herbal medicine chests, 'vanity cases' (sometimes with mirrors) and cupbords ranging from miniature size to wardrobes.

Puppets and Masks: The parchment *wayang kulit* puppets who populate the ancient *Mahabharata* and *Ramayana* sagas in Java's shadow plays are, along with *batik*, the highpoint in the Javanese handicrafts tradition. The intricate hand-cut detail of a Krisna or one of the heroic Pandawa brothers is lacework in leather and an outstanding *wayang kulit* figure may take weeks or even months of pain-staking cutting and painting. Many of the figures 'for sale' would never pass muster with a discrimina-ting puppet-master, but they are mostly well-crafted and make a handsome souvenir.

The *wayang golek* or wooden puppet theater is popular in West-Java and is found occasionally in Central Java (*golek* translates broadly as 'in the round'). West Java draws on the repertoire of the *Mahabharata* and *Ramayana* stories, and also includes the *Panji* stories which originally developed in East Java. Performances in Central Java favor characters from a series of Islamic stories; despite Islamic strictures regarding representation of the human form, the puppets' features are remarkably lifelike, though the "baddies" are suitably demonic. The costumes are sometimes Arabic in inspiration, and sometimes based on 19th Century European military uniforms. West Java's puppets are larger and more stylised.

Wayang klitik puppets, also made of wood and featuring *Panji* characters, are flat and two-dimensional with shallow carving. The moveable arms are made of leather. *Klitik* is dying out, and is rarely performed now except in parts of East Java. Most of the puppets are old, and though crudely worked in comparison with the *wayang kulit* and *wayang golek* figures they have a strong character of their own.

Topeng masks are worn by human actors taking part in 'live' performances of the *Panji* stories, and offer a startling range of smoothly refined heroes and heroines and their excitingly grotesque adversaries. Good masks and puppets are finely worked and deserve a place on your shopping list.

Leathergoods: Pierced, tooled and colored parch-ment in the *wayang kulit* style also makes attractive lampshades, bookmarks and other serviceable souvenir items. Buff-colored embossed leather from Yogyakarta comes in a wide array of bags, cases, belts, pouches and open sandals; the leather ages to a rich, light mahogany color which can be helped along with a liberal dose of coconut oil or a good leather soap. Prices are inexpensive, but you should check the stitching.

Krises: The armorer's art died years ago in Java, and with it died the ability to produce a good kris (*keris*) or dagger. Nobody can now follow the extraordinary metallurgical skill which enabled the smith to fold and re-fold two or even three types of iron to produce a blade with successive areas of light and dark metal like contour lines on a good map (a process frequently but incorrectly known as 'damascening'). The *kris*, either straight or wavy-bladed, is reputedly endowed with supernatural qualities, and the blade itself is the repository of the soul of the weapon's first or bravest owner. The blade was of much greater importance than the grip or scabbard, even though these were often beautifully carved and ornamented.

Today, within Java, an outstanding blade may change hands for Rp.1,000,000. Good blades, finely inlaid with gold, occasionally turn up in antique shops and are in the Rp.100,000 to Rp.250,000 range (you won't find them on display, but they will be shown if your interest seems deep enough). Some attractive *krises* can be found at a much lower price, and a good souvenir will cost around Rp.5,000 to Rp.10,000. The so-called "Majapahit kris," with the hilt and blade forged from a single piece of metal, will be a modern reproduction.

Basketry and Weaving: Pandanus leaf, rotan (rattan) bamboo and innumerable husk and leaf fibers are used to make a bewildering array of baskets, hats, fruit bowls, placemats, drink coasters, fans and mats. Woven wares are an essential feature of Indonesian homes (which often have plaited bamboo walls that last for up to 10 years with an annual coat of line wash) and what you'll see for sale almost always has a practical purpose. Tangerang and Tasikmalaya (famous among other things for its floormats of *mendong* or dried straw) are major weaving centres, though woven goods can be bought almost anywhere. They're inexpensive, and you can have a lot of fun foraging through village markets for something that takes your eye.

Pottery and Ceramics: The standard of modern 'creative' potting in Java is not high. On the other hand, a lot of village-made terracotta is simple and attractive, and if weight is no problem you might like to snap up a *kendi* (water jar) or one or two of the money boxes in the shape of birds, animals and mythical beasts found around Yogya; they may be brightly and even garishly painted or simply fired to a rich brick color. For fun you might spend a few *rupiah* on a handful of terracotta kitchen toys: crudely finished but delightful, they include every useful item from the cooking pot and the *kendi* through to a miniature charcoal brazier. If you have an eye for European bric-à-brac you may spot some minor treasures in the way of English, Dutch and French household pottery or porcelain. The place to look is the jam-packed antique and artifact shops, and especially the markets in such cities as Jakarta, Solo and Malang.

Tortoise-shell: Strictly speaking a misnomer: "tortoise-shell" comes from the carapace of members of the turtle family, and since turtles abound in Indonesia's coastal waters there is a thriving industry in tortoise-shell ornaments and souvenirs ranging in color from a dark translucent red through browns, blacks and greys to ivory-white. Rings, combs, bracelets, cigarette cases, ornamental boxes, salad spoons and fans are among the inexpensive items you can find in most souvenir shops and at many roadside stalls.

Jewlery and Metalwork: Some of the world's most delicate filigree silverwork is made in Indonesia. The main centers are Kendari in Sulawesi, Kota Gedang in Sumatra and Kota Gede on the outskirts of Yogyakarta; work from all three areas can be found in Java, and interesting pieces also come from Bali.

Lace-like flowers, butterflies, stars, birds and purely symbolic or ornamental designs are patiently pieced together until the addition of a hoop or pin turns them into exquisite rings or brooches. Bracelets clasps and cufflinks are also made, and the silver artisan's work includes boxes, trays, coffee sets, candlesticks and flatware. In Yogya, if you have the time, you can arrange for special orders. Silver is sold at a fixed price gram, so for once forget about bargaining. The silver content is high, with grades of 800 and 925, or 835 and 900 (compared with the British sterling standard of 950 and the U.S. standard of 930).

Filigree jewelry follows traditional designs. Modern jewelry can also be found (mainly in Jakarta) and is mostly silver combined with local precious or semi-precious stones such as agate, onyx, moonstone, jasper, carnelian and various kinds of workable quartz; settings range from crude to excellent. Uncut or roughly polished stones are readily available, but know what you're looking for or take along a friend who's a knowledgeable rockhound.

Antique or curio shops, preferably of the rather "junky" sort, occasionally yield up old dress jewelry (iron buckles with silver inlay, cut-steel faceted buckles), Madurese silver anklets, and gold filigree work from Aceh.

Painting: Somewhere in Java, and especially in Jakarta, you'll come across an open-air display of large canvases featuring rose-tinted views of volcanos and pink evening light on fields of *padi.* They are not great art, but are a pleasant change from the heavy, politically-inspired social realism which was once popular in Indonesia. Some good painting can be found in Bandung and Yogyakarta, and *batik* painting has many fresh and interesting offerings. *Batik* paintings are designed for hanging, not for wearing; the centuries-old wax-and-dye technique takes the place of oils and canvas, and the artists draw from many cultural traditions. Many of the pieces inspired by the *Ramayana* and similar epics, glowing in reds, oranges and yellows, make beautiful 'light boxes' when framed and lit from behind. Yogyakarta also offers some intriguing abstract '*batik*' paintings.

Curios: Java is a wondrous source of out-of-the-ordinary mementoes and souvenirs, ranging from the stunningly beautiful to the odd and preposterous. You might negotiate the purchase of a brightly painted *becak.* You could start a collection of *kretek* (clove cigarette) packets, or of distinctively and often humorously, labeled patent medicines. You can buy bronzes, porcelain. ivories, Dayak beads, Chinese wedding beds, old Dutch Delftware, tattered bundles of pre-1968 *rupiah*, stamps issued in Yogyakarta by the 'rebel' nationalists during the struggle for independence, musical instruments of extraordinary shape, comic books of the *Ramayana* story or the folded *batik* head-dresses traditionally worn in Central Java. Old oil-burning or kerosene lamps, many of them collector's items, are still in good supply. You might find a *kacip* or betelnut cutter made from iron inlaid with gold or silver, or perhaps a simple but striking *sirih* set with all its little pots and compartments for the lime, nut, leaves and other bits and pieces that go to make up a "betelnut" quid. There are intricate models of schooners from Maluku, made entirely of dried cloves, there are ships fashioned from crude rubber; there are water vessels made from huge stems of bamboo or from dried gourds the size of footballs; there are the copper *cap* or stamps used for hand-blocking *batik* patterns; and the list goes on until your imagination runs dry, for there's something of interest in every corner of this incredible island.

Antiques:

Caveat Emptor: There are reasons for practicing

purchase with caution. Certain categories of antiques and artifacts are either wholly banned from export, or may be exported only after clearance from the relevant authorities. Secondly, reproductions can cause problems when you're seeking outward customs clearance as the personnel concerned are not experts in the fine arts. Thirdly, the excellence of many modern reproductions or items 'in the style of' may be exploited by some dealers. Fourthly, you are supposed to have an export clearance for any 'antique' more than 50 years old, and in some cases you may have to pay export duty.

Prehistoric and Hindu-Javanese Antiques: Anything at all dating from the year dot up to around 1600 A.D. will almost certainly fall within this classification, particularly bronze bells, priests' water vessels, statuettes, gold ornaments and anything in stone that may have come from a temple or an archaeological site. Such items, unless otherwise certified, are National Treasures and must not be removed from the country.

Porcelain: In the past decade vast quantities of Chinese "blue and white" export porcelain from the Sung and Ming dynasties, and many outstanding examples of what is broadly termed "Annamese" ware from Indochina (including pieces from Annam proper, Sawankolok and Sukothai), have been unearthed in various parts of the Indonesian archipelago, particularly in Maluku and Sulawesi, and taken out of the country. Many similar pieces are still being found, and while not all pieces are considered National Treasures, they should be considered to be so unless cleared for export.

Ethnographic Artifacts: This is a difficult category to define in terms of what is restricted or prohibited. Many genuine pieces of ethnographic or anthropological interest are neither rare nor especially valuable, and are still being made in reasonable quantities. On the other hand, the removal from Indonesia of a painted and decorated skull from Kalimantan, or a carved ancestor figure from Toraja, should not be attempted without prior consent from the *Central Museum*.

Coins: Restrictions on the export of coins are a fairly recent innovation, and in part a case of closing the stable door after the horse has bolted. In the late 60s and early 70s the catalogs of coin dealers in Amsterdam reflected increases of at least 100 percent a year in the value of certain Dutch coins once used in Indonesia, and many a speculator paid his return air fare to Java and still made a handsome profit on coins bought in small towns and even through regular dealers who hadn't caught up with European trends. All coins more than 50 years old are now banned from export unless otherwise cleared, though in the case of VOC (Dutch East India Company) copper coins and Chinese *cash* (round coins with a square hole in the centre) you needn't worry.

Authenticity: There is little deliberate misrepresentation of antiques in Java. Good dealers will gladly refund your money if a piece proves to be other than what they claim. Four-or-five-hundred-year-old temple ornaments, like genuine bank notes, don't grow on trees, and if they ever do come up for sale they will probably be offered to the Central Government, or if not essential for the national collection may be sold to a private collector or museum through international channels . . . so that beautiful little bronze *Ganesa* statuette you admire so much is probably half a year old, if that. Accordingly, if you're buying a reproduction be sure you're buying at a reproduction price, *not* the price of the genuine article.

Similar caveats apply to the buying of porcelain. Much of what is available is genuine. Much is not, and the slightly coarse textures and glazes of Annamese ware (for example) are reasonably easily reproduced, and can defeat the eye of all but the expert . . . but even he is not always infallible, and a dealer may sell a "wrong" piece in good faith. If you're buying because you *like* a piece, or have fallen in love with its shape, its color, its texture, its crackle glaze, the fact of its being old or new is probably far less important than the pleasure it gives you. However, if age is a genuine consideration, but you have doubts, get yourself and your proposed purchase down to the Central Museum for an expert appraisal.

Furniture can also be tricky, complicated by a thoroughly honest tendency to imitate what is or has been considered good. There are hundreds of tiny hole-in-the-wall workshops in Jakarta and other places where skilled craftsmen are turning out superb imitations of antique furniture, and this has been done for generations. It is often extremely difficult, and in some cases impossible, to distinguish between a genuine early 18th Century chair and a lovingly copied model made 100 or 150 years later. There are fine Javanese chests, boxes and cabinets for sale, often with Chinese-influenced red and gold carving. Many have been crudely restored, but most still appear to be authentic.

Clearance: If you suspect that you have bought or are harboring a "National Treasure" there is only one sensible thing to do. HAVE IT CHECKED AND CLEARED. The onus for obtaining a clearance rests entirely with the buyer, though good and reputable dealers will always help you with the paperwork, and in many cases will actually obtain a clearance for you. Prehistoric and Hindu-Javanese antiquities can be cleared through offices of the Archaeological Service *(Pusat Penelitian Purbakala dan Peninggalan Nasional)*, located at Jakarta (Jln. Cilacap 4), Prambanan and Mojokerto. Certain genuine Hindu-Javanese antiquities may be kept in a private collection in Indonesia, but should be registered and *not* exported. **Porcelain** can only be cleared through the Curator of Porcelain at the Central Museum in Jakarta; the abundance of Chinese and Annamese stoneware and porcelain in the art and antique shops suggests that it is not necessary to have every piece checked, but once again if you are in doubt, do the wise thing. The last court of appeal in all cases is the Central Museum and its authorities.

Customs: If you have bought a high-quality reproduction (and some are excellent) of a Hindu-Javanese work of art it is advisable to have

Insight Guides
java
Insight Guides
singapore
Insight Guides
thailand
Insight Guides
philippines
Insight Guides
hong kong
Insight Guides
korea
Insight Guides
bali
Insight Guides
malaysia
Insight Guides
sri lanka
Insight Guides
florida
Insight Guides
burma
Insight Guides
hawaii
APA PRODUCTIONS
Insight Guides
mexico
APA PRODUCTIONS
Insight Guides
nepal
APA PRODUCTIONS

Outside of the capital there are interesting museums in Trowulan (fine terracotta wares from the Majapahit kingdom), Mojokerto (some outstanding stone sculpture of the Hindu-Javanese period), Yogyakarta and Solo.
Museums are open from 8 a.m. to around 2 p.m. and admission fees are low.

Art Galleries

The **Balai Seni Rupa Jakarta,** the Jakarta Art Gallery, at Taman Fatahillah, opened in August 1976 with an excellent exhibition of Indonesian painting during the past hundred years. The late President Sukarno's extensive collection of art at the **Bogor Presidential Palace** may be seen only with permission. The **studio gallery of Affandi** (internationally the best known of Indonesia's painters) was in 1973 given government's accolade as a national gallery. (Many artists also run small galleries in Bandung (where art training flourishers at I.T.B.) and in Yogyakarta.

Bookstores

Bookstores in Java rarely carry books in *Inggiris* although a few of the big bookstores in Jakarta may.

B.P.K. GUNUNG MULIA
Jl. Kwitang 22; tel. 372208
GUNUNG AGUNG BOOKSTORE
Jl. Kwitang 5; tel. 344678, 346069, 352562, 354566
GRAMEDIA BOOKSTORE
Jl. Gajah Mada 109; tel. 627809
Jl. Pintu Air 72; tel. 343800; 360971
INDIRA BOOKSTORE
Jl. Sam Ratulangi 37; tel. 342653
Jl. Melawai V6; tel. 770584
KALMAN BOOKSTORE
Jl. Kwitang 11; tel. 364334
TROPEN BOOKSTORE
Jl. Pasar Baru 113; tel. 362695, 363542
SARI AGUNG BOOKSTORE
Jl. Kebon Sirih 94; tel. 365868, 366313
Sarinah Department Store, Jl. M.H. Thamrin; tel. 320096
IKHTIAR BOOKSTORE
Jl. Majapahit 6; tel. 341226, 341551

The Unexpected

If you like to get out and about on foot, you'll no doubt meet at least one roving band of street entertainers somewhere in Java. It might be a miniature circus: two men, two monkeys, a dog and perhaps a large snake providing 10 minutes' entertainment for around Rp.100 or Rp.200. A band of four raggedly appealing children with home-made instruments will serenade you for Rp.10 each. An old man or woman will tap out pure *gamelan* melodies on a portable *gender* (bronze keys suspended above resonating bamboo tubes) for a token payment of Rp.10 to Rp.25. And, of course, there are the unexpected performances of *wayang kulit, wayang golek, kuda kepang* (horse trance dance) or *reog* (with a huge tiger mask) which you may come across during your travels, especially if you venture off the beaten track.

Festivals

Festivals and celebrations, both religious and secular, reflect that Java is colorfully woven into the many calendars of Indonesia. On certain days of the moon calendar offerings are made to volcanic gods and on certain days of the sun calendar mystical reunions occur between the living and the souls of their ancestors.
Labuhan, which means "offering," is a ritual to please Nyai Loro Kidul, the legendary goddess of the Indian Ocean. This ritual usually takes place the day after the Sultan's birthday. A procession leaves the *kraton* in Yogyakarta at 8 a.m. heading for Parangkusumo on the south coast of Java where the Sultan's old clothes are put out to sea on a raft to placate the Queen of the South Seas. Similar rituals are held at the crest of the volcanos, Merapi and Lawu.
Galungan is a Balinese celebration and can be viewed at the Balinese temple in Megelang 42 kilometers outside Yogya. This Hindu festival occurs every 210 days after **Nyepi,** the Balinese New Year, and marks the reunion of the people of Bali with the souls of their ancestors. There are temple offerings, *gamelan* music, village decorations and dances, the best of which is in Yogyakarta 10 days after **Kuningan.** On Kuningan to complete spiritual purification, people bathe in Holy Springs.
Another pilgrimage is made to the Holy Spring of Sengdang Sono in Menoreh Mountains in southern central Java. In May and October thousands of Javanese Catholics climb a narrow footpath which leads to the Promason Church and continue on over the "Road of the Cross" another 1½ kilometers to the shrine. Candles are lit and prayers offered at the spring under the Sono tree, which is dedicated to the Holy Virgin. Devotees sometimes take a flask of the holy water with them when they depart.
Kasada is a spectacular midnight ceremony on the rim of the active volcano Mount Bromo in the Tengger region of eastern Java. The ceremony begins at dawn when priests and thousands of worshippers carry rice, fruit, flowers and vegetables on bamboo poles. After the priests conduct the purification ceremony, a long procession of people slowly wind up the mountain to the volcano's rim. Here the worshippers cast their offerings into the crater hoping that in retun they will be blessed by Betoro, the God of Bromo.
In the summer of the sun (solar) calender **Tumplaik Wajik** or the preparing of *gunungan* (rice mounds decorated with vegetables), eggs and cakes can be seen in the Yogyakarta 'kraton.' The making of the rice mounds is accompanied by the rythmic pounding blocks and chanting to ward off evil spirits. The *gunungan* is blessed and handed out to the people. This occurs two days before Grebeg Mulud.
Saparan, a thanksgiving ceremony is held every Sapar, the second month of the Javanese calendar in the village of Ambar Ketawang (Gambing) about five kilometers west of Yogyakarta. The ceremony was initiated to placate the spirits to prevent fatal accidents during the time when people made their living by extracting limestone from the surrounding hills. Effigies or *bekakak* made of sticky rice with

coconut syrup-filled necks are carried by a festive procession along the limestone hillsides to a digging spot where they are beheaded and sugar syrup sprouts out of the wounds like blood.

Sekaten begins at the stroke of midnight one week before Grebeg Mulud, the day commemorating the birth of the Prophet Mohammed. The festival begins in Yogyakarta where big fairs are held on the square north of the *kraton.* There are continuous prayer sessions in the mosque west of the *kraton* and two ancient and sacred *gamelan* Sekati are played continuously for the entire week. At noon of the seventh day, great processions of palace guards wearing striped shirts, bright red pointed headwear armed with swords carrying *gunungan* parade in 100 platoons while firing rifles in the air. Sweets, ballons, pin wheels, handicraft and folk art are sold by vendors. Sekaten festivals are held in the Surakarta, Kanoman and Kesepuhan (Cirebon) 'kratons.'

On **Waicek Day** at Borobudur, the world's greatest Buddhist shrine, a full moon festival commemorates the birth, death and enlightenment of the Lord Buddha. Thousands of yellow and white robed Buddhist priests and followers chant and walk slowly from Menduk, a small temple near Borobudur. At 4.01 a.m. the procession of worshippers, each carrying a lighted candle, ascend Borobudur and circle the temple in a clockwise direction toward the main stupa at the top. This is one of Indonesia's most impressive ceremonies.

Nightlife

Cabarets, nightclubs and discotheques are popular in large cities like Jakarta, Semarang and Surabaya. International hotels generally offer a cabaret act of some kind, but prices are high and the quality is often questionable. The most consistently good entertainers on the high-priced, after-dark rounds are Filipino groups (not perhaps what you came to Java for?). Check with a good tour operator for recommendations, and make sure you've got a fat wallet if you decide to take the plunge.

Dancing, Western-style, is more acceptable now than it was in 1961 when students in Yogyakarta demonstrated against it and the Javanese author of a guidebook was happy to note that although "owing to the Dutch Djakarta had been provided with dancing halls and the like . . . (dancing) won't flourish as long as the Oriental character prevails within the Indonesian society." In big city hotels and nightcubs, and in some hill resort hotels, dancing gets moving at about 9 p.m. and roars on until an hour or so after midnight, though some places are open as late as 4 a.m. on weekends and holidays. Live bands are the norm, and dance hostesses are generally available for around Rp.5,000 an hour or (in the resort towns) Rp.5,000 for a couple of hours.

Massage Parlors

A comparatively recent phenomenon, limited to the cities (the big ones) and some hill resorts. They are increasingly popular but the government has put a halt on any further building (poker-machines were banned rather abruptly in August 1973, after only a brief appearance). Some massage parlors have baths, all serve liquor, and all of them offer a weary gentleman a very self-indulgent means of relaxation. You are charged by the hour, and prices start at a modest Rp.5,000 an hour.

Sports

In the years since Indonesia hosted the Fourth Asian Games at **Senayan Sports Complex** (Jakarta) in 1962, sport has played an increasingly important role in Indonesian life. The best known figure internationally is Rudi Hartono, whose defeat at the hands of Dane, Sven Pri, in the 1973 Thomas Cup almost ranked as a national disaster. Hartono has since won more Thomas Cup titles than anyone else, but now concentrates on coaching Indonesia's rising young badminton stars. Indonesia always collects a goodly share of medals at international meets, and the emphasis on sport has meant more and more facilities which can also be used by the active visitor.

Getting into it . . . It's fairly easy to arrange a game of golf or tennis in the big towns. An 18-hole championship golf course was opened at Sawangan in July 1973 as part of a large country club development project, and there are other good courses around Java. Hill and mountain resort areas always have hardcourts for tennis, and a quick set in the fresh, crisp air is ideal pre-breakfast exercise. The newest large hotels usually have swimming pools, though the charge to non-guests is high at times (up to Rp.500 for a swim is more heating than cooling); coastal and mountain resorts have beaches and freshwater pools, and most big towns have public swimming pools (*kolam renang*) where the entry fees range from Rp.100 to Rp.300. For water-skiing try the waters around the **Thousand Islands** just north of Jakarta, or drop in at the **Surabaya Watersports Club;** the placid surface of **Jatiluhur Reservoir** on the northern route to Bandung is popular, and facilities have been opened at **Karangkates Dam** in East Java. The west coast from Merak to Labuhan has some great spots for skin-diving and is within a few hours' drive of Jakarta; there is good swimming and snorkelling to be enjoyed at **Pasir Putih** (not far from Surabaya), as well as on the far south coast of East Java; the northeast corner of Madura has some very pretty and seldom used beaches.

Most hill and mountain resorts offer ponies for riding and trekking. The beasts mostly stick to a fast walk, though they can sometimes be encouraged to canter or (rarely) to gallop. There are some beautiful trails to follow in the high country, especially through East Java and in the south of Central and West Java. There are also magnificent areas for dedicated bushwalkers and hikers. Some of the paths are easy going, but there are some which will tax the hardiest trekker (though for genuine mountaineers and rock-climbers there is little offering).

If you feel like a game of badminton there are almost as many players as there are people, and as many courts (albeit primitive in some cases) as there are *padi*-fields: five minutes with one of the locals will leave you satisfactorily exhausted. Table tennis or ping pong has been another favorite since long before China was rediscovered, but only play if you don't mind being thrashed by a 10-year-old!

In Jakarta you can also indulge in ten-pin bowling and ice-skating.

. . . and watching: There is not a lot of organized spectator sport in Java, and apart from badminton and football (soccer) you'll see little outside of Jakarta. The capital is one of the few places apart from Spain, the Philippines or Latin America where you can watch *jai alai:* the speed of the ball makes it a very ooooh-aaaaah sort of game (the price of your admission ticket also entitles you to your first betting slip if you're that way inclined). Basketball, baseball, volleyball, track and field events and the various martial arts (judo, tae kwan do, karate) are also popular. Jakarta also offers horse-racing on Sundays, greyhound racing three nights a week, and even a skydiving club.

There's ram fighting at Maribaya (near Bandung), bull fighting near Bondowoso and Situbondo in East Java (beast against beast, *not* the Spanish version), and the famous Madura bull races, *kerapan sapi,* a noisy colorful spectacle best seen in regional heats and finals during August and September, but scheduled for monthly meets at Bangkalan in West Madura. Cock-fighting is also popular. It is not the same as the Balinese version (in which the use of razor-sharp steel spurs bloodily resolves the combat in a matter of minutes), but is much more a trial of strength and wiliness, and is seldom fatal. Although banned in most of Java, the sport refuses to die.

Photography

A still or movie camera (or both) should be high on your list of things-to-bring. Whether you're toting a hip-pocket Instamatic or a few thousand dollars' worth of Leica or Hasselbad equipment, you'll inevitably wish that you had more room or more money for more film. Java and its people are superbly photogenic. The attitude towards photography is free and easy, and most people enjoy having their picture taken. However, it is polite, and in the case of older people, essential, to ask permission first (sign language for this request is adequate). A very discreet telephoto may circumvent an impasse. You should also check out the propriety of photographing or filming religious buildings or monuments, though refusal is unlikely. The use of a flash is generally O. K. Check first.

Camera and film care

In Java's tropical climate you'll get better results by protecting your camera and film from excessive exposure to heat and humidity. Never leave a camera lying in direct sunlight or in a hot car, since heat gives color film a greenish overtone which cannot be corrected in processing; if you don't want to leave your camera in your room, carry it with you (even if you're not using it) rather than storing it in a place that can get hot. If you carry a camera case, packets of silica gel will help prevent damage through humidity. Space permitting, a useful do-it-yourself film storage container can be made by cutting a few holes in a block of polystyrene foam.

When you move out of air-conditioning into the hot outside world, beware of condensation on external and internal lens surfaces; it's worthwhile removing the lens (if you can) for a quick check. Moisture should be allowed to evaporate in its own time, since wiping it off can leave a smear or even cause permanent damage. It is not advisable to leave film in your camera for anymore from a week at most without taking a few shots; the emulsion may sweat and stick, causing ruinous wavy lines (or worse). It's better to miss a few shots on a roll then risk spoiling which you already have.

When to Shoot

Very few travelers can afford the luxury of waiting for perfect light, and all too often it's a matter of catch-as-catch-can when you're sticking to a schedule. Nonetheless, beware the noonday sun when light and shade contrasts are much greater than they may seem. From around 10 a.m. to 3 p.m. the color quality of sunlight along the equator is very different from that in places like Europe, Japan, the United States or Australia: color tend to flatten and lose their brilliance, and the problem is often compounded by hazy conditions; although your exposure readings seem to be perfect the result may be slightly disappointing and "washed out." Deliberately underexposing by half a stop or even more can help, as will the use of a daylight or haze filter, but try to take your shots in the early morning or late afternoon when colors are richer and warmer, and the sidelighting gives better depth to most subjects.

Film and Processing

Major cities and towns, and the big hotels, are your best sources of film, and you should have little trouble finding black and white, color transparency and print stock made by Kodak, Agfa and Fuji in a range of ASA/DIN ratings and 35 mm format; larger format stock such as 9 mm = 9 mm, is harder to come by. In smaller shops, or those which don't seem to have a big turnover, be sure to check the expiry date on the carton. Black and white and color stock for Super-8 movie cameras is available in major cities. Film prices are high.

Avoid local processing if possible, even for black and white. The quality varies enormously. Carefully stored exposed film should survive several months before processing.

Language

'Unity in Diversity'

Indonesia's motto, *Bhinneka Tunggal Ika* (unity in diversity) is seen in its most driving, potent form in the world of language. Although there are over 250 distinct languages and dialects spoken in the archipelago, the one national tongue, *Bahasa Indonesia,* will take you from the northernmost tip of Sumatra through Java and across the string of islands to Irian Jaya.

Bahasa Indonesia is both an old and new language. It is based on Malay, which has been the *lingua franca* throughout much of Southeast Asia for centuries. Sailors, traders, and Islamic missionaries spoke what became known as marketplace or 'Bazaar' Malay, a simplified version of the sophisticated Malay spoken on the Malay Peninsula.

In 1929, while the country was still under colonial rule, the All Indonesia Youth Congress wisely urged the development of a single national language, based not upon colloquial Bazaar Malay but upon the pure classical Malay of the Peninsula. This language was admirably suited to Indonesia's needs, since it was the basis of many of the regional languages and, like them, contained many words of Sanskrit and Arabic origin. As a symbol of national pride and unity, *Bahasa Indonesia* spread rapidly, incorporating many new words so that today, although similar, it is quite distinct from Malay.

In Java, the two major regional languages are Sundanese (in West Java) and Javanese, the high complex language of Central and East Java; Madurese is also spoken in parts of East Java and on the island of Madura. However, in Java, as in other parts of Indonesia, *Bahasa Indonesia* is all you need to know unless you get into remote areas far from the usual tourist track.

Although formal Indoneisan is a complex language demanding serious study, the construction of basic Indonesian sentences is relatively simple. Indonesian is written in the Roman alphabet and, unlike some Asian languages, is not tonal. There are no articles in Indonesian: *rumah* means "a house." To make a plural, you simple double the noun: *rumah-rumah* means "houses" and is normally written as *rumah2.*

Another help for beginners is the lack of complicated verbal tenses. To denote time, a few key adverbs are used, the most useful being *sudah* (already) denoting the past, *belum* (not yet) flexibly indicating what is about to or never to happen, and *akan* (will) denoting the future.

When speaking *Bahasa Indonesia* you need to keep a few basic rules in mind. Adjectives always follow the noun: *rumah* (house) and *besar* (big) together are *rumah besar* meaning "big house." When constructing a sentence, the order is usually subject-verb-object: *saya*(I) *minum* (drink) *air* (water) *dingin* (cold): *saya minum air dingin.*

The possessive is made by putting the personal pronoun after the noun: *rumah saya* means "my house."

Indonesians always use their language to show respect when addressing others, especially when a younger person speaks to his elders. The custom is to address an elder man as *bapak* or *'pak* (father) and an elder woman as *ibu* (mother), and even in the case of slightly younger people who are obviously VIPs this form is suitable and correct. *Bung* (in West Java) and *mas* (in Central and East Java) roughly translate as "brother" and are used with equals, people your own age whom you don't know all that well, and with hotel clerks, taxi drivers, tour guides and waiters (it's friendly, and a few notches above "buddy" or "mate"); *nyonya* is polite when speaking with a married woman, *nona* with an unmarried woman.

To achieve standardization of spelling in Malaysia and Indonesia, *ejaan baru* (new spelling) was introduced in both countries in August 1972. All publications printed since then use the new form, and many signs have been altered to conform to the new spelling, though you may still come across old spellings from time to time.

Listed below are a few general guidelines on the pronunciation of *Bahasa Indonesia* which, with minor exceptions, is written phonetically with much the same sound values as Italian. The pre-1972 spellings, where applicable, are in brackets. The best way to acquire the correct pronunciation is of course, to listen to the way Indonesians speak. Once you start to use the language you will find that most people are eager to help and to understand you.

a	short as in 'father' (*apa* = what, *ada* = there is)
ai	rather like the 'i' in 'mine' (*kain* = material, *sampai* = to arrive)
k	hard at the beginning of a word as in 'king,' hardly audible at the end of a word. (*kamus* = dictionary, *cantik* = beautiful)
kh (ch)	slightly aspirated as in 'khan' or the Scottish 'ch' in 'loch' (*Khusus* = special, *khabar* = news)
ng	as in 'singer' never as in 'danger' or 'Ringo' (*bunga* = flower, *penginapan* = cheap hotel)
ngg	like the 'ng' in 'Ringo' (*minggu* = week, *tinggi* = high)
r	always rolled *rokok* = cigarette, *pertama* = first)
u (oe)	as in 'full,' never as in 'bucket' (*umum* = public, *belum* = not yet)
y (j)	as in 'you' (*saya* = I, or me, *kaya* = rich)
c (tj)	like the 'ch' in 'church' (*candi* = temple, *kacang* = nut)
e	1. often unstressed as the barely sounded 'e' in 'open' (*berapa*, sounding like *b'rapa* = how much?) 2. sometimes stressed, sounding somewhere between the 'e' in 'bed' and 'a' in 'bad' (*boleh* = may, *lebar – wide)*
g	hard as in'golf' never as in 'ginger' (*guntur* = thunder, *bagus* = very good)
h	generally lightly aspirated (*hitam* = black, *lihat* = to see)
i	either short as in 'pin' or a longer sound like 'ee' in 'meet' (*minta* = to ask for, *ibu* = mother)
j (dj)	as in 'John' (*jalan* = road or street, *jahit* = to sew)

Two minor points about spelling. Despite the new rules you will find many instances where people's names continue to be spelled with the old 'oe' rather than the current 'u'; some may change, but most stick to their birthright, including the President whose name is Soeharto and only rarely used by the press as Suharto. Less important are the subtle distinctions in Central Java between two forms of 'o' and the liquid sounds of 'l' and 'r'; the niceties are of interest only to experts in phoenetics, but in practical terms it means that the city of Solo may also appear as Sala, and that the Siva temple at Prambanan may be written (in its popular form) as Lara Janggrang, Lord Jonggrong or Roro Jonggrang . . . and they are all correct.

In airline offices, travel agencies, medium to large hotels, and major stores, you'll find that English is widely understood. Many Indonesians over the age of 35 also speak Dutch with varying degrees of excellence. Other European and Asian languages are less well served. Avoid slang or regional usages as far as possible, and unless your listener is obviously fluent in your language, speak slowly and clearly. Even a smattering of *Bahasa Indonesia* (the Indonesian language) is a help, and its use will be appreciated.

Although its roots are ancient, Indonesian as the official national language is only as old as the Republic itself, and the "first language" of many people in Java (even if they speak impeccable Indonesian) is still likely to be language they learned at mother's knee: Sundanese, Javanese or Madurese. In many rural villages and hamlets Indonesian scarcely exists, though there will always be someone who knows enough to understand you or your guide.

A Basic Guide To Bahasa Indonesia

Greetings and Civilities

thank you (very much)	*terima kasih (banyak)*
please	*silahkan*
good morning	*selamat pagi*
good day (roughly 11 a.m. to 3 p.m.	*selamat siang*
good afternoon, evening	*selamat sore*
good night	*selamat malam*
goodbye (to person going)	*selamat jalan*
goodbye (to person staying)	*selamat tinggal*
I'm sorry	*ma'af*
welcome	*selamat datang*
please come in	*silahkan masuk*
please sit down	*silahkan duduk*
what is your name?	*siapa nama saudara?*
my name is ...	*nama saya ...*
where do you come from?	*saudara datang dari mana?* or *dari mana?*
I come from ...	*saya datang dari ...*

Pronouns and Forms of Address

I	*saya*
you (singular)	*kamu (to children) saudara, anda*
he, she	*dia*
we	*kami (not including the listener)*
we	*kita (including the listener)*
you (plural)	*saudara-saudara, anda*
they	*mereka*
Mr.	*Tuan/'Pak/Mas/'Bung*
Mrs.	*Nyonya/Ibu*
Miss	*Nona*

Directions and Transport

left	*kiri*
right	*kanan*
straight	*terus*
near	*dekat*
far	*jauh*
from	*dari*
to	*ke*
inside	*didalam*
outside of	*diluar*
between	*antara*
under	*dibawah*
here	*disini*
there	*disana*
in front of	*didepan, dimuka*
at the back	*dibelakang*
next to	*disebelah*
to ascend	*naik*
to descend	*turun*
to walk	*jalan*
to drive	*stir, bawa*
pedicab	*becak*
car	*mobil*
bus	*bis*
train	*kereta-api*
airplane	*kapal terbang*
ship	*kapal laut*
bicycle	*sepeda*
motor cycle	*sepeda motor*
where do you want go?	*mau kemana?*
I want to go to ...	*saya mau ke ...*
stop here	*berhenti disini, stop disini*
I'll be back in five minutes	*saya akan kembali lima menit*
turn right	*belok kekanan*
how many kilometers?	*berapa kilometer jauhnya?*
slowly, slow down	*pelan-pelan/perlahan-lahan*

Important Places

hotel	*hotel, penginapan, losmen*
shop	*toko*
train station	*stasiun kereta-api*
airport	*lapangan terbang*
cinema	*bioskop*
bookshop	*toko buku*
petrol station	*pompa bensin*
bank	*bank*
post office	*kantor pos*
swimming pool	*tempat pemandian, kolam renang*
Immigration Dept.	*Departemen Immigrasi*
tourist office	*kantor parawisata*
embassy	*kedutaan besar*

Spending the Night

room	*kamar*
bed	*tempat tidur*
bedroom	*kamar tidur*
bathroom	*kamar mandi*
toilet	*kamar kecil*
towel	*handuk*
bedsheet	*seprei*
pillow	*bantal*

water	*air*
soap	*sabun*
fan	*kipas angin*
to bathe	*mandi*
hot water	*air panas*
cold water	*air dingin*
to wash	*cuci*
to iron	*gosok*
clothes	*pakaian*
shirt	*kemeja*
trousers	*celana*
dress	*baju, rok*
Where is a hotel?	*Dimana ada hotel?*
How much for one night?	*Berapa harganya satu malam?*
Please wash these clothes	*Tolong cuci pakaian-pakaian ini*

Eating

restaurant	*restoran, rumah makan*
dining room	*kamar makan*
food	*makanan*
drink	*minuman*
breakfast	*makan pagi*
lunch	*makan siang*
dinner	*makan malam*
boiled water	*air putih, air matang*
iced water	*air es*
ice	*es*
tea	*teh*
coffee	*kopi*
cordial	*stroop*
beer	*bir*
fresh orange juice	*air jeruk*
milk	*susu*
bread	*roti*
butter	*mentega*
rice	*nasi*
noodles	*mie, bihun, bakmie*
soup	*soto*
chicken	*ayam*
beef	*daging (sapi)*
pork	*babi, daging babi*
lamb	*domba*
goat (also sometimes 'mutton')	*kambing*
liver	*hati*
brains	*otak*
fish	*ikan*
prawns	*udang*
vegetables	*sayur*
fruit	*buah*
banana	*pisang*
pineapple	*nanas*
coconut	*kelapa*
mango	*mangga*
egg	*telur*
solf-boiled egg	*telur setengah matang*
fried egg	*telur mata sapi*
dumpling (small)	*pangsit*
dumpling (large)	*bakpao*
sugar	*gula*
salt	*garam*
pepper	*merica, lada*
soya sauce	*kecap*
vinegar	*cuka*
sweet	*manis*
sour	*asam*
bitter (without sugar)	*pahit*
hot (temperature)	*panas*
hot (spicy)	*pedis, pedas*
cold	*dingin*
'supreme'	*istimewa*
boiled	*rebus*
fried	*goreng*
served in stock	*godok*
sauce	*kuah, saus*
cup	*cangkir*
plate	*piring*
glass	*gelas*
spoon	*sendok*
knief	*pisau*
fork	*garpu*

Shopping

shop	*toko*
money	*uang*
change (of money)	*uang kembali*
to buy	*beli*
price	*harga*
expensive	*mahal*
cheap	*murah*
fixed price	*harga pas*
How much is it?	*Berapa?/Berapa harganya?*
It is too expensive.	*Itu terlalu mahal.*
Do you have a cheaper one?	*Adakah yang lebih murah?*
Can you reduce the price?	*Bisa saudara kurangkan harganya?*
What is this?	*Apa ini?*
I'll take it.	*Saya akan ambil ini.*
I don't want it.	*Saya tidak mau.*
I'll come back later.	*Saya akan kembali nanti.*

Time

day	*hari*
night	*malam*
today	*hari ini*
morning (to about 10.30)	*pagi*
noon (broadly 10.30 to 3 p.m.)	*siang*
evening (3 to 8 p.m.)	*sore*
now	*sekarang*
just now	*baru saja*
soon, presently	*nanti*
always	*selalu*
before	*dahulu, dulu*
when (= the time that)	*waktu*
when? (interrogative)	*kapan?*
tomorrow	*besok*
yesterday	*kemarin*
minute	*menit*
hour	*jam*
week	*minggu*
month	*bulan*
year	*tahun*
past (the hour)	*liwat*
to (before the hour)	*kurang*
What is the time?	*Jam berapa sekarang?*
Seven o' clock	*Jam tujuh*

Half-past seven	*Setengah delapan (i.e. half to eight)*
It is 10 to eight.	*Jam delapan kurang sepuluh.*
It 10 past eight.	*Jam delapan liwat sepuluh.*

Numbers and Days of the Week

1. one	*satu*
2. two	*dua*
3. three	*tiga*
4. four	*empat*
5. five	*lima*
6. six	*enam*
7. seven	*tujuh*
8. eight	*delapan*
9. nine	*sembilan*
10. ten	*sepuluh*
11. eleven	*sebelas*
12. twelve	*duabelas*
13. thirteen	*tigabelas*
14. fourteen	*empatbelas*
15. fifteen	*limabelas*
16. sixteen	*enambelas*
17. seventeen	*tujuhbelas*
18. eighteen	*delapanbelas*
19. nineteen	*sembilanbelas*
20. twenty	*duapuluh*
21. twenty-one	*duapuluh satu*
30. thirty	*tigapuluh*
40. forty	*empatpuluh*
58. fifty-eight	*limapuluh delapan*
100. one hundred	*seratus*
263. two hundred and sixty-three	*duaratus enampuluh tiga*
1,000 one thousand	*seribu*
Sunday	*Hari Minggu*
Monday	*Hari Senin/Senen*
Tuesday	*Hari Selasa*
Wednesday	*Hari Rabu*
Thursday	*Hari Kamis*
Friday	*Hari Jum'at/Juma'at*
Saturday	*Hari Sabtu*

Handy Words and Phrases

yes	*ya/ia*
no	*tidak, tak* (also *nggak*)
(that's) correct	*betul*
(that's) wrong	*salah*
much, many	*banyak*
very much, very many	*banyak sekali*
and	*dan*
but	*tetapi, tapi*
if	*jika, kalau*
with	*dengan*
this	*ini*
that	*itu*
like this	*begini*
like that	*begitu*
similar to	*seperti*
here	*sini, disini*
there	*sana, disana*
very nice	*bagus*
more	*lebih*
less	*kurang*
because	*karena*
perhaps	*barangkali, mungkin*
about (approximately)	*kira-kira*
then	*kemudian, lalu*
good, alright	*baik*

Some verbs

There are several verbal prefixes such as *me- mem- men-, meng-,* and *ber-*. They can be confusing. You will be understood if you just use the root of the verb.

bring	*bawa*
carry	*angkat*
take	*ambil*
give	*kasi, beri*
buy	*beli*
sell	*jual*
ask/ask for	*tanya/minta*
speak	*bicara*
see	*lihat*
try	*coba*
look for	*cari*
wash	*cuci*
want	*mau*
can (permission)	*boleh*
can (possible, though commonly signifying permission as well)	*bisa*
speak	*bicara*
tell/say	*bilang/berkata*
I don't understand.	*Saya tidak mengerti.*
I don't speak Indonesian.	*Saya tidak bisa bicara Bahasa Indonesia.*
I speak ony a little Indonesian.	*Saya bisa bicara sedikit saja Bahasa Indonesia.*
Please speak slowly	*Tolong bicara pelan-pelan.*

Interrogatives

who	*siapa*
what	*apa*
when	*kapan*
where (location)	*dimana*
where (direction)	*kemana*
why	*kenapa, mengapa*
how	*bagaimana*
how much, how many	*berapa*
which, which one	*yang mana*

A few more nouns

cigarette/clove cigarette	*rokok/kretek*
matches	*korek api*
train (railway)	*kereta-api*
house	*rumah*
paper	*kertas*
newspaper	*surat khabar, koran*
hair	*rambut*
map	*peta*
place	*tempat*
stamp (postage)	*prangko, perangko*
electricity	*listrik*
foreigner	*orang asing*
tourist	*turis, wisatawan*

Useful adjectives

big	*besar*
small	*kecil*
young	*muda*
old (person)	*tua*

old (thing)	*lama*
new	*baru*
beautiful	*cantik*
good	*baik*
no good	*tidak baik*
hot	*panas*
cold	*dingin*
delicious	*enak*
clean	*bersih*
dirty	*kotor*
red	*merah*
white	*putih*
blue	*biru*
black	*hitam*
green	*hijau*
yellow	*kuning*
gold	*mas*
silver	*perak*

Understanding signs

Many Indonesian words have been borrowed from other languages, and quickly reveal their meanings: *sekolah, universitas, mobil, bis, akademi, sektor, proklamasi* and *polisi.* Other important signs leave you guessing; the following short list may help you.

open	*buka, dibuka*
closed	*tutup, ditutup*
entrance	*masuk*
exit	*keluar*
don't touch	*jangan pegang*
no smoking	*dilarang merokok*
push	*tolak*
pull	*tarik*
gate	*pintu*
ticket window	*loket*
information	*keterangan*
public	*umum*
hospital	*rumah sakit*
pharmacy	*apotik*
ticket	*karcis*
house (institutional sense)	*wisma*
central	*pusat*
city	*kota*
district	*daerah*
zoo	*kebun binatang*
market	*pasar*
church	*gereja*
golf course	*lapangan golf*
customs	*bea dan cukai*

Filling in forms

Forms are an unavoidable part of travel. Within Indonesia few forms carry translations into other languages so here are a few key words and phrases to help you out.

name	*nama*
address	*alamat*
full address	*alamat lengkap*
male, female	*laki-laki, perempuan*
age	*umur*
date	*tanggal (tgl.)*
time	*jam*
departure	*berangkat*
marital status	*kawin*
religion	*agama*
nationality	*kebangsaan*
professionpekerjaan	*pekerjaan*
identification (passport, etc.)	*surat keterangan*
issued by	*pembesar yang memberikan*
purpose of visit	*maksud kunjungan*
signature	*tanda tangan*

Further Reading

Much has been written about Indonesia and Java. The following suggestions are therefore directional rather than comprehensive; titles marked with an asterisk (*) are highly recommended.

Increasing numbers of periodic tourist publications with up-to-date information on coming events, hotels, local entertainment and culture are being published in English. The Indonesian Directorate General of Tourism has some good booklets and brochures of a general nature. Useful regional publications include *Business & Pleasure in Jakarta, Welcome to Yogyakarta, Welcome to East Java, Jakarta's Visitor Guide, Destination Indonesia* and *Papineau's Guide to Jakarta.*

Good overall maps of Java (and of Indonesia) have been published by the Directorate General of Tourism and by Pertamina (the national oil company), but they are not accurate in fine detail or in terms of road conditions. Detailed regional maps are difficult to find. Adequate maps of cities like Jakarta, Bandung, Yogyakarta and Surabaya are available, and you will find the P.T. Pembina publication *Peta Sembilan Kota* (Maps of Nine Cities) useful as a general guide.

General History

Coedes, G., *The Indianized States of Southeast Asia,* trans. Susan Brown Cowing, East-West Centre Press, Honolulu, 1968.

Day, Clive, *The Dutch in Java,* Oxford University Press, 1966.

Hall, D.G.E., *A History of South-East Asia,* Macmillan, 1964.

________, *Atlas of South-East Asia,* Macmillan, 1964.

*Harrison, Brian, *South-East Asia, A Short History,* Macmillan, London, 1966.

Raffles, Sir Thomas Stamford, *The History of Java* (2 vols.), Oxford University Press, 1965.

Vlekke, Bernard H.M., *Nusantara: A History of Indonesia,* Van Hoeve, The Hague, 1959.

Wurtzburg, C.E., *Raffles of the Eastern Isles,* Hodder and Stoughton, London, 1954.

*Zainu'ddin, Ailsa, *A Short History of Indonesia,* Cassell Australia, Melbourne, 1968.

Art and Culture

*Bernet Kempes, A.J., *Ancient Indonesian Art,* Harvard University Pres, Cambridge, Mass., 1959.

da Franca, Antonio P., *Portuguese Influence in Indonesia,* P.T. Gunung Agung, Jakarta, 1970.

*Holt, Claire, *Art in Indonesia: Continuities and Change,* Cornell University Press, New York, 1967.
Moebirman, *Wayang Purwa: The Shadow Play of Indonesia,* published by courtesy of Van Deventer-Masstichting, The Hague, 1960.
Tirtaamidjaja, N., *Batik: Pattern and Motif,* English text by Benedict R. Anderson, Penerbit Djambatan, Jakarta, 1966.
Ulbricht, M., *Wayang Purwa: Shadow of the Past,* Oxford University Press, Kuala Lumpur, 1970.
*Wagner, Frits A., *Indonesia: The Art of An Island Group,* Crown Publisher, New York, 1959.
Winstedt, Richard, *The Malays: A Cultural History,* Routledge & Kegan Paul, London, 1961.
Wirjosuparto, Sutjipto, *Rama Stories in Indonesia,* Bhratara Publishers, Jakarta, 1969.
Zimmer, Heinrich (ed. Joseph Campbell), *Myths and Symbols in Indian Art and Civilization,* Harper Torchbooks, New York, 1962.

Sociology and Religion

Anderson, Benedict R., *Mythology and the Tolerance of the Javanese,* Cornell University Press, New York, 1965.
*Geertz, Clifford, *The Religion of Java,* The Free Press of Glencoe, London, 1960 (also paperback, 1964).
McVey, Ruth T. (ed.), *Indonesia: Its People, Its Society, Its Culture,* Human Relations Area File Press, New Haven, Conn. 1963.
*Takdir Alisjabhana, S., *Indonesia: Social and Cultural Revolution,* trans. Benedict R. Anderson, Oxford University Press, 1966.

Politics, Revolution and Economics

Bartlett, Anderson G. (ed.), *Pertamina: Indonesian National Oil,* Amerasia, Jakarta and Singapore, 1972.
Brackman, Arnold C., *The Communist Collapse in Indonesia,* W.W. Norton, New York, 1968.
Douwes Dekker, E. (Multatuli), *Max Havelaar or the Coffee Auctions of the Dutch Trading Company,* Heinemann, London, 1967.
Geertz, Clifford, *Agricultural Involution,* University of California Press, 1963.
Kahin, George McT., *Nationalism and Revolution in Indonesia,* Cornell University Press, New York, 1952.
Kartini, Raden Adjeng, *Letters of a Javanese Princess,* trans. Agnes L. Symmers, W.W. Norton, New York, 1964.
K'tut Tantri, *Revolt in Paradise,* E.H. Garland, London, 1960.
van Leur, J.C., *Indonesian Trade and Society,* van Hoeve, The Hague, 1955.
Sjahrir, Sutan, *Out of Exile,* John Day, New York 1949.
Sukarno, *An Autobiography,* as told by Cindy Adams, Bobs Merrill, New York, 1965.

Natural History-Geography

Dobby, E.H.G., *Southeast Asia,* London, 1966.
Fisher, C.A., *Southeast Asia: A Social, Economic and Political Geography,* London, 1966.
Wallace, A.R., *The Malay Archipelago,* London, 1869, reprinted New York, 1962.

A Miscellany

Indonesia, and Java in particular, have been sadly ignored by novelists writing in English, perhaps as a result of the prolonged Dutch presence. The country has occasionally been used as a hastily sketched background for thrillers like Eric Ambler's *Passage of Arms* and adventure stories like Alistair MacLean's *South by Java Head,* but nobody has written fiction involving the place and its people (with wit, sympathy and perception) in the way that Kipling did for India.

Attenborough, David, *Zoo Quest for a Dragon,* Pan Books, London, 1961.
Bartlett, J., Fowler, G., and Cale, R., *Java, A Garden Continuum,* Amerasian Ltd., Hong Kong, 1974.
Conrad, Joseph, *Almayer's Folly,* J.M. Dent, London, 1947.
Courlander, Harold, *Kantchil's Lime Pit and Other Stories from Indonesia,* Harcourt, Brace & World, New York, 1950.
Epton, Nina, *The Palace and the Jungle,* Oldbourne Press, London, 1955.
Forster, Harold, *Flowering Lotus,* Longmans, Green & Co., London, 1958.
Introducing Indonesia, American Women's Association, Jakarta, 1973 (reprint).
Lubis, Mochtar, *Twilight in Jakarta,* Hutchinson, London, 1963.
Southall, I., *Indonesia Face to Face,* Landsdowne Press, Melbourne, 1964.
________, *Indonesian Journey,* Landsdowne Press, Melbourne, 1965.
Williams, Masslyn, *Five Journeys from Jakarta,* Collins, Sydney, 1966.

Appendix/Useful Addresses

Airlines (International)

Aeroflot Soviet Airlines, Sahid Jaya Hotel, Jalan Jend Sudirman 86, tel. 584315, 584316.

Air India, Hotel Sari Pacific, Jalan Thamrin, tel. 325534, 325470.

Air New Zealand, c/o Sabang Metropolitan Hotel Unit G001.

Air Niugini, Hotel Borobudur Inter-continental, Jalan Lap. Banteng Selatan, tel. 371306.

Airlanka Ltd, Kartika Plaza Hotel, Ground Floor, tel. 322849, 332006.

Alitalia, Hotel Sheraton, Jalan M.H. Thamrin, tel. 322008, 321220 ext. 736.

Biman Bangladesh Airlines, PP Building, Jalan Thamrin, tel. 324635, 320727.

British Airways, The Jakarta Mandarin, Jalan Thamrin, tel. 333207, 333092, 333198, 333572.

British Caledonian Airways, c/o Bigg Air Services, Ground Floor, Kartika Plaza Hotel, Thamrin 10, tel. 322849, 332006, 321108 ext. 275, 273.

Cathay Pacific Airways Ltd, BDN Building, Jalan M.H. Thamrin, tel. 327807; Hotel Borobudur Inter-continental, tel. 370108. Reservations: tel. 326807, 327807.

China Airlines, St. Maria House, Jalan Ir. H. Juanda, tel. 354448, 364449, 353195.

Czechoslovak Airlines, Wisata International Hotel, Jalan M.H. Thamrin, tel. 320308 ext. 135 or 136, 320408, 325530.

Garuda Indonesian Airways, Jalan Angkasa, tel. 417808 (4 lines). Nusantara Building, Ground Floor, Jalan Thamrin, tel. 333408, 330464, 333909 ext. 2116 or 2117. Hotel Borobudur Inter-Continental, tel. 359901, 370108 ext. 2241 or 2242, 370709.

Japan Air Lines, President Hotel, Jalan Thamrin 59, tel. 322207.

K.L.M. Royal Dutch Airlines, Hotel Indonesian Sheraton, Jalan M.H. Thamrin, tel. 320708 (5 lines).

Korean Airlines, c/o Amaran International Courier, 3rd Floor, Hotel Borobudur Inter-Continental, tel. 357777, 357744, 357679, 348683.

Lan Chile, Jalan Raden Saleh 6, tel. 354267.

Lufthansa German Airlines, Asoka Hotel, Jalan M.H. Thamrin, tel. 323400, 320632, 321104.

Malaysian Airlines System, BDN Building, 8th Floor, Jalan Thamrin, tel. 320909 (4 lines).

Northwest Orient, Hotel Sari Pacific, Jalan Thamrin, tel. 324659, 320558, 326439.

Pakistan International Airlines, Oriental Building, Jalan Thamrin 51, tel. 357542, 357545 ext. 298 or 299.

Pan American World Airways, Hotel Borobudur Inter-Continental, tel. 361707 (5 lines), 370108 ext. 2114-2117.

Philippine Airlines, Hotel Borobudur Inter-Continental, Jalan Lap. Banteng Selatan, tel. 370108 ext. 2310, 2312, 2314 or 2336.

Quantas, BDN Building, Jalan Thamrin, tel. 327707 (5 lines), 326707 (6 lines).

Royal Dutch Airlines, Jalan M.H. Thamrin, Hotel Indonesian Sheraton, tel. 320708.

S.A.S. Scandinavian Airlines, BDN Building, Jalan Thamrin, tel. 320607 (7 lines).

Sabena, Belgian World Airlines, Hotel Borobudur Inter-Continental, Jalan Lapangan Banteng Selatan, tel. 372039, 371915.

Singapore Airlines, Sahid Jaya Hotel, Jalan Jend. Sudirman 86, tel. 584021, 584041, 583711, 583691.

Swiss Air, Hotel Borobudur Inter-Continental, Jalan Lap. Banteng Selatan, tel. 373608 (3 lines).

Thai International, BDN Building, Jalan Thamrin, tel.320607 (7 lines).

U.T.A. (Union De Transport Airlines), Jaya Building, Jalan Thamrin 12, tel. 323609, 323507 (3 lines).

Airlines (Domestic) in Jakarta

Bouraq Indonesian Airline, Jalan Patrice Lumumba 1, tel. 354395, 357640, 357940.

Deraya, Jalan Pintu Air, tel. 340219.

Derazona, Wisma Kosgoro, Jalan M.H. Thamrin, tel. 322168.

Garuda Indonesian Airway (GIA), Jalan Ir. H. Juanda 15 (Head Office), tel. 370709; Kemayoran Airport, tel. 410808; Halim Perdanakusuma Airport, tel. 884156; Wisma Nusantara Building, Jalan M.H. Thamrin, tel. 373909; Hotel Borobudur Inter-Continental, tel. 359901 ext. 2116, 2117.

Mandala Airlines, Jalan Veteran 1/34, tel. 368107 (5 lines).

Merpati Nusantara Airlines (MNA), Jalan Patrice Lumumba 2, tel. 314608, 413672; Kemayoran Airport, tel. 348031, 348038.

Pelita Air Service, Jalan Abdul Muis 52, tel. 357389.

Sempati Air Transport, Jalan Merdeka Timur 7, tel. 348760, 37911.

Seulawah Air Service, Jalan Patrice Lumumba 18 BD, tel. 354207.

Zamrud Aviation Corporation, Kartika Plaza Hotel, Room 282, tel. 321008 ext. 8282.

Note: Due to the expansion of the telecommunications network in several cities still in progress, certain telephone numbers are subject to change.

Accommodations

JAKARTA

Luxury (US$100-up)

Borobudur Inter-Continental, Jalan Lap. Banteng Selatan, P.O. Box 329 JKT, tel. 370108.

Jakarta Hilton International, Jalan Jend. Gatot Subroto, P.O. Box 3315 JKT, tel. 583051, 587981.

The Jakarta Mandarin, Jalan M.H. Thamrin, P.O. Box 3392 JKT, tel. 321307.

Sari Pacific, Jalan M.H. Thamrin no. 6, P.O. Box 3138 JKT, tel. 323707.

Expensive (US$60-100)

Holiday Inn Orchid Palace, Jalan Letjen S. Parman Slipi, P.O. Box 2791 JKT, tel. 596911, 593115 (direct).

Horison, Taman Implan, Jaya Ancol, P.O. Box 3340 JKT, tel. 680008 (20 lines).

Hotel Indonesia Jakarta, Jalan M.H. Thamrin, P.O. Box 54 JKT, tel. 320008, 322008.

Hyatt Aryaduta Jakarta, Jalan Prapatan 44-46, P.O. Box 3287 JKT PUSAT, tel. 376008 (8 lines).

President Hotel, Jalan M.H. Thamrin 59, tel. 320508.

Putri Pulau Seribu Paradise, Jalan M.H. Thamrin No. 9, Jakarta Theater Building, tel. 359333, 359334.

Moderate (US$20-50)

Asoka, Jalan M.H. Thamrin 28-30, P.O. Box 3076 JKT, tel. 322908.

Garden, Jalan Kemang Raya, Kebayoran Baru, P.O. Box 41 KBY, tel. 715808.

Interhouse, Jalan Melawai Raya 18-20, Kebayoran Baru, P.O. Box 128 KBY, tel. 716408.

Kartika Plaza, Jalan M.H. Thamrin no. 10, P.O. Box 2081, tel. 321008 (15 lines).

Kebayoran Inn, Jalan Senayan 57, Kebayoran Baru, tel. 716208.

Kemang, Jalan Kemang Raya, Kebayoran Baru, P.O. Box 163 KBY, tel. 793208.

Marcopolo, Jalan Cik Ditiro 19, tel. 375409 (9 lines).

Menteng 1, Jalan Gondangdia Lama 28, tel. 325208; Jalan Cikini Raya 105, tel. 325543, 326311.

Monas, Jalan Medan Merdeka Barat 21, tel. 375208.

Natour Transaera Hotel, Jalan Merdeka Timur 16, P.O. Box 3380 JKT, tel. 351373.

Inexpensive (less than US$20)

Bali International, Jalan K.H. Wahid Hasyim 116, tel. 345058.

Djakarta, Jalan Hayam Wuruk 35, tel. 377709 (6 lines).

Jalan Jaksa No. 5, off Jalan Kebun Sirih.

Pondok Soedibjo, Jalan Keboh Sirih 23.

Wisma Delime, 5 Jalan Jaksa.

Wisma Esther, Jalan Mataram Raya 113.

BANTEN AND THE WEST COAST

Expensive (US$25-50)

Anyer Beach Motel, Jalan Raya Karang Bolong, Anyer, Serang Banten, tel. 381-382 Cilegon.

Carita Krakatau Beach, Jalan Carita Kec. Labuan, Kao. Pandeglang, Banten, Hotel Menteng, tel. 325208 ext. 5.

Guest House Krakatau Steel, Komplek PT. Krakatau Steel, Kota Baja, Cilegon, Banten.

Merak Beach Hotel, Jalan Raya Merak, Banten, tel. 15 Merak.

Moderate (US$10-25)

Marcopolo Pulorida Village, Florida, Banten.

Inexpensive (less than US$10)

Gondang, Jalan Raya Merak No. 30, Cilegon, Banten.

Penginapan, Karangantau Indah, Banten.

Wisma Kasihsayang, Jalan Tirtayasa, Serang.

BOGOR, PUNCAK AND THE SOUTH

Luxury (US$50-up)

Samudra Beach Hotel, Pelabuhan Ratu, Sukabumi, tel. 23 Pelabuhan Ratu.

Expensive (US$25-50)

Bukit Indah Hotel & Cottages, Jalan Raya Cipanas, Ciloto, Cianjur, tel. 49 Cianjur.

Bukit Raya, Sindanglaya, Cipanas, Cianjur, tel. 0255 — 2605.

Evergreen, Jalan Raya Puncak Km. 84, Bogor, tel. 4075 Code 9.

Karya Jasa "Wisma," Jalan Raya Puncak Km. 88, Cianjur, tel. Puncak 13.

Ussu International, Jalan Cisarua — Puncak, tel. 4499 Code 9.

Moderate (US$10-25)

Cibogo, Jalan Raya Cipayung, tel. 4143 Code 9.

Genggong Village Hotel, Km. 30 Cisalak, Cimanggis, Kabupaten Bogor, tel. 870875.

Sanawisata, Kampung Prabon, Ciloto, Puncak, Cianjur, tel. 29 Puncak.

Sindanglaya, Jalan Raya Pasekon 43, Cipanas, Cianjur, tel. (0255) 2116.

Inexpensive (less than US$10)

Bayu Amarta, Karang Pamulang No. 31, Pelabuhan Ratu, Sukabumi.

Pondok Dewata Motel, Pelabuhan Ratu, Sukabumi.

Salak, Jalan Ir. H. Juanda No 8, Bogor, tel. 22091, 22092, 22093.

Teluk Biru, Jalan Tenjo Resmi, Pelabuhan Ratu, Sukabumi.

BANDUNG

Luxury (US$50-up)

Panghegar, Jalan Merdeka No. 2, P.O. Box 506, tel. 57584 (4 lines).

Expensive (US$25-50)

Istana, Jalan Lembong 22 — 24, tel. 57240, 58240, 56871.

Kumala Panghegar, Jalan Asia Afrika 140, P.O. Box 507 BD, tel. 52141, 52142.

Savoy Homann Hotel, Jalan Asia Afrika 112, P.O. Box 9, tel. 58091.

Moderate (US$10-25)

Braga, Jalan Braga No. 8, tel. 51685.

Grand Hotel Lembang, Jalan Raya Lembang 288, Lembang, tel. (022) 82392.

Grand Hotel Preanger, Jalan Asia Afrika 81, P.O. Box 124 BDG, tel. 58061, 58062.

Suka Rasa, Jalan Tamblong 36.

Trio, Jalan Gardujati No. 55-61, tel. 615055, 615059.

Inexpensive (less than US$10)

Brajawijaya, Jalan Pungkur No. 28, tel. 50673.
Gania Plaza, Jalan Bungsu No. 30, tel. 56557.
International, Jalan Veteran 32.
Melati Baru, Jalan Kebonjati 24, tel. 56409.
Sahara, Jalan Otto Iskandardinata 3, tel. 51684.

FROM BANDUNG TO YOGYAKARTA

Moderate (US$10-25)

Lembur Kuring, Tarogong, Garut.
Sari Panas, Jalan Cipanas, Taragong, Garut.

Inexpensive (less than US$10)

Losmen Mini I, Pangandaran.
Nasional, Jalan Kenanga 19, Garut.
Santosa, Jalan Gunung Sabeulah No. 45, Tasikmalaya, tel. 41202.
Wisma Dinar, Pangandaran.
Wisma Sawarji, Pangandaran.

YOGYAKARATA

Luxury (US$50-up)

Ambarrukmo Palace, Jalan Laksda Adisucipto, Yogyakarta. P.O. Box 10 Yogyakarta, tel. 88488, 88984.

Expensive (US$25-50)

Airlangga Guest House, Jalan Prawirotaman No. 4, tel. 3344.
Arjuna Plaza, Jalan P. Mangkubumi No. 48, tel. 3063.
Batik Palace, Jalan Pasar Kembang 29, P.O. Box 115 Yogyakarta, tel. 2149.
Mutiara Hotel, Jalan Malioboro 18, P.O. Box 87, tel. 3272, 4530, 4531.
Natour Garuda Hotel, Jalan Malioboro, P.O. Box 43, tel. 2113, 2114.
Puri Artha Cottages & Restaurant, tel. 5934 (2 lines).
Sri Wedari, Jalan Laks. Adisucipto, P.O. Box 93 Yogyakarta, tel. 88288 (3 lines).

Moderate (US$10-25)

Duta Guest House, Jalan Prawirotaman 20, Yogyakarta, tel. 5219.
Gajah Guest House, Jalan Prawirotaman No. 24, tel. 2479.
Gajahmada Guesthouse, Bulak Sumur, Kampus, Universitas Gajah Mada, tel. 88461, 88688.
Sri Puger, Jalan M.T. Haryono, tel. 5545.
Sumaryo Guest House, Jalan Prawirotaman No. 18/A, Yogyakarta, tel. (0274) 2852.

Inexpensive (less than US$10)

Asia Afrika, Jalan Pasar Kembang 25.
Aziatic Hotel, Jalan Sosrowijanyan 6.
Hotel Kota, Jalan Pasar Kembang.
Intan, Jalan Sosrokusuman DN. 1/16.
Prambanan, Jalan Adisucipto No. 6, tel. (0274) 4709.
Ratna, Jalan Pasar Kembang No. 17 A.

THE NORTH COAST

Expensive (US$25-50)

Karlita Bar & Restaurant, Jalan Brigjen, Katamso No. 27, Tegal, tel. 41314, 41121.
Nirwana, Jalan Dr. Wahidin 11, Pekalongan, P.O. Box 36 Pekalongan, tel. 41691, 41446.
Omega, Jalan Tuparev 20, Cirebon, P.O. Box 23 Cirebon, tel. 3072, 3073, 5023.
Patrajasa "Cirebon" Motel, Jalan Tujuh Pahlawan Revolusi, No. 11 Cirebon, P.O. Box 68 Cirebon, tel. 3792, 3793.

Moderate (US$10-25)

Grand Hotel Cirebon, Jalan Siliwangi 110, Cirebon, tel. 2014, 2015, 2286, 2287.
Hayam Wuruk, Jalan Hayam Wuruk 152 — 158, Pekalongan, tel. 41823, 21405.
Ramayana, Jalan Gajah Mada 9, Pekalongan, tel. 43.

Inexpensive (less than US$10)

Asia, Jalan Kalibaru Selatan 11, Cirebon, tel. (0321) 2183.
Damai, Jalan Siliwangi 130, Cirebon, tel. (0231) 3045.
Hotel Gadjah Mada, Jalan Gadjah Mada 11A, Pekalongan.
Semarang, Jalan Siliwangi 132, Cirebon, tel. (0231) 3231.
Susana, Jalan Mayjen Sutoyo, Tegal, tel. 41823.

SEMARANG

Luxury (US$50-up)

Patrajasa Hotel/Motel, Jalan Sisingamangaraja, P.O. Box 8 Semarang, tel: 314441, 314445.

Expensive (US$25-50)

Candi Baru, Jalan Rinjani 21, tel. 315272.
Metro Grand Park Hotel, Jalan H. Agus Salim 2-4, tel. 27371.
Natour Hotel Dibya Puri, Jalan Pemuda 11, tel. 27821 (5 lines), 24934.
Sky Garden, Jalan Setlabudi, Gombel, tel. 312733, 312736.

Moderate (US$10-25)

Hotel Dibya Puri, Jalan Pemuda, tel. 25187.
Djelita, Jalan Letjen M.T. Haryono, No. 32-34-36, tel. 23891, 25897.
Gombel Indah, Jalan Dr. Setiabudi, tel. 312876.
Green Guest House, Jalan Kesambi No. 7, tel. 312642, 312787.
Queen Hotel, Jalan Gajah Mada 44-52, tel. 27063.

SEMARANG TO SURABAYA

Expensive (US$25-50)

Kurnia, Jalan Tondonegoro 12, Pati, tel. 81133
Mulia, Jalan Kol. Sunanda 17, Pati, tel. 2118

Moderate (US$10-25)

Menno Jaya Inn, Jalan Diponegoro 40/B, Jepara, tel. 143.
Notosari, Jalan Jalan Kepodang 17, Kudus, tel. 21245.
Purnama, Jalan Raya Tuban — Semarang, Tuban, tel. Tuban 277.

Inexpensive (less than US$10)

Buddha Gaya Whatugong, (5 kilometers north of Ungaran on road to Semarang). Lovely, cheap and quiet Buddhist monastery.
Jaya, Jalan M.T. Haryono 85-87, tel. 23604.
Rahayu, Jalan Imam Bonjol 35-37, tel: 22532.
Hotel Singapore, Jalan Iman Bonjol.
Hotel Tanjung, Jalan Tanjung, Semarang.

SEMARANG TO YOGYAKARTA/SOLO

Moderate (US$10-25)

Beringin, Jalan Jend. Sudirman 60, Salatiga, tel. 81129.
Kopeng Pesanggrahan, Kopeng, Salatiga.
Rawa Pening, Bandungan, Ambarawa.

Inexpensive (less than US$10)

Asrama Mahasiswa Universitas Satya Wacana, Jalan Kartini 11A.
Wijaya, Jalan Raya 105, Lasem, Rembang, tel. 95.

Inexpensive (less than US$10)

Losmen Asia, Jalan Kartini 32, Jepara.

EAST JAVA

Luxury (US$50-up)

Hyatt Bumi Surabaya, Jalan Jend. Basuki Rahmat, No. 124-128 Surabaya, P.O. Box 5130 SBY, tel. 470875 (6 lines), 470525.

Expensive (US$25-50)

Asida, Jalan Panglima Sudirman No. 99, Batu, Malang, tel. 259 Batu.
Bristol, Jalan Pregolan 3, Surabaya, tel. 42379.
Elmi, Jalan Panglima Sudirman 42-44, Surabaya, tel. 471571, 45291.
Garden, Jalan Pemuda 21, Surabaya, tel. 470000, 470009.
Grand Park, Jalan Samudera 3-5-, Surabaya, tel. 270004, 270008.
Majapahit, Jalan Tunjungan No. 65, Surabaya, P.O. Box 199, tel. 43351 (5 lines).
Mirama, Jalan Raya Darmo 72-74, Surabaya, P.O. Box 232 SBY, tel. 69501.
Purnama, Jalan Raya Selecta Batu, Malang, P.O. Box 18, tel. 195 Batu.
Ramayana Hotel, Jalan Basuki Rachmat 67-69, Surabaya, tel. 46321 (9 lines).
Selecta, Jalan Tulungrejo, Batu, Malang, P.O. Box 30 Batu, tel. 25 Batu.

Moderate (US$10-25)

Jane's House, Jalan Dinoyo 100, tel. 67722.
New Flores, Jalan Flores 27-29, Surabaya, tel. 68701.
Olympic, Jalan Urip Sumohardjo 65-67, Surabaya, tel. 43215, 43216.
Pelangi, Jalan Merdeka Selatan 3, Malang, tel. 27456, 27457.
Remaja, Jalan Embong Kenongo 12, Surabaya, tel. 41359.
Royal, Jalan Panglima Sudirman 68, Surabaya, tel. 43547, 43548.
Santoso II, Jalan Selecta — Tulungrejo, Batu, Malang, tel. 66 Batu.
Y.M.C.A., Jalan Jend. Basuki Rachmat 72—74, Malang, tel. 23605.

Inexpensive (less than US$10)

Bamboo Denn Transito, Jalan Pemuda 19, tel. 40333.
Hotel Wisma Nirvana, Jalan Jen Basuki Rachmat, 124A, Malang.
Losmen Selamat, Jalan Kandangan, Pare.
Niagara, Jalan Dr. Sutomo 63, Lawang, Malang, tel. 106.
Sriwijaya, Jalan Desa Pacot, Mojokerto, tel. 12/9 Mojokerto.
Wisma Ganeca, Jalan Sumatra 34A.

BY ROAD TO BALI

Expensive (US$25-50)

Natour Bath Hotel Tretes, Jalan Pesanggrahan Tretes No. 2, Tretes, Pasuruan, tel. (0343) 81161.
Tanjung Plaza, Jalan Wilis No. 7, Tretes, Pasuran, tel. (0343) 81102.

Moderate (US$10-25)

Manyar, Bulusan, Ketapang, Banyuwangi, P.O. Box 36 BWI, tel. (0333) 41741.
Mars, Jalan Imam Syafi'i No. 27, Jember, tel. 41573.
Pelita Concern, Jalan Wilis 19-21, Tretes, Pasuruan, tel. 81802.
Safari, Jalan Setia Kawan AA, No. 26-28, Jember, tel. 21085, 41146, 41897.
Tretes Raya, Jalan Malabar 166, Tretes, Pasuruan, tel. (0343) 81902.
Victoria, Jalan Suroyo 1-3, Probolinggo, tel. 21461, 21462, 21463, 21990.

Inexpensive (less than US$10)

Blambangan, Jalan Dr. Wahidin 4, Banyuwangi, tel. (0333) 21598.

Direksi Perkebuan (Estate Management), Jember.

Handini, Jalan Kartini 38, Jember, tel. (0331) 21496.

Hotel Kemayoran, Jalan Jen. Soedirman, Prolombingo.

Pasangrahan Sidho Muntjul, Pasir Putih.

Pasir Putih Inn, Pasir Putih.

Sido Muncul, Jalan Pasir Putih, Situbondo, tel. 2273 Panarukan, Pasir Putih.

Wisatawan, Jalan Prigen 460, Pandaan, Pasuruan.

Domestic Banks

Bank Bumi Daya, Jalan Kebon Sirih no. 66-70, Jakarta Pusat, tel. 370608; Jalan Lapangan Stasion Kota, Jakarta Kota, tel. 670158.

Bank Dagang Negara, Jalan M.H. Thamrin no. 5, Jakarta Pusat, tel. 321707 (18 lines).

Bank Ekspor Impor Indonesia, Jalan Lapangan Stasion Kota no. 1, Jakarta Kota, tel. 670072, 673122.

Bank Indonesia, Jalan M.H. Thamrin no. 2, Jakarta Pusat, tel. 372408 (30 lines).

Bank Negara Indonesia 1946, Jalan Lada no. 1, Jakarta Kota, tel. 672075.

Bank Pembangunan Daerah Djaya, Jalan Ir. H. Juanda 111/9, Jakarta Pusat, tel. 375708, 352983, 362305.

Bank Pembangunan Indonesia (Bapindo), Jalan Gondangdia Lama no. 2-4, Jakarta Pusat, tel. 321908 (20 lines); Jalan Hayam Wuruk no. 88, Jakarta Pusat, tel. 637709.

Bank Rakyat Indonesia, Jalan Veteran no. 8, Jakarta Pusat, tel. 374208.

Bank Tabungan Negara, Jalan Gajah Mada no. 1, Jakarta Barat, tel. 366598, 360237, 368008.

Bank Umum Nasional, 78 Jalan Cikini Raya, tel. 321607.

Foreign Banks

Algemene Bank Nederland, Jalan Ir. H. Juanda 23, Jakarta Pusat, tel. 362309.

American Express International Banking Corporation, Arthaloka Building, Jalan Jend. Sudirman, Jakarta Pusat, tel. 587401 (9 lines).

Amsterdam Rotterdam Bank, Eurasbank Building 5th floor, Jalan Imam Bonjol 80, Jakarta Pusat, tel. 350500, 356409.

Asia Commercial Banking Corporation Limited, Wisma Hayam Wuruk, 2nd floor, Room 1204, Jalan Hayam Wuruk, Jakarta Pusat, tel. 624109.

Bangkok Bank Limited, Jalan M.H. Thamrin 3, Jakarta Pusat, tel. 349048.

Bank of America, Wisma Antara (Building), Merdeka Selatan 17, 1st Floor — 2nd Floor, tel. 348031, 347031.

The Bank of Tokyo Limited, Wisma Nusantara Building, Jalan M.H. Thamrin 59, Jakarta Pusat, tel. 333409 (10 lines), 333909.

Bank of Credit & Commerce International S.A., Jalan M.H. Thamrin 8, 10th floor, Jakarta Pusat, tel. 359815.

Bank of India, BDN Building, 8th floor, Jalan M.H. Thamrin 5, Jakarta Pusat, tel. 320230.

Bank of Montreal, Wisma Kosgoro, tel. 325345.

Bank of New South Wales, Bangkok Bank Building 5th floor, Jalan M.H. Thamrin 3, Jakarta Pusat, tel. 353758, 345417.

The Bank of Nova Scotia, Wisma Nusantara 14th floor, Jalan M.H. Thamrin 59, Jakarta Pusat, tel. 325508 (5 lines), 330808.

Bankers Trust Company, Wisma Nusantara 7th floor, Jalan M.H. Thamrin 59, Jakarta Pusat, tel. 356146.

Banque De L'Indochino Et De Suez, BDN Building 11th floor, Jalan M.H. Thamrin 5, Jakarta Pusat, tel. 325408, 326497.

Banque De L'Union Europienne, Skyline Building 12th floor, Jalan M.H. Thamrin 9, Jakarta Pusat, tel. 320360.

Banque De Paris Et Des Pays Bas, Hotel Borobudur 3rd floor, Jalan Lapangan Banteng Selatan, Jakarta Pusat, tel. 371259.

Banque Francaise Du Commerce Exterieur, Wisma Nusantara 8th floor, Jalan M.H. Thamrin 59, Jakarta Pusat, tel. 333309 ext. 5486.

Banque National De Paris, Skyline Building 9th floor, Jalan M.H. Thamrin 9, Jakarta Pusat, tel. 323282, 321708 ext. 2650.

Barclays Bank International Limited, Wisma Nusantara 24th floor, Jalan M.H. Thamrin 59, Jakarta Pusat, tel. 333909 ext 6544.

The Chartered Bank, Jalan M.H. Thamrin 53, Jakarta Pusat, tel. 325008 (8 lines).

The Chase Manhattan Bank N.A., Jalan Merdeka Barat no. 6, Jakarta Pusat, tel. 374008, 353753, 353796.

City Bank N.A., Jalan M.H. Thamrin 55, Jakarta Pusat, tel. 354711, 354811.

Credit Lyonnais, Skyline Building 8th floor, Jalan M.H. Thamrin 9, Jakarta Pusat, tel. 321161.

Conrand Hinrich Donor Bank, BDN Building, 2nd floor, Jalan M.H. Thamrin 5, Jakarta Pusat, tel. 322117, 324365.

The Dai Ichi Kangyo Bank Limited, Wisma Nusantara 14th floor, Jalan M.H. Thamrin 59, Jakarta Pusat, tel. 333909 ext. 3223.

European Asian Bank, Euresbank Building, Jalan Imam Bonjol 80, Jakarta Pusat, tel. 358292.

The Export Import Bank Of Japan Limited, Skyline Building 5th floor, Jalan M.H. Thamrin 9, Jakarta Pusat, tel. 321708.

The First National Bank Of Chicago, Hotel Borobudur Inter-Continental 2nd floor, Jalan Lapangan Banteng Selatan, Jakarta Pusat, tel. 320360, 370108.

The Fuji Bank Ltd, Wisma Nusantara 17th floor, Jalan M.H. Thamrin 59, Jakarta Pusat, tel. 333909 ext. 5421.

Habib Bank Ltd, Ramayana Arcade Hotel Indonesia Sheraton, Jalan M.H. Thamrin, Jakarta Pusat, tel. 322008 ext. 777.

The Hong Kong & Shanghai Banking Corporation, Jalan Hayam Wuruk 8, Jakarta Pusat, tel. 377808.

The Indonesia Overseas Bank, Asoka Hotel 2nd floor, Jalan M.H. Thamrin 28-30, tel. 322908.

International Bank Of Singapore Ltd, Wisma Hayam Wuruk 8th floor, Jalan Hayam Wuruk 8, Jakarta Pusat, tel. 358309.

Canada — 225 Albert Street, Suite 1010, Kent Square Building "C," P.O. Box 430. Ottawa,

Ontario, K.2.P.OL9., tel. (613) 236-7403, 236-7404, 236-7405.

Czechoslovakia — Nad Budankaml II/7, 125.29 Prague 5, Smichov, tel. 52 60 41, 52 60 42, 52 60 43.

Democratic People's Republic of Korea — 5 Foreigners Building Moon So Dong, Tai Dong Kang District, Pyong'yang, tel. 206, 297, 298.

Socialist Republic of Vietnam — 50 Pho Ngo Quyen, Hanoi (North Vietnam), tel. 56316, 53353, 53324.

Denmark & Norway — Orehoj Alle I 2900 Hellerup, Copenhagen (Denmark), tel. (01) 62.44.22, (01) 62.54.39.

Ethiopia — Mekanisa Road, P.O. Box 1004, Addis Ababa (Ethiopia), tel. 44.84.55, 44.84.56, 44.34.12.

Korean Exchange Bank, Jalan Gatot Subroto no. 58, Jakarta Selatan, tel. 516581.

Manufacturers Hanover Trust Company, Wisma Nusantara 20th floor, Jalan M.H. Thamrin 59, Jakarta Pusat, tel. 333909 ext. 6537.

Marine Midland Bank, Wisma Nusantara 27th floor, Jalan M.H. Thamrin 59, Jakarta Pusat, tel. 333909 ext. 5400.

The Mitsui Bank Limited, Wisma Nusantara 19th floor, Jalan M.H. Thamrin 59, Jakarta Pusat, tel. 333909 ext. 3287, 3288.

M. M. Warburg/Bringkmann, Awrts, & Company, Jalan Prof. M. Yamin SH. 59, Jakarta Pusat, tel. 346866, 340652.

The National Bank Of Australia, Hotel Borobudur 2nd floor, Jalan Lapangan Banteng Selatan, Jakarta Selatan, tel. 360209, 351452.

Philippine National Bank, BDN Building, 2nd floor, Jalan M.H. Thamrin 5, Jakarta Pusat, tel. 324594.

The Sanwa Bank Limited, Wisma Nusantara 9th floor, Jalan M.H. Thamrin 59, Jakarta Pusat, tel. 333909 ext. 2197.

Societe General, Eurasbank Building 6th floor, Jalan Imam Bonjol 80, Jakarta Pusat, tel. 341492, 352658.

The Sumitomo Bank Limited, Wisma Nusantara 9th floor, Jalan H. Thamrin 59, Jakarta Pusat, tel. 333909 ext. 2190.

Tat Lee Bank Ltd., Gedung Metro Pasar Baru, Jakarta Pusat, tel. 362504, 360486.

The Tokai Limited, Wisma Nusantara 8th floor, Jalan M.H. Thamrin 59, Jakarta Pusat, tel. 333909 ext. 7645, 7646.

The Toronto Dominion Bank, Wisma Metropolitan 3rd floor, Jalan Jend. Sudirman 29, Jakarta Pusat, tel. 584761 ext. 21.

United California Bank, Bangkok Bank Building 5th floor, Jalan M.H. Thamrin 3, Jakarta Pusat, tel. 347693, 353194.

Indonesian Embassies

Afghanistan — Wazir Akhbar Khan Meina, P.O. Box 532, Kabul, tel. 23334, 23338, 23752.

Algeria, Guinea & Mali — 6 Rue Etienne Bailac, B.P. 62 EL — Moradia, Algiers, tel. 58.01.02.56.25.50.

Arab Republics of Egypt, Sudan & Lebanon — 13 Rue Aisha E1 Taimouria, Garden City, Cairo, Tel. 27200, 27209, 27356.

Argentina, Chile & Uruguay — 2901, Mariscal Ramon Castilla, Buenos Aires, tel. 824-6622, 824-6655, 824-7142.

Australia — 8 Darwin Avenue, Jarrumla ACT, 2600, Canberra, tel. 73-3222.

Austria — Cottagegasse 49, 1190 — Wien — Osterreich, tel. 0222/34 25.

Bangladesh — 1075 CWS (A), Gulshan Avenue, Gulshan Model Town, Dhaka 12, tel. 300131, 300132.

Belgium, Luxembourg & E.E.C. — 294, Avenue de Tervuaren, 1150 Brussels, tel. 771.20.12, 771.20.13, 771.20.14.

Brazil & Bolivia — S.C.S.E.D. Central 50 Andar, Brasilia D.F. Cep 70.000, tel. 226-0382, 226-1942, 226-2737.

Bulgaria — 32, Rue G. Gueorguiun — Dej., Sofia, tel. 44-23-49, 44-17-87.

Burma & Nepal — 100, Pydaungsu Yeiktha Road, P.O. Box 1401, Rangoon, tel. 11714, 71362.

Federal Republic of Germany — 2, Kurt Schumacher Strasse, 5300 Bonn I (West Deutschland), tel. 2 1 70 67.

Finland — 37 Eerikinkatu, 00180 Helsinki 18, tel. 64 42 21.

France — 49, Rue Cartambert, 75016 Paris, tel 503.07.60.

Great Britain & Ireland — 38, Grosvernor Square, London WIX 9 AD (England), tel. 01.499.7661.

German Democratic Republic — 110 Berlin — Pankow, Esplanade 9 Berlin (G.D.R.), tel. 482.6944, 482.4532.

Holy See (Vatican) — 42, Piazzale Roberto Ardigo, Roma (Italy), tel. 542 0441.

Hungary — 26, Gorji Fasor, 1068 Budapest, tel. 428-508, 428-585, 428-308, 428-549.

India — 50-A, Chanakyapuri, New Delhi, tel. 692392.

Iraq — 24/6/33 Al-Wathiq Street Alwiyah, P.O. Box 420, Baghdad, tel. 98677, 98679, 98680, 90260.

Iran — 210 Ghaem Magham Farahani Avenue, P.O. Box 1559, Teheran, Tel. 62 68 65, 62 72 51.

Italy — 53 Via Campania, Roma, Tel. 475.9251.

Japan — 9-2, Higashi Gotanda 5 Chome Shinagawa-Ku, Tokyo tel. 441-4201.

Kuwait, Qatar & Bahrain — 32, Nuzha Main Street Block 3, Nuzha Dhohia, P.O. Box 21560, Safat, Kuwait, tel. 514588, 514658, 519923.

Laos — Route Phone Keng, Boite Postale 277, Vientiane, tel. 2373, 2370.

Malagasy Republic — 15 Rue Radama Ler Tsaralalana, Tananarive, tel. 249.15.

Malaysia — P.O. Box 889, Kuala Lumpur, tel. 421011, 421141, 421228.

Mexico & Cuba — 27, Julio Verne, Colonia Polanco, Mexico 5 Df, tel. 520 41 67.

New Zealand & Fiji — 11 Fitzherbert Terrace, Thordon, Wellington, P.O. Box 3543, tel. 736669, 736670, 737119, 737370.

Netherlands — 8, Tobias Asserlaan, 2517 Kc Den Haag, tel. 070-633960.

Nigeria, Ghana & Liberia — 5/B Anifoswoshe Street, Victoria Island, P.O. Box 3473, Lagos (Nigeria), tel. 614601, 610508.

Pakistan — 10/12 Street 4, Shalinar 6/3, Islamabad (Pakistan), tel. 202499.

Papua Niugini — Henao Drive, Sec 67 Lot. 6, Gordon Estate, Boroko, P.O. Box 7165.

Philippines — Salcedo Street Legaspi Village, P.O. Box 372 MCC, Makati, Metro Manila, tel. 85-50-61, 88-03-01.

Poland — Ul Wackeka 9, P.O. Box 33, Warzawa Saska Kepa 00-950, Warzawa (Poland), tel. 17-51-79, 17-84-5.

Republic of Korea — 1-887, Yoido-Dong, Young — deoungpo-ku, Seoul, tel. 7825116, 51175118.

Rumania — 18 Strada Biserica Popa Chitu, Bucharest, tel. 11 77 20, 11 77 29, 11 74 50.

Saudi Arabia — Khalid bin Wahid Street, Sharafiah, Jeddah, P.O. Box 10.

Singapore — 435 Orchard Road, "Wisma Indonesia Singapore," tel. 7362422, 7377422.

Soviet Union & Mongolia — 12, Novokusnetskaya Ulitsa, Moscow (U.S.S.R.), tel. 2316262.

Spain — Calle del Cinca 13, Madrid 2, tel. 458.0649, 458.0567, 458.0948.

Sri Lanka & Maladewa — 10, Independence Avenue, Colombo 7, tel. 91392, 91485.

Surinam — 3, Van Brusslan, Uitvlugt, P.O. Box 157, Paramaribo, tel. 99900, 97070, 99516.

Sweden — 47/V Stradvägen 114 56, Stockholm, tel. 63 54 70, 63 54 74.

Switzerland — 51 Elfenauweg, 3006 Bern, tel. 440983.

Syria & Jordan — 19 Jadet Al Amier, Izeddine Street Sahet Al-Madfa'a, Damascus, tel. 331237, 331238.

Tanzania & Zambia — 299 Upanga Road, Dar es Salaam, Tanzania, P.O. Box 572, tel. 24086, 24087, 240997.

Thailand — 600-602 Petchburi Road, Bangkok, tel. 252-3135.

Tunisia — 93, Avenue Jugurtha (Avenue de Lesseps), Mutuellville, Tunis, tel. 284.359.

Turkey — Cankaya, Abdullah Cevdet Sokak 10, P.O. Box 506, Ankara, tel. 271914, 273934.

United Arab Emirates — Mohammed Sa'if Buthy Building, Flat 101, 102 Hamdan Street, P.O. Box 7256, Abu Dhabi, tel. 825517.

United States of America — 2020 Massachusetts Avenue N.W., Washington D.C. 20036, tel. (202) 293-1745.

Yugoslavia & Greece — Bulevar Oktobarshe Revolucije no. 18, 1104 Belgrade, tel. 662-122.

Venezuela — Calle Roraima Con Avenida, Rio de Janeiro, Caracas, P.O. Box 67061, tel. 91 04 11, 91 06 56.

Foreign Missions in Jakarta

Embassy of The Republic of Afghanistan, Jalan Dr. Kusurma Atmaja SH. 15, Jakarta Pusat, tel. 342677. Open 8 a.m. to 1 p.m. Monday to Friday.

Embassy of Democratic People's Republic of Algeria, Jalan Ciponegoro 8, Jakarta Pusat, tel. 349310, 352694. Open 8 a.m. to 2 p.m. Monday to Thursday; 8 a.m. to 12 noon Friday.

Embassy of The Republic of Argentina, Jalan Panarukan 17, Jakarta Pusat, tel. 348368, 353095. Open 8:30 a.m. to 1:30 p.m. Monday to Friday.

Embassy of Australia, Jalan M.H. Thamrin 15, Jakarta Pusat, tel. 350511 (10 lines). Open: 8:30 a.m. to 3:30 p.m. Monday to Friday.

Embassy of Austria, Jalan Diponegoro 44, Jakarta Pusat, tel. 345811, 348568. Open: 8:30 a.m. to 2:30 p.m. Monday to Friday.

Embassy of The People's Republic of Bulgaria, Jalan Imam Bonjol 34, Jakarta Pusat, tel. 346725, 343926. Open: 8 a.m. to 2 p.m. Monday to Friday.

Embassy of The Socialist Republic of The Union of Burma, Jalan H. Agus Salim 109, Jakarta Pusat, tel. 340440, 347204, Open: 8 a.m. to 3 p.m. Monday to Friday.

Embassy of Canada, Wisma Metropolitan 5th floor, Jalan Jend. Sudirman Kav. 29, Jakarta Pusat, P.O. Box 52/JKT, tel. 584030, 584039. Open: 8 a.m. to 4:45 p.m. Monday to Thursday; 8 a.m. to 1:30 p.m. Friday.

Embassy of The Republic of Chile, Arthaloka Building 14th floor, Jalan Jend. Sudirman no. 2, Jakarta Pusat, tel. 584308, 587611 ext. 292. Open: 9 a.m. to 4 p.m. Monday to Friday.

Embassy of The Czechoslavakia Socialist Republic, Jalan Prof. Moh. Yamin SH.29, Jakarta Pusat, tel. 346480, 344994, 340538. Open: 8 a.m. to 2 p.m. Monday to Friday.

Royal Danish Embassy, Jalan Abdul Muis 34, Jakarta Pusat, tel. 346615. Open: 8 a.m. to 2:30 p.m. Monday to Friday.

Embassy of The Arab Republic of Egypt, Jalan Teuku Umar 68, Jakarta Pusat, tel. 345572, 348181. Open: 9 a.m. to 2 p.m. Monday to Friday.

Embassy of Finland, Jalan Dr. Kusuma Atmaja SH. 15-A, Jakarta Pusat, tel. 346686, 345871. Open: 8 a.m. to 2 p.m. Monday to Friday.

Embassy of France, Jalan M.H. Thamrin 20, Jakarta Pusat, tel. 357311, 347871, 347872, 360572. Open: 8 a.m. to 3 p.m. Monday to Thursday; 8 a.m. to 1:30 p.m. Friday.

Embassy of The German Democratic Republic, Jalan Raden Saleh 56, Jakarta Pusat, tel. 349547, 349548. Open: 8:30 a.m. to 1 p.m. Monday to Friday.

Embassy of The Federal Republic of Germany, Jalan M.H. Thamrin 1, Jakarta Pusat, tel. 323908 (5 lines). Open: 7:30 a.m. to 2 p.m. Monday to Friday; 9 a.m. to 1 p.m. (Saturday).

Her Britannic Majesty's Embassy, Jalan M.H. Thamrin 75, Jakarta Pusat, tel. 341091, 341098. Open: 8 a.m. to 2:30 p.m. Tuesday; 8 a.m. to 5 p.m. Monday.

Apostolic Nunciature (Holy See-Vatikan), Jalan Medan Merdeka Timur 18, Jakarta Pusat, tel. 341142, 341143. Open: 8:30 a.m. to 1 p.m. Mondaty to Saturday.

Embassy of The Hungarian People's Republic, Jalan Rasuna Said, Kav. No. X3, Kuningan, Jakarta Pusat, tel. 587521. Open: 8 a.m. to 2 p.m. Monday to Friday.

Embassy of India, Jalan Kebon Sirih 44, Jakarta Pusat, tel. 342815, 365554. Open: 8 a.m. to 4:30 p.m. Monday to Friday.

Embassy of The Republic Islamic of Iran, Jalan H.O.S. Cokroaminoto 110, Jakarta Pusat, tel. 347807, 347808, 359667. Open: 9 a.m. to 2 p.m. Monday to Friday.

Embassy of The Republic of Iraq, Jalan Teuku Umar 38, Jakarta Pusat, tel. 343988, 344557, 348861. Open: 8 a.m. to 1:30 p.m. Monday to Friday; 8 a.m. to 1 p.m. (Saturday).

Embassy of The Republic of Italy, Jalan Diponegoro 45, Jakarta Pusat, tel. 348339, 347907. Open: 8 a.m. to 1:30 p.m. Monday to Friday.

Embassy of Japan, Jalan M.H. Thamrin 24,

Jakarta Pusat, tel. 324308, 324948, 325140, 325268. Open: 8:30 a.m. to 3 p.m. Monday to Friday; 8:30 a.m. to 12:30 p.m Saturday.

Embassy of The Democratic People's Republic of Korea, Jalan Teuku Umar 72–74, Jakarta Pusat, tel. 346457, 349606. Open: 8 a.m. to 1 p.m. Monday to Friday.

Embassy of The Republic of Korea, Jalan Jenderal Gatot Subroto, Jakarta Selatan, tel. 512309 (4 lines). Open: 8 a.m. to 2 p.m. Monday to Friday; 8 a.m. to 12 noon Wednesday and Saturday.

Embassy of Malaysia, Jalan Imam Bonjol 17, Jakarta Pusat, tel. 354945, 346770, 348243, 350176. Open: 8 a.m. to 2 p.m. Monday to Friday.

Embassy of Mexico, Jalan M.H. Thamrin 59, Jakarta Pusat, Nusantara Building 4th Floor, tel. 348974, 373909 (ext. 2151). Open: 9 a.m. to 2 p.m. Monday to Friday.

Royal Netherlands Embassy, Jalan H.R. Rasuna Said Kav. 5–3, tel. 511515, 361808. Open: 8 a.m. to 2:30 p.m. Monday to Friday.

New Zealand Embassy, Jalan Diponegoro 41, Jakarta Pusat, tel. 357924, 359796. Open: 8:30 a.m. to 1:30 p.m. Monday to Friday.

Embassy of The Federal Republic of Nigeria, Jalan Diponegoro 34, Jakarta Pusat, tel. 345484. Open: 8 a.m. to 2:30 p.m. Monday to Friday.

Embassy of The Kingdom of Norway, Jalan Padalarang 4, Jakarta Pusat, tel. 354556. Open: 8 a.m. to 2 p.m. Monday to Friday.

Embassy of The Islamic Republic of Pakistan, Jalan Teuku Umar 50, Jakarta Pusat, tel. 377502, 350576, 350577. Open: 7:30 a.m. to 2:30 p.m. Monday to Thursday; 7:30 a.m. to 11:30 a.m. Friday.

Embassy of Papua New Guinea, Wisma Metropolitan 4th Floor, Jalan Jenderal Sudirman Kav. 29, Jakarta Pusat, tel. 584604, 584605. Open: 7:30 a.m. to 2:30 p.m. Monday to Friday.

Embassy of The Philippines, Jalan Imam Bonjol 6–8, Jakarta Pusat, tel. 343745, 348917, 349986, 351917. Open: 8 a.m. to 4 p.m. Monday to Friday.

Embassy of Polish People's Republic, Jalan Diponegoro 65, Jakarta Pusat, tel. 320509. Open: 8 a.m. to 2 p.m. Monday to Friday; 8 a.m. to 12 noon Saturday.

Embassy of The Socialist Republic of Romania, Jalan Teuku Cik Ditiro 42/A, Jakarta Pusat, tel. 349524, 354847. Open: 8 a.m. to 2 p.m. Monday to Saturday.

Royal Embassy of Saudi Arabia, Jalan Iman Bonjol 3 Pav. Jakarta Pusat, tel. 346342, 346343, 359838. Open: 8 a.m. to 3 p.m. Monday to Saturday.

Embassy of The Republic of Singapore, Jalan Proklamasi 23 Jakarta Pusat, tel. 346046, 342885. Open: 8 a.m. to 4:30 p.m. Monday to Friday; 8 a.m. to 12:30 p.m. Saturday.

Embassy of Spain, Wisma Kosgoro 14th Floor, Jalan M.H. Thamrin 15, Jakarta Pusat, tel. 325996, 321808 ext. 362, 322869, 322872. Open: 8:30 a.m. to 1:30 p.m. Monday to Friday.

Embassy of The Democratic Socialist Republic of Sri Lanka, Jalan Diponegoro 70, Jakarta Pusat, tel. 321018, 321896, 321996. Open: 8 a.m. to 1 p.m. and 2 p.m. to 4:15 p.m. Monday to Friday.

Embassy of The Kingdom of Sweden, Jalan Tman Cut Mutiah 12, Jakarta Pusat, tel. 349121, 346953. Open: 9 a.m. to 12 noon Monday to Friday.

Embassy of Switzerland, Jalan Latuharhary SH. 23, Jakarta Pusat, tel. 347921, 347922. Open: 7:30 a.m. to 2 p.m. Monday to Friday.

Embassy of The Syrian Arab Republic, Gondangdia Lama no. 38, Jakarta Pusat, tel. 354570. Open: 8 a.m. to 2 p.m. Monday to Friday; 8 a.m. to 1 p.m. Saturday.

Royal Thai Embassy, Jalan Imam Bonjol 74, Jakarta Pusat, tel. 349180, 343762, 348221. Open: 8:30 a.m. to 2:30 p.m. Monday to Friday.

Embassy of The Republic of Turkey, Jalan Iman Bonjol 43, Jakarta Pusat, tel. 349500, 349509, 353709. Open: 8:30 a.m. to 2 p.m. Monday to Friday.

Embassy of The Union of Soviet Socialist Republics, Jalan M.H. Thamrin 13, Jakarta Pusat, tel. 351263, 351477, 342552. Open: 7:45 a.m. to 2:15 p.m. Monday to Friday.

Embassy of The United States of America, Jalan Medan Merdeka Selatan 5, Jakarta Pusat, tel. 340001. Open: 7:30 a.m. to 4 p.m. Monday to Friday.

Embassy of The Socialist Republic of Vietnam, Jalan Teuku Umar 25, Jakarta Pusat, tel. 348759, 347325. Open: 8 a.m. to 2 p.m. Monday to Thursday; 8 a.m. to 12 noon Friday to Saturday.

Embassy of The Socialist Federal Republic of Yugoslavia, Jalan H.O.S. Cokroaminoto, Jakarta Pusat, tel. 346411, 348450. Open: 7:30 a.m. to 2:30 p.m. Monday to Friday.

Hospitals

Budi Kemuliaan Hospital, Jalan Budi Kemuliaan, tel. 342828, 344728.

Cipto Mangunkusumo Hospital, Jalan Diponegoro 71, tel. 343021, 882829.

Fatmawati Hospital, Jalan R.S. Fatmawati, tel. 760124, 764142.

Gatot Subroto Hospital, Jalan Abdul Rachman Saleh 1, tel. 371008.

Husada Hospital, Jalan Mangga Besar 137–139, tel. 620108, 622555.

Islamic Hospital Jakarta, Jalan Letjen. Suprapto, tel. 414208, 414989.

Mintaharja Hospital, Jalan Bendungan Hilir, tel. 581031.

Pershabatan Hospital, Jalan Raya Persahabatan, tel. 481708.

Pertamina Hospital, Jalan Kyai Maja 43, tel. 775890, 775891.

Sint Carolus Hospital, Jalan Salemba Raya 41, tel. 883091, 882401.

Sumber Waras Hospital, Jalan Kyai Tapa, Grogol, tel. 596011, 593122.

Tjikini Hospital, Jalan Raden Saleh 40, tel. 374909, 365297, 363859.

Yayasan Jakarta Hospital, Jalan Jend. Sudirman, tel. 582241, 584576.

Restaurants

JAKARTA

European

Bamboo Den, Jalan Ir. H. Juanda, 4B. Popular place for Western food, especially steaks.

Bayanihan Steak House, Jalan H.A. Salim 103-A.
Bodega Grill, Caringin Shopping Centre, Cilandak, tel. 767798.
The Cellar Bar, Jalan Gondongdia Kecil 8. Good pizzas and other Italian snack food.
Gandhy Steak House, Jalan Melawai VIII/2 Kebayoran Baru; Jalan Gajah Mada No. 82, tel. 270563/272674,
George & Dragon, Jalan Teluk Betung No. 32.
The Green Pub, Jakarta Theatre, 9 Jalan M.H. Thamrin, tel. 325808.
Java Coffee Shop, Hotel Indonesian, Jalan M.H. Thamrin, tel. 320008.
Le Parisien, Hyatt Aryaduta Jakarta Hotel, 44–46 Jalan Prapatan, tel. 376008.
Oasis Restaurant, Jalan Raden Saleh 47. 'The' place for elegant wining and dining in gorgeous surroundings. Expensive.
The Stable, 4th floor, Wisma Hayam Wuruk, Jalan Hayam Wuruk, tel. 360200.
Swiss Inn, Jalan Jend. Sudirman, tel. 583280.
Taman Sari Grill, Jakarta Hilton Hotel, Jalan Jend. Gatot Subroto, tel. 583051.

Indonesian

Anging Mamiri, Horison Hotel, Taman Impian Jaya Ancol, tel. 680008.
Ayam Bulungan, Jalan Bulungan I/64, Kebayoran Baru.
Fatahillah, 14 Jalan Fatahillah, tel. 673842.
Jawa Timur, 67 Jalan Jen. A. Yani, tel. 884197.
Mataram, Borobudur Hotel, Jalan Lapangan Banteng, Selatan, tel. 370108.
Rice Bowl, Nusantara Building, Jalan M.H. Thamrin.
Roda, Jalan Matraman Raya 65–67. The best place in town for hot, spicy Sumatran food. Dozens of dishes brought to the table. You pay only for those you eat. Don't go to the Grill Room next door by mistake.
Satay House Senayan, Jalan Pakubuwono VI/6, Kebayoran Baru.
Satay House Senayan, Jalan Kebon Sirih 31.
Sate Blora Cirebon, Jalan Pemuda no. 47.
Trio, Jalan Gondangdia Lama, No. 29A.
Vic's Viking, Jalan M.H. Thamrin 31. Very popular restaurant serving Western smorgasbord. Also has Indonesian and Chinese food. Moderately priced.

Chinese/Others

Adhyaksa Akbar, 1 Jalan Kiyai Maja, Kebayoran Baru. Spicy Indian food prepared in traditional style.
Angel, Jalan Kendal. Masterly blend of Korean, Japanese, Indonesian and Western cuisines.
Ayothaya, 35A Jalan Ir. H. Juanda, tel. 350921. Thai restaurant.
Bakmi Gajah Mada, Jalan Gajah Mada No. 92.
Bakmi Gajah Mda, Jalan Melawai IV/25, Kebayoran Baru.
Bakmi Hayam Wuruk, Jalan Hayam Wuruk No. 92, tel. 638012.
Cahaya Kota Bar & Restaurant, Jalan K.H. Wahid Hassyim No. 9, Jakarta, tel. 342436, 353105.
Furusato, Sari Pacific Hotel, Jalan M.H. Thamrin, tel. 323707.
Ginza Benkay, President Hotel, Jalan M.H. Thamrin, tel. 320508.
Hayam Wuruk, Jalan Hayam Wuruk 5. One of Jakarta's best Chinese restaurants, specializing in Cantonese cuisine. Try the Tim Sum.
Hong Kong, 27 Jalan Blora, tel. 332324.
Foodstalls. All types of local food can be found nightly at the stalls along Jalan Jen. A. Yani and Jalan Cikapundung Barat (a side street off Jalan Asia Africa).
Jun Njan, 22 Lorong C, Tanjung Priok, tel. 290240. Small, simple, but extremely popular Chinese seafood restaurant. Excellent frogs' legs and prawns. Must reserve table in advance.
Kikugawa, Jalan Kebun Binatang, 111/3. One of Jakarta's nicest Japanese restaurants.
Korean Steak House, Asoka Hotel, Jalan M.H. Thamrin.
New Korea House, Asoka Hotel, Jalan M.H. Thamrin, tel. 322908.
Omar Kayam, Jalan Antara no. 5–7.
Paradise Bar & Restaurant, Jalan Pasir Putih 1/5–6.
Sanur, III/31 Jalan Ir. H. Juanda, tel. 354203.
Tjahaja Kota, Jalan K.H.A. Wahid Hashim 9. Award-winning Chinese restaurant.

BANDUNG

European

Braga, Braga Hotel, Jalan Braga no. 8, tel. 51685.
Sukarsa Steak & Egg, Jalan Tamblong 52, tel. 56968.
Sumber Hidangan, Jalan Braga 20–22. Large popular cafe with pastries, bread, ice-cream. Slightly cheaper than Braga Permai.
Tizi, Jalan Hegarmanak 14, Bandung.

Indonesian

Ayam Bengawan Solo, Jalan Riau 69. Local restaurant popular for its Central Javanese style chicken.
Bale Kambang, Jalan Bungur no. 2, tel. 81101.
Braga Permai Jalan Braga no. 58, tel. 50519, 59176.
Sate Klaten, Jalan Pasir Kaliki 43.

Chinese/Others

Queen, Jalan Dalam Kaum 79, tel. 51561.
Tjoan Kie, Jalan Jend. Sudirman 62–64, tel. 58264.

YOGYAKARTA

European

French Gill, Jalan Mangkubumi (in the Arjuna Plaza Hotel). Tops for juicy steaks and chops.
Gita Bujana Snack & Steak House, Jalan Diponegoro no. 52A, tel. 3742.
Legian Restaurant, Jalan Perwakilan. Delicious, inexpensive Western food served in a roofed garden overlooking Jalan Malioboro. Try smoked fish and

chicken cordon bleu. Best ice cream in Yogya.

Mirota, Jalan Jen A. Yani Supermarket and delicatessen. Large display of cakes and snacks in front; a sandwich bar is at the back.

Puri Artha Restaurant, Jalan Cendrawasih no. 9, tel. 5934, 5935.

Superman's on lane between Jalan Pasar Kembang and Jalan Sorowijayan.

Indonesian

Ayam Goreng NY. Suharti, Jalan Adisucipto Km. 7. tel. 5522.

Gudeg Bu Citro, Jalan Solo (special dish made from jackfruit).

Mama's, Jalan Pasar Kembang.

Moro Seneng Restaurant, Jalan Solo 65, tel. 2949.

Nyonya Suharti Mbok Berek, Jalan Solo, 1 kilometer east of Ambarrukmo Palace Hotel. The best fried chicken in Central Java.

Sinar Budi, Jalan Managkubumi, 41. Padang-style restaurant known for its spicy sauces. *Gulai otak* (curried brains) and *bubur kampiun* with durian (when in season) are superb.

Tri Sono Boga (southwest corner of *alun-alun lor*) Serves *gudeg* and *nasi liwet*, Solo's special dish of rice cooked in coconut milk.

Stalls at north end of Alun Alun Lor (north square of *kraton*). *Sate* and other local food available nightly.

Chinese/Others

Lie Djiong, Jalan Brigjen Katamso 19. Popular Chinese restaurant. Small menu. Excellent *swee kie* (frog legs).

Ramayana, Jalan P. Mangkubumi no. 77, tel. 2067.

SOLO

Indonesian

Madukoro. On the road to Yogya approximately 7 kilometers from Solo. Famous for its fried chicken and *es Madukoro* drink.

Ramayana Restaurant, Jalan Ronggowarsito 2 (Best *sate* and fried pigeon in town).

Timlo Solo, Jalan Jend. Urip Sumiharjo 106. Probably the best place in central Java to sample a variety of authentic native dishes. New, clean, and inexpensive.

Food stalls which set up a night on Jalan Teuku Umar between Jalan Ronggowarsito and Jalan Slamet Riyadi. All kinds of local food. And Jalan Nonongan for lamb *sate*.

Chinese/Other

Centrum, Jalan Kratonan 151. Delicious, more delicately flavored Chinese food than the norm. For an unusual treat, try *sosis kepiting* (crab sausage).

Mataram, Jalan Brig. Jend. Slamet Riyadi 262 (Delicious Chinese delicacies.)

SEMARANG

European

Santana Ice Cream Palace, Jalan Pemuda. Two restaurants serving Chinese food as well as a wide array of ice-ceam concoctions.

Toko Oen, Jalan Pemuda. Huge old-fashioned tea rooms with comfortable cane chairs. Ice-cream, cakes, Western and Indonesian food.

Indonesian

Ayam Goreng Mbok Berek, Jalan Siliwangi no. 376.

Lembur Kuring, Jalan Gajah Mada.

Ya'ik Night Market, Pasar Johar. At night, a *bemo* and taxi park is transformed into Semarang's favorite outdoor eating complex, with dozens of stalls catering to every taste.

Jalan Depok, another good area to find eating stalls at night.

Chinese/Others

Gang Lombok, (off Jalan Pekojan). Rows of small restaurants in area of Klinteng Temple selling excellent Chinese cuisine at moderate prices. 'Hap Kie' and 'Soen' both recommended.

Kit Wan Kie, Gg. Pinggir no. 23-25, tel. 20973.

Rumah Makan Gajah Mada, Jalan Gajah Mada (just off Jalan Depok). Specializes in seafood and fried pigeon. Delicious crab and prawns and other Chinese cuisine.

Phien Tjwan Hiang, Gg. Pinggir no. 86-92, tel. 23529.

Pringgading, Jalan Pringgading no. 54, tel. 288973.

SURABAYA

European

Arumanis Terrace Hugo's/Ceshiang Garden, Hyatt Bumi Surabaya, Jalan Basuki Rachmat, no. 124-128, tel. 470875.

Chez Rose, Jalan Panglima Sudirman. Popular coffee house during the day, transforms into an exclusive restaurant with European cuisine at night.

Indonesian

Phoenix, Jalan Genteng Kali 12 (next door to the "Oriental"). Excellent food.

Santapan Nusantara Bibi & Baba, Jalan Tanjungan no. 76, tel. 41633.

Chinese/Others

Aloha, Jalan Tratap, Waru (by turnoff to airport). Specializes in seafood cooked Chinese-style.

Kiet Wan Kie, Jalan Kembang Jepun 51. Good Chinese food with excellent roast pork.

Miami Seafood Restaurant, Jalan Urip Sumohardjo no. 34, tel. 45189.

Oriental, Jalan Genteng Kali 7, tel. 44631. Large, busy restaurant with very good Chinese food.

Tji Kong, Jalan Pecindilan. Renowned for its fried pigeon and other Chinese dishes.

Shops

JAKARTA

Ardjuna & Craft, Jalan Majapahit 16A Jakarta Pusat, tel. 344251. Statues.

Bakti Budaya, Jalan Bunga 5 — Jatinegara. Jakarta Timur. Export.

Bali Artja, Jalan Palatehan 1/20; Kebayoran. Woodcarvings, Woven items, Silver, and Paintings from West and Central Java.

Bali Internasional, Jalan Wahid Hasyim 116, Jakarta Pusat, tel. 45057/45058. Statues.

Bandung Art Shop, Jalan Pasar Baru 18 C, Jakarta Pusat. Statues.

Banka Tin Art Shop, Jalan K.H.S. Hasyim No. 178, Jakarta Pusat. Tin-Art.

Banuwati Art Shop, Jalan Semarang 14, Jakarta Pusat, tel. 342390. Statues.

Batik Danar Hadi, Jalan Raden Saleh No. 1A, Jakarta Pusat. Painted Batiks.

Batik Keris Cabang, Sarinah Bld. Lt. IV, Jalan M.H. Tharim, Jakarta Pusat. Batiks, Export.

Bergas Art Shop, Kartika Chandra Hotel, Jalan Gatot Subroto, Jakarta Selatan, tel. 583720, 583421. Hand Painted Batiks.

Bintara Art Shop, Jalan Tjiragil blok Q no. 2, Kebayoran Baru, Jakarta Selatan, tel. 771442. Statues.

Borobudur, Jalan Pasar No. 15, Jakarta Pusat, tel. 364642. Statues.

Darma Bhakti CV., Jalan Gandaria Tengah I/21, Kebayoran Baru. Basket Works.

Dewi Batik & Art Shop, Jalan Falatehan I/24, Kebayoran Baru, tel. 772830. Statues.

Djody Art & Curio, Jalan Kebon Sirih Timur 22, Jakarta Pusat, tel. 347730. Statues, Export.

Famous Store, Jalan Pasar Baru 21, Jakarta Pusat. Statues.

Fine Art, Jalan H.A. Salim, Jakarta Pusat. Statues.

G.K.B.I., Jalan Jendral Sudirman 28, Jakarta Pusat, tel. 581022. Hand Painted Batiks, Printed Batiks.

Garuda N.V., Jalan Majapahit 12, Jakarta — Pusat, tel. 342712. Statues.

Harris Art Gallery, Jalan Raya Cipete 41, Jakarta Pusat, tel. 760460. Paintings, Export.

Home Art, Jalan H.A. Agus Salim 41 B, Jakarta Pusat. Statues.

Indonesia Tin Art, Jalan Matraman Raya 54 A, tel. 81299. Tin Handicrafts.

Irian Art & Gift Shop, Jalan Pasar Baru No. 16A, Jakarta Pusat, tel. 43422. Statues.

Jakindra, Jalan Tanah Abang 3/16. All types of Indonesian handicrafts, including those not normally seen elsewhere.

Java Boutique, Jalan Semarang 14, Menteng. A good selection of batiks from every region of Java. Ready-made clothes available.

Djelita Batik Art Shop, Jalan Paletehan I/37 Blok K 5, Kebayoran Baru, Jakarta Selatan, tel. 770347. Hand Printed Batiks.

Johan's Art and Curio, Jalan H.A. Salim 59A. Good selection of porcelain and furniture as well as other old and new items. Very expensive.

Kota Gadang Indonesia Art Shop, Jalan Ir. H. Juanda no. 8, Jakarta Pusat, tel. 347231. Statues.

Kota Indah, Jalan Pasar Baru No. 15, Jakarta Pusat, tel. 357425. Statues.

Lee Cheong, Jalan Majapahit 32. Good reputation for top quality Chinese furniture and porcelain.

Lestari Art Shop, Jalan Ir. H. Juanda 14, Jakarta Pusat. Statues.

Made Handicraft, Jalan Pergangsaan Timur no. 2, Jakarta Pusat. Basket Works, Export.

Maison Young, Jalan Paletehan I/39-B, Kebayoran Baru, Jakarta Selatan. Batiks.

Majapahit Art & Curio, Jalan Melawi 3/4, Kebayoran. Manay interesting Indonesian items as well as Chinese and European antiques.

Multi Redjeki, Jalan Melawai IX Blk M 111/102, Kebayoran Baru, Jakarta Selatan. Statues.

Nouveautex, Jalan H.A. Salim 20. Attractive dress-length batiks as well as printed cotton, linen, voile and silk. Ready-made items on sale.

Pigura Art & Gift Shop, Jalan Paletehan I/41 Kebayoran Baru, Jakarta Selatan, tel. 771143. Statues.

Pura Art Shop, Jalan Paletehan I/43, Jakarta Selatan, tel. 73178. Statues.

Puri Bali Art Shop, Hotel Indonesia Sheraton, Jalan M.H. Thamrin 58, Jakarta Pusat. Statues.

Pusaka Art Shop, Hotel Arya Duta Jalan Prapatan 44–46, Jakarta Pusat. Statues.

Ramayana, Jalan Ir. H. Juanda 14-A, Jakarta Pusat. Paintings.

Ramayana Art Shop, Jalan Pasar Baru No. 15, Jakarta Pusat. Statues.

Royal Batik Shop, Jalan Paletehan I, Kebayoran Baru, Jakarta Selatan. Batiks.

Sida Mukti, Wisma Batik Indonesia, Jalan Dr. Saharjo 311. Manay modern prints and color combinations on cotton.

Shinta Art & Gift Shop, Jalan Melawai VI/17–19 Blk. M, Lt. III — Kebayoran Baru, Jakarta Selatan, tel. 774788. Statues.

Srikandi Batik Shop, 'Hias Rias' Shopping Complex, Jalan Cikini Raya 90. Small store packed with traditional and modern batiks, as well as '*lurik*' (homespun) suitable for furnishing. Inexpensive batik slippers and sandals and other odds and ends suitable for gifts.

Toni's Gallery, Jalan Paletehan I/31, Kebayoran Baru, Jakarta Selatan, tel. 770036. Satutes.

Urip Store, Jalan Paletehan I/40 Blok K.V., Kebayoran Baru, Jakarta Selatan. Statues.

BANDUNG

Agam Gift Shop, Jalan Asia Afrika 88, tel. 52884. Balinese Lace Work.

Aneka Lukisan, Jalan Cihampelas 96. Paintings, Batiks, Embroidered Textiles, *Angklung*, Flutes, Vases, Flowers.

Batik Semar Solo, Jalan Dalam Kaum 40, tel. 57432. Statues, Flutes, Ceramics.

"Cupu Manik" Handicraft Industry, Jalan Kebon Kawung Gg. Umar 2. Statues, Flutes, Ceramics.

E. Sukatma Muda Puppet Wayang Studio, Jalan Mohammah Ramdhan 4. *Wayang*.

Karya Nusantara P.T. Jalan Asia Afrika 94, tel. 51036. Paintings, Statues, Textiles.

Leather Palace, Jalan Braga 67. Up-to-date leather shoes, Handbags, Coats, Hats, and Belts, all made locally.

Lumayan Shop, Jalan Cicendo 5. Paintings, Statues, Basket Works, Laceworks.

Luwes Art Shop, Jalan Braga 46, tel. 57875. Paintings, Statues, Ceramics, *Angklung* Flutes.

"Mayang Sari" Saung Angklung, Jalan Moch. Toha, Gg. Madurasa 275. *Anklung/Degung, Kecapti/*Flutes, Drums/Trumpets, Export.

M. Sukama Store, Jalan Braga 88, tel. 52943. Statues, Puppets (*Wayang*), Javanese Traditional Head-dresses.

Naini's Fine Arts, Jalan Tambong 26. Good paintings and Souvenirs.

Panonjaya, Jalan Tamblong 64. Batiks, Basket Works, Toys/Flowers Vases, Wall Decorations, Ashtrays, Embroideries, Albums, Paintings.

Pritico Store, Jalan Braga 72, tel. 50371. Paintings, Batiks.

Rumah Batik Pritico, Jalan Braga 52. Good selection of batik lengths and ready-made clothing. Fixed prices, well displayed.

Saung Angklung. Jalan Padasuka 118, tel. 71714. Wayang. *Angklung*. Lamp Shades.

Sin Sin, Jalan Braga 47. Good reputation as fair and honest antique dealers.

Souvenir Shop. Jalan Raya 280, Lembang.

Tasin Factory Store. Jalan Braga 24, te. 57494.

Tatarah, Jalan Braga 51C. Paintings and some jewelery.

YOGYAKARTA

Affandi, Jalan Solo, next to river. Work of Indonesia's most famous artist displayed along with work of other local artists.

Gallery Amri, Gampingan (off Jalan Wates). Large selection of batiks and oil paintings by Amri Yahya. Distinctive abstract style in strikingly flamboyant colors. A second building displays prints, oils and sculptures by a number of lesser known, but accomplished artists.

"An Suryanto" Art Studio, Jalan Kadipaten Kidul Kp. IV/19. Paintings, Batiks.

Antiques Art Shop, Jalan Kota Gede. Paintings, Leather puppets (*Wayang*).

Ardianto Batik, Jalan Pajeksan no. 21. Batik.

"Aris Shoes" Handicraft, Jalan Kauman 14. Slippers, Shoes, Belts.

Arjuna Art Shop, Jalan Sala no. 110. Statues, Export.

Asmopawiro, Jalan Let. Jen. Haryono 20. House with small selection of moderately priced antiques. Fine krises for sale.

Asri (Fine Arts College), Gampingan, off Jalan Wates. Can watch students at work and see display of their work between 8 a.m. and 1 p.m.

Balai Penelitian Kerajinan (Handicrafts Research Center), Jalan Sidobali, Muja-muju. A government workshop developing all manner of goods made from natural materials. Hours same as Batik Research Center.

Bangong Kussudiardjo, Jalan Wates 9. Large display of batik paintings by this well-known dancer and painter. Also work of other artists and small selection of handmade jewelery for sale.

B.S. Store, Jalan Ngasem no. 10. Leather Handicraft.

Batik Indah Raradjongrang, Jalan Tirtodipuran 6A. Batik.

Batik Paintings, Jalan Kadipaten Kidul no. 16. Paintings, *Wayang*.

Batik Soemiharjo, Jalan Mangkuyudan 15A. Good batik paintings by Soemiharjo. Also batik cloth and clothing in modernistic design.

"Bu Karti" Batik Store, Jalan Taman Kp. III/36. Batik.

Budi Murni, Jalan Muja-muju 21 (near Gembira Loka zoo). Jackets and travel bags in finished leather and suede. Also women's handbags in "batik-on-leather" design.

Edi Store, Jalan Malioboro 13A, tel. 2997. Statues, Textiles from Sumba. *Wayang* puppets.

Effendi Abunyamin Art Shop, Taman Kp. 3/107. Paintings, Carved Designs.

F. Agus, Jalan Taman Siswo Mg. III/102. Batik paintings by a good, young artist with a clean, vibrant sense of composition.

Gallery Lod, Western edge of Taman Sari. Display of paintings by several young batik artists. Prices very reasonable.

Ganeca Art Shop, Jalan Ambarukmo 109. *Wayang*.

Garuda Art Shop, Jalan Pangeran Mangkubumi 105. Paintings, Batik.

Hastirin Store, Jalan Malioboro no. 99. *Wayang*, Carvings from Jepara, Ivory.

H.S. Silver Store, Jalan Mandongan Kota Gede. Paintings, Silver.

Indonesian Art, Jalan Malioboro 193. *Wayang*. Turtle shell, Ivory.

Indonesian Arts & Crafts "S.S." Jalan Kemasan no. K6V, Kota Gede. Silver Handicrafts.

Jul Shop Curio & Antiques, Jalan Pangeran Mangkubumi 29, tel. 2157. *Wayang*, Antique Cupboards, Wood carvings, Krises, Masks.

"Kusuma" Shoes Handicraft & Carvings Leather Bags, Jalan Kauman 50. Basket Works, Leather Handicrafts.

Ledjar, Jalan Mataram DN I/370. Good new *wayang kulit* puppets.

Madusari Art Shop, Jalan Malioboro 129. Batiks, Paintings.

Maha Dewa Art Shop, Jalan Taman Garuda 8. Statues (Human), Leather Bags, Basket Works, Rattan Chairs, Export.

Mahkota Art Shop, Jalan Kemasan Kota Gede. Paintings, *Wayang*, Ivory Handicrafts.

M. D. Silver, Jalan Keboan Kota Gede. Paintings, *Wayang*, Silver Handicrafts.

Moelyosoeharjo, Jalan Taman Sari 37B. Old and new *wayang kulit* puppets. Good quality.

Naga Art Shop, Jalan Malioboro no. 61. Paintings, Statues, Basket Works, Export.

Pusaka Art Shop, Jalan Taman Garuda no. 22. Basket Works, Rattan Chairs, Leather Bags.

Rama Store, Jalan Sala 76. Statues.

Sabda Art Shop, Jalan Taman Garuda 10. Paintings.

Sanggar Batik Printing, Kadipaten Kidul no. 23. Paintings.

Saptohoedojo, Jalan Solo (near entrance to airport). Tasteful Artworks, Ceramics, Batik Clothing and Handicrafts. All outrageously overpriced.

Seni Sono Gallery, Jalan Senopati, almost opposite Post Office. Occasional displays of the work of local and foreign artists. Banners outside advertise current show.

Setia, Jalan Malioboro 165. Leather Bags, Silver Decorations.

Setia, Jalan Malioboro 79. Statues, Basket Works, Export.

S.S. Shop, Jalan Maioboro no. 55, Yogyakarta. Statues, Leather (*Wayang*) Puppets, Silver, Masks.

"Sidamukti" Art Shop & Batik Painting, Jalan Taman Kp. III/103A. Paintings, Carved Designs, *Wayang* puppets.

Soed Amri Boutique, (at Gallery Amri). Batik lengths and clothing. Gorgeous men's shirts that are breathtakingly expensive.

Souvenir Shop, Jalan Malioboro 19. Statues, Carved Designs, Porcelains, Export.

Stupa Batik Printing, Jalan Pasar Kembang no. 17. Paintings, Statues from Stones, Export.

Surya Kencana Batik C.V., Ngadinegaraan ud 7/98. Paintings, Batik.

Tan Jam An, Jalan Sangaji 2 (just north of Tugu Monument). Selection of ready-made silver jeweleries and other items. Will make jewelery to your designs. Owners very helpful.

Tjokrosuharto, Jalan Panembahan 58. Large selection of souvenirs, batik, silver, *wayang kulit* figures, dancers' costumes.

Tobal Batik (The Flower Market), Jalan Pasar Kembang no. 19. Batik.

Toko Kerajinan Wayang Kulit, Jalan Taman Sari 37B, tel. 2873. Carved Designs, (*Wayang*) Lamp shades & things, Souvenirs.

Tom's Silver C.V., Jalan Kota Gede. Paintings, Silver Handicrafts.

Wama Sentral Batik Studio, Jalan Prarimosono no. 3. Batiks.

Wijayakusuma, Jalan Pajeksan 21 (old name of street is Gandekan). Antiques and art objects assembled by the artist, Ardiyanto. Classy and expensive.

Yarindrata, Pekapalan 5 Alun-Alun Utara. Statues, *Angklung*, Coconut Shell, Sisal.

Yogya Kembali Store, Jalan K.H.A. Dahlan no. 8, tel. 3830. Paintings, Batiks, Slippers, Bags, Hats.

SURAKARTA (SOLO)

Batik Danar Hadi, Jalan Dr. Rajiman 8. Elegantly appointed store which sells a large selection of clothings and batik cloths. Fine assortment of traditional Solo-style natural dye tulis batiks.

Batik Keris, Jalan Yos Sudarso 37.

Batik Semar, Jalan Pasarnongko 132.

Bedoyo Srimpi, 116 Ronggo Bharsito (corner of Hayam Wuruk).

Eka Hartono CV., Jalan Dawung Tengah 11/38. Statues, Carved Designs.

Goci Batik (Slameto), Karagan 291, Panularan. Carved Designs, Ceramics.

K.R.T. Harjonegoro, Jalan Kratonan 101. Small selection of high quality batiks, both traditional and modern, handwaxed on all types of cloths.

Mirah Delima, Jalan Kemasan RT XI. Selection of antiques as well as handicrafted reproduction chairs.

Pasar Kelwer, Jalan Secoyudan. Vast array of batik and *lurik*. Choose carefully and be sure to bargain.

Pasar Trewindu, Jalan Diponegoro (near Mankunegaran Palace). For fascinating collection of bric-a-brac, junk and occasional good antiques. Best place to buy old oil lamps.

Seni Kerajinan Usaha Pelajar, Nayu Barat I/8, Nusukan. Paintings, Carved Designs (*Wayang*), Leather Handicrafts.

Singowidodo, Jalan Urip Sumoharjo 117 (road to Surabaya). An Aladdin's cave bursting with every type of antiques and junks. Good selection of fossils, rocks and stones.

Trisani Batik & Art Shop, Jalan Bhayangkara 2. Paintings, Batik.

Toko Parto Art, Jalan Slamet Riyadi 103. All types of antiques sold here and at 'Pak Partosuwarno's home, where excellent reproductions of antique carved cupboards are made.

Tom Harry, Jalan Kampung Kepunton RT 21/RK 1. Paintings, Carved Designs.

The Mangkunegaran Palace also maintains a shop where visitors may buy masks and *wayang* figures in leather, wood and on scrolls.

SURABAYA

Bali Art Shop, Jalan Jendral Basuki Rachmat 143, tel. 45933. Paintings, Statues, Carved Designs, Antique Earthen Pitchers, Bronze, Majapahit Stones, Export.

Bangun Art Shop, Jalan Raya Darmo 5. Paintings.

Indian Publication Agency, Jalan Pasar Besar 17-19, tel. 41566. Paintings, Statues, Good collection of books.

Kendedes Art Shop, Jalan Baliton 67, tel. 40469. Batiks, Embroideries, Basket Works, Silver rings, Export.

Kundandas Art Shop, Jalan Tunjungan 97, tel. 43927. Paintings, Statues Carved Designs, Batiks, Embroidered Textiles, Basket Works, Silver handicraft, Shell handicrafts, Wax statues.

Mie Lie Paintings, Jalan Bubutan 32. Paintings, Carved Designs.

Pinguin Art Shop, Taman A. IS. Nasution 45, tel. 40650. Statues, Antique Lamps, Porcelains.

Rochim Art Shop, Jalan Raya Darmo 27. Statues, Carved Designs.

Sarinah, Jalan Tunjungan 7, Paintings, Statues, Carved Designs, Basket Works, Silver, Brass, Spoon Ceramics.

Sudimampir, Jalan Jendral B. Rachmat 122, tel. 43376. Paintings, Statues, Carved Designs, Batiks, Songket Textiles, Basket Works, Silver handicrafts, Bamboo Basket Works.

Wing On, Jalan Jendral Baduki Rahmat, tel. 472037. Paintings, Statues, Songket Textiles, Basket Works, Silver.

SEMARANG

Galendra Art Shop, Jalan Pemuda no. 13. Paintings, Statues, Ceramics.

G.K.B.I., Jalan Pemuda no. 48. Batiks.

Kerta Niaga P.T., Jalan Stadion. Statues,

Ceramics, Gerabah, Batik.

La Vogue, Jalan Pemuda 43. Small collection of European and Chinese antiques.

Mustika Mas, Jalan Pemuda 58. Two shops, side by side, selling souvenir items and antiques.

Panjang, Jalan Widoharjo 31. Statues, Carved Designs (wayang & animals), Silver, Leather *wayang* puppet, Export.

Toko Pandjang, Jalan Widohardjo 31A. Six rooms brimming with fine examples of Java's crafts. Across the street a warehouse of finely carved teak furniture.

Tours and Travel Agents

JAKARTA

Agaphos Tours & Travel, 16 Jalan Gajah, Mada, tel. 375476.

Antar Arah Ltd., 1-7 Jalan Pinangsia, tel. 672563.

Batemuri Tours Ltd., Wisata International Hotel, Jalan M.H. Thamrin, tel. 320408.

Bayu Buana, 4P Jalan Pinangsia Timur, tel. 674741.

Carnation, 24 Jalan Menteng Raya, tel. 344027.

Djengger Tour & Travel, 94-96 Jalan Kramat Raja, tel. 343339.

Gama Travel, 111/4A Jalan Pembangunan, tel. 353535.

Golden Bali Tours, 121 Jalan Barito, tel. 712232.

Ista, Hotel Indonesia Sheraton, Jalan M.H. Thamrin, tel. 321909.

Kartini, Asoka Hotel, Jalan M.H. Thamrin, tel. 324493.

Kintamani, 28, Jalan Cikini Raya, tel. 343246.

Kostour, 60 Jalan Senen Raya, tel. 342091.

Koswara Travel, 12 Jalan Merdeka Utara, tel. 360856.

Mitra, Wisma Hayam Wuruk, 8 Jalan Hayam Wuruk, tel. 366445.

Musi Holiday, 30 Jalan Cikini Raya, tel. 322709.

Natourin, 16 Jalan Merdeka Timur, tel. 351373.

Natrabu, 29A Jalan Agus Salim, tel. 371709.

Nitour Inc., Jalan Majapahit, tel. 340955.

Pacto Travel, 88 Jalan Cikini Raya, tel. 324011.

Pantravel, Hotel Kartika Plaza, Jalan M.H. Thamrin, tel. 320908.

Ray Tour & Travel, 79-A Jalan H.O.S. Cokroaminoto, tel. 352349.

Satriavi, 32 Jalan Prapatan, tel. 353543.

Siem Travel, 11 Jalan H. Samanhudi, tel. 343403.

Surya Tours & Travel, 111 Jalan Hayam Wuruk, tel. 634508.

Tedjo Express, Jalan Guntur, 823473.

Tomaco, Jakarta Theatre Building, Jalan M.H. Thamrin, tel. 354551.

Tunas Indonesia Tours & Travel, 29 Jalan Majapahit, tel. 347390; Jakarta Hilton Hotel, Jalan Gatot Subroto, tel. 586170.

Universal Travel, 18A Jalan Pintu Kecil, tel. 677795.

Usaha Express, 41 Jalan Kopi, tel. 670045.

Vaya Tour, 38 Jalan Batu Tulis, tel. 356584.

Wirontono Travel, 35 Jalan Antara, tel. 341562.

YOGYAKARTA

Jatayu, Jalan Sukun Lor 30, tel. 3486.

Indonesia Tours, Hotel Sri Wedari, tel. 88288.

Intan Pelangi, Jalan Malioboro, tel. 3173, 3372.

Milangkori, Jalan Jend. Sudirman, tel. 2325.

Intras Tour, Jalan Malioboro, tel. 3611.

Natrabu, Hotel Ambarrukmo, tel. 88488 ext. 705.

Nitour Inc., Hotel Ambarrukmo, tel. 88488 ext. 137.

Pacto, Hotel Ambarrukmo, tel. 88488 ext. 703.

Royal Holiday, Hotel Ambarrukmo, tel. 88488 ext. 8752.

Satriavi, Hotel Ambarrukmo, tel. 88488 ext. 742.

Vaya Tour, Hotel Ambarrukmo, tel. 88488 ext. 121.

Vista Express, Hotel Ambarrukmo, tel. 88488 ext. 719.

Tunas Indonesia, Hotel Ambarrukmo, tel. 88488 ext. 744.

Sri Rama, Wisma LPP, tel. 88380.

Tourista, Jalan Kemetiran Lor 16, tel. 5498, 88117.

Universal, Jalan Kemetiran Lor 16, tel. 3254.

Places of Worship

MOSQUES

Al Azhar, Jalan Singamangaraja, Kebayoran.
Al Hikmah, Jalan M.H. Thamrin 9.
Al Mujahidin, Jalan Dr. Semeru Raya.
Baitul Taqwa, Jalan Matraman Raya 132.
Baitur Rahim, Jalan Medan Merdeka Utara.
Darus Saadah, Jalan Let. Jend. Suprapto 16.
Istiqlal, Jalan Pintu Air.
Sunda Kelapa, Jalan Sunda Kelapa.

PURA (HINDU BALI TEMPLE)

Pura Dalem Purnajati, Cilincing
Pura Rawamangun
Pura Senayan

TEMPLES

Lalitawistara
Tri Ratna (Kwan Im)

CHURCHES

English

Anglican/Episcopal — All Saint Church, Jalan Arif Rahman Hakim 5, tel. 345508.

Baptist — Kebayoran Baptist Church, Jalan Tirtayasa Raya 1, tel. 711799.

Charismatic Worship — Hotel Hyatt Aryaduta, tel. 777368.

Community Church — Effatha Church, Jalan Iskandarsyah II, tel. 772325.

Roman Catholic — St. Yohannes, Jalan Melawai 197, tel. 774556.

German

Protestant — All Saints' Church, Jalan Arif

Rahman Hakim 5, tel. 76265.
Roman Catholic — Immaculata Convent's Chapel, Jalan Sambas III/17 Blok B, tel. 773864.

Italian

Roman Catholic — St. Mary's The Queen, Jalan Suryo 62 Blok Q, tel. 773640.

Dutch

Reformed — Emmanuel Church, Jalan Merdeka Timur, tel. 342895.
Roman Catholic — Budi Mulia's Chapel, Jalan Gunung Sahari 91, tel. 360373.

Chinese

Roman Catholic — St. Mary's Of Fatima, Jalan Kemenangan III/47, tel. 273922.

Korean

Protestant, Emmanuel Church, Jalan Merdeka Timur, tel. 342895.

French

Roman Catholic, Canisius College's Chapel, Jalan Menteng Raya 64, tel. 774556.

Indonesia

Protestant, Immanuel Church, Jalan Merdeka Timur 10, tel. 342895.
Roman Catholic — Cathedral, Jalan Katedral 7, tel. 367746.

INDEX

For quick access to and understanding of the places and terms of Java, the following index-glossary identifies important entries as well as refers to the pages on which they appear. Page references in **boldface** indicate a section devoted to that entry; while page references in *italics* are for illustrations or maps.